D1129681

CONFEDERATE SUPPLY

Duke Historical Publications

RICHARD D. GOFF

CONFEDERATE SUPPLY

1969
Duke University Press
Durham, N. C.

L.C.C. card no. 68–57274

Printed in the United States of
America by Kingsport Press, Inc.

For NANCY

PREFACE

Before pursuing the subject of the supply problems of the Confederacy, some introductory comments on the sources and the proper delineation of the subject area are necessary. Source materials for the study of Confederate supply come from two major areas, each presenting its special problems. On the one hand, many of the "official" papers of the various departments and bureaus of the Confederate government and of the men who ran them had been lost, and the remaining sources are sometimes too spotty to provide balanced judgments on some aspects of the Confederate supply effort. Davis's papers are not very informative, and the personal papers of the Secretaries of War and top supply officials, with the exception of the Gorgas diary, are virtually nonexistent. Official papers of the various supply bureaus are few, except for those of the Quartermaster Department, and here, too, there are large gaps. Still, there is enough information in these sources to explain the creation and transformation of official supply policy and also to suggest the various motivations of the Richmond administrators. To a lesser degree, these materials give some insight into public reaction to government policy. On the other hand, an enormous quantity of papers of average Confederate citizens, of newspapers, etc., have been amassed over the years in a formidable number of depositories. These materials provide little insight into the creation and implementation of government supply policies and do little to explain supply problems from the point of view of the Confederate officials. These materials do sometimes reveal public reaction to government policy, reactions often colorful and often contradictory. Indeed, "public opinion" on a given matter is a notoriously slippery concept to isolate and identify. So vast is the bulk of materials that would have to be sifted that any comprehensive analysis of reaction to government policy would be the labor of decades and the results would be worthy of separate study and publication. Faced with these problems in sources, I have elected to concentrate on "official" sources and study the evolution of Confederate supply policy, recording "public opinion" only where a sampling of unofficial materials, especially in newspapers, indicates that there was some consensus in the public mind about some specific policy or problem.

The materials which pertain to official supply policy, while uneven, are still too voluminous in many areas to be assimilated properly unless the concept of "Confederate supply" is rigorously limited. In this study, finance, diplomacy, politics, conscription, private contributions, state supply efforts, the navy, and the army in the Trans-Mississippi have been subordinated in one degree or another to one dominant theme: the Confederate government's management of supplies for the armies east of the Mississippi. Besides this limitation in "breadth" a further limitation of "depth" had to be imposed. Technological information about manufacturing processes, farming methods, railroad management, techniques of blockade running, purchasing procedures, and the routine of distributing supplies in the field had to be omitted to give adequate attention to the problem-solving, policy-making, administrative, and organizational aspects of the Confederate supply effort.

In presenting this study of Confederate supply management, I have interwoven three strands: the history of the individual supply bureaus —their problems and their development; the evolution of general supply policies by the civilian leadership of the Confederate war effort; and the effect of supply factors on strategy and campaigning. This approach, so far as I know, adds a new perspective to Confederate history. In pursuing this plan, I believe new ground has also been broken in presenting the activities of the Quartermaster's and Subsistence departments, in developing the evolution of a number of supply policies, and in suggesting the interrelationship of supply factors to a number of specific campaigns. One of the major conclusions of this study, that Davis mismanaged Confederate affairs, concurs with a substantial body of historical opinion.

In preparing this study, I received assistance from a number of libraries, depositories, and individuals. I particularly wish to acknowledge the assistance of the staffs of the Duke University Library, the Library of Congress, the National Archives, the Tulane University Library, the University of North Carolina Library, the Virginia Historical Society, and the Virginia State Library. Professor Donald Disbrow of Eastern Michigan University secured materials used in this study. Professor Robert Woody of Duke University was generous with time and advice in the initial stages of this project, and members of the Duke University Department of History encouraged its publication. My greatest appreciation goes to my wife, Nancy, for her indispensable encouragement, criticism and hard work.

RICHARD D. GOFF

CONTENTS

SHORT TITLE KEY TO ABBREVIATIONS

War Department Collection of Confederate Records, National Archives (Record Group 109)

QMDELR	Quartermaster's Department, Endorsements on Letters Received
QMDLS	Quartermaster's Department, Letters Sent
QMDSW	Quartermaster's Department, Communications with the Secretary of War
QMDTS	Quartermaster's Department, Telegrams Sent
WDAA	War Department, Appropriations Accounts
WDCP	War Department, Communications with the President
WDLR	War Department, Letters Received
WDLS	War Department, Letters Sent
WDRTR	War Department, Registers of Telegrams Received
WDTR	War Department, Telegrams Received
WDTS	War Department, Telegrams Sent
RG 109	General prefatory citation to all items in Record Group 109 not given one of the special citations listed above

Other Abbreviations

Debates	[Proceedings of the First and Second Congresses of the Confederate States of America], *Southern Historical Society Papers*
Journal	*Journal of the Congress of the Confederate States of America*
Messages	Richardson, *A Compilation of the Messages and Papers of the Confederacy*
OR-1	*War of the Rebellion: A Compilation of the Official Records of the Union and Confederate Armies,* Series 1
OR-4	*War of the Rebellion: A Compilation of the Official Records of the Union and Confederate Armies,* Series 4

ORN-1	*Official Records of the Union and Confederate Navies,* Series 1
ORN-2	*Official Records of the Union and Confederate Navies,* Series 2
PRSD	Papers Relating to the Subsistence Department, C.S.A., Virginia Historical Society
RG 56	General Records of the Department of the Treasury, Confederate Records, National Archives (Record Group 56)
Statutes, I	*Statutes at Large of the Provisional Congress of the Confederate States of America*
Statutes, II	*Public Laws of the Confederate States of America* (all sessions)

Note on Terminology

The names of the supply bureaus vary in official Confederate documents. The terms employed herein are those most frequently used, i.e., "Subsistence Department" rather than "Commissary Department," or "Commissary General's Department"; and "Quartermaster's Department" rather than "Quartermaster General's Department." The latter two terms should not be confused with "Quartermaster General's Office," which applied to the central office of the bureau in Richmond, and not to the bureau as a whole.

CONFEDERATE SUPPLY

CHAPTER ONE

TRYING TO ORGANIZE

. . . *It was not the improved* arm, *but the improved* man, *which would win the day. Let brave men advance with flint locks and old-fashioned bayonets, on the popinjays of the Northern cities—advance on and on, under the fire, reckless of the slain, and he would answer for it with his life, that the Yankee would break and run.* —— Henry A. Wise, April 12, 1861*

Before undertaking a study of the supply policies of the Confederacy, it is important to consider whether or not secession politics had already determined the course of the Confederate supply effort before the war broke out. The war-making potential of the eleven Confederate states was so markedly inferior to that of the entire slave section of fifteen states that the failure of the secessionists to carry the Border States into the Confederacy certainly weakened, and possibly eliminated, any reasonable chances for Confederate independence.

In developing this point, the first step is to compare on a broad basis the resources of the fifteen Slave States with those of the Free States.[1] Compared to the Free States, the Slave States displayed marked disadvantages should a war break out between the sections. The financial base and the transportation network of the Slave States were feeble. Their industrial output was comparatively miniscule: except for cotton yarns, factory production in the Slave States ranged from 8 per cent to

* Cited in John Beauchamp Jones, *A Rebel War Clerk's Diary at the Confederate States Capital* (2 vols.; New York: Old Hickory Bookshop, 1935), I, 18. Cited hereinafter as Jones, *War Clerk's Diary*.

1. The material in the following section on resources has been taken from a number of tables in the following volumes of The Eighth Census of the United States: *Population of the United States in 1860; Compiled from the Original Returns of the Eighth Census, under the Direction of the Secretary of the Interior, by Joseph C. G. Kennedy Superintendent of [the] Census* (Washington, 1864); *Agriculture of the United States in 1860; Compiled from the Original Returns of the Eighth Census, under the Direction of the Secretary of the Interior, by Joseph C. G. Kennedy Superintendent of [the] Census* (Washington, 1864); *Manufactures of the United States in 1860; Compiled from the Original Returns of the Eighth Census under the Direction of the Secretary of the Interior* (Washington, 1865). The material in numerous tables was recombined in various manners and rounded off, so that nearly all figures presented are the writer's own compilation.

13 per cent of the Free State output of crude and bar iron, coal, clothing, cotton sheeting, woolens, and shoes.

In other aspects the economy of the Slave States compared more favorably with that of the Free States. Southern agriculture displayed the potential to sustain a prolonged war effort: the Slave States produced nearly all of the rice, sugar, sweet potatoes, peas, and beans in the United States, more corn than the Free States, and a substantial wheat crop. Draft and food animals were abundant, although inferior in quality. Cotton land could be converted to augment food production and still leave sufficient cotton for producing textiles and as barter for purchasing supplies. Nor was the manpower factor, on its face, unduly ominous. Canceling out the disloyal and disinterested on both sides and calculating that the slave population would release a larger proportion of white adult males for the Confederate armies, the Free State advantage in manpower was slightly over two to one. Assuming the Slave States would fight a defensive war, these odds hardly constituted a formidable disparity.

The overall comparative weakness of the slave section was aggravated by a marked disparity in economic development between the Upper South and the Cotton States. The Cotton States had little to offer a sustained military effort. Transportation and communication were unco-ordinated patchworks. The agricultural products of this area displayed distinct practical limitations. There was an abundance of corn, sweet potatoes, sugar, rice, peas, and beans; but most of these crops were highly perishable and of little use for supplying armies which were defending the borders, since transportation depended upon the existing rickety railroad system. The farmers produced little in the way of surplus grains and fodder crops, but their vaunted King Cotton was useful for fibers, barter, and money. Perhaps the most positive characteristic of agriculture in this region was its potential for converting cotton land to the production of major food crops for the armies. Animals for food and labor were in relative abundance, but many of the horses and most of the beef cattle were virtually inaccessible in Texas. Industry consisted of some cotton factories in the Georgia–South Carolina Piedmont, a cluster of clothing and shoe shops in New Orleans, and little else.

In contrast to the cotton South, the seven upper slave states, an area extending from Delaware and North Carolina to Missouri, comprised a land of grains, meat, and some semblance of heavy industry. One third of the wheat grown in the United States came from this belt, plus a scattering of food and feed grains such as oats, rye, buckwheat, and barley—and, of course, plenty of corn. Beef cattle and swine flourished in this area, located close to lines of transportation and to the armies defending the borders of a slave republic. Industrially, these states produced 60 per cent of the cotton textiles in the slave states and over 90 per cent of the pig iron, bar, sheet, and railroad iron, and coal. Two thirds of the white adult males of the entire region lived in these seven states.

With the bulk of the military resources of the slave section located in the Upper South, the failure of the secessionists to carry Missouri, Kentucky, and Maryland into the Confederacy was the first major Confederate disaster. A political-military line was drawn through the Upper South's grain and industrial belt, surrendering to the Union at the outset one third of the grains and animals of the slave states, one third of the fighting men, and over one half of the already feeble industrial output. In addition, it exposed the remaining farms and shops of the Confederacy's war economy to easy conquest. A march southward of 150 miles through Virginia and Tennessee would carry Union troops to nearly all of the significant iron mills, coal mines, flour mills, grain fields, and slaughterhouses of the Confederacy. However, in the patriotic fervor of the spring of 1861, few, if any, Confederates knew or cared about such considerations.

. . .

Although the politicians who assembled at Montgomery in February 1861 were primarily concerned with constructing the constitutional and civil framework of their new Confederacy, the prevailing uncertainty concerning relationships with the United States soon induced them to devote time and thought to national defense. In his inaugural address on February 18, after commenting on civil matters, President Davis made a cursory obeisance to historic military tradition, avowing that the main reliance for the defense of the Confederacy would be placed on the state militias. He then pushed on to his main point, declaring that "the present condition of affairs" made it "advisable" that Congress create a navy and "a well-constructed and disciplined army, more numerous than would usually be required of a peace establishment."[2] Congress responded swiftly. The first Congressional defense measure initiated the prime pattern in the Confederate war

2. *Messages,* I, 34.

effort—letting the President do it. The contacts of Jefferson Davis as former Secretary of War were one of the most valuable military assets of the Confederacy, and Congress moved to exploit it. On February 20 Davis signed a bill authorizing the President or the Secretary of War (although such an office did not yet exist) to make contracts for the purchase and manufacture of heavy ordnance and small arms and for machinery to manufacture small arms and munitions of war, to employ artisans and agents, and to establish powder mills, "on such terms as in his judgment the public exigencies may require."[3] Shortly thereafter, Congress created the War Department and set up the office of Chief of the Bureau of War to handle the department's paperwork.[4] On February 26 the President signed a bill creating the general staff of the regular army, although that army had not been authorized. This act provided the basic administrative agencies for the conduct of the war —the supply bureaus. It created the Adjutant and Inspector General's Department, the Quartermaster's Department, the Subsistence Department, and the Medical Department. Slightly enlarged during the ensuing months, these departments consisted of the bureau chief, usually visualized as a colonel, and six to eight assistants ranked variously from lieutenant-colonel to captain, plus a few clerks.[5] Finally, Congress created in the Treasury Department the office of Second Auditor, assisted by eleven clerks, for the sole purpose of auditing War Department accounts.[6]

After Congress had created the administrative aspect of war-making, it proceeded to establish an army and to empower the government to make war with it. On February 28 the President signed an omnibus bill which authorized him to receive arms and munitions and to conduct war. It also vaguely provided for military forces. The act authorized

3. "An Act to Provide Munitions of War, and for Other Purposes," Feb. 20, 1861, *Statutes*, I, 28–29.

4. "An Act to Establish the War Department," Feb. 21, 1861, *ibid.*, p. 32; "An Act to Create the Clerical Force of the Several Executive Departments of the Confederate States of America, and for Other Purposes," March 7, 1861, *ibid.*, pp. 52–53.

5. "An Act for the Establishment and Organization of a General Staff for the Army of the Confederate States of America," Feb. 26, 1861, *ibid.*, pp. 38–39; "An Act to Increase the Military Establishment of the Confederate States, and to Amend the 'Act for the Establishment and Organization of the Army of the Confederate States of America,'" May 16, 1861, *ibid.*, pp. 114–116.

6. "An Act to Appoint a Second Auditor of the Treasury," March 15, 1861, *ibid.*, p. 66; "An Act to Increase the Clerical Force of the Treasury Department, in the Bureau of Second Auditor," May 21, 1861, *ibid.*, p. 151.

him "to assume control of all military operations in every State."[7] It further authorized the President to accept state military units which might be offered to the Confederate States "in such numbers as he may require, for any time not less than twelve months, unless sooner discharged," the troops to receive the same pay and allowances and to be under the same rules and regulations as the yet uncreated provisional army.[8]

On March 6 legislation establishing a regular army and a provisional army reached the President's desk. One act created the "Army of the Confederate States of America," incorporating the staff departments previously authorized and, as later amended, adding a corps of engineers, a corps of artillery, eight regiments of infantry, and two of cavalry. Pay of officers and men was precisely described; enlisted men were to receive one ration per day, in kind if possible, and a yearly allowance of clothing; quartermasters and commissaries were to be bonded.[9] A second act authorized the President to accept up to 100,000 volunteers for twelve months' service and provided for their organization. These volunteers, when mustered into service, were to be armed either by the states or by the Confederate government and paid by the Confederate government. Enlisted men were to be furnished rations in kind, but the men were to furnish their own clothing, the cost of which would be commuted by the government.[10]

Between February 20 and March 6, therefore, in a spurt of legislation, the Confederate Congress created the framework for a flexible military system suitable to the uncertain times. The Executive had been given the power to make war on behalf of the several states, directed by the President through the Secretary of War and implemented by the staff and supply bureaus. The government had obligated itself to raise and equip a small regular army for the long-range future, to equip immediately for service at Charleston and Pensacola a small force of men mustered by the states, and to pay for the time, clothing, arms, and food for a short-term force of 100,000 men if the future should bring war.

As Congress created offices and armies the politics of appointments proceeded apace. The very day on which Davis signed the War De-

7. "An Act to Raise Provisional Forces for the Confederate States of America, and for Other Purposes," Feb. 28, 1861, *ibid.*, p. 43. 8. *Ibid.*, pp. 43–44.

9. "An Act for the Establishment and Organization of the Army of the Confederate States of America," March 6, 1861, *ibid.*, pp. 47–52.

10. "An Act to Provide for the Public Defense," March 6, 1861, *ibid.*, pp. 45–46.

partment bill into law, he sent forward the nomination of Leroy Pope Walker, the Alabama Democratic party stalwart, as Secretary of War. Walker was not Davis's first choice, and Davis apparently knew little about him from personal contact but accepted him on advice from his political advisers, probably to give Alabama a place in the Cabinet. Congress confirmed Walker before it recessed that evening.[11] Both Davis and Walker then began immediately to cast about for men to fill the positions opened up by the General Staff bill of February 26.

Despite the tradition that Southerners were fierce fighters and presumably would not have stooped to anything as unmartial as a supply post, a substantial number of men sought positions in the staff departments.[12] One man, Abraham C. Myers, fought for appointment. Born in South Carolina and a West Point graduate, Myers had performed brilliantly in the Mexican War, where in the unlikely capacity of a division supply officer he had the distinction of receiving two brevet promotions for acts of gallantry at Churabusco and Resaca de la Palma.[13] General Taylor had been so impressed with Myers that he had put him in command of quartermaster operations for the whole army.[14] After the war Myers had filled a number of important administrative posts under Joseph E. Johnston, U.S. Quartermaster General, and in 1861 was chief quartermaster of the Southern Department, with headquarters in New Orleans.[15] A secessionist, Myers surrendered the government stores in his possession to the state of Louisiana, handed in his resignation on January 28, and became Quartermaster General of Louisiana.[16]

On February 7 he wrote to William Porcher Miles, South Carolina representative to the Provisional Congress and later chairman of the Military Affairs Committee of the Permanent Congress, to ask Miles to round up Congressional support for his preferment:

> After you have established a provisional Government, one of the first things to be done I presume will be the creation of an Army for the Southern Confederacy. We have a small regular

11. Rembert Wallace Patrick, *Jefferson Davis and His Cabinet* (Baton Rouge, 1944), p. 104; *Journal,* I, 73.

12. See files for spring of 1861, WDLR.

13. Ellsworth Eliot, Jr., *West Point in the Confederacy* (New York, 1941), p. 402. Cited hereinafter as Eliot, *West Point.*

14. Wigfall to Clay, Aug. 13, 1863, Clement Claiborne Clay Papers, Duke University Manuscript Department.

15. Eliot, *West Point,* p. 402.

16. Myers to Kilburn, Jan. 28, 1861, *OR*-1, I, 408; Myers to Miles, Feb. 7, 1861, William Porcher Miles Papers, Southern Historical Collection, University of North Carolina.

> Army in this State of which I am Quarter Master General. I beg the favor of you to bear this in mind when the same office is being fitted for the Confederate Army and to co-operate with the delegation from Louisiana in promoting my claims. I have said nothing on this subject to anyone.[17]

Myers's qualifications and his political manipulation brought results. In response to a wire from Walker, Myers went to Montgomery, where in an interview with Davis he asked for service in the Quartermaster's Department.[18] Apparently Davis told Myers he would be put in temporary control of the bureau, for on March 15, Walker sent to Congress Myers's nomination as a lieutenant-colonel in the Quartermaster's Department.[19] On March 16 the nomination was duly confirmed.[20] Myers wired his acceptance from New Orleans and then wrote to Miles:

> The Qmr. place [Acting Quartermaster General] I accept, because it really gives the best opportunity to claim the 1st. No one I understand is spoken of now. I will act as Chief of the Department until they attempt to put some one over me and then I will resign if the attempt succeeds.[21]

On March 25, 1861, General Orders No. 1 proclaimed Myers as "Acting Quartermaster-General of the Confederate States."[22]

While the Quartermaster General had politicked to secure his position, the future Chief of Ordnance had to be coaxed. A West Pointer from Pennsylvania, Josiah Gorgas had seen service in the Mexican War and had married into the Gayle family of Alabama politicians, being stationed from time to time in ordnance posts in the South after the Mexican War.[23] After refusing an earlier proposal, Gorgas was prompted by personal difficulties in the United States ordnance service

17. Myers to Miles, Feb. 7, 1861, *ibid.*

18. Walker to Miles, March 14, 1861, WDTS, XXXIII, 4; Myers to Miles, March 14, 1861, William Porcher Miles Papers, Southern Historical Collection, University of North Carolina. 19. *Journal*, I, 154, 156. 20. *Ibid.*

21. Myers to Miles, March 19, 1861, William Porcher Miles Papers, Southern Historical Collection, University of North Carolina.

22. General Orders No. 1, Adjutant and Inspector General's Office, 1861 Series, March 25, 1861, *OR*-4, I, 188.

23. Frank E. Vandiver, *Ploughshares into Swords: Josiah Gorgas and Confederate Ordnance* (Austin, 1952), pp. 41 ff. Cited hereinafter as Vandiver, *Confederate Ordnance.*

to inquire of Walker if the original offer still held.[24] Walker replied, "Yes, and come at once."[25] On April 8, 1861, probably after personal consultations between Gorgas and Davis at Montgomery, Special Orders No. 17 announced: "Major Josiah Gorgas, of the Corps of Artillery and Ordnance, is assigned to duty as Chief of the Bureau of Ordnance."[26] Actually, as "Chief of the Bureau of Ordnance," Gorgas's position was a nebulous one. Unlike the Quartermaster's Department and the Subsistence Department, there was no official Ordnance Department. There was a corps of artillery, created for the regular army and intended for field service, and there was authorization for the President to contract for ordnance production. But that was all. However, even at this period, the need for centralized administration of the production and distribution of ordnance demanded the creation of a *de facto* Ordnance Department, which took its place with the other supply bureaus.

Myers and Gorgas, whatever the real reason for their selection, were West Pointers whose military careers had been based on quartermaster and ordnance service; the processes leading to the accession of Lucius Bellinger Northrop to the post of Commissary General of Subsistence are more obscure. Northrop was a South Carolinian and a West Pointer, a plebe during the year that Davis was a senior. Northrop rose to the rank of captain of cavalry, serving at one point under Davis. Long stretches of sick leaves finally led to his being dropped from the army rolls in 1848.[27] Davis, John C. Calhoun, and Pierce Butler had worked to have Northrop reinstated, and he had been continued on the rolls in an inactive capacity while building up a medical practice in Charleston,[28] finally resigning his army commission in January 1861. Apparently Davis remembered Northrop and decided to employ him in some capacity, for Walker telegraphed Northrop on March 11, 1861, and again on March 13 to see if his health would allow him to accept the position of captain in the Subsistence Department.[29] Northrop, who

24. Beauregard to Gorgas, Feb. 27, 1861, WDTS, XXXIII, 3; Gorgas to Walker, March 12, 1861, WDLR; Vandiver, *Confederate Ordnance,* p. 53; Myers to Walker, n. d., WDTR.

25. Walker to Gorgas, March 26, 1861, WDTS, XXXIII, 34.

26. Special Orders No. 17, Adjutant and Inspector General's Office, 1861 Series, April 8, 1861, *OR*-4, I, 211.

27. Eliot, *West Point,* p. 403; RG 109, Adjutant General's Office Personal Files—Lucius Bellinger Northrop.

28. RG 109, Adjutant General's Office Personal Files—Lucius Bellinger Northrop.

29. Walker to Northrop, March 11, 1861, WDTS, XXXIII, 12; Walker to Northrop, March 13, 1861, *ibid.,* p. 13.

had been serving as a paymaster for South Carolina, accepted immediately.[30] What occurred after Northrop left for Montgomery on March 20 is unknown, but Davis must have been impressed with him; for on March 27 General Orders No. 9 announced that "Lieutenant-Colonel Lucius B. Northrop, of the Subsistence Department, is assigned to duty as Acting Commissary-General of Subsistence."[31] Davis apparently considered Northrop as only a temporary expedient, for Walker offered two other men the post of Commissary General. After Richard Griffith refused, Walker telegraphed Captain William Maynadier at the Frankford Arsenal in Pennsylvania, offering him the appointment of Commissary General.[32] Maynadier declined, however, and there is no evidence that anyone else was approached for the position, which Northrop continued to administer by default.[33] Under the circumstances, it seems hardly fair to claim, as some have done, that Davis schemed to put in an old crony.

. . .

At the same time they were creating offices and finding officials, Congress and the Executive were also beginning to accumulate supplies. On February 21, the day after the President had signed the act empowering him to contract for ordnance, Davis authorized Raphael Semmes to set out for the North to make purchases and contracts. Davis suggested the Hazard Powder Company in Connecticut as a likely prospect and suggested that an "artificer named Wright" at the Washington Arsenal might sell a cap machine. Davis also told Semmes to buy the improved rifle-making machinery then for sale at Harper's Ferry, to contract for the establishment of a friction-primer plant in the Confederacy, to buy all the artillery he could find, and to bring back as many armorers and skilled men as possible from the United States ordnance depots.[34] It was also in these early days that the Confederate administration formed its important connection with the Tredegar Iron Works. The Tredegar establishment in Richmond was still in the United States, but that did not prevent interested parties

30. Northrop to Walker, March 12, 1861, WDTR; Northrop to Walker, March 13, 1861, *ibid.*

31 General Orders No. 9. Adjutant and Inspector General's Office, 1861 Series, March 27, 1861, *OR*-4, I, 191.

32. Thomas Hay, "Lucius B. Northrop: Commissary General of the Confederacy," *Civil War History,* IX, No. 1 (March 1963), 6; Walker to Maynadier, April 9, 1861, *OR*-4, I, 215. 33. Maynadier to Walker, April 15, 1861, *ibid.*, p. 221.

34. Davis to Semmes, Feb. 21, 1861, *ibid.*, pp. 106–107.

from bringing Joseph R. Anderson, the proprietor, to Montgomery by March 1 to begin negotiations with the Confederate government.[35]

Despite this initial display of vigor on the part of the President, the politicians who managed procurement in early March before the army professionals took over operated in a rather perfunctory fashion, perhaps because they did not believe that war would break out. Contractors in both the United States and in the Confederacy had scented lucrative possibilities in supplying the new army, and a rising tide of offers to supply arms, equipment, clothing, and food began to flood the Montgomery offices of the War Department.[36] The only offers that Walker routinely accepted were those of arms, food, and equipment made by the states and contracts which the states wished to transfer to the Confederate government,[37] perhaps because Davis wished to assume control of the existing military potential of the Confederacy. When it came to the offers of private parties, Walker, undoubtedly with the approval of Davis, began to pick and choose, and chiefly to reject. Walker haggled over prices of a large lot of ordnance stores offered from Washington and in the end ordered only a few pistols and rifles.[38] He pressed into service the secretary of the Congress, Johnston Jones Hooper, who specialized in polite refusals to Confederate contractors and appears to have declined offers from most manufacturing establishments worthy of the name in the seven states of the Confederacy. Under the direction of the Secretary of War, Hooper's most notable refusals included an offer by the Phoenix Iron Works of New Orleans to sell shot and shell, an offer to sell the Selma powder works to the Confederacy, the offer by the Gregg family's famed Graniteville Mill in South Carolina to make up tent cloth, and other contracts for shot and shell and quartermaster supplies.[39]

Even the limited commitments of March cost money. On March 11 Congress appropriated $7,183,995.17 to support for twelve months a force of 5,000 volunteers in service and to provide for any new

35. Clayton to Walker, Feb. 27, 1861, WDLR; Semmes to Walker, Feb. 28, 1861, *OR*-4, I, 118–119. 36. See files for spring of 1861, WDLR.

37. Walker to Brown, March 20, 1861, *OR*-4, I, 179; Walker to A. B. Moore, April 9, 1861, *ibid.*, p. 179; Walker to Brown, May 13, 1861, *ibid.*, p. 315.

38. Forsyth to Walker, April 8, 1861, *ibid.*, p. 210; Walker to Forsyth, April 9, 1861, *ibid.*, p. 212; Walker to Forsyth, April 9, 1861, *ibid.*, p. 213.

39. Watts *et al.* to Walker, Feb. 22, 1861, *OR*-4, I, 107–108; Leroy to Walker, March 11, 1861, WDLR; Hooper to Leroy, March 23, 1861, WDLS, I, 75; Gregg to Walker, March 14, 1861, WDLR; Hooper to Gregg, March 22, 1861, WDLS, I, 65; Gilmore to Walker, March 26, 1861, *OR*-4, I, 191; Hooper to Gilmore, March 29, 1861, *ibid.*, p. 194; Holbrook to Walker, March 20, 1861, WDLR; Hooper to Holbrook, March 22, 1861, WDLS, I, 65.

units which might be accepted.[40] To equip for twelve months the regular army, which as yet existed only on paper, Congress appropriated $6,533,760.00 with a proviso suggested by the President that the monies not spent on the regular army could be used to support any new units of volunteers which might be mustered into the Confederate service.[41] The civil expenses of the War Department, meanwhile, entailed an appropriation of only $59,000.[42] Finally, on March 16, the last day of the session, Congress, at the President's request, appropriated an additional $110,000 for the purchase of munitions.[43]

By April the new supply chiefs were in office, but before they had an opportunity to estimate their needs and resources and make out a program for steady procurement, hostilities at Fort Sumter altered the entire situation. On the one hand, the state of war made it imperative for the Confederacy to raise and equip the large volunteer forces authorized, and this threatened to be beyond the immediate resources of the supply bureaus. On the other hand, the accession of Virginia, North Carolina, and Tennessee brought into the Confederacy the great bulk of the manufacturing and much of the food-producing potential of the new nation, and these resources turned what would have been a forlorn hope of winning a war of attrition into a possibility.

President Davis set the pace for mobilization. He called for Congress to assemble in special session so that it could vote new measures and new money, and before it assembled, he called on his bureau chiefs to estimate the costs of supporting the full force of 100,000 volunteers allowed by law. Davis had also decided to accept volunteers as fast as they were now offered, and he sent them to Virginia and Pensacola. To facilitate matters, Walker dropped his earlier role as contract evaluator

40. "An Act Making Appropriations for the Support of Three Thousand Men for Twelve Months, to be Called into Service at Charleston, South Carolina, under the Third and Fourth Sections of An Act of Congress 'To Raise Provisional Forces for the Confederate States of America, and for Other Purposes,'" March 11, 1861, *Statutes,* I, 58; "An Act Making Appropriations to Carry Out the Provisions of 'An Act to Provide for the Public Defense,'" March 12, 1861, *ibid.,* p. 61.

41. "An Act Making Appropriations for the Support of the Regular Army of the Confederate States of America for Twelve Months, and for Other Purposes," March 11, 1861, *ibid.,* pp. 58–60; Davis to Congress, March 6, 1861, *Messages,* I, 57–58.

42. "An Act Making Appropriations for the Legislative, Executive, and Judicial Expenses of Government, for the Year Ending the Fourth of February, Eighteen Hundred and Sixty-two," March 15, 1861, *Statutes,* I, 63–65.

43. "An Act Making Additional Appropriations for the Support of the Army, for the Year Ending the First of March, Eighteen Hundred and Sixty-one," March 16, 1861, *ibid.,* p. 88; Davis to Congress, March 15, 1861, *Messages,* I, 58.

to serve as the President's foil in dealing with the states on matters of equipment and transportation of the troops. The President arrogated to himself all matters of appointing officers and assigning ranks and precedents of command.[44]

On April 29 Congress reconvened and assumed its role in the mobilization project. It authorized the President to accept units without making a formal call on the states and thus enabled men from outside the Confederacy to enter the service more easily, and it also authorized him to accept volunteers "for the duration."[45] Units which volunteered for the duration were given priority in being accepted and armed by the government. Finally, to support an army of 100,000 men until the spring of 1862, Congress appropriated over $39,000,000, treble the previous total cost of the war effort.[46]

Meanwhile the chiefs of the supply bureaus were attempting to create effective organizations and trying to stay abreast of their rapidly expanding responsibilities. The Ordnance Department was the center of greatest concern because of its comparative poverty in resources, and Major Gorgas struggled to secure arms, ammunition, and equipment under the pressure of political and public concern. He left to his civilian bosses the task of hounding the state governments to give up ordnance supplies, while he concentrated on distribution and production. In dealing with the states, Gorgas requested that arms be issued to troops after they had rendezvoused for active service, in order to prevent state governors from making "perplexing and mischievous requisitions"[47] on the arsenals. He estimated that 159,000 small arms of every description, including flintlocks, had been seized from the United States arsenals within the limits of the Confederacy, with an unknown (but small) number in private hands, and some 429 cannon.[48] He had some 330,000 pounds of cannon powder, 162,000 pounds of musket and rifle powder, and 3,200,000 small-arms cartridges.[49] Trans-

44. Walker to Governors A. B. Moore, Brown, Magoffin, and T. V. Moore, April 22, 1861, *OR*-4, I, 231–232.

45. "An Act to Raise an Additional Military Force to Serve During the War," May 8, 1861, *Statutes,* I, p. 104; "An Act to Make Further Provisions for the Public Defense," May 11, 1861, *ibid.*, p. 106.

46. "An Act Making Appropriations in Addition to Those Already Made for the Military Service of the Confederate States of America, for the Fiscal Year Ending the Eighteenth of February, One Thousand Eight Hundred and Sixty-two," *ibid.*, pp. 123–124.

47. Gorgas to Walker, May 4, 1861, *OR*-4, I, 280.

48. Gorgas to Walker, May 7, 1861, *ibid.,* p. 292; Gorgas to Walker, April 20, 1861, *ibid.,* pp. 227–228.

49. Gorgas to Walker, April 20, 1861, *ibid.,* pp. 227–228.

lating small-arms powder into cartridges, his total might perhaps reach 4,500,000 cartridges, or only some 30 rounds per available small arm, and that amount only if the cartridges could be differentiated into the proper calibers. The ordnance manual called for 200 rounds per man.

With a miniscule ordnance reserve to service an army projected at 100,000 men it was imperative for Gorgas to begin production of new supplies. The Confederate government had taken over the use of the former United States arsenals and depots, but their productive capacities were depressingly limited. Only the Richmond Arsenal was immediately equipped to manufacture small arms. The other establishments, those at Nashville, Baton Rouge, Mongtomery, Mount Vernon, Charleston, Augusta, and Savannah, were in a position to make only accouterments, plus cartridges if supplied powder.[50] The Confederate government controlled no facilities for making heavy ordnance, powder, or small arms in the quantities needed. For heavy ordnance, Gorgas contracted with the only two private firms capable of heavy casting, the Etowah works outside Atlanta and Tredegar in Richmond.[51] For powder he began to make arrangements with those contractors whom he could find in Tennessee, North Carolina, Louisiana, and Alabama and sent agents to explore the Appalachian foothills for niter caves.[52] He encouraged North Carolina to expand its tiny small-arms factory at Fayetteville and also negotiated with private contractors who professed to be able to produce small arms. Finally, apparently thinking in terms of preparing for a long war, he arranged to send Caleb Huse abroad as Confederate agent empowered to buy and ship ordnance supplies.[53] Private contracts and Huse's purchasing would not come to fruition for months, however. Meanwhile, Gorgas envisioned setting up a complex of government ordnance works that could supply the armies without reliance on private contracts.[54] But if any military action were to be fought that summer, the Confederacy would have to make do with what it had inherited from the United States.

Quartermaster General Myers was also making progress. He began to advertise for bids from contractors for the tents and camp and garrison equipage that he was to furnish both the regular army and the volunteers and for the uniforms that he was to furnish the regular army.[55] The official uniform of the regular army was to consist of a semi-annual issue of one blue flannel shirt, four pairs of grey flannel

50. Vandiver, *Confederate Ordnance,* pp. 59, 61. 51. *Ibid.*
52. *Ibid.,* p. 75. 53. *Ibid.,* p. 61. 54. *Ibid.,* p. 59.
55. See, for example, Myers to Walker, April 12, 1861, WDLR.

trousers, three pairs of red flannel undershirts, four pairs of cotton drawers, three pairs of wool stockings, two pairs of boots, one blanket, one leather stock, and one cap, all for a total cost of $26.95.[56] By mid-April five thousand sets had been ordered from contractors in New Orleans.[57] The commutation to be paid the volunteers who furnished their own clothing was set by Congress at $21 semi-annually;[58] but Myers, on getting reports of the condition of the swarms of volunteers who were being accepted after Fort Sumter, saw that many men could not or would not furnish themselves with the standard issue. Although the textile-producing states on the eastern seaboard were able to make arrangements to clothe their men and receive reimbursement from the Confederate government, it was soon obvious that the Confederate government would have to supply many of the volunteers with clothing. By June Myers was calling on his New Orleans contractors to furnish 1,500 sets of clothing a week and was trying to make arrangements with mills in Georgia and Virginia to increase the sources of supply.[59]

As early as May Myers reached the conclusion that the Confederacy did not have enough blankets, flannel, shoes or woolen cloth for uniforms to equip the tiny regular army, much less meet the burgeoning needs of the volunteers. He suggested that measures be taken to obtain these articles from Europe.[60] But unlike Gorgas, he did not press the matter, waiting instead for the Secretary of War to take the initiative. As a result, nothing was done.

To collect quartermaster supplies and hold them subject to requisitions by the field armies, Myers established a series of quartermaster depots, which he moved northward as the limits of the Confederacy expanded. He set up the first depots at Montgomery, San Antonio, Charleston, New Orleans, and Mobile;[61] but after the second secession he added posts at Nashville, Lynchburg, and Richmond, to the immediate rear of the armies forming in Tennessee and Virginia.[62]

Another important responsibility of the Quartermaster General was

56. Myers to Walker, April 18, 1861, QMDSW, p. 8.

57. Myers to Galt, April 19, 1861, QMDLS, XIII, 38.

58. "An Act Concerning the Transportation of Soldiers and Allowance for Clothing of Volunteers, and Amendatory of the Act for the Establishment and Organization of the Army of the Confederate States," May 21, 1861, *Statutes*, I, 126.

59. Myers to Galt, June 5, 1861, QMDLS, XIII, 166.

60. Myers to Walker, May 13, 1861, *OR*-4, I, 314–315.

61. Myers to posts, March 28, 1861, QMDLS, XIII, 13.

62. Myers to Williams, April 24, 1861, *ibid.*, pp. 50–51; Myers to Cabell, April 24, 1861, *ibid.*, pp. 51–52.

to provide for transportation. The "gay blades" of the Confederacy compounded difficulties in collecting wagons for the army units by the enormous impedimenta that they insisted on taking into the camps before combat and marching experience enlightened them. Supply transportation from the rear to the armies appeared to be easier to arrange. Myers made numerous contracts for hiring steamboats to haul supplies and men about on the rivers and inland waters of the Confederacy, and few problems arose on that score.[63] The railroads, too, appeared to pose no problem. Commissary officials, anxious to secure a dependable supply of transportation for subsistence stores, approached Myers to suggest that he arrange for through freight schedules, but Myers was opposed to such controls over the railroad companies and set out to guarantee adequate shipping facilities by voluntary agreements with them.[64] In a series of railroad conventions held at Montgomery, Chattanooga, and Richmond from April to July the railroads of the Confederacy patriotically agreed to transport soldiers at two cents per mile per man (civilian fares averaged four and one half cents per mile) and also agreed to carry military supplies at half the local freight rates. In addition, they promised to accept payment in bonds or treasury notes at par if ordinary currency were not available.[65] With such agreements the Quartermaster General rested well content.

Material is fragmentary on the work of the Commissary General, but Northrop, inexperienced in comparison with Gorgas or Myers, and perhaps less tradition-bound, soon demonstrated his penchant for basing actions on theory. Technically Northrop's responsibility was to collect those foodstuffs called for by the regulation army ration in sufficient quantities to feed the troops; but he immediately envisioned controlling the entire Confederate food markets.[66] Unfortunately for

63. A typical case of the steamboat arrangements of the Quartermaster's Department can be found in Myers to Cruger, March 7, 1863, *ibid.*, XVII, 104–105.

64. "Substance of the Testimony of Lieutenant-Colonel Frank G. Ruffin before a Joint Committee of Congress, January [23], 1865," PRSD, p. 40. Cited hereinafter as "Ruffin Testimony," PRSD.

65. Walker to the Railroad Presidents, April 25, 1861, *OR*-4, I, 238; Robert C. Black III, *The Railroads of the Confederacy* (Chapel Hill, 1952), pp. 52–56; Resolution of the Montgomery Railroad Convention, April 30, 1861, *OR*-4, I, 269. Cited hereinafter as Black, *Confederate Railroads.*

66. Northrop to Walker, September 9, 1861, *OR*-1, V, 835–836. Northrop's obligation was to furnish the troops with the following daily ration, based on the standard U. S. army ration tables:

per individual ration: ¾ lb. pork or bacon or 1¼ lbs. fresh and/or salt beef.
18 ounces of bread or flour or

his theories, he ran into difficulties at once. He sought to buy the non-perishable components of the army rations in large quantities to guard against future exigencies, but he found that provision sellers wanted currency rather than treasury notes or bonds and the Secretary of the Treasury could not supply him with enough bank notes or specie.[67] In addition, there were not enough supplies of such items as coffee, vinegar, and soap for stockpiling even if funds had been available.[68] To save money, Northrop made contracts for large amounts of meat and breadstuffs from outside the limits of the Confederacy, but the outbreak of hostilities disorganized those arrangements.[69]

Many of Northrop's stockpiling ideas were good theory thwarted by unfortunate circumstances, but other aspects of his theorizing tended to conflict with common sense, as events in Virginia demonstrated. With the approval of Davis, Northrop refused to pay higher prices for flour demanded by producers in proximity to the troops at Manassas but rather filled up large depots with the cheaper flour of south-central Virginia and offered northern producers only the Richmond market prices less transportation costs, on the argument that the Washington markets were closed to the producers of northern Virginia and that without a Confederate army for customers farmers would have to sell their wheat at Richmond and deduct transportation costs.[70] Northrop forbade commissary agents in northern Virginia to pay the higher local prices and supplied the troops from Richmond as long as the prices in

---

12 ounces of hard bread or 1¼ lbs. corn meal.

per 100 rations: 8 qts. peas or beans or 10 lbs. rice.
6 lbs. coffee.
12 lbs. sugar.
4 qts. vinegar.
1½ lbs. tallow or 1¼ lbs. adamantine or 1 lb. sperm candles.
4 lbs. soap.
2 qts. salt.

There were a number of authorized substitutes and variations for troops on the march and under special conditions.

67. Northrop to Davis, Aug. 21, 1861, Dunbar Rowland, ed., *Jefferson Davis, Constitutionalist: His Letters, Papers, and Speeches* (10 vols.; Jackson, Mississippi, 1923), V, 124–127. Cited hereinafter as Rowland, *Jefferson Davis.*

68. *Ibid.* 69. *Ibid.*

70. Sir Frederick Barton Maurice, ed., *An Aide-de-Camp of Lee, Being the Papers of Colonel Charles Marshall, Sometime Aide-de-Camp, Military Secretary, and Assistant Adjutant General on the Staff of Robert E. Lee, 1862–1865* (Boston, 1927), p. 46.

northern Virginia remained above Richmond market levels. He is alleged to have pointed to the large Richmond mills and stated, "Here are my magazines; I will bring those gentlemen to terms."[71] Army officers and others pointed out that when the transportation costs of shipping the flour from Richmond to Manassas were added to the Richmond price, the cost of the flour was virtually the same as that asked in the vicinity of the armies.[72] Somehow, to the officers at Manassas, it was just too strangely theoretical to watch local farmers load their flour on cars to be sent to Richmond, while carloads of government flour, some originally from the vicinity, arrived regularly from Richmond. In addition, the constant transportation of flour back and forth from northern Virginia monopolized valuable freight space on the overworked railroads. Most damaging, Northrop's scheme left the food-producing areas nearest the enemy untouched, providing the enemy with food if they should advance.[73]

. . .

The Manassas campaign presented an acid test of the Confederate supply system. For one thing, Manassas provided a portent for the future, for it revealed in microcosm many of the supply problems that would continue to plague the Confederate supply effort for years to come. In addition, the supply situation at Manassas affected the prospects of the Confederacy's capturing Washington and thus winning a short war.

By the first of June the War Department and the supply bureaus had set up their offices in Richmond, closer to the scene of impending battle and closer, also, to the multiplying evidences of confusion, inefficiency, and general inadequacy in preparing the volunteers for field operations. Troops had been collecting near Manassas and in the Shenandoah Valley since May, and by June over 30,000 men were encamped, many without sufficient arms, ammunition, and clothes, or regular food supplies.[74] Pungent comments on the condition of the troops abound, but Colonel Edmund Kirby Smith's statement that his men were "so illy provided with everything from arms to

71. *Ibid.* 72. *Ibid.*

73. For a typical press attack on Northrop's plan, see *Daily Richmond Examiner,* April 15, 1862.

74. Alfred Roman, *The Military Operations of General Beauregard in the War between the States, 1861 to 1865, Including a Brief Personal Sketch and a Narrative of His Services in the War with Mexico, 1846–8* (2 vols.; New York, 1883), I, 98, 113. Cited hereinafter as Roman, *Beauregard.*

clothing that they are scarcely efficient to take the field" suffices.[75] Colonel James Chesnut, the prominent South Carolina politician, bespoke the common conclusion: "The opinion prevails throughout the army that there is great imbecility or shameful neglect in the War Department."[76]

In reality the causes for the failure of supplies were not as morbidly romantic as imbecility or shameful neglect. The causes were prosaic—inadequate supplies and inexperienced administrators. The railroad system, which funneled into a single track leading to Manassas, was unable to carry all of the volunteers, their mountains of impedimenta, and their daily food supply; and as a result, food and ammunition piled up at depots all along the way. Meat was weeks in coming from Tennessee, while flour and ammunition piled up at Fredericksburg.[77] At Manassas the military complicated matters by retaining freight cars as storehouses instead of unloading them and putting them back into service.[78] Even if the railroad system had been adequate, the Ordnance Department did not have enough ammunition to pass out more than fifty to seventy rounds per man.[79] Despite the volunteers' anxious determination to look the part of a soldier, the Quartermaster's Department could not supply enough uniforms and boots; and the soldiers who had not been able to procure clothing and boots from home markets or from their state governments had to be content with their own civilian togs and shoes. Tents, blankets, and camp and garrison equipage were unavoidably in short supply. Food rations did not match those called for in the manuals, because vegetables, sugar, coffee, vinegar, and soap could either not be found in the quantities needed or could not be regularly shipped in from across the country. The troops soon had to content themselves with a monotonous diet of corn meal, flour, bacon, and beef.

The melancholy situation of inadequate resources was compounded

75. Kirby Smith to Mrs. Kirby Smith, June 2, 1861, Edmund Kirby-Smith Papers, Southern Historical Collection, University of North Carolina.

76. Chesnut to Mrs. Chesnut, June 22, 1861, Mary Boykin Chesnut, *A Diary from Dixie, As Written by Mary Boykin Chesnut, Wife of James Chesnut, Jr., United States Senator from South Carolina, 1859–1861, and Afterward an Aide to Jefferson Davis and a Brigadier-General in the Confederate Army,* ed. Isabella D. Martin and Myrta Lockett Avary (New York, 1929), pp. 75–76. Cited hereinafter as Chesnut, *Diary from Dixie.*

77. Northrop to Davis, Aug. 21, 1861, Rowland, *Jefferson Davis,* V, 127–128; Myers to Ashe, July 18, 1861, QMDLS, XIII, 313.

78. Northrop to Davis, Aug. 21, 1861, Rowland, *Jefferson Davis,* V, 128.

79. Vandiver, *Confederate Ordnance,* p. 75.

by administrative inexperience and inefficiency. Most of the field officers and supply officials were new to their tasks and committed many errors, usually errors of omission. In particular, the supply officers in the field were either negligent of or unfamiliar with proper requisitioning procedures and kept the bureau officials in Richmond in ignorance of the nature and quantities of supplies needed by the men. The field quartermasters and commissaries also distributed the available supplies unequally, with the result that some units missed whole days of being fed, while supplies rotted at the depots for lack of proper storage facilities.[80] The quartermasters and commissaries attached to the field units were ostensibly appointed and controlled by their bureau chiefs in Richmond, but they were actually selected by the commanding officers of the units and felt a loyalty and responsibility to their field commanders rather than to the Richmond administrators. At the lower levels, this divided loyalty made little practical difference in comparison with the general inexperience in requisition and distribution; but in the higher echelons it bred trouble. On occasion, Myers and the chief army quartermasters clashed over transportation and storage policy. However, the most serious controversies occurred between Northrop and the chief commissaries of commanding generals P. G. T. Beauregard and Joseph E. Johnston, Captain W. H. Fowle and Colonel R. B. Lee. Both Fowle and Lee were ordered by their commanders to buy locally to feed the men. Northrop, interested in controlling prices, forbade them to buy locally and asked them instead to depend on supplies from Richmond. Northrop was supported by Davis in his endeavors and eventually succeeded in getting both subordinates removed.[81] Before Lee was removed, however, he had the satisfaction of seeing railroad transportation difficulties force Northrop to abandon his idea of shipping all food from Richmond and to allow the field commissaries to buy supplies in the vicinity.

To complicate matters, Johnston and Northrop clashed over the diet of the men. Regulations called for the issue of bacon three or four times a week, but transportation difficulties delayed shipping the bacon in from Tennessee, where the Subsistence Department was getting the best prices. As a result, the commissaries issued bacon only one or two times a week and the rest of the time supplied the men fresh beef from

80. Beauregard to Miles and Chesnut, July 29, 1861, Roman, *Beauregard,* I, 121; Northrop to Davis, July 21, 1861, Rowland, *Jefferson Davis,* V, 124–127.

81. Roman, *Beauregard,* I, 72; Northrop to Davis, July 21, 1861, Rowland, *Jefferson Davis,* V, 127–128.

the herds of cattle gathered in the vicinity of the camps.[82] The "fresh" meat, however, because of delays in slaughtering and in local transportation and field distribution, was often spoiled before it reached the troops. In addition, many of the men did not know how to cook beef properly.[83] Johnston complained about the shortage of bacon, and ex-medic Northrop, ever the theoretician, replied, "The experience of mankind, confirmed by scientific research, proves that a diet of fresh meat exclusively is conducive to health and that an admixture of salt meat is not more so."[84] And so it went, both before and after the battle.

When the men marched out to fight on July 21, according to the military manuals they were already beaten. They had neither the ammunition, clothing, nor diet to be effective. Thus, from the very first battle many soldiers, officers, and supply officials learned to disregard traditions and manuals. On the other hand, too many commanders, dismayed in their very first campaign by supply shortages, became reluctant to fight unless their armies were supplied up to traditional standards. Perhaps this was why Joseph E. Johnston proved to be so cautious during the war. Who should be a better judge of what an army needed to fight and win than the former Quartermaster General of the United States Army?

The Confederates won the battle of Manassas in spite of supply deficiencies, but the unsatisfactory supply situation may have contributed vitally to the failure of the Confederacy to follow up the victory, capture Washington, and win the war. On the evening of the battle, Davis advised immediate pursuit; but the generals, probably impressed by the disarray of their own men, evaded compliance, and a rainstorm during the early hours of the next morning ended the matter for the moment.[85]

There is little evidence of what was proposed or discussed concerning pursuit during the next few days. Apparently Beauregard wished to advance in early August, but Johnston did not wish to make the attempt. If Johnston did veto Beauregard's idea, the state of supplies may well have been a factor; for the shipments of bacon and hard bread had become even more erratic than before the battle, while both the infantry and the artillery were short of wagons and teams.[86]

The glittering temptation of an advance on Washington lingered on into the autumn. In a conference at Fairfax Court House on September

82. Northrop to Davis, Aug. 21, 1861, Rowland, *Jefferson Davis,* V, 124–127.
83. *Ibid.* 84. *Ibid.,* p. 126. 85. Roman, *Beauregard,* I, 114–117.
86. *Ibid.,* pp. 125–126.

30 and October 1, Davis listened as generals Johnston, Beauregard, and Gustavus Smith unfolded a plan to take the offensive. The plan involved crossing the Potomac while a covering force remained in the original works to distract the enemy. The generals said such an operation called for an increase in the forces at Manassas from the current force of 40,000 men to 60,000. The additional 20,000 would be obtained by withdrawing regular forces from the west and from other points and allowing reserves to take the places of the temporarily departed troops.[87] Davis objected that he could not, presumably for political reasons, withdraw regular troops from other parts of the Confederacy to reinforce the Manassas army, and he also noted that there were no arms to equip new men above the 2,500 arms in the current army reserves.[88] The generals were unwilling to advance with the 40,000 men they had, and so the troops continued to sit in camp until the following spring.[89] Those military experts who feel that 60,000 men could have captured Washington and who also feel that this was the Confederacy's only opportunity to win can thus blame the supply situation for the downfall of the Confederacy, for even if the President had been willing to transfer regular troops to Virginia, there were no arms available to supply the reserves. The abandonment of the "on to Washington" scheme is the first, and quite possibly the most important, instance of the manner in which supply deficiencies shaped strategy.

Manassas supply confusion and post-Manassas supply shortages became the focus of public and official criticism and controversy. On July 29 Beauregard precipitated the furor. He wrote to William Porcher Miles and James Chesnut, his friends in the South Carolina congressional delegation, reciting specific post-Manassas shortages and claiming that Washington could have been taken as late as July 24, but

> The want of food and transportation had made us lose all the fruits of our victory. We ought at this moment to be in or about Washington. . . . God only knows when we will be able to advance; without those means we can neither advance nor retreat. . . .

87. The statements of Johnston, Beauregard, and Smith relating to this conference are found in *OR*-1, V, 884–887. See also Roman, *Beauregard,* I, 137–139, 142–145; Gustavus W. Smith, *Confederate War Papers* (New York, 1884), pp. 14–20, 33–36; Joseph E. Johnston, *Narrative of Military Operations, Directed during the Late War between the States* (New York, 1874), pp. 74–77, cited hereinafter as Johnston, *Narrative of Military Operations*; cf. Jefferson Davis, *The Rise and Fall of the Confederate Government* (2 vols.; London, 1881), I, 449–451.

88. *Ibid.* 89. *Ibid.*

> Cannot something be done towards furnishing us more expeditiously and regularly with food and transportation?[90]

On August 1 he wired Myers that some of his brigades were "destitute" of transportation and requested a hundred wagons.[91] Myers answered that he could send the wagons but complained that he had not heard of any deficiencies and since military operations were "never divulged," it was "impossible to anticipate" the general's wants.[92]

While Myers defended himself, Miles and Chesnut read Beauregard's letter to Congress and caused a sensation. Already impressed with months of complaints from soldier constituents,[93] the congressmen passed a resolution of inquiry offered by Chesnut on August 1 and sent it on to the President. It inquired about the condition of the Subsistence Department and whether or not the President had received "any authentic information going to show a want of sufficient and regular supply of food for the Army of the Confederate States, or any portion of it, now in the field."[94] There could have been no surer method of enraging Jefferson Davis than for Congress to inquire into the efficiency of some part of the executive branch, and he was quick to reply. No man to tolerate wrong-doing, he had written to Johnston that if unsatisfactory affairs in the commissariat were the result of "neglect" by subsistence officers in the bureau or in the field, "investigation and the proper correction" would be undertaken, not only to end specific abuses but also to "deter others."[95] To Congress, however, the President replied immediately that the condition of the commissariat

> is, in my judgment, quite as good as was reasonable to expect. The occupation of the railroads in the transportation of troops and munitions of war has interfered with the collection of the desired supply of bacon, but no complaint of insufficiency of rations has reached me until within a few days past.[96]

At the end he noted that inquiries and investigations had been inaugurated to correct abuses and to prevent their recurrence.[97] Meanwhile, Davis ferreted out the source of the mischief and wrote Beauregard

90. Roman, *Beauregard,* I, 121–122.

91. Beauregard to Myers, Aug. 1, 1861, *ibid.,* p. 122.

92. Myers to Beauregard, Aug. 1, 1861, *ibid.,* p. 125.

93. For example, one correspondent claimed that his regiment had received only one issue of vegetables between July 19 and September 7, 1861; *Daily Richmond Examiner,* Sept. 7, 1861.

94. *Journal,* I, 305.

95. Davis to Johnston, Aug. 1, 1861, *OR*-1, V, 767.

96. Davis to Congress, Aug. 1, 1861, *Messages,* I, 125–126.

97. *Ibid.*

that Myers and Northrop felt themselves "unjustly arraigned" and continued: "As for myself, I have endeavored to anticipate wants and any failure which has occurred from imperfect knowledge might have been best avoided by timely requisition and estimates."[98] As to the lost opportunities, Davis reminded Beauregard that information about the state of Union weakness was unknown at the close of the battle of Manassas and that under the known circumstances of that time it would have been "extremely hazardous to have done more than was performed."[99] Beauregard, in his reply, admitted that it would have been impossible to advance on July 21 or 22, but he still maintained that Washington could have been taken as late as July 24.[100]

Despite Davis's letter-writing, criticism of the supply services continued. Mrs. Chesnut noted in her diary:

> Now, if I were to pick out the best abused one, where all catch it so bountifully, I should say Mr. Commissary-General Northrop is the most "cussed" and villified [*sic*] man in the Confederacy. He is held accountable for everything that goes wrong in the army.[101]

In this acrimonious atmosphere Northrop wrote several long letters to Davis, analyzing and justifying his methods of purchasing and explaining his actions to keep the men at Manassas regularly supplied. At the end of one of these he added:

> I have done my best for our Common cause, but if the Executive or Legislative Powers can find any one to do better, I pray it may be done. I do not flinch from duty but I neither cringe nor cling to office.[102]

On second thought, however, he deleted his tempting offer. Undoubtedly, Northrop need not have been so circumspect, for Davis was satisfied with his performance or at least was apparently determined not to give Congress the satisfaction of seeing Northrop removed. As Congressman Miles put it in a letter to Beauregard, "The President has not the remotest idea of removing Colonel Northrop. On the contrary, he is under the impression that he has done everything in his power in his department."[103]

98. Davis to Beauregard, Aug. 4, 1861, *OR*-1, II, 507–508.
99. *Ibid.*
100. Beauregard to Davis, Aug. 1, 1861, Roman, *Beauregard,* I, 123–124.
101. Chesnut, *Diary from Dixie,* pp. 97–98.
102. Northrop to Davis, Aug. 21, 1861, PRSD.
103. Miles to Beauregard, Aug. 6, 1861, Roman, *Beauregard,* I, 128.

It was a different matter, however, with Leroy Pope Walker. During the summer the Secretary of War had shown increasing signs of strain in managing the War Department and had fallen under criticism from the public and the press.[104] John B. Jones, the "Rebel War Clerk," noted in his diary with cold-blooded precision the Secretary's faltering, inefficient labors and picked up for posterity Walker's despairing comment that "no gentleman can be fit for office."[105] More important, Davis himself apparently had become convinced that Walker could not handle the position, and the President increasingly took over the routine details of the office.

Congress also pressed Walker. Late in August, as the session was moving towards its close, Congress, undaunted by the earlier rebuff from the President, began to direct War Department business. It passed a resolution calling on the Secretary of War to furnish the troops with ovens to bake hard bread and also to supply fresh vegetables if possible.[106] Congress also considered enacting new legislation concerning the composition of the daily ration but refrained after Walker stated point-blank that the present regulations were sufficient.[107] Finally, on August 27, Congress appointed a special committee of five

> to inquire into the organization and administration of the Medical, Commissary, and Quartermaster's Departments, with power to continue said inquiry during the recess, and to report at the next session of Congress what changes in the laws and regulations relating thereto are necessary and proper.[108]

The Secretary of War wrote a polite letter to the committee, informing them that the War Department "cheerfully concurs in the objects of your Committee" and affording them all possible facilities to expedite their inquiries.[109]

Public disappointment with the failure to seize Washington,

104. Jones, *War Clerk's Diary,* I, 77. 105. *Ibid.,* p. 64.

106. "A Resolution to Provide Troops in the Field with Bread and Fresh Provisions," Aug. 31, 1861, *Statutes,* I, 214.

107. Walker to Chilton, Aug. 31, 1861, Leroy Pope Walker Official Letter Book, Library of Congress.

108. Walker to Miles, Atkins, Preston, Waul, and Venable, Sept. 4, 1861, *OR*-4, I, 598–599; *Journal,* I, 374, 395, 399–401, 413, 415–416.

109. Walker to Miles, Atkins, Preston, Waul, and Venable, Sept. 4, 1861, *OR*-4, I, 598–599.

Congressional investigations into the conduct of the War Department and its bureaus, and Davis's private estimates of the Secretary's efforts all apparently combined to induce Walker to tender his resignation, probably quite a salutary decision for the war effort.[110] Walker delayed his official resignation until September 10, after Congress had adjourned, presumably to give Davis the opportunity of naming an acting successor without having to submit a nomination to Congress in the heated circumstances of the moment, a nomination that would be seized as a pretext for "sounding off" on the executive conduct of the war.

The press, while not overlooking supply problems and the general inefficiency of the army during the summer campaign, usually praised Walker's performance. Comments ranged from a temperate noting of "good intentions" to the *Daily Richmond Examiner*'s eulogy, ending in "Well done, good and faithful servant."[111] Davis appointed Judah P. Benjamin as Acting Secretary of War.

. . .

Although post-Manassas euphoria obscured the fact from many Confederates, the possibility of a short war was fast fading away, and a much magnified war of attrition loomed as the order of the future. The record of the Confederate supply effort to the autumn of 1861 showed little promise that the Confederacy would rise to the burgeoning demands of a full campaigning season. The effort to put into the field an army of 100,000 men had resulted in an unsettling display of confusion and conflict, understandable in view of the inexperience on the part of all concerned but hardly a record to engender confidence in the ability of the civilian and military leaders to manage a war effort many times larger than the Manassas episode. Except for such ideas as overseas procurement of ordnance and control of the national subsist-

110. Davis to Walker, Sept. 9, 1861, *ibid.*, p. 600; Walker to Davis, Sept. 10, 1861, *ibid.*, pp. 602–603; Walker to Davis, Sept. 10, 1861, *ibid.*, p. 603; Davis to Walker, Sept. 15, 1861, *ibid.*, pp. 613–614; for examples of various reasons advanced for Walker's resignation, see Jones, *War Clerk's Diary,* I, 63–64; Burton J. Hendrick, *Statesmen of the Lost Cause: Jefferson Davis and His Cabinet* (Boston, 1939), p. 182; Stephen R. Mallory Diary entry, Sept. 4, 1861, Southern Historical Collection, University of North Carolina; Patrick, *Jefferson Davis and His Cabinet,* pp. 113–120. Cf. John H. Reagan, *Memoirs, with Special Reference to Secession and the Civil War,* ed. Walter Flavius McCaleb (New York and Washington, 1906), pp. 108, 160.

111. *Richmond Enquirer,* Sept. 18, 1861; *Daily Richmond Examiner,* Sept. 17, 1861; Richmond *Daily Dispatch,* Sept. 17, 1861.

ence market, there was little evidence as yet that the supply chiefs or their superiors saw any necessity for departing from traditional prewar arrangements for equipping a small force of regulars. Quite possibly losing the Border States to the Union before the war began had made the task of adequately supplying the Confederate armies impossible from the beginning.

CHAPTER TWO

GAUGING THE UNKNOWN

You are somewhat in error as to the resources of the C. S. . . . You do not know how difficult it is to get any, the most common, thing heretofore abundant. —— A. C. Myers to J. B. Magruder, August 21, 1861*

In the autumn of 1861, as it became apparent that the United States was undertaking massive preparations to renew the war in 1862, Confederate officials saw that they would have to expand their own preparations. Even though the War Department had been unable properly to equip and manage 100,000 men, Congress, in response to the President's request, authorized the addition of as many as 400,000 men to the army.[1] The supply bureaus, led by their new Secretary of War, Judah P. Benjamin, thus had to prepare for a vastly expanded war effort. In addition, the magnitude of the new preparations forced Confederate administrators and legislators to grope for new and efficient procurement policies.

One response to such increased responsibilities was the abandonment of all pretense of providing for the more remote areas of the Confederacy. The isolation of the far west became official during the autumn of 1861 when Myers announced to his Texas quartermasters that they would have to fend for themselves or trade with Mexico for supplies because there was no surplus in the east to ship to them.[2] At the same time, Myers ordered these quartermasters to send the wool in their area east to the factories. The Ordnance Department had nothing to spare for the Texas area either, and the Subsistence Department paid only enough attention to dispatch agents to bring beef and wheat back east.

Except for limiting their operations in the west, the supply bureaus prepared to meet their multiplied responsibilities. The focal point of

* QMDLS, III, 426.

1. Message to the Third Session of the Provisional Congress, July 20, 1861, *Messages,* I, 123; "An Act to Provide for the Public Defense," Aug. 28, 1861, *Statutes,* I, 176; "An Act Making Appropriations for the Public Defense," Aug. 21, 1861, *ibid.,* p. 187.

2. Myers to Maclin, Aug. 28, 1861, QMDLS, XIII, 453; Myers to Minter, Sept. 14, 1861, *OR*-1, II, 105.

concern during the fall and winter was the ordnance service, which faced the largest deficiencies. Gorgas had expanded the physical plant of his bureau enormously but had as yet produced little in the way of ordnance supplies. A chain of some twenty depots, laboratories, armories, and arsenals engaged in government manufacture stretched from Richmond to San Antonio, and the Ordnance Department had made numerous contracts with private concerns for everything from cartridge paper to heavy artillery. But results were meager. Many of the government establishments were little more than storage depots, while others were in varying states of renovation. Lack of skilled manpower shackled ordnance production from the very beginning.

The small-arms situation caused the greatest headaches. The original stocks of weapons taken from former United States arsenals and state and private collections had long ago been put in the hands of the troops, and by the fall some 200,000 volunteers had been turned away from government service for lack of arms to give them.[3] The Secretaries of War, Benjamin as well as Walker, and state governors badgered their subordinates and each other over little caches of unassigned antiquities, and the Secretary of State took it upon himself to supply funds for purchases in the border states.[4] By winter only the Richmond Arsenal produced small arms for the government—at the feeble rate of 1000 a month. Gorgas expected to add another 500 a month in the spring from the Fayetteville Arsenal but did not know what to expect from the tiny Asheville establishment.[5] Contracts with private parties predicted the delivery of 66,000 small arms, but delivery was highly uncertain.[6] By the end of the winter Benjamin reported to Davis that small arms production was so "woefully deficient" that it provided only one tenth of the projected needs for an expanded army.[7] The picture was so gloomy that pikes were made regular weapons for the Confederate service, and if it had not been for the importation of 15,000 small arms during the winter, the fighting capacity of the army would have been severely hampered at the opening of campaigning.[8] On the other

3. Walker to Davis, July 24, 1861, *OR*-4, I, 497; Tyler to Congress, Aug. 12, 1861, *ibid.*, p. 555. 4. Hunter to Gwaltney, Aug. 5, 1861, *ORN*-2, I, 234–235.

5. Gorgas to Benjamin, Sept. 26, 1861, *OR*-4, I, 622.

6. Benjamin to Davis, Report of the Secretary of War, Feb. —, 1862, *ibid.*, p. 959. 7. Benjamin to Davis, March 12, 1862, WDCP, XXXIX, 83–84.

8. Davis to Brown, April 11, 1862, Rowland, *Jefferson Davis,* V, 230. See also "An Act to Provide for Keeping All Firearms in the Armies of the Confederate States in the Hands of Effective Men," April 10, 1862, *Statutes,* II, 26; Vandiver, *Confederate Ordnance,* p. 86. Editorial support for the pike was widespread. See, for example, Richmond *Daily Dispatch,* Feb. 18, 1862; Mobile *Advertiser and Register,* Feb. 5, 1862.

hand, field and coastal artillery was apparently in greater supply, and contracts with the Tredegar works in Richmond and the Etowah works in Georgia promised adequate production.[9]

Powder and ammunition supplies had seemed adequate in the summer. The Secretary of War had pronounced adequate for a year's supply the 20,000,000 cartridges and 200,000 pounds of rifle and cannon powder reported on hand.[10] Construction was underway in the fall for a large plant in Augusta which it was hoped would supply all the needs of the Confederacy.[11] In addition, mills in Raleigh, Nashville, New Orleans, and South Carolina, as well as small contractors, added to the reserve.[12] A new plant in Nashville had contributed 100,000 pounds of powder by the spring of 1862.[13] Moreover, the bureau's seven arsenals were capable of producing 225,000 cartridges per month, although the production of field ammunition had barely commenced.[14]

Although Gorgas had an immediate powder reserve and the capacity to produce a respectable amount of ammunition, there were unsolved problems in providing the components. There was a nationwide shortage of niter, the chief component of the powder. The Confederacy had potential sources of niter, especially in the Southern Appalachians and in the Trans-Mississippi, but access to the caves was difficult and the extraction process relatively unrewarding in a country where speculation in everyday commodities had become a more lucrative profession. The price of saltpeter, or niter, rose quickly from ten cents to forty cents a pound and would have gone higher, except for the fact that the army received authorization to impress the saltpeter while paying forty cents.[15] Some private plants were engaged in the production and refining of saltpeter, particularly at New Orleans and Nashville, but their production fell far below the needs of the army.[16]

Other materials needed by the Ordnance Department were available

9. Vandiver, *Confederate Ordnance,* pp. 62–63.

10. Walker to Cobb, July 31, 1861, *OR*-4, I, 510–511; Tyler to Congress, Aug. 12, 1861, *ibid.,* p. 555.

11. George Washington Rains, *History of the Confederate Powder Works* (Augusta, Georgia, 1882), p. 10. Cited hereinafter as Rains, *Powder Works.*

12. *Ibid.,* p. 4; Bledsoe to Memminger, Oct. 4, 1861, WDLS, II, 382; *Proceedings of the Court of Inquiry Relative to the Fall of New Orleans* (Richmond, 1864), *passim.* Cited hereinafter as *New Orleans Court of Inquiry.*

13. Rains, *Powder Works,* p. 6.

14. Gorgas to Benjamin, Sept. 26, 1861, *OR*-4, I, 622.

15. Polk to Davis, Aug. 7, 1861, *ibid.,* p. 535; Bledsoe to Lovell, Feb. 2, 1862, WDLS, V, 83.

16. Rains, *Powder Works,* pp. 4–5; *New Orleans Court of Inquiry, passim.*

to a certain extent, but the quantities varied. Sulphur was easily attainable, especially from sources developed in the sugar-cane country, and copper was in good supply as long as the large Ducktown mine in southeastern Tennessee was safe.[17] There were major lead deposits at Wytheville, Virginia, and minor ones in North Carolina, if properly developed, but the ordnance service needed alternative sources of both lead and copper.[18]

This unstable supply of powder components could have meant the end of the war by default by the summer of 1862, and consequently the government moved to subsidize the munitions industry. Gorgas suggested the creation of a special corps for extracting niter and developing metal resources.[19] Congress duly created a niter corps, headed by Gorgas's assistant, Major Isaac St. John, under the direction of the Chief of Ordnance.[20] The pressures of ordnance shortages forced Congress to loosen the purse strings, and in so doing it involved the government in an extensive underpinning of the Confederate economy. Two acts authorized advances of 50 per cent to encourage the private production of niter and small arms and the mining of coal and iron.[21] Congress appropriated $1,000,000 for the purchase of niter and for the exploration and working of niter caves and $1,500,000 to buy iron and to pay contractors for casting shot and shell. It earmarked an additional $1,000,000 for advances by the Navy Department to stimulate iron manufacturing, and still another $2,000,000 for the manufacture of small arms.[22] Still, Ordnance organization and Congressional subsidizing of private manufacturing looked to a future supply of arms and munitions. Both were still in short supply when spring campaigning opened.

. . .

17. Benjamin to Davis, Report of the Secretary of War, Feb. —, 1862, *OR*-4, I, 959; Davis to the House of Representatives, March 13, 1862, *Messages,* I, 199.

18. Tyler to Congress, Aug. 12, 1861, *OR*-4, I, 555.

19. Gorgas to Benjamin, March 12, 1862, *ibid.,* pp. 990–991.

20. "An Act for the Organization of a Corps of Officers for the Working of Nitre Caves and Establishing Nitre Beds," April 11, 1862, *Statutes,* II, 27–28.

21. "An Act to Encourage the Manufacture of Saltpetre and of Small Arms," April 17, 1862, *ibid.,* pp. 33–34; "An Act Supplementary to the Act Entitled 'An Act to Encourage the Manufacture of Small Arms,'" April 19, 1862, *ibid.,* p. 38.

22. "An Act Making Further Appropriations for the Expenses of the Government in the Treasury, War, and Navy Departments, and for Other Purposes," April 19, 1862, *ibid.,* pp. 37–38. An example of an iron contract proffered by the War Department may be found in Benjamin to Messrs. Hoyt, *et al.,* Jan. 3, 1862, WDLS, IV, 81–82.

The Quartermaster's Department faced the greatest increase in responsibilities because a new act of Congress made that bureau responsible for providing clothing for all the troops. Previously, the act of May 21 had required that the individual soldier furnish his own clothing in the quantities specified by army regulations. The Quartermaster's Department would then pay $21 to each man every six months as commutation.[23] The new legislation required the Secretary of War "to provide, as far as possible, clothing for the entire forces of the Confederate States upon the requisition of the [regimental] commander."[24] Commutation was still paid to any individual who supplied himself and to the governor of any state which supplied clothing to its own men in the Confederate service.[25]

Myers also had to expand his traditional pay and transportation obligations and extend his contracts for tents and camp equipage. Although faced with the problem of securing enough duck for tent material, he scraped together enough tents to supply the expanded army.[26] His chief worry, however, was his new responsibility for supplying clothing to the troops where private and state efforts had failed. The bureau would be particularly responsible for clothing the "refugee" troops from Missouri, Kentucky, and Maryland, whose home states could not or would not supply them. During 1861 the bulk of the clothes came from private sources, but the bureau enlarged its contracts with the cotton and woolen factories and with shoe shops. In contracting for clothing, Myers apparently made what arrangements he could with those factories that were willing to sell a portion of their production to the government at the prices Myers considered to be reasonable.[27] However, many factories chose to sell in large part or in entirety in the civilian market in order to take advantage of the higher prices to be found there. Myers agreed to make no contracts with the

23. "An Act Concerning the Transportation of Soldiers, and Allowances for Clothing of Volunteers, and Amendatory of the 'Act for the Establishment and Organization of the Army of the Confederate States,'" May 21, 1861, *Statutes*, I, 126.

24. "An Act to Amend the Second Section of 'An Act Concerning the Transportation of Soldiers, and Allowances for Clothing of the Volunteers and Amendatory of the "Act for the Establishment and Organization of the Army,"'" Aug. 30, 1861, *ibid.*, p. 198. 25. *Ibid.*

26. Myers to Curry, Aug. 10, 1861, QMDLS, XIII, 386; Myers to Randolph, March 5, 1862, QMDSW, pp. 227–228.

27. Myers to Benjamin, Feb. 28, 1862, QMDSW, pp. 103–105; Myers to Randolph, March 5, 1862, *ibid.*, pp. 227–228.

mills of the largest textile state, North Carolina, in return for that state's undertaking the responsibility of clothing its own troops.[28]

He estimated in the summer of 1861 that the supply of woolen cloth, blankets, and shoes in the Confederacy was so small that both private and state efforts to secure these items for army use would fail and that the entire responsibility for supplying these items would fall on him. He sent special purchasing agents around the country to buy up odd lots of shoes and blankets on the local markets, pushed shoemaking contracts to the utmost, and arranged to buy extensive quantities of wool in Texas to be shipped east for manufacture.[29] He knew that such purchasing efforts would be entirely inadequate, and as early as August he estimated that of 1,600,000 pairs of shoes needed to supply the army for one year only 300,000 could be secured inside the Confederacy. The rest would have to come from abroad. He also estimated that he would need to import 800,000 yards of gray wool cloth, 500,000 pairs of wool socks, 500,000 flannel shirts, and large quantities of blankets and uniforms to supply the army for one year.[30]

To make distribution of his accumulations more efficient, Myers reorganized the post system set up earlier in the year. He relieved the quartermasters at the numerous posts in the larger towns and commercial centers of their responsibilities for storing goods in their areas and set up several large supply depots in their stead. The number fluctuated, but in general there were about half a dozen depots, one in each major military command area. These depots were the centers of accumulations of goods by purchase and contract, and, later, by their own manufacturing. The depots distributed the quartermaster supplies to the troops of the military department, upon the requisition of the field quartermasters. For the supply of the two large field armies Myers designated Richmond and Nashville as his main depots and allowed them to draw on the accumulations at other depots if necessary.[31]

By the spring of 1862 good fortune had smiled upon the Quartermaster General to the extent that he could announce to the Secretary of

28. Elizabeth Webb, "Cotton Manufacturing and State Regulation in North Carolina," *North Carolina Historical Review,* IX, No. 2 (April 1937), 117 ff.

29. Myers to Benjamin, Feb. 28, 1862, QMDSW, pp. 103–105.

30. Myers to Walker, Aug. 10, 1861, *ibid.,* p. 29.

31. Myers to Stevenson, Sept. 10, 1861, *Miscellaneous Correspondence and Orders of the Adjutant and Inspector General's Office and Correspondence of the Quartermaster General's, Ordinance and Engineer Bureaus, of the Confederate States, 1861* (Washington, 1876), p. 44; Myers to Benjamin, Feb. 28, 1862, QMDSW, pp. 103–105.

War: "The success which has attended . . . [depot] operations is shown by the fact that they have been enabled to meet every important demand made upon them."[32] The evidence suggests, however, that reserve accumulations were scanty and the troops indifferently clothed and equipped. The bureau had supplied most of the tents and camp equipment out of its own efforts, but the clothing had been in great measure supplied by the states, by individuals, and by timely arrivals of goods through the blockade, as, for example, the large numbers of uniforms run in by Fraser and Company at Charleston.[33] Myers had not specifically stated that his bureau could successfully cope with the waste and losses involved with the impending months of campaigning across half a continent, but Benjamin unwisely translated his bureau chief's satisfaction with past performance into the ringing claim that "It will hereafter be in the power of the [Quartermaster's] Department to furnish all that is required. . . ."[34]

• • •

The Subsistence Department, working with the most productive section of the economy, was the bureau most able to fulfil its basic responsibilities from the domestic market, with little need to rely on civilian contributions or overseas purchases. In their intimate and expanding intercourse with the domestic economy, however, the commissaries had to contend with nagging problems of shortages, financial derangement, and transportation inefficiencies—problems that foreshadowed the disasters of the future.

As early as midsummer of 1861 the Commissary General, in estimating the trends of the subsistence market, had decided to suspend procurement by bids in order to forestall speculators. Instead, the bureau, by purchasing large quantities of the basic ration components of meat and bread, would create a general reserve for the armies.

For flour Northrop at first returned to his early idea of making a standard price based on the price of principal markets in the Confederacy and deducting transportation costs for flour bought elsewhere.[35] There was much outcry against this practice, and in the end Northrop failed in his objective of holding down prices by monopolizing pur-

32. Myers to Benjamin, March 5, 1862, QMDSW, pp. 227–228.

33. *Ibid.*; Samuel Bernard Thompson, *Confederate Purchasing Operations Abroad* (Chapel Hill, 1935), p. 43. Cited hereinafter as Thompson, *Confederate Purchasing*.

34. Benjamin to Davis, Feb. —, 1862, *OR*-4, I, 959.

35. Examples of this practice can be found in Ruffin to Northrop, Jan. —, 1862, *ibid.*, pp. 876–878.

chases on the market at fixed rates. His chief contract for flour in this period illustrates his defeat. The Haxall and Crenshaw Company at Richmond held a contract for 25,000 bushels of flour at $5.25 per bushel, while firms in Fredericksburg and Petersburg, holding contracts at 20,000 bushels each, received $5.00. The Haxall and Crenshaw contract also called for delivery of 25,000 additional bushels and pegged the price to a sliding scale of 50 cents rise per barrel for each 10 cents rise in the price of wheat above its base price of $1.00 per bushel. By January 1862 Haxall and Crenshaw were entitled to a price of $6.76 per barrel.[36] The flour purchased in Virginia was adequate for the Army of Northern Virginia, and the bureau purchased a large bakery which regularly supplied hard bread. In addition, the bureau had accumulated by January 2,700 barrels of hard bread in reserve at Richmond and 330,000 pounds at Manassas.[37]

Meat posed a special problem. In August Northrop predicted that the Confederacy would not have enough swine to feed both the army and the plantation slaves, nor enough beef east of the Mississippi to feed the large armies stationed there.[38] To make the most of his limited opportunities, he worked out three general principles: he employed civilian agents of experience to locate and bring in the meat; he bought outside the army lines in Kentucky in gold at a price up to 25 per cent premium, a price which was one third lower than the Confederate market; and he made contracts with every meat packer in Tennessee at liberal rates—the government taking 48 to 53 per cent of the net weight of the swine in bacon and surrendering the traditional "fifth quarter" to the beef packers.[39] In this manner Northrop attempted to ensure that the government would have a share of all available meat. In addition, the government established packing plants at Thoroughfare Gap near Johnston's army and at Richmond. For fresh beef, the bureau left the local commissaries in areas of surplus cattle to make their own arrangements, but the bureau made large contracts for the supply of fresh beef for isolated posts in Texas, the Indian Territory, West Arkansas, and Missouri, and for certain posts on the Gulf coast.[40]

These efforts to secure meat produced gratifying results. In October 1861, Major Frank Ruffin, Northrop's chief assistant, reported the slaughter of 116,000 hogs and 26,500 cattle east of the Mississippi for

36. *Ibid.*, pp. 876–878. 37. *Ibid.*, pp. 877–878.
38. Northrop to Davis, Aug. 21, 1861, Rowland, *Jefferson Davis,* V, 127.
39. Ruffin to Northrop, Jan. —, 1862, *OR*-4, I, 873–876.
40. Northrop to Benjamin, Nov. 27, 1861, *ibid.,* pp. 756–757.

a total yield of 29,818,888 rations of salt meat, enough, he estimated, to feed 225,000 men for 120 days after December 1, or at four salt rations a week for seven months. To complete the ration and provide three days of fresh beef per week for the seven months, field commissaries would have to secure 50,000 cattle.[41] In addition, the bureau secured bacon west of the Mississippi.[42]

By January 1862, at the end of the packing season, contracts for slaughtering totaled 249,000 hogs and about 75,000 cattle east of the Mississippi.[43] Local commissaries had been unable to find enough cattle to supply fresh beef three times a week and were using up salt meat faster than Ruffin had predicted. Ruffin now estimated that there was enough bacon on hand to reach next year's packing season and enough salt beef to reach the summer, when fresh beef would be available again.[44] The bureau had also made arrangements to increase the amount of fresh meat available in the summer by contracting for the driving of cattle from Texas to Mississippi for the winter and then moving the herds to the armies by summertime.[45]

A positive factor in the meat situation at that time was that all the packing was done in the vicinity of the armies. There was little trouble with railroad delays, and large reserves of meat were beginning to accumulate at points in Tennessee and Virginia. On the other hand, figures stress how the Subsistence Department depended upon the armies' ability to hold their positions on the borders of the Confederacy. Of 249,000 hogs slaughtered, 193,200 came from Tennessee, two thirds of these from the Nashville area; 20,000, purchased with gold, came from Kentucky; 35,300 came from Virginia; and 500 from North Carolina. Of the cattle slaughtered, two thirds came from Tennessee and the rest from Virginia.[46] The Confederate armies were, in fact, their own meat packers. If the armies held, there would be meat the next winter, and in 1863. If not—

The bureau was not as successful in acquiring the subordinate components of the official ration. Coffee, vinegar, and soap had become scarce, and purchasing agents bought at high prices whatever they could find. In an attempt to assure a more stable supply of items in high demand, Northrop entered into a number of contracts to manufac-

41. Ruffin to Northrop, Oct. 19, 1862, Jefferson Davis Papers, Duke University Manuscript Department.

42. RG 56, Item 68 (Contract Box), *passim.*

43. Ruffin to Northrop, Jan. —, 1862, summary of appended contracts, *OR*-4, I, 878–879.

44. *Ibid.,* p. 875.

45. Northrop to Davis, Aug. 21, 1861, Rowland, *Jefferson Davis,* V, 124–127.

46. Ruffin to Northrop, Jan. —, 1862, *OR*-4, I, 878–879.

ture vinegar, whiskey, and soap.[47] Molasses, sugar, and vegetables were abundant in certain areas, but troops not blessed with local supplies were at the mercy of transportation delays. The bureau found itself hampered by the fact that provision sellers in general demanded payment in bankable funds; the Treasury Department met bureau requisitions with large proportions of bonds, which the prospective sellers refused.[48] The railroads displayed a marked reluctance to expedite shipments of commissary stores, with the result that the sugar and molasses which the bureau had managed to secure reached the troops in Tennessee and Virginia only after several months' delay.[49] Unit and post commissaries secured vegetables locally while the season lasted, to the extent of their acceptable funds. Salt contracts at Saltville, Virginia, netted some 32,000 bushels per month, and 40,000 bushels purchased in Nashville supplied the extensive meat packing operations in Tennessee and Kentucky.[50]

On January 18, 1862, Northrop reported to the Secretary of War: "All subsistence stores that are allowed to the Army have to the fullest capacity of our country been obtained, and no essential supplies have ever failed to be ready for transportation when and where required, timely notice having been given to this department."[51] Benjamin, with his penchant for super-optimism, immediately translated Northrop's statement into the claim that, given adequate transportation, "No apprehension whatever need be entertained of our ability to feed any number of men that we think proper to keep under arms from our own resources."[52] Actually, it is doubtful whether Northrop had made much of a claim if one strips the provisos away from his statement. One phrase needs special comment. "The fullest capacity of our country" meant, as it had at Manassas, that the troops received salt or fresh meat and flour or corn meal and only sporadic amounts of anything else. Their fare also varied considerably with the efficiency of their unit commissaries, who were chosen by the unit commanders for reasons best known to them. The men complained about their diet and many did not know how to cope with the flour ration, cooking up a gummy mess in their skillets to wolf down with their bacon and beef and often

47. Northrop to Benjamin, Jan. 18, 1862, *ibid.*, p. 870; Northrop to Davis, Aug. 21, 1861, Rowland, *Jefferson Davis,* V, 124–127.

48. Northrop to Davis, Aug. 21, 1861, Rowland, *Jefferson Davis,* V, 124–127.

49. Northrop to Benjamin, Jan. 18, 1862, *OR*-4, I, 870.

50. Ruffin to Northrop, Jan. —, 1862, *ibid.*, p. 878.

51. Northrop to Benjamin, Jan. 18, 1862, *ibid.*, pp. 871–872.

52. Benjamin to Davis, Feb. —, 1862, *ibid.*, pp. 959–960.

becoming ill.[53] Scurvy occasionally cropped up, but the chief cause of the sickness and death so prevalent in the camps of the Confederate armies in the late summer and the fall was the primitive sanitation conditions—the inevitable by-product of untrained officers and men. The incidence of sickness greatly declined by spring, however, although the ration remained as monotonous as ever.[54] The troops had developed veteran stomachs by the time they faced the enemy. On the other hand, most of the officers, who supplied themselves from the surrounding markets, found provisions in abundant quantities, and at least one general, transferred from Manassas, commented about the luxurious living he had had to forego.[55]

Still, the Confederate troops complained in a mighty fashion to all who would listen. The men broadcast their fearful tales to their Congressmen, but the investigating committee which had chased Walker from office reported back to Congress that the army was "well fed" and abundantly supplied, although the committee did recommend changing the official ration to substitute items in more general supply and suggested the installation of baking ovens to save the troops from their flour ration.[56] So, amidst complaints and compliments, shortages and surpluses, the Subsistence Department, together with its sister bureaus, awaited campaign time.

. . .

While the supply bureaus struggled with magnified problems on their level, the expanded war effort brought forth nationwide problems of railroad management, inflation, allocation of manpower, and foreign procurement, problems which demanded high level policy decisions on the part of Congress, the Secretary of War, and the President. Haltingly, in the autumn and winter of 1861–62, Confederate leaders began to attack these problems.

By the first winter of the war, the railroads were displaying signs of wear and tear, and the laissez-faire spirit of railroad owners was also eroding. Although the Chattanooga Railroad Convention on October 4

53. An English Combatant, *Battle-Fields of the South, from Bull Run to Fredericksburg; with Sketches of Confederate Commanders, and Gossip of the Camps* (New York, 1864), pp. 14, 123–124, 316, 318.

54. Benjamin to Davis, Dec. —, 1861, *OR*-4, I, 794; Northrop to Davis, Aug. 21, 1861, Rowland, *Jefferson Davis,* V, 124–127.

55. Kirby Smith to Mrs. Kirby Smith, March 10, 1862, Edmund Kirby-Smith Papers, Southern Historical Collection, University of North Carolina.

56. *Journal,* I, 653–654, 678, 720; text of report is in *OR*-4, I, 886–887.

had raised government transportation rates, certain railroad owners did not hesitate to propose measures for government aid such as loans, the detailing of skilled laborers, and government-financed railroad shops.[57] The President's message to Congress contained references to the need for improving transportation facilities and particularly mentioned the need for closing the Greensboro-Danville railroad gap.[58] In response, Congress appropriated $1,000,000 to construct the link and thus set a precedent for government aid to the railroads.[59] Two other measures followed immediately. A bill to lend $150,000 to complete the Selma-Meridian gap moved easily through Congress,[60] and the President sent a special message to the Senate to save a bill which appropriated $1,500,000 to complete the railroad connection between Houston and New Iberia, Louisiana, under the mistaken impression that it would link Texas with the Confederacy.[61]

While there was support for government subsidies for railroads, there was little enthusiasm at this stage in the war for government competition. Although William Goodman, President of the Mississippi and Central, suggested that the government build its own trains and appoint a general superintendent of railroads, backed by a squad of agents and messengers, to co-ordinate railroad service,[62] the Quartermaster General himself opposed such a proposal. Myers, a conservative, rejected the idea of a superintendent, agents, and messengers because such a plan would lessen the obligation of the railroad companies to fulfil their contracts with efficiency, and he opposed the idea of government trains because the railroads would not take care of them.

57. Circular, Quartermaster Department, Dec. 13, 1861, QMDLS, XIV, 442; Houston to Walker, received Sept. 14, 1861, *OR*-4, I, 612–613; Goodman to Davis, Sept. 22, 1861, *ibid.*, p. 616; Brown to Benjamin, Jan. 12, 1862, *ibid.*, p. 839.

58. Message to the Fifth Session of the Provisional Congress, Nov. 18, 1861, *Messages,* I, 139–140; message to the Fifth Session of the Provisional Congress, Dec. 17, 1861, *ibid.*, p. 152.

59. *Journal,* I, 548, 566, 731–734, 766–770, 781–782, 784; "An Act to Provide for Connecting the Richmond and Danville and the North Carolina Railroad, for Military Purposes," Feb. 10, 1862, *Statutes,* I, 258–259. As the above act became law, the *Daily Richmond Examiner* commented that the link would already have been completed except for the "mulish selfishness of villages in Virginia and Carolina." Actually, the link was not completed until May 1864.

60. "An Act to Provide for the Connection of the Railroad from Selma, in Alabama, to Meridian, in Mississippi," Feb. 15, 1862, *Statutes,* I, 276.

61. *Debates,* XLV, 160; *Journal,* II, 197–198; "An Act to Aid the Construction of a Certain Line of Railroad in the States of Louisiana and Texas," April 19, 1862, *Statutes,* II, 34–35.

62. Goodman to Davis, Jan. 25, 1862, *OR*-4, I, 880–882.

It would be better, he thought, if it became necessary, for the government to build engines and cars and sell them to the railroads.[63]

Nor was Congress willing to go further. Proposals to create a "military chief of transportation" and government transportation agents and to put the main trunk lines under military control[64] were suppressed. Senator Preston of Virginia, representing a state that had already seen inefficiency of railroad management demonstrated at Manassas, went so far as to offer a resolution calling on the Committee on Military Affairs to inquire into the "necessity and propriety of the government taking possession of all the railroads in the Confederacy, and repairing, working, and managing the same, so as to render them the most effective for the transportation of troops, munitions of war, and supplies."[65] This proposal received no support from the Quartermaster's Department or from Congress. Although the government had taken its first step towards a comprehensive railroad policy, it was too early in the war to resort to centralization.

By autumn prices in the domestic marketplaces of the Confederacy had become so inflated that the Confederate supply officials began to resort to a questionable tool of procurement—impressment. Across the land there were shortages of hardware, furnishings, transportation equipment, and ration components. Speculators bought up supplies and hoarded them to make prices rise, and the supply bureaus found themselves unable to purchase many needed items. American military precedent conceded to the Secretary of War and the commanding generals the right to appropriate private property under emergency conditions. Benjamin and Walker had both attempted to impress railroad equipment in moments of transportation crises, although both had backed down in the face of resulting outcry.[66] In addition, field commanders had resorted to occasional acts of impressment during the previous summer's campaigning.

Frustrated by the speculators, the Quartermaster General and the Commissary General persuaded the Secretary of War to confer general impressment powers upon them and through them upon the bureau purchasers. In November Myers sent a circular to all quartermasters,

63. Myers to Davis, Jan. 31, 1862, *ibid.*, pp. 896–897.

64. *Journal*, I, 654, 720–721; text is in *OR*-4, I, 884–885; Debates, XLIV, 198; *Journal*, II, 87.

65. *Debates*, XLV, 147–148, 152; *Journal*, II, 215, 251–254.

66. Black, *Confederate Railroads*, p. 68; Benjamin to Myers, Sept. 24, 1861, *OR*-4, I, 617; Benjamin to Brown, Sept. 30, 1861, *ibid.*, p. 634.

conferring upon them official authority to impress, but only if "absolutely demanded by the public necessities."[67] Impressing officers were ordered to show written authority, give receipts, make payments on the spot at market prices, and make reports to the Quartermaster General's Office.

Despite circumspect procedures, conferring the power of impressment on myriads of supply minions, a departure from tradition, soon increased the incidence of impressment. However, the civilian heads, the field commanders, and the supply chiefs apparently felt little apprehension that the practice of impressment might become seductive for the impressing agents and demoralizing to the public; no doubt they believed that the practice would remain local, insignificant, and occasional.

Conscription was the most radical policy inaugurated during the winter of 1861–62. Alarmed at the magnitude of Union preparations and convinced that flagging patriotism would not provide an army of adequate size through volunteers, the Davis administration created the first draft in American history. Such a decisive step was remarkable compared with the conservatism with which the administration usually handled innovations in policy.[68] The Conscription Act of April 16, 1862, called up all men eighteen to thirty-five for three years unless the war ended sooner. As for the sticky question of exemptions, the act struck a reasonable balance between expediency and responsibility. Traditional political and social pressures dictated the exemption of "professionals" on the one hand—teachers, doctors, ministers, government officials—and common sense indicated that skilled labor be husbanded by the exemption of ordnance, railroad, and textile workers.[69] The main flaws in conscription policy were the provision allowing substitutes and the rejection of a bill providing for the detailing of artisans and mechanics.[70]

One prospect of enhancing domestic procurement proved to be too revolutionary for Congress. A bill proposing to limit the production of cotton for 1862 clashed with the great economic interests of the Confederacy and was swept away by gusts of state's rights doctrine and

67. Circular, Quartermaster General's Department, Nov. —, 1861, *OR*-4, I, 767.

68. Albert Burton Moore, *Conscription and Conflict in the Confederacy* (New York, 1924), pp. 9–11.

69. "An Act to Further Provide for the Public Defense," April 16, 1862, *Statutes*, II, 29–32; "An Act to Exempt Certain Persons from Enrollment for Service in the Armies of the Confederate States," April 21, 1862, *ibid.*, pp. 51–52.

70. *Debates*, XLIV, 197; *Journal*, II, 87, 92.

dark prognostications for the future of slavery. Instead, Congress contented itself with a resolution urging the restriction of cotton acreage for the sake of growing of more food.[71]

. . .

Faced with deficiencies at home, the War Department from its earliest moments turned to foreign sources to supply the armies. Private citizens showered advice upon War Department officials and submitted plans for importing supplies.[72] Even the Quartermaster General himself, succumbing to temptation, concocted complex plans for slipping goods past the Union blockading fleet.[73] The War Department considered many proposals, but officials found it difficult to work out effective plans. Two major trends of supplying goods from Europe (one could not call them plans) set in. In one approach the War and Navy departments sent agents abroad to contract for supplies. The agents paid the European contractors on delivery and then arranged for large tramp steamers to carry the goods to Bermuda, Nassau, and occasionally to Havana, the agents paying the freight. At these ports other Confederate agents supervised the repacking of the shipments and placed the goods into smaller lots on light, fast steamers to run into Confederate ports past the blockaders. Here the government paid the high freight rates and took the cargoes. Sometimes large freighters steamed directly from England to Confederate ports, especially in the early part of the war when the blockade was inefficient and the captures few.[74] The second approach was for the War Department to rely on private initiative to bring supplies to the government's attention. Government officials bought goods from private blockade runners as they arrived and gave out contracts to private individuals to go to Europe, buy the goods, ship them to the Confederacy, and resell to the government at some predetermined rate. Payments at home and abroad were to be in money, because cotton was embargoed.

At this time Caleb Huse, the agent dispatched to Europe by the War Department, was at his most effective in securing supplies for a Con-

71. *Debates,* XLIV, 147, 150, 160, 163–166, 169–171; *Journal,* II, 57, 67, 69, 72, 80; *ibid.,* V, 76.

72. Marshall to Walker, Aug. 13, 1861, *OR*-4, I, 558; Humphries to Walker, Aug. 15, 1861, *ibid.,* p. 560; Warren to Walker, Aug. 16, 1861, *ibid.,* p. 564; Bisbie to Benjamin, Jan. 16, 1862, *ibid.,* pp. 843–845.

73. Myers to Wood, Sept. 23, 1863, QMDLS, XIV, 84.

74. For an extended discussion of Confederate purchasing and shipping practices, see Thompson, *Confederate Purchasing, passim.*

federacy desperately in need of arms and munitions of any kind. The government supplied him with all the specie that it could command in bills of exchange and letters of credit, and by September remittances to Huse totaled $1,400,000 in sterling exchange.[75] With this money Huse paid off old contracts, made new ones, and, in addition to ordnance stores, purchased quartermaster, medical, and engineering supplies. During the fall three ships loaded with government stores arrived, and four more arrived during the early spring. These seven ships together brought in 15,000 small arms, plus powder, saltpeter, and other ordnance supplies, as well as blankets, shoes, and uniforms.[76] While it is difficult to give any precise evaluation of Huse's contribution for any given period, it is probable that the goods which he shipped in this period enabled the Ordnance and Quartermaster's bureaus to equip most of the soldiers instead of falling critically short.

Even at this early stage of the war, officials began to question their practice of relying upon private parties to buy goods abroad and resell them to the Confederate government, for few goods seemed to come in by this system. Critics of the practice, however, were faced with the problem that the government was unable to get enough money to Europe to have government agents buy all the needed supplies. Rather, there was the possibility that the government would not even have enough specie to meet needs at home.

To meet the specie shortage, the Quartermaster General, among others, suggested cotton as a medium of exchange. Although Myers had made contracts in the summer with "capitalists," as he termed them, to ship in 300,000 pairs of shoes and 100,000 blankets, he found that the contracts predicated sales at Confederate market prices, prices already advanced 100 per cent.[77] More important, he was not satisfied that the goods arranged for earlier would ever come in. He wished to drop contracts with private parties and rely exclusively upon agents in Europe to contract at European prices, using remittances from home to pay for the goods and paying for freight in advance. If there was no money available, Myers suggested an alternative system, that of having contractors ship goods to the Confederate States, to be paid for in cotton there. Myers also felt that the agent-purchasing

75. Tyler to Gorgas, Sept. 12, 1861, WDLS, II, 251; Benjamin to John Fraser and Company, Sept. 25, 1861, *ibid.*, p. 354.

76. Myers to Benjamin, Feb. 28, 1862, QMDSW, p. 196; Thompson, *Confederate Purchasing*, pp. 23, 43.

77. Myers to Walker, Aug. 10, 1861, QMDSW, p. 29; Myers to Walker, Aug. 24, 1861, *ibid.*, p. 33; Thompson, *Confederate Purchasing*, pp. 18–19.

system could be improved. He was dissatisfied with the rates that Huse was paying and requested in October 1861 that Major J. B. Ferguson of his bureau be sent abroad to purchase for the Quartermaster's Department.[78] Benjamin vetoed the suggestion, remarking that he preferred to have contracts made with private parties. So the matter rested for the moment.[79]

Myers's proposition to pay for goods in cotton was the first official indication that a change in fiscal policy was impending. Up to this point, the Confederacy as a whole was in the grasp of the "King Cotton" embargo aimed at securing foreign recognition and ruining Union finances. Although there was no effective national embargo act,[80] state and local pressures largely prevented cotton exportations. In the face of expanded needs for a prolonged war, however, many were beginning to claim that the best way to win the war was the more mundane method of equipping a superior military force to defeat the enemy in battle. Since the government had used up its specie, it would have to supply the army by buying cotton and selling the cotton for specie abroad.

The government had already used cotton indirectly to help the army by spending the proceeds of the government produce loan for supplies.[81] Expanded in August to the sum of $100,000,000, the produce loan envisioned that the planters would pledge a portion of their crops to the government, sell the crops on the general market for specie, and

78. Myers to Benjamin, Oct. 10, 1861, *OR*-4, I, 688.

79. Bledsoe to Myers, Oct. 18, 1861, WDLS, II, 418.

80. The acts specifying the embargo on cotton and its destruction in the presence of the enemy include: "An Act to Regulate the Destruction of Property under Military Necessity and to Provide for the Indemnity Thereof," March 17, 1862, *Statutes*, II, 2; "An Act to Prohibit the Exportation of Cotton from the Confederate States, Except through the Seaports of said States, and to Punish Persons Offending Therein," May 21, 1861, *ibid.*, I, 152–153; "An Act to Extend the Provisions of an Act Entitled 'An Act to Prohibit the Exportation of Cotton from the Confederate States, Except through the Seaports of Said States, and to Punish Persons Offending Therein,' Approved May Twenty-one, Eighteen Hundred and Sixty-One," Aug. 2, 1861, *ibid.*, p. 170; "An Act to Prohibit the Transportation and Sale of Certain Articles in any Part or Place within the Confederate States, in the Possession of the Enemy, and to Prohibit the Sale, Barter, or Exchange of Certain Articles Therein Named, to Alien or Domestic Enemies," April 19, 1862, *ibid.*, II, 46.

81. "An Act to Authorize a Loan and the Issue of Treasury Notes and to Prescribe the Punishment for Forging the Same, and Forging Certificates of Stocks and Bonds," May 16, 1861, *Statutes*, I, 117–118; "An Act to Authorize the Issue of Treasury Notes and to Provide a War Tax for Their Redemption," Aug. 19, 1861, *ibid.*, pp. 177–183.

then exchange the specie for twenty-year 8 per cent government bonds. The government would use the specie for buying army supplies. However, the available specie was soon taken up and large amounts of cotton pledged to the government on the loan sat idly in warehouses and plantations awaiting a buyer with specie.[82]

By winter the administration had decided to ship cotton to pay for military supplies. The Secretary of the Treasury and Congress secured cotton to pay for supplies by partially transforming the nature of the produce loan. The Hypothecation Act of April 21, 1862, authorized the Secretary of the Treasury to accept from subscribers to the produce loan payment in cotton, tobacco, and other agricultural products in kind, in lieu of specie, total subscriptions not to exceed $35,000,000. The government could ship these products abroad to be sold and then apply the proceeds to the debts of the purchasing agents, or it could store the cotton to meet the private contracts for goods from abroad. Besides paying directly for contracts, the government used the produce-loan cotton to secure capital for buying supplies by offering it as an investment. Congress authorized Memminger to issue Produce Certificates based on this cotton, certificates which entitled the buyer to a specified lot of cotton. Both contractor and certificate holder could ship out the cotton to any neutral port.[83] Treasury agents set out immediately to secure the cotton, and cotton began to pay for the war effort. Benjamin also tried to use cotton as credit by offering the agent of an English commercial house in New Orleans, on authorization from Davis, $1,000,000 in cotton at Confederate prices plus commission if the commercial house would advance $1,000,000 in specie to Confederate agents abroad.[84] The Confederate government would store and insure the cotton at its own expense and deliver it in England at the end of hostilities. The loss of New Orleans smashed this plan.

Although Davis and Benjamin had taken a step towards solving their foreign purchasing problem, they simultaneously compounded that problem by making cotton contracts with private parties instead of turning all purchasing operations over to government agents in Europe. The contracts usually called for an open quantity of certain specified ordnance and quartermaster stores. After inspection in Eu-

82. Richard Cecil Todd, *Confederate Finance* (Athens, Georgia, 1954), pp. 36–39.

83. Benjamin to Chauvin, Dec. 30, 1861, *OR*-4, I, 820; Benjamin to Fallon, Jan. 28, 1862, *ibid.*, pp. 882–883.

84. Benjamin to Forstall, Jan. 17, 1862, *ibid.*, pp. 845–846.

rope, the goods would be paid for on delivery, at the risk of the shipper, at a Confederate port. The government would pay 50 per cent profit in cotton at current Confederate market prices. The shipper took out the cotton at his own risk.[85] This arrangement promised lucrative profits, for London cotton prices were already four times Confederate prices. Many offered to make contracts on this basis.[86] Such contracts offered an opportunity for buying the most expensive items on the market and invited invoice padding and double books. Some contractors delayed deliveries to wait for the cotton price in Europe to rise. Some failed to find the necessary capital or sold the contracts to others, with the general result that the contracts were never fulfilled.[87] The private contract system would remain an incubus on overseas procurement for years to come.

· · ·

As the war effort expanded, financial complications proliferated. By the autumn of 1861 the rising costs of domestic and overseas procurement soon forced the bureaus into a monthly scramble to meet commitments. This situation may be illustrated by considering the fate of the Quartermaster's Department estimates. In July, Myers, on orders to estimate the money that he would need to equip four hundred new regiments through February 18, 1862, made his estimates in the usual fashion, allowing for pay and commutation and for camp and garrison equipage, doubling his estimate ratio for transportation. The total figure came to $132,958,973.[88] Other bureau estimates are not available, but all supply chiefs were undoubtedly stunned when Congress appropriated only $57,000,000 on August 21, 1862, to meet the expenses of the entire War Department.[89] Walker divided the money, allotting $39,500,000 to the Quartermaster's Department, $12,000,000 to Subsistence, $1,000,000 each to Medical and Engineering, and $3,500,000 to Ordnance.[90] All bureaus soon ran short. In November the

85. Todd, *Confederate Finance,* p. 41; "An Act to Authorize the Exchange of Bonds for Articles in Kind, and the Shipment, Sale or Hypothecation of Such Articles," April 21, 1862, *Statutes,* II, 47.

86. Frank L. Owsley, *King Cotton Diplomacy: Foreign Relations of the Confederate States of America,* 2nd. ed., revised by Harriet Chappell Owsley (Chicago, 1959), p. 387.

87. Some shady practices are described in McRae to Memminger, Oct. 7, 1863, *OR*-4, II, 982–985.

88. Myers to Walker, July 21, 1861, QMDLS, pp. 22–24.

89. "An Act Making Appropriations for the Public Defense," Aug. 21, 1861, *Statutes,* I, 187.

90. Walker to Memminger, Sept. 4, 1861, *OR*-4, I, 599.

bureaus were asked to prepare new estimates of the expenses for the entire army from February 18 to April 1, 1862. Myers complained that he had only $23,000,000 left, which would pay only for November expenses, leaving him with no money from then until February 18.[91] Gorgas, saddled by heavy overseas expenditures, ran out of funds completely by December and needed $1,750,000 to meet expenditures of that month.[92]

Benjamin had undoubtedly received a number of gloomy predictions, for he sent around to the various bureaus to find out what they needed to get through to February 18. In December he sent to the President an appropriation request totaling $90,634,508, which represented deficiencies until February 18 and estimates for the period from February 18 to April 1.[93] In doing this, he remarked that he had shaved estimates of the bureau heads, not wishing to play the game of exaggerating amounts needed in anticipation of Congressional cuts, a thought which would have occurred to an ex-Senator. He did not, however, cut Quartermaster estimates, which totaled $72,323,701. The Secretary of War predicted that future monthly expenditures of the War Department would average $24,000,000 for the duration of the war.[94] While waiting for Congress to act, Myers became so strapped for funds that he had to secure Congressional approval to pay the volunteers with funds earmarked for pay of the virtually nonexistent regular army.[95] Shortly thereafter Congress appropriated to the penny the sums that Benjamin had asked for and provided an extra $1,113,400 for the purchase of molasses to supplement the ration, as Benjamin had previously urged.[96] In March, Gorgas, reduced to approximately $3,000, had to get Congressional authorization to transfer $3,000,000 from unexpended Quartermaster funds to the Ordnance Department.[97] Thus the bureaus scrambled through until April.

Hardly had the bureaus finished making up their deficiencies when it

91. Gorgas to Benjamin, Dec. 4, 1861, *ibid.*, p. 776.

92. Myers to Benjamin, Nov. 18, 1861, QMDSW, pp. 58–61.

93. Benjamin to Davis, Nov. [30], 1861, *OR*-4, I, 764–765.

94. *Ibid.*

95. Myers to Benjamin, Dec. 14, 1861, QMDSW, pp. 68–69; "An Act Providing for the Transfer of Certain Appropriations," Dec. 18, 1861, *Statutes,* I, 224.

96. "An Act Making Appropriations for the Expenses of the Government, in the Legislative, Executive, and Judicial Departments, for the Year Ending the Eighteenth of February, Eighteen Hundred and Sixty-Two," Dec. 24, 1861, *Statutes,* I, 230–231; "An Act Making Appropriations for the Expenses of the Government in the Legislative, Executive, and Judicial Departments, From the Eighteenth of February to the First of April, Eighteen Hundred and Sixty-Two, and for Other Purposes," Feb. 15, 1862, *ibid.*, pp. 268–270.

97. "An Act to Transfer Funds from the Quartermaster's to the Ordnance Department," Jan. 30, 1862, *ibid.*, pp. 256–257.

was time to make new estimates for the support of the army from April 1 to December 1, 1862. Myers estimated for 475 regiments, in view of the fact that Davis was currently asking Congress to provide more men by conscription, and asked for $195,271,748 or $24,375,000 per month;[98] total estimates were $256,296,888.58.[99] Remembering his success in getting from Congress all he had asked for after he had shaved bureau estimates, Benjamin cut the figures approximately 21 per cent. Noting that the Quartermaster figure alone equaled his publicly announced estimate for total monthly expenses, he cut the Quartermaster estimates along with the others. The final requests sent to Congress were: Quartermaster, $155,000,000; Subsistence, $29,000,000; Ordnance, $11,000,000; Medical, $2,400,000; Engineer, $1,800,000.[100] With "incidentals" the amount totaled $199,883,725.58, which was duly appropriated by Congress.[101]

. . .

The effort to produce and equip an army cannot be explained by discussing the activities of the Confederate government alone. The government would have fallen well short of equipping the armies if it had not been for the aid of state and local authorities and the voluntary offering of the people. State participation in the war effort is a major subject meriting separate treatment, and only incidental references can be given in this study. The summer and autumn of 1861 marked the peak of private voluntary contributions, however, and deserve notice.

Although precise data are unavailable, it is possible that home-front contributions to Confederate supply made the difference between actual want and minimum comfort. In the summer of 1861, in the first flush of enthusiasm and while there was still something to give, the contributions poured in on the troops in such amounts that Congress passed a number of bills and resolutions to provide for the orderly distribution of the goods to the soldiers.[102] As the troops went into winter quarters, the contributions still came in. Jones remarked in his

98. Myers to Benjamin, March 11, 1862, QMDSW, pp. 117–121.

99. Benjamin to Davis, March 12, 1862, *OR*-4, I, 989.

100. *Ibid.*

101. "An Act Making Appropriations for the Support of the Government from April First to the Thirtieth of November, Eighteen Hundred and Sixty-Two, and for Objects Hereinafter Expressed," April 3, 1862, *Statutes*, II, 7–10.

102. "A Resolution to Dispose of Donations Made by Certain Churches on the Late Fast Day," June 30, 1861, *ibid.*, I, 212; "An Act to Make Provisions for the Care of Supplies for the Sick and Wounded," Aug. 2, 1861, *ibid.*, p. 170; "An Act Providing for the Reception and Forwarding of Articles Sent to the Army by Private Contributions," Aug. 31, 1861, *ibid.*, p. 209.

diary on this subject again and again, once bursting out, "Never was there such a patriotic *people* as ours. Their blood and their wealth are laid upon the altar of their country with enthusiasm."[103] Again, "The fathers and mothers and sisters of our brave soldiers continue to send their clothing and provisions. *They* do not relax in the work of independence."[104] Pollard estimated that $3,000,000 in contributions came in during the last quarter of 1861 alone.[105] The diaries and reminiscences of the period constantly reiterate the theme of the stitch, stitch, stitch of women on the home front and need not be discussed here. The statement of Benjamin is ample testimony to the importance of private individuals to the early war efforts of the Confederacy:

> The supplies of clothing, shoes, tents and other articles embraced within the scope of the duties of the Quartermaster's Bureau, could not possibly have been furnished in time for the wants of the present winter had not the entire population aided with common accord the efforts of the Government to prevent our brave defenders from suffering for want of needful protection from exposure.[106]

As the Confederate citizens gave to help outfit and feed the soldiers, their opinion of the quality of the government's efforts was undoubtedly reaching and reinforcing the views of their Congressional leaders. The action of the Senate on nominations during the winter may well serve to give perspective on the public image of the efforts of the various bureaus. The Senators thoroughly chewed over Northrop's nomination for promotion to full colonel and confirmation as Commissary General and postponed their decision until the end of the session, when they then paradoxically confirmed the nomination by the one-sided vote of 43–3.[107] Myers's nomination for promotion to full colonel and confirmation as Quartermaster General was approved on the day it arrived.[108] Northrop's bureau appears to have been as efficiently run as those of Myers and Gorgas, but despite high praises heaped on his head by his superior,[109] Northrop's unpopularity stood out in contrast

103. Jones, *War Clerk's Diary,* I, 83.   104. *Ibid.,* p. 102.

105. Edward A. Pollard, *Southern History of the War* (2 vols. in one; New York, 1866), I, 224 n.   106. Benjamin to Davis, Feb. —, 1862, *OR*-4, I, 959.

107. *Journal,* I, 495–508, 568, 718, 811. "Orient," in the *Daily Richmond Examiner,* (Sept. 1, 1863) claimed that Congress would not approve Northrop's nomination and rank until Myers's nomination and rank had been sent in and confirmed.   108. *Journal,* I, 841, 844.

109. Davis, *The Rise and Fall of the Confederate Government,* I, 303, 310, 315; Benjamin to Davis, Feb. —, 1862, *OR*-4, I, 959–960.

to the good reputation which Gorgas and Myers enjoyed.[110] Press attacks on the Commissary General had already begun, and the *Daily Richmond Examiner* was pursuing a vendetta against Northrop with such comments as "Have we a commissariat, or have we only a stupid piece of official machinery called Commissary General, whose only claims to distinction and usefulness are that he was the college chum of President JEFFERSON DAVIS!"[111] Personality factors and the fortunes of war were already laying the groundwork for one of the Confederacy's traditional villains.

When the spring of 1862 opened with a series of defeats, the full force of public irritation and disappointment fell on the Secretary of War's office. Like Walker before him, Judah P. Benjamin was ousted as a political scapegoat. As a routine administrator Benjamin was probably an improvement on Walker, but he was handicapped by his non-military background. He seems to have made little positive contribution to the supply effort except to encourage and praise the bureau chiefs and to pass on innovations that they suggested. On the other hand, his ideas and practices concerning overseas procurement delayed the bureau chiefs in setting up an efficient system. Apparently the pressure for his ouster resulted from a combination of blame for supply deficiencies and the military defeats of the spring of 1862, complicated by the antipathies of certain army officers and Congressmen and a hostile press which railed against "a cabinet of dummies" and "men unequal to the high trusts committed to them."[112] Benjamin's replacement was George Wythe Randolph, a politician who had served as a Confederate artillery officer.

· · ·

110. Myers's prospects were aided materially by his close friendship with the chairman of the military affairs committees of the House and Senate of the Permanent Congress, Congressmen William Porcher Miles and Senator Edward Sparrow. Pollard and DeLeon also sang his praises: see Pollard, *Southern History of the War,* I, 535–536; Thomas Cooper DeLeon, *Four Years in Rebel Capitals: An Inside View of the Confederacy from Birth to Death* (Mobile, Alabama, 1890), p. 114.

111. *Daily Richmond Examiner,* May 21, 1862.

112. The editorials quoted are from the *Daily Richmond Whig,* Feb. 23, 1862, and the Atlanta *Southern Confederacy,* May 22, 1862. See also the *Daily Richmond Examiner,* March 3 and March 6, 1862. Giving military defeats as a cause for Benjamin's resignation is a commonplace among students of Confederate history. The point about Benjamin's unpopularity among certain army officers is raised by John H. Reagan in his *Memoirs, with Special Reference to Secession and the Civil War,* p. 160.

One year after the outbreak of hostilities, despite the optimistic pronouncements of Benjamin that except for small arms the Confederacy "evinced the capacity of providing all that is necessary to the maintenance of . . . independence,"[113] the Confederacy in fact had not succeeded in supplying her troops adequately. The armies had been fed on a monotonous diet of meal and meat, had been indifferently clothed and equipped, and were critically short of arms and ammunition.

More sobering than the slipshod results of the first year of the Confederate supply effort was the degree to which the supply bureaus had depended on good luck. Success in running the blockade had made the difference between disastrous shortages and nagging deficiencies, but the Union blockade was beginning to tighten. Commissary hopes of furnishing meat and bread depended on good weather, on holding Tennessee and Northern Virginia, and on maintaining access to the Trans-Mississippi. The Quartermaster's Department had been greatly aided by individual and state contributions of clothing; but the domestic market was fast contracting. Another important variable was the morale of the citizens at home. The home-front had begun to display abundant signs of rising prices, hoarding, and speculation. It was already an open question whether the Confederate citizens would continue to display the patriotism necessary to forbear from exploiting the shortages in the country.

While the spotty results of the supply operations were everywhere apparent, the public and the politicians at this stage of the war generally understood that the reasons for deficiencies were not bureau incompetence or corruption but rather the suddenness and magnitude of the task and the natural scarcity of war materials. The President and the Secretaries of War held the bureau heads in high esteem, and the chiefs were also supported by Congress and by the country at large, except for some objections to Northrop. Whatever the estimate of past performance, could the bureaus, by expanded operations and increased efficiency, reduce their dependence on luck, sustain the armies, and withstand the wastage and losses of a long campaign? Part of the answer would lie in the vigor and insight of civilian leadership.

Civilian administration of the supply effort up to the spring of 1862 displayed both positive and negative elements. In terms of an efficient chain of command, the central position of the Secretary of War had proved almost irrelevant. Caught in a politically expendable position,

113. Benjamin to Davis, Feb. —, 1862, *OR*-4, I, 959.

Walker and Benjamin, with their civilian backgrounds, found their powers of decision closely circumscribed by the bureau chiefs' expertise on the one hand and by the President's determination to make all important decisions on the other. The Secretaries had not co-ordinated bureau operations, allowing the bureaus to act independently of each other and even to compete with each other for supplies. Most of the sensible innovations in supply arrangements, both in individual bureau administration and in general supply policy, had been initiated by the bureau heads rather than by the Secretaries, a condition that speaks well of the quality of bureau leadership but not of that of the Secretaries. Since the President himself decided the fate of major proposals, the quality of the Confederate supply effort to a large extent rested on the capacity of the President and, to a lesser degree, of Congress, to develop insight commensurate with the expanding war effort.

On the face of it, the major policy decisions of the Confederate officials did display some flexibility and insight in the sense of often making intelligent reactions to emerging problems. The government had allocated manpower, turned cotton into a basis for credit abroad, subsidized ordnance manufacturing and railroad construction, and encouraged conversion from cotton to provision raising. These programs were impressively innovative, considering the peculiarly conservative nature of Confederate political, social, and economic ideology.

In a deeper sense, however, the leadership of the civilian officials during the first year of the Confederate war effort displayed characteristics which portended disaster. So far, the policies of the Davis administration had been reactions to problems grown too dangerous to ignore. There was little indication that those responsible for the success of the Confederate supply system understood that their duty was to anticipate problems, to plan ahead for maximum use of domestic resources, for efficient procurement of necessary supplies from abroad, and for efficient co-ordination of bureau activities in the transportation and distribution of goods. To expect an implementation of a centralized war program at this early stage of the war, of course, would be to demand a superhuman display of insight and a renunciation of tradition amounting to genius. Still, the penchant on the part of the Confederate leaders for reacting to problems rather than planning for the future demonstrated a pedestrian mentality that boded ill for the Confederacy if the problems of making war should multiply.

CHAPTER THREE

REORGANIZING FOR THE LONG HAUL

The Government has employed an army of barnacles to go out in swarms like the locusts of Egypt, into every section and neighborhood, to buy up what the army needed. Many of these agents knew no more of business than a Comanche Indian knew of mathematics. —— Jackson *Daily Southern Crisis,* January 16, 1863.*

The Union onslaught in the spring of 1862 devastated the Confederate war effort. The United States military machine wrenched away the border areas, the Mississippi Valley, most of the coast and harbors, and transformed large areas of the Confederacy into a no-man's land subject to sporadic destruction. The area from which the Confederacy could draw provisions was sharply reduced, and except for some minor losses of territory in 1863, the Confederacy operated within these limits for the next two years. In addition, the Confederates lost much of their supply reserves in the retreats and squandered them amidst inter-command bickering. The privations of the Confederate armed services in subsequent months and years stemmed in large part from the defeats of the spring of 1862.

On the other hand, the 1862 debacle led to some beneficial developments. Sudden destitution, coupled with the growing realization that the war would be a prolonged one, to be decided in part by intelligent use of resources, spurred the Confederate administration to revamp supply organizations and to create more effective supply policies.

Every immediate aspect of the campaigns of the spring of 1862 hurt the supply services. Union operations on the coast, for example, severely restricted blockade running as a source of supply. Many ports and sounds were seized or blocked up, and the blockading squadrons, which could now concentrate off Wilmington, Charleston, and Mobile, raised the percentage of captures. The Union found the Texas coast

* Quoted in John K. Bettersworth, ed., *Mississippi in the Confederacy: As They Saw It* (Baton Rouge, 1961), p. 290.

and the Rio Grande more difficult to control, but supplies arriving here could not be shipped eastward by land. Altogether, the Union severely constricted available sea entries and ended the era in which large numbers of private blockade runners slipped easily into Confederate ports and rivers. Captures rose from an estimated one in eight to one in four, and blockade running began to concentrate in the hands of those few who could stand the high overhead of securing or constructing ships suitable for blockade running and also absorb the loss of some of the ships. The needs of the domestic market continually enhanced the profit of bringing in goods solely on private account, and such profits tempted private blockade runners to ignore the less lucrative business of shipping government supplies. Consequently, as will be seen, the government had to reconsider its importation methods.

In Virginia, although McClellan's peninsular campaign fizzled, the Confederates incurred severe supply losses. In moving to protect the Capital against McClellan, General Johnston abandoned his position outside Washington and uncovered all of Virginia east of the Shenandoah Valley and north of the Rappahannock River and thus exposed large areas of Virginia's flour and beef belt to the enemy. At this juncture Manassas became the scene of, and Johnston, Northrop, and Davis the principal participants in, another vicious wrangle, this time over a "sport" in the history of Confederate logistics, a veritable plethora of foodstuffs. By January shipments by railroad and the activities of the nearby meat packing plant at Thoroughfare Gap had accumulated five million pounds of rations, plus enough cattle to feed Johnston's army for forty-five days.[1] Johnston began to demand that the foodstuffs be sent away and the accumulation trimmed to fifteen days' supply.[2] He did not, however, inform Davis of his plans for withdrawal, and Davis apparently forbade the transfer of the food until he knew where Johnston was going so that the food could be put in storehouses at the proper place.[3] Johnston suddenly decided to break camp, but the vast stocks of food, including the mountain of private impedimenta accumulated by the volunteers over the months in camp, delayed his withdrawal for a day.[4] Even so, the army abandoned over one million pounds of foodstuffs, some already rotten from improper storage. Davis and Northrop denounced Johnston for his precipitate

1. Johnston, *Narrative of Military Operations*, p. 98.
2. *Ibid.*; J. E. Johnston to Davis, Feb. 25, 1862, *OR*-1, V, 1081.
3. Rowland, *Jefferson Davis*, V, 208.
4. Johnston, *Narrative of Military Operations*, p. 103.

withdrawal and waste, especially since his position was not threatened. In his turn, Johnston inveighed against materials having been accumulated despite his protests.[5]

Later Davis censured Johnston for abandoning his lines at Williamsburg without sufficient notice, because supplies that could have been salvaged were unnecessarily lost.[6] Worse still, Confederate authorities at Norfolk were surprised by Johnston's retreat. The army abandoned a large amount of ordnance stores, and the Confederacy lost forever its principal naval yards, containing most of the apparatus for large-scale shipbuilding, as well as the main shops for casting naval shot and shell and for constructing maritime engines.[7] Although the navy had saved most of the machinery and had moved it to a new laboratory at Charlotte, the transfer involved damaging delays in naval construction and ordnance output.[8] The affairs at Manassas and Norfolk rankled so much in the minds of the principals that they debated the matter in letters and memoirs after the war.[9]

Disasters in the west dwarfed the losses in Virginia. The initial losses of fortified spots on the river systems, such as Fort Donelson or Island No. 10, were the fruits of inept strategic concepts rather than results of supply deficiencies. Special efforts had been made to have the strong points well fortified with ammunition and food, and no post fell because of immediate supply difficulties. Rather, the posts fell either because too few men were available to hold the generously conceived and engineered posts, or because strategic circumstances rendered them untenable.[10]

The consequences that followed the loss of forts Henry and Donelson may well have been the greatest single supply disaster of the war. The forts controlled access to central Tennessee and northern Mississippi, Alabama, and Georgia. They protected the largest provision-rais-

5. Davis to Phelan, Feb. 18, 1865, Rowland, *Jefferson Davis,* V, 494–495; Davis to Northrop, May 20, 1879, *ibid.,* VIII, 391–392; Davis to Northrop, April 28, 1878, *ibid.,* 187; Johnston, *Narrative of Military Operations,* pp. 98, 444–446; *Daily Richmond Examiner,* April 15, 1862.

6. Davis to Phelan, Feb. 18, 1865, Rowland, *Jefferson Davis,* V, 494–495; cf. Johnston, *Narrative of Military Operations,* p. 449.

7. Report of the Secretary of the Navy, Feb. 27, 1862, *ORN*-2, II, 153–154.

8. Report of the Secretary of the Navy, Aug. 16, 1862, *ibid.,* p. 250.

9. Davis to Northrop, May 20, 1879, Rowland, *Jefferson Davis,* VIII, 391–392; Davis to Northrop, April 28, 1878, *ibid.,* p. 187; Johnston, *Narrative of Military Operations,* pp. 98, 444–446.

10. These statements are based upon investigation of campaign reports in *OR*-1. For Fort Donelson, e.g., see *OR*-1, VII, 269–334, 429–437.

ing areas in the Confederacy, the nexus of the Confederate railroad network, and large supply accumulations. Nashville, for example, was a great administrative center for the Confederate supply system. Procurement and distribution for the armies in Tennessee, Kentucky, Arkansas, and Missouri were centered there, and the city held a substantial part of those reserves the Confederacy had been able to scrape together to face the 1862 campaigning year. There were large government warehouses filled with quartermaster and commissary property, and the Ordnance Department maintained two powder mills and a depot. The protection of these supplies was a major responsibility for the field commander of the district, Albert Sidney Johnston, and for the supply officials in charge of government materials, but no one exercised that responsibility when Grant took Fort Henry on February 6 and Fort Donelson on the sixteenth, and thus wrenched open the door to the Confederate heartland. While Grant had been busy at the forts, Johnston had been hurriedly evacuating his base at Bowling Green, Kentucky, and abandoning his packing plants at Clarksville, Tennessee, putting to the torch large amounts of provisions that he could not carry away in his precipitate retreat south to Nashville.[11] On arriving at Nashville, he heard of the fall of Fort Donelson and marched his men through the city and away to the south.[12] Johnston left no men to direct the evacuation of government stores or to keep the panic-stricken civilians in hand until Floyd's men arrived from Fort Donelson. The supply officials stationed in Nashville apparently had not made arrangements to remove the supplies in case of evacuation, and when the crisis was upon them, they panicked like the civilians. It was alleged that Major V. K. Stevenson, principal quartermaster for the western depots and president of the Nashville and Chattanooga Railroad, fled the city immediately in his private railroad car.[13] When Floyd reached the city with his troops on the seventeenth, he found the government storehouses virtually in the possession of what he termed

11. Trousdale Testimony, *Report of the Special Committee on the Recent Military Disasters at Forts Henry and Donelson, and the Evacuation of Nashville* (Richmond, 1862), p. 82. 12. *Ibid.*, p. 80.

13. Forrest to Committee of the House of Representatives, n. d., *OR*-1, VII, 429–431. The investigating committee apparently found the performance of the supply bureaus satisfactory. "Timon," in the Charleston *Courier*, March 31, 1862, commented, "I have the most reliable authority for stating that their conduct, and especially that of the Quartermaster-General, in regard to prudence, economy, integrity and efficiency, have [*sic*] made a most favorable and satisfactory impression on the Committee."

the "rabble," and he had to order his cavalry to keep the mobs at bay with drawn sabers while his men worked for four days loading trains and sending stores off to Chattanooga.[14] A cloudburst which washed out the railroad bridges in the Nashville area ended the evacuation of supplies, and when Buell marched in on the twenty-third, immense if unspecified amounts of quartermaster and commissary stores fell into the hands of the Union troops.[15] The materials which had been saved were scattered through depots further south and the machinery of the powder works sent on to the new plant at Augusta.[16] Atlanta subsequently became the general depot for the west.

The most serious result of the Henry-Donelson episode was the loss of the iron-producing areas of the lower Tennessee Valley and a substantial part of the most valuable meat region of the Confederacy. One third of the hogs packed in 1861 for the use of the Confederate armies had come from areas now surrendered permanently to the Union.[17] The daily diet of the Confederate soldiers in later campaigns amply demonstrated the magnitude of this loss.

To compound these disasters, Union cavalry dashed south across Tennessee and swept into Huntsville, Alabama, permanently breaking up the railroad line from Memphis to Chattanooga, the main east-west trunk line in the Confederacy. Any hopes of regaining the use of this line were snuffed out when the Confederates lost the battle of Shiloh and evacuated the railroad junction at Corinth. From that time communication between Virginia and Mississippi for both strategic and supply purposes depended on a conglomeration of rail and wagon transportation from Richmond to Mobile (by way of Atlanta and Montgomery) and thence back north into Mississippi.

If communication with Mississippi had been rendered difficult, the loss of Memphis and New Orleans made communication with Texas little more than a theory. From the north, Union forces took Confederate positions on the upper Mississippi and captured Memphis, another important Confederate supply depot. General Lovell had prepared in depth the defense of New Orleans, and he had at hand adequate artillery and ammunition to defend that area against a land attack.[18] However, delays by the Secretary of the Navy in letting contracts and

14. Forrest to Committee of the House of Representatives, n.d., *OR*-1, VII, 429–431; Floyd to Brewster, March 22, 1862, *ibid.*, pp. 427–429.

15. A. S. Johnston to Benjamin, Feb. 25, 1862, *ibid.*, pp. 426–427.

16. *Ibid.*

17. Ruffin to Randolph, Nov. 8, 1862, PRSD.

18. Lovell Testimony, Proceedings of Court Martial on the Fall of New Orleans, *Or*-1, VI, 560–566.

various problems in securing plating materials contributed to the failure of the naval defense.[19] The Confederates acted with intelligence and speed and succeeded in removing most of the military property of the Confederate government and of the state of Louisiana.[20] The naval ordnance machinery was sent to Atlanta and army ordnance equipment moved to Selma.[21]

While the removal of the government stores had minimized material losses, long-term consequences of the fall of New Orleans were almost as catastrophic as the loss of Nashville and middle Tennessee. The Crescent City was the second largest general manufacturing city in the Confederacy, producing large amounts of shoes and clothing; in addition, an extensive ordnance complex there had supplied the Army of Tennessee, the navy, and military establishments on the Gulf.[22] New Orleans was also the center of naval construction for the Gulf, second only to Norfolk in importance.[23] Beyond the intrinsic value of the city, the fall of New Orleans provided a base for the extension of Union control northward up the Mississippi Valley, enabling the Union forces virtually to eliminate the movement of cattle, horses, sugar, wool, and molasses east across the river and the movement of arms and equipment westward. Union possession of New Orleans also closed a valuable network of channel entries for blockade runners and tempted Confederates to sell their embargoed cotton.

During the early months of 1862 vicissitudes of campaigning had diminished the reserves of the supply services, but campaigning had not been affected by supply shortages. During the "defensive" campaigns in the early summer of 1862 the Confederate armies were adequately supplied with food and clothing and, with the exception of Kirby Smith in eastern Tennessee, minimally provided with arms. Later in the year, however, supply problems became a factor both in strategic planning and in the degree of success in conducting campaigns, remaining an important consideration to the end of the war. By August the material losses of the spring manifested themselves most strikingly in exhausted quartermaster stores. Kirby Smith described his men as ragged and barefooted,[24] and Lee reported that his army lacked "much of the materials of war, . . . [was] feeble in transportation, the animals being much reduced, and the men . . . poorly pro-

19. *Ibid.*, pp. 599–611. 20. *Ibid.*, pp. 560 ff. 21. *Ibid.*
22. *Ibid.* 23. *Ibid.*
24. Kirby Smith to Mrs. Kirby Smith, Aug. 21, 1862, Edmund Kirby-Smith Papers, Southern Historical Collection, University of North Carolina.

vided with clothes, and in thousands of instances . . . destitute of shoes."[25] Despite these shortages, planning for the Kentucky and Maryland invasions proceeded. The main considerations in undertaking these campaigns, of course, were the factors of strategy, diplomacy, morale, and recruitment. In addition, supply officials hoped to replenish the commissariat partially even if the offensive operations failed in their larger objectives. Lee hoped to gather subsistence and forage in Maryland, while the commissaries were busy in the rear gleaning the cattle, wheat, and forage of northern Virginia.[26] In addition, the Commissary General was interested in securing a large part of the Kentucky hog crop,[27] and he scraped together some gold for the commissary agents who were to follow Bragg and Kirby Smith in order to buy and drive in the hogs.[28] In the execution of the autumn campaigns, however, supply procurement was aborted by campaign failures, failures which were in part affected by supply problems.

One problem common to both campaigns was that the armies, operating off the railroads and hobbled by a shortage of field transportation and inadequate food reserves, had to subsist off the land and thus to gauge strategic considerations to the practicability of foraging. In the Kentucky campaign, Bragg claimed that he had left his strategic position at Munfordville because he could not feed his army.[29] The validity of Bragg's claim has been disputed down to the present.[30] Regardless of what happened at Munfordville, the eventual retreat from Kentucky illustrates the complex interrelationship between the supply situation and campaigning. Bragg claimed that the retreat was hastened by his inability to subsist his men,[31] while the precipitation of the withdrawal prevented the commissary agents from getting out

25. Lee to Davis, Sept. 3, 1862, *OR*-1, XIX (2), 590.

26. Lee to Davis, Aug. 30, 1862, Douglas Southall Freeman, ed., *Lee's Dispatches: Unpublished Letters of General Robert E. Lee, C.S.A., to Jefferson Davis and the War Department of the Confederate States of America, 1862–1865, from the Private Collection of Wymberly Jones De Renne* (New York and London, 1915), pp. 71–73. Cited hereinafter as Freeman, *Lee's Dispatches*; *Daily Richmond Examiner*, Sept. 5 and Sept. 12, 1862.

27. Northrop to Seddon, Jan. 12, 1863, *OR*-4, II, 351.

28. *Ibid.*

29. Bragg to Cooper, Sept. 25, 1862, *OR*-1, XVI (2), 876. Kirby Smith had claimed an abundance of supplies at Lexington. See Kirby Smith to Bragg, Sept. 15, 1862, *ibid.*, p. 830.

30. For a sympathetic review of Bragg's Kentucky campaign which presents all sides of Bragg's strategic, subsistence, and logistical problems, see Grady McWhiney, "Controversy in Kentucky: Braxton Bragg's Campaign of 1862," *Civil War History*, VI, No. 1 (March 1960), 5–42.

31. Bragg to Cooper, May 20, 1863, *OR*-1, XVI (1), 1093.

the cattle and hogs which they had purchased to feed the army during the winter.[32]

Bragg's subsequent position at Murfreesboro protected southern and eastern Tennessee and enabled the commissaries to secure and pack meat from this area. Before the battle of Murfreesboro, Bragg reported that his army's "health and general tone . . . were never better."[33] There were no reported supply shortages to hamper the troops on the battlefield, but Bragg's strange retreat interrupted meat packing operations for the winter and, as it turned out, permanently surrendered the bountiful lands of middle Tennessee to the Union. Bragg subsequently chose to scatter his army in winter quarters in the fertile lands of southern Tennessee around Fayetteville and Tullahoma rather than in the Appalachian foothills to protect Chattanooga, because the hills were too barren to maintain his men. Of course, the lack of subsistence reserves was partly due to his retreats and abandonment of productive areas, but Bragg commented that there would have been even less meat if he had not saved eastern Tennessee in the summer of 1862 and if he had not held much of that state during the autumn.[34]

Supply problems also affected the Maryland campaign. Lee's men were weary after Second Manassas, and this weariness and the failure of the shoe supply caused large-scale straggling.[35] The Quartermaster's Department had not been able to recover from the spring debacles and was unable to replace the thousands of shoes that wore out on the stony northern Virginia and Maryland pikes. This straggling depleted Lee's army and hampered the campaign, but it was a minor consideration compared with McClellan's lucky discovery that Lee had divided his forces. The campaign was aborted before the commissaries operating in Lee's rear could gather supplies.

The disasters of the spring of 1862 and the demands of the long campaigning season which followed had strained the supply bureaus beyond their capacity, highlighting the previous winter's inadequate accumulation. As a result, during the fall and winter of 1862–63, the bureaus magnified and diversified their efforts to furnish materials, and the Quartermaster's and Subsistence bureaus created a new organizational format that would last throughout the war. During this period Randolph resigned and was replaced by James A. Seddon. The change

32. Cummings to Ruffin, Oct. 25, 1862, PRSD.
33. Bragg to Davis, Nov. 24, 1862, *OR*-1, XX (1), 421.
34. Bragg to Ewell, Feb. 24, 1863, *ibid.,* XXIII (2), 648.
35. Lee to Cooper, Aug. 19, 1862, *ibid.,* XIX (1), 151.

did not affect supply policies controlled at the bureau level, the policies being considered in this chapter. Randolph's role will be evaluated in a subsequent chapter in connection with supply policies determined at the higher, civilian level of policy-making.

. . .

The Ordnance Department suffered the least from the spring defeats, a fortunate circumstance in view of the fact that it had been the least successful of the bureaus in fulfilling its obligations. Although three large ordnance-producing centers, New Orleans, Norfolk, and Nashville, had fallen into the hands of the enemy, most of the invaluable machinery at these places had been saved, and general losses of matériel during all the retreats had been small.[36]

Indeed, as the Confederate defeats mounted, good fortune in blockade running began to ease that bureau's critical shortages in small arms. From April 27 to August 3, 1862, so Gorgas reported, 48,410 stand of arms arrived in the holds of blockade runners; and after that, importations averaged about 10,000 a month.[37] Captures, especially those on the Virginia battlefields, may have contributed as many as 80,000 arms and a number of cannon.[38] Domestic small-arms production had crept up to 2,050 per month in government arsenals and to 1,550 in private shops,[39] but domestic production remained a negligible source of supply. The arsenals held machinery capable of much higher production, but the factories were throttled by a shortage of skilled labor.[40] By autumn the Ordnance Department was meeting all requisitions for small arms regularly and had built up a reserve of some 10,000.[41] In fact, the bureau felt confident enough to attempt to ferry 18,000 arms across the Mississippi to alleviate the desperate shortages of the western troops.[42] Figures on cannon production are lacking, but Gorgas claimed that enough cannon had been captured and manufactured to satisfy the needs for both fixed emplacements and field artillery.[43]

Gorgas also faced new shortages, this time in lead and leather. The supply of lead ore from available mines, despite the best exertions of

36. Gorgas to Randolph, Aug. 20, 1862, *OR*-4, II, 65–66.
37. Gorgas Memorandum, Aug. 16, 1862, *ibid.,* p. 52.
38. Randolph to Davis, Aug. 12, 1862, *ibid.,* pp. 47–48.
39. Gorgas to Seddon, Jan. 7, 1863, *ibid.,* p. 299. 40. *Ibid.*
41. Randolph to Shorter, Oct. 11, 1862, WDTS, XXXIV, 378.
42. Vandiver, *Confederate Ordnance,* pp. 138–139.
43. Gorgas to Seddon, Nov. 15, 1863, *OR*-4, II, 955 ff.

the Niter and Mining Corps, reached only three or four tons a day, an inadequate amount for the needs of the army.[44] The Corps collected scrap lead from mines and from the battlefields, brought it across the Mississippi from Mexico and Texas, and began to import from abroad.[45] Still there was not enough to allow the laboratories to make cartridges to their full capacity.[46] Leather for accouterments was a vexing rather than crippling problem, but serious enough to cause a number of clashes between the Ordnance and Quartermaster's bureaus over the control of stocks of the valuable material.[47] Two other raw materials, sulphur and copper, remained in good supply.[48]

Perhaps the greatest success of the Ordnance Department was in taking fundamental steps to overcome its most serious problem, the saltpeter shortage. The blockade runners were beginning to bring in quantities of saltpeter, and the new Niter and Mining Corps, although hamstrung by the spring retreats, was laying the groundwork for a more certain domestic supply. After losing caves in Arkansas, Alabama, Tennessee, and Virginia,[49] the Corps found itself reduced to one large cave in Georgia and a few small scattered caves which together produced only 500 pounds a day.[50] A quick survey soon brought to light new sources, which the Corps divided into development districts. With money provided by Congress, the Corps encouraged private parties to enter the niter production business. However, private sources proved unreliable and when the government took over production, using details from the armies,[51] niter production boomed. Whereas the April 15–June 1 output totaled 25,000 pounds, June production was 35,000 pounds. Production rose to 2,000 pounds a day in August, and St. John hoped to reach 3,000 pounds a day if the Corps could overcome "lamentable" transportation.[52] By October the Corps had collected 200,820 pounds of niter and had brought 38,000 pounds over the Mississippi from Mexico, while artificial niter beds set up by the bureau totaled 120,000 cubic feet.[53] St. John's establishment had grown by December to more than 1,100 men, agents, clerks, physical exempts, army details, free Negroes, and impressed slaves.

In order to keep production up to a satisfactory level, St. John

44. St. John to Randolph, July 31, 1862, *ibid.*, p. 30. 45. *Ibid.*

46. Vandiver, *Confederate Ordnance*, p. 148.

47. General Orders No. 97, Adjutant and Inspector General's Office, 1862 Series, Dec. 1, 1862, *OR*-4, II, 219.

48. St. John to Randolph, July 31, 1862, *ibid.*, p. 30. 49. *Ibid.*, pp. 28–30.

50. *Ibid.*, p. 27. 51. *Ibid.* 52. *Ibid.*, p. 29.

53. St. John to Seddon, Dec. 3, 1862, *ibid.*, pp. 222–223.

demanded success in the battlefield: first, the Confederate armies must hold eastern Tennessee and southwest Virginia; second, because of the failure of private capital, military authorities must provide for adequate transportation and details to push the work forward in the inaccessible areas.[54] The War Department authorized the Corps to use conscripts and to call for details as needed, for "this service is second to no other engaged in the public defense."[55] In addition, the War Department gave the Corps authority to seize the products of defaulting contractors.[56]

The contributions of the Corps had been so impressive that Congress, on April 22, 1863, created the Niter and Mining Bureau, a separate and independent bureau of the War Department.[57] In addition to its normal responsibility for the mining of iron ore, coal, lead, copper, and saltpeter and for the artificial production of niter, the new bureau was to centralize under its jurisdiction all War Department contracts for the manufacture of iron and to determine priorities for its use.[58]

To receive the increased supply of saltpeter, the Ordnance Department opened its huge new powder works at Augusta. The Augusta mills produced 1,000,000 pounds of powder for the Confederacy in the span of a year after it commenced operations on April 10, 1862, at a cost of $1.08 per pound compared with the price of $3.00 for blockade-run powder.[59] Works at Raleigh and Richmond and a few small contractors around the country supplemented the Augusta output.[60] Despite a nagging shortage of lead, eight Ordnance laboratories produced 170,000 rounds of small-arms ammunition and up to 1,350 rounds of field ammunition daily.[61] Heavy expenditures of ammunition during 1862, however, prevented the accumulation of any substantial reserves.

Sooner than any other bureau, the Ordnance Department felt the manpower pinch. From the earliest days of the war the shortage of skilled armorers had held the production of small arms below the

54. *Ibid.*

55. General Orders No. 99, Adjutant and Inspector General's Office, 1862 Series, Dec. 5, 1862, *ibid.*, p. 228.

56. General Orders No. 14, Adjutant and Inspector General's Office, 1863 Series, Feb. 3, 1863, *ibid.*, pp. 380–381.

57. "An Act to Establish a Nitre and Mining Bureau," April 22, 1863, *Statutes*, II, 114.

58. Myers to Glover, QMDLS, XVII, 426; General Orders No. 85, Adjutant and Inspector General's Office, 1863 Series, June 16, 1863, *OR*-4, II, 594–595.

59. Rains, *Powder Works*, p. 12. 60. *Ibid.*

61. Vandiver, *Confederate Ordnance*, p. 148.

capacity of the arsenals. While unskilled labor, often women, could do much of the work of assembling the cartridges and preparing ammunition packages, the bureau early found that it needed to accumulate all the foundrymen, miners, and laborers it could find; and Gorgas had been active in seeing that munitions workers were exempted from the very start of the conscription era. Yet skilled men remained in such short supply that the bureau began early to examine the possibility of bringing in skilled labor from abroad.[62]

By the spring of 1863 the Chief of Ordnance had reason to enter in his diary: "My Department is in a very satisfactory condition. . . ."[63] From the beginning Gorgas had enjoyed both exclusive controls over the raw materials he needed and top priority in transportation, advantages denied, for instance, to the Subsistence Department with eventual catastrophic results to the commissariat. Thus freed to concentrate on production and importation, Gorgas had by 1863 secured enough ordnance stores to equip the armies for the present, and, although dogged by shortages in raw materials and skilled workmen, had created a physical plant equal to the demands of the future except for the manufacture of small arms. The Niter and Mining Bureau, as efficient as its youth would permit, could be expected progressively to reduce dependence on the blockade for raw materials if the armies protected the vital mineral-producing areas. Since the Ordnance Department was dependent for the immediate future on importations to counterbalance domestic shortages in raw materials and small arms, Gorgas had evolved an effective system of getting needed supplies into the Confederacy. In one year the Ordnance Department had been transformed from the most deficient to the most efficient of the supply bureaus.

. . .

Unlike the Ordnance Department, the Quartermaster's Department experienced damaging setbacks as a consequence of the spring retreats. The loss of New Orleans, Nashville, and Memphis wiped out the surplus stocks that the bureau had been able to scrape together during the winter. This loss had been compounded by the wasteful actions of the troops during the campaign season. Many supplies received cavalier treatment at the hands of undisciplined soldiers on the march. The men threw away everything not absolutely required to preserve body

62. *Ibid.*, pp. 167–168.

63. Frank E. Vandiver, ed., *The Civil War Diary of General Josiah Gorgas* (University, Alabama, 1947), p. 15. Cited hereinafter as Vandiver, *Gorgas Diary.*

and soul: extra underwear, boots, overcoats, mess equipment, knapsacks, canteens, sidearms, cartridge boxes—even their blankets.[64] The Quartermaster General charged that some commanders actually encouraged wastefulness by allowing unit quartermasters to requisition more than their troops needed.[65] In the spring Myers stated that he could not fulfil requisitions for forty thousand uniforms and sent the following circular to the commanding generals:

> The destruction of large quantities of public stores which had attended the abandonment of different military positions and posts and the general want of economy in their use by the troops have greatly reduced the resources of the Quarter Master Department. The issue of any article must hereafter be curtailed if not discontinued, and it will be impossible to supply tents or tent flies to the army during the summer months. . . . The practice heretofore of applying for . . . stores by staff officers of brigades and regiments without the approval of the General Commanding has interfered materially with the careful and economical disposition of the supplies of this department.
>
> The resources from which such stores are supplied have become seriously limited and the strictest economy is essential throughout the army. I request that I may have your co-operation in enforcing its observance in your command.[66]

During the course of the year, staff-line conflicts sharpened between the Quartermaster's Department and the army commands. When Bragg removed the chief quartermaster assigned to his district and then replaced him with a man not in the Quartermaster service,[67] Myers wrote to Randolph:

> It is necessary to have distinctly defined, the line of demarcation, between the authority of the Qm. M. department and that of a general commanding, in regard to the appointment of principal quarter masters.
>
> This Department is responsible to no small extent, for the action of its subordinates. Their accountability is with it, and they should be under its control. If a general can, at will, displace an

64. Carlton McCarthy, *Detailed Minutiae of Soldier Life in the Army of Northern Virginia, 1861–1865* (Richmond, 1882), pp. 16–28, 42 ff.

65. General Orders No. 67, Army of Northern Virginia, June 12, 1862, John T. Pickett Papers, Library of Congress.

66. Myers to Generals Commanding, May 21, 1862, QMDLS, XVI, 226.

67. Myers to Randolph, Aug. 8, 1862, QMDELR, pp. 28–29.

> officer selected by the Dept., and substitute another over whom it can exercise no control, embarassment and difficulties may readily arise.[68]

Nothing was done. In the fall, commanders in the Mississippi Valley intercepted some cloth bound from the Trans-Mississippi to the Army of Northern Virginia. This time Myers succeeded in getting the Secretary of War to rule that field commanders could not interfere with quartermaster arrangements for the transportation and distribution of supplies.[69]

Efforts to supply the Army of Northern Virginia in the fall and winter of 1862–63 revealed inefficient performance on the part of the field quartermasters, who were generally picked by the officers commanding individual units. By September Lee's army was critically short of quartermaster supplies, particularly shoes, underwear, and blankets.[70] However, field quartermasters failed to notify Myers of these shortages through official channels. Instead, Lee wrote directly to Randolph and Davis, who passed the general's requests on to Myers. The Quartermaster General sent supplies continually during the fall, but as late as December inspection reports continually noted units of the Army of Northern Virginia that were "badly clothed and shod."[71]

Myers found the condition of the Army of Northern Virginia a source of irritation. On October 1 he told Randolph that he had received no requisitions from Lee's quartermaster and that he had no way of knowing the condition of the army units if the quartermasters would not send in their requisitions by normal channels. "The troops, as far as I am informed, are not in need."[72] This failure of the unit quartermasters officially to report their needs was embarrassing to Myers. On one occasion Seddon asked Myers why Lee kept asking for

68. *Ibid.* 69. Myers to Randolph, Nov. 6, 1862, QMDSW, pp. 228–229.

70. Newspaper accounts of the condition of Lee's men vary widely. See *Charleston Daily Courier,* Oct. 9, 1862; Mobile *Advertiser and Register,* Oct. 4, 1862; *Weekly Columbus Enquirer,* Oct. 21, and Dec. 22, 1862; Richmond *Enquirer,* Nov. 12 and Nov. 14, 1862.

71. Lee to Myers, Sept. 21, 1862, *OR*-1, XIX (2), 614; Randolph to Myers, Sept. 26, 1862, *OR*-4, II, 96; Myers to Randolph, Sept. 26, 1862, QMDSW, p. 205; Myers to Randolph, Oct. 1, 1862, *ibid.,* p. 209; Randolph to Lee, Nov. 12, 1862, WDTS, XXXIV, 414; Lee to Seddon, Dec. 2, 1862, *OR*-1, XXI, 1041; Myers to Seddon, Jan. 19, 1863, QMDSW, p. 260; Chilton to Hood, Nov. 14, 1862, *OR*-1, XIX (2), 718–719. Cf. Lee's statement just before Fredericksburg that his army "was never in better health or in better condition for battle than now." Lee to Davis, Dec. 6, 1862, *OR*-1, XXI, 1050.

72. Myers to Randolph, Oct. 1, 1862, QMDSW, p. 209.

supplies if the bureau had met all requisitions as Myers had reported.[73]

In spite of inefficiency in the field, supplies moved forward to Lee's army. In December the Quartermaster's bureau had forwarded to Lee all the shoes that it had on hand at Richmond.[74] In addition, Seddon, at Lee's request, impressed large quantities of shoes held by speculators in Richmond and sent them forward to the army.[75] Seddon noted in a letter to Lee at this time that in order to supply all the Confederate armies with quartermaster stores, he had had to resort to "contracts which, under less stringent necessity, I would not have tolerated."[76] By January the War Department was transporting supplies regularly to Lee's army, as much as 5,000 of each item daily, although reports still indicated that certain commands were not clothed and shod.[77] The fledgling Secretary of War, not overly impressed by the state of the supply bureaus, wrote to Lee somewhat sardonically:

> The Quartermaster-General gives me flattering assurance that, from domestic sources, through instrumentalities he has been arranging and has now brought into operation, he will from this time forth be more and more able to provide these indispensable articles, especially shoes. I trust it may so prove.[78]

While embroiled in an inefficient distribution system, the Quartermaster General directed himself to more pressing problems of depleted reserves. He scoured the local markets and even borrowed surplus navy blankets.[79] In addition, he gave out more contracts to private individuals to supply quartermaster goods from abroad for payment in cotton. In this connection the disasters of the spring had demonstrated to Myers's superiors the necessity for importing supplies; Myers finally received permission to send Major J. B. Ferguson, a former merchant, abroad as a special agent to purchase quartermaster stores.[80] In his major effort to alleviate the destitution of his bureau, however, Myers moved to take control of essential domestic resources. Where there was not enough for both army and citizens, as in wool and leather, the bureau attempted to create a monopoly. For the manufacturing of cloth,

73. New to Perkins, Jan. 19, 1863, *OR*-1, XXI, 1097–1098.

74. Seddon to Lee, Dec. 4, 1862, *ibid.*, p. 1045. 75. *Ibid.* 76. *Ibid.*

77. Myers to Seddon, Jan. 19, 1863, QMDSW, p. 260; New to Perkins, Jan. 19, 1863, and endorsements, *OR*-1, XXI, 1097–1099.

78. Seddon to Lee, Dec. 4, 1862, *OR*-1, XXI, 1045.

79. Myers to Randolph, June 10, 1862, QMDLS, XVI, 286.

80. Smith to Randolph, July 31, 1862, *OR*-4, II, 30–31; Randolph to Memminger, Oct. 20, 1862, *ibid.*, p. 133.

wool was as scarce as cotton was plentiful, and Myers assigned one depot quartermaster in each state the responsibility of buying up all the wool that could be secured in that state.[81] As early as May Myers succeeded in purchasing the entire wool crop of Texas, and he waited to see if he could get it across the Mississippi.[82]

Myers knew that the growing manpower shortage gave him one important advantage in wresting enough supplies out of the textile market to supply the troops—Congress had given the War Department control of exemptions for textile workers.[83] Early in the year textile manufacturers had contributed to the bureau's embarrassing shortages by defaulting on contracts and blaming the conscription officers for carrying off workers.[84] To ensure adequate production, Myers persuaded the Secretary of War to use his authority in the summer of 1862 to detail workers for the textile mills.[85] Assured of a co-operative industry dependent on the War Department for workers, Myers increased the size of contracts for the production of cotton and woolen cloth. In the fall, new legislation limited the prices charged by textile mills using exempted workers to 75 per cent profit above cost of production. This arrangement held down the prices which the bureau would have to pay for materials, although the mills complained that they could easily command twice that profit on the open market.[86] The War Department put further pressure on the textile mills by detailing workers for only sixty days, renewing the details only if the supply officials were satisfied that the companies were discharging their responsibilities to the government.[87] In order to capitalize on the sixty-day detail, the Quartermaster's Department often contracted for only one month at a time.[88]

Figures on quartermaster arrangements and contracts are incomplete for any year before 1863, but fragmentary material illustrates the

81. Myers to South Carolina Quartermasters, June 11, 1862, QMDLS, XVI, 289.

82. Myers to Randolph, May 24, 1862, *ibid.*, p. 235.

83. "An Act to Exempt Certain Persons from Military Duty, and to Repeal an Act Entitled 'An Act to Exempt Certain Persons from Enrollment for Service in the Army of the Confederate States, Approved 21st April, 1862,'" Oct. 1, 1862, *Statutes*, II, 77–79.

84. Myers to Randolph, May 23, 1862, *OR*-4, I, 1127.

85. *Ibid.*

86. "An Act to Exempt Certain Persons from Military Duty, and to Repeal an Act Entitled 'An Act to Exempt Certain Persons from Enrollment for Service in the Army of the Confederate States, Approved 21st April, 1862,'" Oct. 1, 1862, *Statutes*, II, 77–79.

87. General Orders No. 50, Adjutant and Inspector General's Office, 1862 Series, July 18, 1862, *OR*-4, II, 8.

88. RG 56, Item 68 (Contract Box).

struggle the bureau made to overcome its deficiencies. The Quartermaster's Department had negotiated contracts with most of the mills of Mississippi, Virginia, Georgia, and South Carolina and had received from the latter two states during the autumn of 1862 a monthly total of 88,000 yards of woolen cloth and 864,000 yards of cotton fabrics.[89] Contracts arranged in the city of Augusta illustrate the methods and expenses of the bureau in procuring cloth. For the month of December 1862, contracts for yard goods with four firms in Augusta totaled 2,400 yards of wool yarns, 10,000 yards of hickory striping, and 42,000 yards of Osnaburg cottons at a cost of $28,500.[90] A fifth factory contracted to sell its entire month's production of ¾ and ⅞ sheeting, and another sold its entire production of Osnaburgs at 40 cents a yard.[91] A contract for January 1863, with the famous Graniteville Mill across the river called for 100,000 yards of sheeting totaling $43,020, computed on a price per yard basis.[92]

Since most of the factories supplied the bureau with cloth only, the government set up a series of shops to make up clothing and uniforms. Soldiers' wives and other women provided an abundant labor force, as they were desperate for work in the face of runaway domestic prices. Columbus, Georgia, for example, was described at this time as a "vast workshop" in which the government had set up shops to take the production of the Eagle Cotton Mills and make it into soldiers' uniforms.[93] The women employed were paid $2 per suit and averaged four suits or $8 per week at a time when $40 provided a week's bare subsistence.[94]

There was a glaring flaw in the arrangements of the Quartermaster's Department. The bureau had agreed in 1861 not to make contracts with the North Carolina mills in return for North Carolina's clothing her own troops.[95] Thus the bureau had forfeited a share in at least one third of the textile production of the Confederacy.

By the time of the summer shortages of 1862 it was all too obvious that the government would have to share in North Carolina textile production. On August 19 Myers wrote to Randolph, recommending

89. Browne to Davis, Dec. 23, 1862, Jefferson Davis Papers, Duke University Manuscript Department.

90. RG 56, Item 68 (ContractBox), Contracts Nos. 18, 27, 28.

91. *Ibid.*, Contracts Nos. 25, 29. 92. *Ibid.*, Contract No. 34.

93. Jones to Davis, Jan. 6, 1863, Jefferson Davis Papers, Duke University Manuscript Department. 94. *Ibid.*

95. Elizabeth Webb, "Cotton Manufacturing and State Regulation in North Carolina," *North Carolina Historical Review*, IX, No. 2 (April 1937), 117 ff.; Myers to Clark, June 12, 1862, QMDLS, XVI, 292–293.

the repeal of the commutation system. He argued that the market price for soldier's clothing far exceeded the commutation money advanced and that "duty" dictated that the bureau furnish the clothing, "although it cannot claim to be prepared to fully clothe the army in the field. . . ."[96] On October 8, 1862, Congress repealed the old commutation system and required that the Quartermaster's Department henceforth furnish clothing instead of money to the troops.[97] While humanity may have induced Myers to ask for the end of the commutation system, North Carolina was also on his mind. He twice wrote to Governor Zebulon Vance of North Carolina, asking him to transfer all of the state's contracts for clothing to the Confederate government and declaring that the government would pay no more commutation money. He did promise that once the state transferred the contracts, the bureau would set up a shop in Raleigh to make up uniforms.[98] Myers observed that this move was necessary for "systematizing and extending" arrangements for army clothing.[99] Vance replied that he would have to take up the matter with the state legislature,[100] but the legislature apparently took no action to end the agreement and allow the Quartermaster's Department to come into the state, despite the fact that the state would get no more commutation money. In 1863 Congress extended the responsibility of the Quartermaster's Department to the clothing of state militia in Confederate service.[101] Myers thus had the responsibility of furnishing clothing to all the Confederate troops and to a large part of the state militia, without the resources of North Carolina.

Myers was also concerned with solving the leather shortage. He ordered his quartermasters to pay the Subsistence Department for hides and take them to the tanneries, but this source proved inadequate.[102] Since the tanners had to worry about their exemptions, the bureau soon demanded one half of the output of the tanners, with the

96. Myers to Randolph, Aug. 16, 1862, QMDSW, pp. 187–188.

97. "An Act to Repeal the Law Authorizing Commutation for Soldier's Clothing, and to Require Clothing to be Furnished by the Secretary of War in Kind," Oct. 8, 1862, *Statutes*, II, 69.

98. Myers to Vance, Dec. 8, 1862, Governor's Letter Book No. 47, North Carolina State Department of Archives and History.

99. Myers to Vance, Sept. 17, 1862, *ibid.*

100. Barnes to Myers, Oct. 14, 1862, *ibid.*

101. "An Act to Allow Commutation for Clothing to the Militia in Actual Service of the Confederate States," April 30, 1863, *Statutes*, II, 131.

102. Myers to South Carolina Quartermasters, June 12, 1862, QMDLS, XVI, 294; Myers to Calhoun, June 23, 1862, *ibid.*, p. 329; General Orders No. 64, Adjutant and Inspector General's Office, 1862 Series, Sept. 8, 1862, *OR*-4, II, 78.

option of buying the remaining half at prices not to exceed $1 per pound.[103] These tanned hides were then sent east to new government shoe shops in Richmond, Atlanta, and Columbus. A Congressional act detailed 2,000 workers from the army and paid them 35 cents per pair.[104] By the winter of 1862–63 the system was working out well, with the prospect of increased production in the future. The chief quartermaster at the Columbus post had received 1,000,000 pounds of leather during the fall and hoped to produce 1,500 pairs of shoes per day.[105] Myers's shoe experts anticipated supplying shoes through the winter at least.[106]

Another source of anxiety for the bureau was a shortage of draft animals, artillery horses, and fodder. Special agents had been at work buying animals since 1861, but as early as March 1862 Myers admitted that "So great . . . had been the destruction of horses in the public service that the demand for them has of late, exceeded the supply."[107] The situation deteriorated even more, and Myers cautioned Randolph that an increase in artillery companies might be impossible for lack of horses.[108] In April Randolph gave the bureau permission to impress horses if necessary, and in July he extended the permission to include forage.[109] Myers purchased a large supply of draft animals in Texas early in 1862, but the animals were marooned on the far side of the Mississippi by a series of adverse circumstances.[110] Nevertheless, the bureau managed to supply most of the draft animals and artillery horses needed in 1862.[111]

Myers assumed responsibility for problems technically outside his jurisdiction when he tried to relieve the concurrent shortage of cavalry horses. Although by regulations each cavalryman furnished his own mount, there were few horses fit for cavalry purposes. Again it was Texas. A special agent went to Texas late in 1862 to buy up those he could find, get them across the Mississippi, and resell them at cost to the cavalrymen.[112]

The horse supply continued to dwindle. Major A. H. Cole, the

103. Browne to Davis, Dec. 23, 1862, Jefferson Davis Papers, Duke University Manuscript Department. 104. *Ibid.* 105. *Ibid.* 106. *Ibid.*

107. Myers to Lee, March 26, 1862, QMDLS, XV, 496.

108. Myers to Randolph, June 5, 1862, *ibid.*, XVI, 267.

109. Randolph to Myers, April 17, 1862, WDLS, VII, 225; Myers to Carrington, July 24, 1862, QMDLS, XVI, 412–413.

110. Myers to Davis, March 4, 1863, *OR*-4, II, 417.

111. Kean endorsement, Nov. 20, 1862, on Lee to Randolph, Nov. 20, 1862, *OR*-1, XXI, 1016. 112. Lee to Randolph, Nov. 10, 1862, *ibid.*, XIX (2), 709.

Inspector General of Field Transportation, under the orders of the Quartermaster General, reported to the Secretary of War early in 1863 that the number of horses in the possession of the Confederate government was "just barely enough to get on with."[113] He commented, "To keep up this number is my most anxious wish, that we shall ever increase it I cannot hope."[114] He explained that the Confederacy was consuming twenty thousand draft and artillery horses a year, only five thousand of which were lost in active service, the rest being starved, diseased, abandoned, or sold.[115] Thus, army and domestic losses were consuming horses faster than the Cis-Mississippi could replace them by natural increase.[116] Besides the regular domestic farm and drayage work, the war effort placed an additional demand on civilian horses and mules for such temporary work as hauling army supplies to the railroads and collecting the tax-in-kind. The horses of the civilians were thus worn out faster, and the civilians were even less willing to sell healthy animals outright to the government. Cole hoped to make some purchases east of the Mississippi but pointed out that to maintain the armies adequately he would need hard cash to purchase horses and mules in the Trans-Mississippi, the power to impress judiciously, and finally the establishment of government infirmaries to reduce the rate of wastage.[117]

The fodder shortage was more acute than the deficiency of horses. In 1862 commanders of military districts all over the Confederacy forbade the exportation of forage from their districts and attempted to accumulate a reserve.[118] This practice brought the field commanders into conflict with Quartermaster agents, who were often trying to purchase supplies for stricken commands in other military districts. Myers persuaded the Secretary of War to rule that commanders of districts in immediate contact with the enemy should not forbid the exportation of forage by Quartermaster agents, but rather that such commanders should use up their supplies as they found them instead of building reserves that might be taken by the enemy.[119]

113. Cole Memorandum, n. d., RG 109, Entry 43, Quartermaster's Department Telegrams Received. 114. *Ibid.* 115. *Ibid.* 116. *Ibid.*

117. Cole to Lawton, March 15, 1863, QMDLS, XVII, 107; Cole to Myers, July 2, 1863, *OR*-4, II, 615.

118. General Orders No. 101, Army of Tennessee, July 18, 1862, *OR*-1, XVII (2), 650; Waddy Circular, Department of Mississippi and East Louisiana, Dec. 12, 1862, *ibid.*, p. 794.

119. Myers to Randolph, April 26, 1862, QMDSW, p. 148; Bledsoe to Myers, May 6, 1862, WDLS, VII, 340.

As the fodder shortage worsened, the Quartermaster General began to grope toward priorities. The two main field armies needed over 5,300 bushels of corn daily—the burden of 21 railroad cars.[120] The surplus fodder of Alabama, Georgia, and Florida was designated for Bragg's men in Tennessee and for Beauregard's men in South Carolina; the surplus of North Carolina would be reserved for the Army of Northern Virginia.[121] The railroads were already responsible for distributing ordnance and quartermaster stores to all the armies and food to the Army of Northern Virginia. Now the army commanders would have to look to the railroad depots for fodder as well.

As early as May 1862 the fodder shortage in Virginia was particularly acute. Myers empowered Major Charles S. Carrington to divide the state into forage districts, each under the command of a special officer whose duty was to organize each district and "develop fully the resources and capacity of the particular section entrusted to him."[122] Despite special organization of resources, the supply of forage had run out for the Army of Northern Virginia by the winter of 1862–63. By February the situation had reached crisis proportions, and Lee had to scatter his cavalry so widely to subsist the animals as to render it almost useless. Virginia could no longer produce a surplus over civilian needs for the maintenance of the army.[123] Not only would Lee have to depend on North Carolina to send fodder by rail for his animals so that he could concentrate his forces for defense, but he would also have to increase his demands if he expected to accumulate a reserve to carry with him in the event of any offensive campaigning. The demand for forage shipments soon involved bitter recrimination with railroad officials, who were especially opposed to transporting bulky fodder. Seddon sent Major Carrington as a special envoy to Governor Vance to secure his co-operation in getting forage regularly sent out of eastern North Carolina by railroad, and Carrington used special impressment powers to commandeer railroad trains to haul forage to Virginia.[124] Vance loaned thirty thousand bushels of corn,

120. Cole Memorandum, n. d., RG 109, Entry 43, Quartermaster's Department Telegrams Received. 121. *Ibid.*

122. Myers to Carrington, QMDLS, XVI, 250.

123. Lee to Davis, Feb. 24, 1862, Freeman, *Lee's Dispatches,* pp. 71–73; Cole Memorandum, n. d., RG 109, Entry 43, Quartermaster's Department Telegrams Received.

124. Seddon to Carrington, May 20, 1863, WDLS, XII, 72–73; Seddon to Carrington, April 8, 1863, WDTS, XXXV, 9; Carrington to Seddon, April 8, 1863, WDRTR, XXXVII, 108; Seddon to Vance, Feb. 25, 1863, WDLS, XI, 249; Seddon to French, Feb. 20, 1863, *ibid.,* X, 202.

reserved for feeding the wives of North Carolina soldiers, to the Confederate government to meet the emergency in Virginia. Seddon gratefully accepted Vance's suggestion that state agents locate part of the North Carolina corn crop for the convenience of Confederate purchasing agents.[125] Davis did his part to help by strongly emphasizing the need for forage in his appeal to the citizens of the Confederacy to devote themselves to raising provisions rather than cotton.[126] The forage shortage persisted doggedly through the spring of 1863. War Department officials could only hope that when corn and oats came in, Lee could obtain enough local provender to free his army of the daily watch for railroad trains.[127]

In the spring of 1863 Myers reorganized his bureau. The change was demanded by his vastly expanded purchasing and manufacturing activities and by a history of conflicts between staff officers reporting to Richmond and field commanders and field quartermasters. He divided the Confederacy into eleven purchasing districts, each district composed of one state, except the Tenth District, which contained Arkansas and Missouri, and the Eleventh, which included Tennessee and Kentucky. A "principal purchasing officer" was to exercise exclusive control over purchasing and contracts in each district and to regulate prices for buying army supplies. No subordinates of one principal purchasing officer could purchase in the district of another. These officers were to send in to the Quartermaster General's Office monthly returns of materials purchased, manufactured, issued, and on hand. The accumulated quartermaster supplies were to be collected in a series of depots designed to be near the fields of operation of the Confederate armies and located at the following places: Richmond and Staunton, Virginia; Raleigh, North Carolina; Atlanta and Columbus, Georgia; Huntsville and Montgomery, Alabama; Jackson, Mississippi; Knoxville, Tennessee; Little Rock, Arkansas; Alexandria, Louisiana; and San Antonio, Texas. The principal purchasing officer was not subject in any way to the army commanders, as he administered these depots under the "exclusive control" of the Quartermaster General's Office. Chief Quartermasters of each army were to cease general purchasing operations, except for forage and fuel, unless "absolute" necessity dictated otherwise or unless the army was in enemy country.

125. Vance to Seddon, Feb. 28, 1863, *OR*-4, II, 413; Myers to Echols, March 7, 1863, QMDLS, XVII, 103.

126. Lee to Davis, April 16, 1863, Clifford Dowdey and Louis Manarin eds., *The Wartime Papers of R. E. Lee* (Boston and Toronto, 1961), pp. 434–435.

127. Myers to Lee, March 19, 1863, QMDLS, XVII, 119.

Instead, the Chief Quartermasters were required to send requisitions for the supply of their armies to the Quartermaster General's Office, which checked the requisitions and, if it approved them, ordered the appropriate district purchasing officer to issue the supplies from his depots. The exceptions to this district arrangement were Major Dillard at Columbus, who had control of leather from Tennessee, Alabama, Georgia, and South Carolina for shoemaking, and Major Carrington, who could roam the Confederacy to provide forage for the armies in Virginia and North Carolina.[128] This arrangement greatly aided the bureau in husbanding its limited resources. On the whole, Myers had, by mid-1863, built up a going and growing concern.

. . .

The Subsistence Department did not sustain the immediate losses that befell the Quartermaster's Department, but the long-range consequences of the disasters of the spring of 1862 eventually assumed the proportions of a major subsistence catastrophe. The Confederate armies were still in the mid-course of their series of retreats when on April 28 Randolph approved a severe reduction in the meat ration for the entire army. The daily bacon and pork ration was reduced from three fourths of a pound to one half pound and beef from one and one quarter pounds to one half pound. To compensate for this reduction, the flour and meal ration was increased to an amount not to exceed one and one half pounds total.[129]

Northrop provided an elaborate justification for this reduction, and if his estimates represented an accurate analysis of the situation, he presented a sober picture of the transformed state of the Confederate commissariat. In part Northrop's reasons were precautionary. While the bureau had ample supplies for the present, despite losses on retreats, much of what would have been the next year's meat packing areas had been lost and might never be regained. Therefore the bureau had to extend the present stock of meat as long as possible until the results of the next packing season were known. The bureau had planned to extend the meat rations with large purchases of molasses and sugar, for which Congress had appropriated special money, but the loss of the lower Mississippi Valley made this plan undependable. The

128. Circular, Quartermaster General's Office, March 24, 1863, *OR*-4, II, 453–456; Circular, Quartermaster General's Office, March 12, 1863, QMDLS, XVII, 119.

129. Circular, Subsistence Department, April 28, 1862, *OR*-4, II, 414.

problem of railroad officials who were reluctant to handle subsistence stores with dispatch was now compounded by the steadily declining physical condition of the railroads themselves. Consequently, the bureau could not depend on regular transportation of supplies into areas of short supply. Both the session-to-session appropriations, which usually resulted in the bureau's running out of funds, and the impossibility of securing bankable funds in the amounts demanded by provision sellers precluded long-range contracts and forced the bureau into day-to-day purchasing.[130] Some of these arguments smack of rationalization, but there was no doubt that the bureau was in trouble.

The field commanders objected to the reduction of the ration in the midst of apparent plenty, and the manner in which they finally cooperated appears to have matched their personalities. At Corinth Beauregard ignored the order and even increased the ratio in those components which were in abundant local supply.[131] Northrop went to Randolph about it, and there ensued a pungent interchange between Corinth and Richmond, with charges of waste on the one hand and of creating scurvy on the other, an interchange which finally brought Davis and Surgeon General Moore into the picture.[132] Beauregard was assigned soon after to another military district, and his successor, General Bragg, reported rations on hand good for sixty days.[133] However, Northrop suspected that the western armies never really made the ordered reduction.[134] Johnston, who had abandoned food at Manassas, now feared that the reduction of the meat ration meant that there were no reserves to feed his army while it defended Richmond or to sustain it if he had to retreat. It took Lee and Davis, as well as Northrop, to assure Johnston that an abundance of supplies existed for the present in Virginia but that the ration reduction was necessary as a precautionary measure against future shortage. By policy, the Richmond depot held ten days' supply for 100,000 men. Also, the depot at Lynchburg held 5,000,000 bacon rations and 10,000 cattle. Other de-

130. Northrop to field commissaries, April 27, 1862, *OR*-1, XXX (4), 553.

131. Beauregard to Cooper, May 1, 1862, *ibid.,* X (2), 478; Beauregard to Cooper, May 19, 1862, *ibid.,* pp. 530–531.

132. Randolph to Beauregard, May 27, 1862, WDTS, XXXIV, 246; Northrop to Randolph, May 31, 1862, *OR*-1, X (2), 571–572. For other factors relating to sickness at Corinth, see the *Weekly Columbus Enquirer,* May 20 and May 27, 1862; the *Daily Charleston Courier,* June 26, 1862.

133. Bragg to Cooper, June 29, 1862, *OR*-1, XVII (2), 628.

134. Northrop endorsement of Feb. 25, 1863, on Johnston to Seddon, Feb. 4, 1863, *ibid.,* XXIII (2), 625–626.

pots held supplies at Gordonsville, Charlottesville, Danville, and if needed, at Charlotte and Atlanta.[135]

Although Northrop knew that the armies had enough supplies for the summer's campaigning, his efforts to build up reserves for the fall and winter from shrunken territories received another blow, this time from the weather. Severe drought set in through the upper Confederacy[136] and nullified any potential increased food production that might have come about by agricultural conversion in 1862 from cotton to foodstuffs and provender. Wheat production dropped, low corn production in turn cut the bacon supply, and herds of cattle on their way from Texas were halted by the shortage of grass or arrived across the Mississippi in emaciated condition.[137] Hopes of dredging up surplus animals from the lower South to send to the armies on the borders gave way to fears that there would not be enough bacon and beef to feed the local garrisons, or even enough corn meal.

The corn meal shortage in the Deep South reached such proportions in the summer of 1862 that flour from 1861 reserves was dispatched from Virginia by railroad to local garrisons, the last time that Virginia was to feed any other section.[138] By September the exhaustion of the 1861 stocks and the short 1862 wheat crops produced a scarcity of flour in Virginia as well. Randolph closed the borders of that state to further exports by the government or by private citizens and sanctioned the impressment of flour stocks held by speculators.[139] Prices had reached such proportions that the bureau persuaded Congress to appropriate $6,823,800 for the purchase of flour, but stocks were so scanty that the bureau had expended only $2,650,000 of it by the end of March 1863.[140]

In November, Northrop and Ruffin notified the Secretary of War that the evil day was at hand—the bureau could not guarantee meat stocks beyond January 1863. The pair advanced numerous reasons for the situation. Drought had extinguished the surplus meat supply in the Deep South and had prevented bringing in Texas cattle.[141] Virginia,

135. Cole to Johnston, May 13, 1862, *ibid.*, XII (3), 513; Lee to Johnston, May 13, 1862, *ibid.*

136. Northrop endorsement of Dec. 15, 1862, on Bragg to Cummings, Dec. 1, 1862, PRSD.

137. *Ibid.;* Northrop to Seddon, Jan. 12, 1863, *OR*-4, II, 350–351.

138. Myers to Northrop, April 29, 1862, QMDLS, XVI, 149.

139. Randolph to Morfit, Sept. 26, 1862, WDLS, IX, 30; Randolph to Davis, CSWP, XXXIX, 188–189; Jones, *War Clerk's Diary,* I, 182.

140. WDAA, XLI, 37.

141. Northrop endorsement on Lee to Seddon, Jan. 26, 1863, *OR*-1, LI (2), 674.

North Carolina, and Tennessee meat packing, drawn from a greatly reduced area, had totaled only 170,000 hogs and 4,000 cattle, as compared with 250,000 hogs and 40,000 cattle the previous year. Besides, the 1862 animals were thinner and more wastefully packed because of interior salt.[142] The army had aggravated the situation by "the waste committed by the soldiers, and permitted in some corps and perpetuated in others by the generals in command."[143] Fresh beef was almost exhausted. The army would have 37,400,000 salt rations from stock on hand and from products of meat packing if the armies adhered to the half pound ration. This would feed 374,000 men for a hundred days on a daily salt meat diet.[144] Using the declining fresh meat supply to eke out the salt rations and figuring from October 1, the date of the last returns of stocks on hand, "it would be imprudent to estimate full supplies to January, and a fatal error to rely on full supplies after that time in any quarter."[145] The bureau had done everything, so Northrop averred, except to trade cotton for food brought in through the enemy lines. Northrop soon began a campaign to get permission to do this, a campaign discussed elsewhere.[146]

The meat situation was gloomy enough for the Confederate armies as a whole, but the Army of Northern Virginia faced a particularly dismal future. Virginia no longer had enough surplus food to support the army, and food would have to come in from farther south. Through most of the fall Lee had succeeded in subsisting his troops on the countryside, adding bacon shipped in from Virginia depots by railroad and flour from reserves accumulated by Randolph's impressments. In this period of relative plenty, Lee abandoned the reduced meat ration which had theoretically been in effect in all armies of the Confederacy since April 28, and restored the full meat allotment to compensate for the disappearance of vegetables from the ration.[147] In addition, he apparently ignored Northrop's directive to extend the meat ration with the necks and shanks; such portions were not officially a part of the

142. Northrop Report, [Nov. 18, 1862], *OR*-4, II, 192–193; Ruffin to Randolph, Nov. 8, 1862, PRSD.

143. Ruffin to Northrop, Nov. 3, 1862, *OR*-4, II, 159.

144. Northrop Report, [Nov. 18, 1862], *ibid.*, pp. 192–193.

145. Ruffin to Northrop, Nov. 3, 1862, *ibid.*, p. 159–160.

146. Northrop endorsement, Nov. 16, 1862, on Cummings to Northrop, Nov. 10, 1862, PRSD; Northrop Report, Nov. [21], 1862, *ibid.*; Northrop endorsement, Dec. 15, 1862, on Bragg to Cummings, Dec. 1, 1862, *ibid.*; Northrop to Seddon, Jan. 19, 1863, *OR*-4, II, 351.

147. Northrop to Randolph, Nov. 3, 1862, *OR*-4, II, 158.

meat rations.[148] Thus Lee's men were consuming meat at a faster pace than Northrop had envisioned, but Northrop brought the matter to the attention of Randolph, who notified Lee to enforce the reduced ration.[149]

By December it was apparent that stocks for Lee's army would last only through the month; nothing was left in Virginia to purchase or impress. However, Northrop waited to order up supplies from the south until he saw that Lee had won the Battle of Fredericksburg and would be able to hold Richmond.[150] On December 16 Northrop ordered supplies to be shipped from the bureau's reserves at Atlanta and Charlotte across the eccentric Confederate railroad network.[151] The railroads failed miserably for reasons to be examined later. From January 1 to March 25 only four hundred thousand pounds of meat reached Lee from the south.[152] As a consequence, the bureau reduced the ration of the Army of Northern Virginia to one-fourth pound of salt meat a day and planned to substitute sugar for the deficiency when available.[153] Lee complained about being singled out for the reduction, and Northrop pontificated:

> The intervention of commanding officers with the ration is unauthorized and unadvisable for many reasons; but under existing circumstances it is mischievous . . . . It is not to be expected, and it is not the fact that commanding generals are [the] most competent judges of the subsistence resources of the country and should not be permitted to issue any order respecting rations whatever . . . .
>
> Privation is to be looked for, and encouragement is all that the generals can beneficially do beyond calling the attention of the Secretary of War to existing things.[154]

The Army of Northern Virginia remained on short rations and hand-to-mouth provisioning until late in the spring.[155]

148. Northrop endorsement on Lee to Seddon, Jan. 26, 1863, *OR*-1, LI (2), 674.

149. Randolph to Lee, Nov. 14, 1862, *ibid.*, XIX (2), 716–717.

150. Northrop endorsement, Feb. 16, 1863, on Lee to Seddon, Feb. 11, 1863, *ibid.*, XXV (2), 613. 151. *Ibid.*

152. Seddon to Wadley, March 25, 1863, *OR*-4, II, 457.

153. Lee to Seddon, Jan. 23, 1863, *OR*-1, XXI, 1110–1111.

154. Lee to Seddon, March 27, 1863, Dowdey and Mavarin, eds., *The Wartime Papers of R. E. Lee,* pp. 419–420; Northrop to Seddon, March 2, 1863, *OR*-4, II, 414.

155. Jones, *War Clerk's Diary,* I, 297.

The seriousness of the problem stimulated many plans for supplying Lee's men. Lee and others suggested exchanging the additional sugar supplement for bacon but the Commissary General refused:

> It is not proposed by this Bureau to diminish its supplies or resources by barter; it is better to use the sugar, and to impress all the bacon that can be found, consistently with leaving a supply for the family; after that, barter would be beneficial.[156]

Lee then suggested an appeal to the people to send in contributions or to sell their surpluses, but Northrop, as usual unwilling to pursue any plan that did not fit into his system of operations, refused.[157]

In spite of Northrop's veto, Lee's suggestion of appealing to the people met a fate different from that of the sugar exchange proposition. Jones, the "Rebel War Clerk," came across Lee's letter and Northrop's veto in his usual course of digesting War Department correspondence. Jones took it upon himself to write the President, offering to administer the appeal himself; and after a round of references, Seddon sent Jones a polite refusal.[158] Congress, meanwhile, had passed a joint resolution on April 4, urging that the people, "instead of planting cotton and tobacco, shall direct their agricultural labor mainly to the production of such crops as will ensure a sufficiency of food for all classes and for every emergency. . . ."[159] At the request of Congress the President published an address to the people on April 10, explaining the army's situation and urging them to plant provisions and forage. He also appealed to the people to relieve a "temporary" shortage of meat by following a plan of the Secretary of War for sending in contributions and aiding the government in purchasing.[160] Jones wrote in his diary: "This is *my* plan, so politely declined by the Secretary! Well, if it will benefit the government, the government is welcome to it; and Mr. Seddon to the credit of it."[161]

In addition to his general appeal, Davis wrote the governors, urging

156. Northrop endorsement, Jan. 24, 1863, on Lee to Seddon, Jan. 24, 1863, *OR*-1, XXI, 1101; Seddon to Carter, April 20, 1863, WDLS, X, 468.

157. Northrop endorsement on Lee to Seddon, Jan. 26, 1863, *OR*-1, LI (2), 675.

158. Jones, *War Clerk's Diary*, I, 262–265; Jones to Davis, February 19, 1863, and endorsements by Northrop and and Seddon, *OR*-4, II, 405; Seddon to Jones, Feb. 27, 1863, *ibid.*, p. 412.

159. "Joint Resolution Relating to the Production of Provisions," *Statutes*, II, 166–167.

160. "Address to the People of the Confederate States," April 10, 1863, *Messages*, I, 331–335.

161. Jones, *War Clerk's Diary*, I, 290.

them to see to the most effective measures for forwarding provision surpluses to the Confederate armies, and he took special care to hurry along action on Lee's persistent demands.[162] Seddon made more practical arrangements and devoted all his energies to "ransacking the Confederacy," as he put it.[163] As the crisis wore on into March, he urged his field commanders to consider arrangements for trading through the enemy lines: "Even illicit dealing with persons of doubtful position or mercenary natures might be encouraged to the extent of procuring supplies, particularly of meat."[164] More drastic, and more effective to judge by the subsequent outcry, was his widespread and continued impressment of flour in the Virginia mills and warehouses.[165]

"The Commissary General gets more and more gloomy and complains heavily of department commanders robbing the little stores he is able to scrape together for the future," Kean reported during Lee's provision crisis.[166] Specifically, the Army of Tennessee had been eating up part of Lee's bacon supply. Although Bragg had his own packing plant at Fayetteville, Tennessee, and had access to the hog-raising areas of eastern Tennessee, he continued to call on Major Cummings, the Subsistence Department's packing agent in Tennessee, to send up bacon which the bureau had intended as a reserve for Lee's army.[167] Bragg may actually have been unable to provision his men completely from local resources and may have needed some of the reserve stores. In any case, an order from Bragg prohibiting the exportation of Cummings's hogs from Tennessee brought Northrop into Seddon's office in an effort to save his general reserves. He maintained that Bragg could feed himself without dipping into bureau reserves and thus consuming what would undoubtedly be needed by Lee's men.[168] Seddon, however, as was his tendency with army commanders, gave no orders but merely sent Bragg a suggestion:

> Unless the needs of your Army imperatively require the retention and present consumption of these hogs, I recommend the with-

162. Davis to Brown, Jan. 27, 1863, *OR*-4, II, 376; see also circular from Davis to governors of the Confederate States, Nov. 26, 1862, Rowland, *Jefferson Davis,* V, 378.

163. Seddon to Johnston, March 3, 1863, *OR*-1, XXIII (2), 657–658.

164. *Ibid.*

165. Jones, *War Clerk's Diary,* I, 267–268, 271.

166. Edward Younger, ed., *Inside the Confederate Government: The Diary of Robert Garlick Hill Kean, Head of the Bureau of War* (New York, 1957), p. 40. Cited hereafter as Younger, *Kean Diary.*

167. Cummings to Northrop, Nov. 10, 1862, PRSD; Cummings to Northrop, Dec. 10, 1862, *ibid.*

168. Northrop to Seddon, Jan. 12, 1863, *OR*-4, II, 350–351.

> drawal of all impediments and prohibitions to their removal. It is hoped that it may be practicable for you at least in large measure to subsist your Army on the provisions remaining in your Department unappropriated by the General Commissariat.[169]

This process of Northrop's protesting against raids on his supplies followed by the Secretary's suggesting that the generals abstain was repeated a number of times during the winter with Johnston, Breckinridge, Samuel Jones, and other military district commanders, apparently with little effect.[170] Johnston, for example, in the month of April 1863 alone had called up over 1,000,000 pounds of bacon from general reserves, which he may or may not have needed.[171]

While indirect competition between military districts for supplies frequently occurred during the early years of the Confederacy, Pemberton's open war on General Buckner's district caused such an upheaval in the Southwest that it forced even the permissive Secretary of War to take action. Early in December Pemberton had begun to make arrangements to subsist himself completely from within the confines of the Department of Mississippi and East Louisiana. To do this he received permission to exclude procurement agents from other districts, and on his own authority he forbade the exportation of foodstuffs and provender from his district.[172] This latter action may have prevented speculators from carrying off the surplus in his district, but it also cut off Mobile, in General Buckner's Department of the Gulf, from its normal source of provisions and caused suffering in that city.[173] Buckner tried to arrange for provisions for both civilians and soldiers in his district but discovered that agents from Pemberton's district were poaching.[174] In turn, Northrop objected to Buckner's interference with bureau purchasing in the lower Chattahoochee, an area normally left in complete control of the Subsistence Department.[175] Meanwhile, in March 1863, Pemberton secured permission to disengage his district completely from any connection with the purchasing agents working directly for the Subsistence Department, so that he could subsist his men

169. Seddon to Bragg, Jan. 13, 1863, WDLS, VIII, 432.

170. Seddon to Johnston, Feb. 23, 1863, *ibid.*, X, 298–299; Seddon to Jones, March 14, 1863, WDTS, XXXIV, 477.

171. Northrop to Seddon, June 4, 1863, *OR*-4, II, 574.

172. For Pemberton's management of subsistence affairs in his Department of Mississippi and East Louisiana, see *OR*-1, XXIV (3), *passim;* for Seddon's position, see Seddon to Wadley, March 23, 1863, WDTS, XXXV, 1.

173. Seddon to Buckner, April 4, 1863, WDLS, X, 391–392.

174. *Ibid.*

175. *Ibid.*

exclusively by the exertions of his own army commissaries.[176] Northrop was probably not unhappy with this arrangement, for he could then absolve himself of responsibility for affairs in a military district in which he claimed foodstuffs had rotted for lack of care and which he maintained had been generally mismanaged by Pemberton's chief commissary, Major Reed.[177] Northrop did demand that Pemberton send out of his district the stocks of molasses and sugar that the bureau had painstakingly scraped together from across the Mississippi to eke out the 1863 meat ration. Pemberton, however, wanted to hold this molasses and sugar and the Commissary General had to badger the Secretary of War at length to get authority to have even a part of the stocks sent out of the district in time to avoid the onslaught of Grant.[178] By this time affairs at Mobile had reached such a pass that Seddon grudgingly consented to allow Buckner to share army provisions with the civilians.[179] This development so provoked Seddon that he finally agreed to Northrop's plans for a centralization of purchasing arrangements.

Northrop hoped that his new plan would result in a "thoroughly drained" Confederacy and that it would eliminate competition among bureau agents and army commissaries. Under this plan a Chief Commissary directed purchasing in each state. Each state was divided into districts under district purchasing commissaries, these districts again divided into subdistricts under subcommissaries and agents. The Chief Commissary took reports of purchases, prices, and accumulations made to him every ten days by his subordinates, consolidated them, and sent them on each month to the Commissary General's Office. He also arranged for depots and subdepots with an eye to safety and economical use of field and rail transportation.[180] While the purchasing of supplies was centralized in the bureau and in great part removed from the field commands in a manner similar to the arrangements of the Quartermaster's Department, the distribution of supplies was not so centralized. The Chief Commissaries of the armies did not have to submit their requisitions to the central office in Richmond, but rather sent their requisitions to the Chief Commissaries of the states in which

176. Seddon to Pemberton, March 16, 1863, WDTS, XXXIV, 478.

177. Northrop to Seddon, Jan. 23, 1863, *OR*-1, XXIV (3), 634–635.

178. Seddon to Pemberton, Feb. 17, 1863, WDTS, XXXIV, 461; Seddon to Pemberton, March 12, 1863, *ibid.*, p. 476; WDAA, XLI, 10.

179. Seddon to Buckner, April 4, 1863, WDLS, X, 392.

180. Circular, Subsistence Department, April 15, 1863, *OR*-4, II, 290–293.

the armies were stationed or through which they intended to pass. In addition, commissaries of one state or district could draw directly on depots of other states for additional supplies.[181]

Seddon weakened this plan by deferring to the generals. Northrop had wanted to acquire complete control over the collection of subsistence without the interference of army commanders, just as Myers had done, but Seddon merely requested the commanders to allow the Subsistence Department agents to procure subsistence in each military district. Seddon's letter to Buckner is typical of the spirit of the new arrangement:

> I have decided to confine each Commander to subsidiary operations in obtaining supplies to his own Department and to require of the Commissary General through the Bureau officers and agents to be active in all, collecting supplies, accumulating at Depots and preparing to distribute and meet requisitions from the various Armies, according to their respective needs. On this plan it is expected of each Commander, as it is evidently on a large run his true policy, not to interfere with or thwart the operations of the Bureau officers but to give them all countenance and co-operation, and to make the operations of his army officers conform to their standard of prices and generally subsidiary in their character. . . . I wish you always distinctly to prefer the accumulation at depots should be made by the Bureau officers, so far as with equal convenience they can, and that your officers confine themselves to present supply unless where they enjoy superior advantages for establishing Depots and making accumulations. With this general guiding view, I trust you will have no difficulty in operating harmoniously and to the advantage of the service with the Commissary General and his officers.[182]

Little could be expected of a military policy based on "co-operation" rather than obedience.

The winter distress of the Subsistence Department led to the creation of another important supply weapon—the tax-in-kind, often called the tithe. Destined to be one of the props of the Subsistence Department, the tithe cut through the Gordian knot of inflation, speculation, impressment, and hoarding by simply taking a portion of the subsist-

181. *Ibid.;* Randolph to Lee, Nov. 14, 1862, *OR*-1, XIX (2), 716–717.
182. Seddon to Buckner, April 4, 1863, WDLS, X, 391–392.

ence stocks of the country as taxes. Suggested by Memminger, among others, as a means of reducing the monetary demands of the War Department, the measure was so eminently sensible that little record of debate occurs in the journals of Congress.[183] The tax-in-kind provisions were but one part of a stringent tax bill produced by Congress on April 24, 1863, in an attempt to finance the war and sustain the armies in a more responsible manner than by wearing out the printing presses in the Treasury Department and the pencils of the impressing officers.[184] As implemented by the War Department, the tithe worked as follows: when market time for each crop arrived, the local tax assessor would estimate the quantity owed. In case of disagreement with the producer local appraisers would decide the matter. In estimating, the same farmer could reserve certain amounts of food for himself and then was to deliver one tenth of his taxable field crops and the equivalent of one tenth of his hogs in the form of cured bacon to a government depot, if such depot was not more than eight miles away. There he received a receipt. If the farmer did not deliver his tithe within two months after the appraisal, agents levied a 50 per cent fine and took steps to collect the tithe.[185]

To administer the tithe, Congress created a new group in the Quartermaster's Department called post quartermasters. A Chief Quartermaster headed this division in each state, and under him, a District Quartermaster took charge in each Congressional district. In each district the Chief Quartermaster designated a series of depots. Post quartermasters were to administer these depots and each post was to receive assistance from any additional agents that might be needed. Subordinates sent monthly returns up through channels to the Quartermaster General's Office while holding the goods in readiness for the appropriate distributing quartermasters and commissaries, or in the case of staples, for treasury agents.[186]

Reflecting the prevailing suspicion of quartermaster and commissary fidelity and honesty, Congress sought to prevent fraud by elaborate provisions. The local assessor sent one copy of his estimates to the appropriate army auditor and took one copy to the post quartermaster,

183. *Debates,* XLIX, 137; *Journal,* III, 290. For favorable press comments, see the Augusta *Tri-Weekly Constitutionalist,* April 26, May 3, Aug. 19, 1863; *Daily Richmond Examiner,* April 3, 1863.

184. "An Act to Levy Taxes for the Common Defence, and Carry on the Government of the Confederate States," April 24, 1863, *Statutes,* II, 122–126.

185. ***Ibid.***

186. *Ibid.;* Seddon to Smith, June 1, 1863, WDLS, XIII, 317–319.

whose receipt was filed in the office of the local collector of taxes. The post quartermaster now found himself officially responsible for the tithes listed in the estimates—before they arrived. If circumstances indicated that any estimates could not be collected in whole or in part, the quartermaster proceeded to the auditor's office, where he received a "Warrant of Relief" absolving him of responsibility for holding the particular goods.[187]

Amidst subsistence problems and bureau reorganization, the armies survived the winter of 1862–63. Lee and Johnston both reported their men in good condition, and outside observers confirmed this.[188] The lack of vegetables for Lee's men caused medical officers to worry about possible scurvy, but the short rations do not seem to have affected the men adversely in a physical sense.[189] Actually, short rations appear to have been confined to the unfortunate Army of Northern Virginia, a few garrison troops, and civilians on army rations. Incomplete evidence, including some reports of depot accumulations, strongly suggests that the field armies in the Southwest and the Trans-Mississippi ate their fill and did not experience the official reduction in the meat ration. Major B. J. Semmes, the depot commissary for Bragg's army, reported the troops "in splendid condition" in the spring of 1863[190] and wrote his wife:

> The people generally I understand are fearful of starvation. . . . This is sheer nonsense. The south is fully able to feed her army and people and none know it better than the Commissary Department. Our supplies are immense and you surely must be mistaken about the bad fare of our men in the Army of Pemberton. This army I know is plainly but well fed and there are large depots of subsistence in Alabama & Georgia which we do not touch. . . . Some sections it is true are short in their supply but many others have a large surplus.[191]

187. "An Act to Levy Taxes for the Common Defence, and Carry on the Government of the Confederate States," April 24, 1863, *Statutes,* II, 122–126.

188. Younger, *Kean Diary,* pp. 38–39; Johnston to Davis, Feb. 12, 1863, *OR*-1, XXIII, 632; Kirby Smith to ——, Dec. 28, 1862, Edmund Kirby-Smith Papers, Southern Historical Collection, University of North Carolina, Johnston to Kirby Smith, April 18, 1863, *ibid.*

189. Guild to Moore, Jan. 9, 1863, *OR*-1, XXI, 1084–1085.

190. Semmes to Mrs. Semmes, March 29, 1863, Mr. and Mrs. Benedict Joseph Semmes Papers, Southern Historical Collection, University of North Carolina.

191. Semmes to Mrs. Semmes, April 16, 1863, *ibid.*

Still, some troops had been on short rations, and while short rations may not have been detrimental for stationary troops in winter encampment, it was questionable to assume that short rations would physically sustain troops during active campaigning, to say nothing of morale. The civilian workers performing heavy duty for the Niter and Mining, Ordnance, and Engineer bureaus, who were supplied army rations, complained that they did not have enough to eat in order to do their work.[192]

By the spring of 1863 the Subsistence Department had obviously slipped badly in performance and in public estimation. Its problems were compounded by vitriolic attacks from part of the Richmond press. Besides their anger over Lee's army's being on short rations, the newspapers were outraged because widespread impressment of foodstuffs in Virginia had created hoarding on the farms and food shortages in the Confederate capital. The *Daily Richmond Whig* was foremost in howling for Northrop's scalp. He had "criminally neglected his duties, or was incompetent to their performance."[193] Indeed, "Through his remissness, the army is reduced to the point of starvation."[194] His "past inefficiency, whether the result of incompetency or treason, is so gross, and in its effects so disastrous, that nothing can excuse or palliate it. The starvation of the army is the ruin of the cause."[195]

In large part the victim of circumstance, the bureau was plagued with deficiencies and harassed by too many imponderables to plan with confidence. The bureau's food surplus was unequally distributed, and in Virginia food was in short supply. Inflation and shortage of funds combined to hamper purchasing. Because of undependable transportation facilities over which the bureau had no control, perishable elements of the ration could not be shipped long distances and thus remained in unequal supply, especially complicating the feeding of the Army of Northern Virginia. Situated in a rapidly developing wasteland, Lee's men would have to depend on local impressments to obtain flour, fresh beef, and occasional vegetables; on the railroads from the Deep South for cornmeal and some bacon; and on the railroads, the fortunes of war, and the co-operation of other army commanders for meat from eastern Tennessee. For the future, however, the Subsistence Department had hopes for several things: more effective control over procurement under Northrop's new organization, increased railroad

192. Vandiver, *Confederate Ordnance,* pp. 164–165.
193. *Daily Richmond Whig,* April 22, 1863. 194. *Ibid.*
195. Quoted in *Weekly Columbus Enquirer,* April 28, 1863.

efficiency, successful campaigns that held and regained productive areas, good weather, agricultural conversion, tax-in-kind accumulations, and, if necessary, blockade running.

. . .

The rapid growth of the bureaus proliferated money problems. In the spring of 1862 the main problem had been the persistent shortage of Treasury notes. The Treasury, in fulfilling bureau money requisitions, remitted half in Confederate interest-bearing bonds, which occurred in denominations no smaller than $100. The services strove to use as many of these bonds as possible, and the transportation contracts of the Quartermaster's Department, for example, stipulated that payment would be half in bonds. Still there were too many bonds to disburse and not enough Treasury notes. Myers and Gorgas protested continually, but Northrop made the greatest number of complaints.[196] Provision sellers, Northrop noted, had from the beginning of the war demanded bankable funds and refused bonds; he gloomily predicted that if he did not have his allotment almost entirely in notes, it would be "almost if not absolutely impossible for this department to feed the armies of the Confederacy."[197] The Treasury Department replied that the expenses of the War Department were enormously high and that the Treasury could not possibly furnish the War Department with the amount of notes demanded. Randolph, after making a routine query to his bureau heads to see if they could cut expenses and being assured that they could not, lectured Memminger: "It must be borne in mind that our scale of preparation is regulated to some extent by the preparations of the enemy, and cannot be reduced below a certain limit without subjecting us to great risk of overthrow."[198] But the Treasury could do no better, and Randolph decided in July that since notes were in short supply, supply personnel and field commanders would have to purchase subsistence first and then pay the troops with the residue of notes, if any.[199] This aggravated the already haphazard pay situation,

196. Randolph to Davis, April 7, 1862, *OR*-4, I, 1050; Randolph to Memminger, April 17, 1862, WDLS, VII, 275.

197. For example, see Northrop to Randolph, April 29, 1862, *OR*-4, I, 1101.

198. Randolph's endorsement, Aug. 4, 1862, on Childs to Gorgas, July 29, 1862, RG 56, Item 92, Miscellaneous Correspondence; Myers to Randolph, Aug. 2, 1862, QMDSW, pp. 194–195.

199. Joynes to Memminger, April 24, 1862, WDLS, VII, 293; Randolph to Northrop and Myers, April 24, 1862, *ibid.*, pp. 294–295; Randolph to Pemberton, July 8, 1862, George Wythe Randolph Papers, Confederate Museum, Richmond, Virginia.

and on September 4 Myers notified Randolph that none of the troops had been paid in four months and that some had not been paid for six or eight months.[200] The Treasury Department replied that they were facing technical delays in lithographing notes and passed all these facts on to a Congressional investigating group.[201] These activities accomplished little, apparently, for on October 10 Myers reported $15,000,000 in unfulfilled pay requisitions.[202] Finally, Congress relieved the problem in September and October by putting an estimated $140,000,000 in new Treasury notes into circulation; after this, complaints of note shortages faded away.[203]

As the problem of Treasury notes eased, the larger problem of increasing levels of expenditures for the war effort became more persistent. The inflated price levels of late 1862 had swollen government expenses enormously; accumulated total expenditures of the government, over 90 per cent of which was spent by the War Department, had more than quadrupled, from $70,000,000 in November 1861, to $329,000,000 by August, 1862.[204] The rate of expenditure was so headlong that the $199,000,000 appropriated for War Department expenses until December 1, 1862, was running out by September. Myers sounded the alarm first. Already annoyed by Benjamin's cutting his estimate for expenses to December 1, 1862, he was further angered by Randolph's slashing his estimate for funds for December from $26,576,568 to $18,838,049.[205] On September 26 he wrote Randolph that only $33,000,000 remained for the bureau's use until December 1, yet expenses averaged $24,500,000 per month in the summer and would be higher in the winter when fuel costs were added. It would take an additional $27,000,000 to get through to December plus every penny of the $12,000,000 cut from his December estimates, an additional total of $39,000,000.[206] This was the turning point in the battle over shaving estimates. Randolph capitulated. He had already sent in to Congress his reduced December estimates and did not care to lose face by revising that total. Instead he sent in a request for a deficiency appropriation of $39,000,000.[207]

To provide for expenses, Congress passed two acts which appro-

200. Myers to Randolph, Sept. 4, 1862, QMDSW, pp. 207–208.
201. *Ibid.*
202. Myers to Randolph, Oct. 10, 1862, CSWP, XXXIX, 179.
203. Todd, *Confederate Finance,* p. 109.
204. *Ibid.,* p. 64.
205. Myers to Randolph, Sept. 4, 1862, QMDSW, pp. 194–195.
206. Myers to Randolph, Sept. 26, 1862, *ibid.,* pp. 206–207.
207. Randolph to Davis, Sept. 18, 1862, CSWP, XXXIX, 188.

priated $127,000,000 for War Department use from December 1, 1862, to February 1, 1863.[208] In addition to regular expenses, the bills included the deficit requests of the supply bureaus, money to continue iron and niter contracts, and a special appropriation for the Subsistence Department to buy flour.[209] By the end of the year, the expenditures of the government had almost doubled from August, now totaling $582,000,000.[210] Still the bureaus could not meet their obligations. Desperate needs in the Ordnance Department resulted in the transfer of $8,000,000 from the Quartermaster's Department, eventually leaving the latter bureau short of funds; yet by February Ordnance funds were down to less than $30,000.[211]

In January Seddon assembled estimates for expenses from February 1 to June 30, 1863, and sent in a total request for the War Department of $242,977,065.23, a level of expenses averaging almost $50,000,000 monthly. This average made Benjamin's year-old prediction of $23,000,000 an exercise in naïveté.[212] Congress had just approved this sum[213] when Northrop sent in a new estimate, which indicated that his former estimate of $46,656,500, just approved by Congress, was far too low. The cost per ration, 25 cents in 1861, now stood at $1.12. Counting special contingencies, the bureau needed an additional $74,168,026 to get through until June 30.[214] By April the Ordnance Department had only $943,000 left of its appropriation of $15,900,000, and when Congress appropriated some $363,000,000 for expenses from July 1 to December 31, 1863, it must have done so with the feeling that even this amount would prove insufficient.[215]

208. "An Act Making Appropriations for the Executive, Legislative, and Judicial Expenses of the Government for the Month of December, 1862," Oct. 9, 1862, *Statutes,* II, 72–74; "An Act Making Appropriations for the Support of the Government for the Month of January, Eighteen Hundred and Sixty-Three, and for Certain Deficiencies and Other Purposes Therein Mentioned," Oct. 13, 1862, *ibid.,* pp. 81–84. 209. *Ibid.* 210. Todd, *Confederate Finance,* p. 64.

211. Myers to Seddon, Jan. 9, 1863, QMDSW, p. 259.

212. Summary of War Department estimates for the period Feb. 1, 1863—June 30, 1863, *OR*-4, II, 294.

213. "An Act Making Appropriations for the Support of the Government, for the Period from February First, to June Thirtieth, Eighteen Hundred and Sixty-Three, Inclusive, and to Supply Deficiencies Arising Prior Thereto," Feb. 10, 1863, *Statutes,* II, 94–97.

214. Estimate of funds required to subsist 475,000 men from Jan. 1 to June 30, 1863, March 5, 1863, *OR*-4, II, 418.

215. "An Act to Make Appropriations for the Support of the Government of the Confederate States of America, For the Periods Therein Mentioned," May 1, 1863. *Statutes,* II, 136–140.

Faced with the astronomical expenses of the War Department, Congress stiffened the tax laws but still found no other recourse but to issue more Treasury notes. The one-time shortage of notes was now transformed into an innundation. The act of March 3, 1863, empowered the Secretary of the Treasury to issue $50,000,000 per month in new Treasury notes, and issues under this act eventually totaled $517,000,000.[216] The trends of the time were unmistakable. The fevered home market and the gigantic scope of the war effort had already tripled War Department expenses in one year, and the only answer for the moment seemed to be the issue of notes, since Congress had not seen fit to strike directly at inflation. Where this paper-money finance would lead, no one knew.

. . .

By early 1863 the supply bureaus had created the basic policies for domestic procurement and production that they would pursue, with some modifications, to the end of the war. The bureaus had increasingly diverted the productive capacities of the country to satisfy the needs of the war effort by regulating existing industries and erecting their own establishments when private resources had proved insufficient. In addition to controlling production, the bureaus had succeeded to a large extent in wresting control of the distribution of supplies from the field commands, in order to conserve war materials. In assuming all these responsibilities, the bureaus had swollen enormously, and with the mushrooming bureaucracy had undoubtedly come inefficiency and corruption. Still, within the bounds imposed by the Confederacy's natural deficiencies, by human limitations in perception and foresight, and by fortunes of war, the bureaus continued to forge competent records in meeting their specific problems. There were larger, national problems, however, which affected all the bureaus; and for solutions to these problems the bureau chiefs turned to Congress, to the Secretaries of War, and to the President.

216. Todd, *Confederate Finance,* p. 111.

CHAPTER FOUR

GROPING AT THE TOP

The Department has been energetic only in the very doubtful policy of impressments. —— R. G. H. Kean, April 1, 1863*

By the autumn of 1862 the civilian leaders of the Confederacy, pressed by events, moved to modify current supply policies and to create new programs. One policy that demanded re-examination was conscription. As late as the summer, the government appeared to have few fears about a shortage of fighting men under the Conscription Act of April 16, 1862, although officials had opened up new categories of exemptions.[1] The Secretary of War exempted civilian purchasing agents of the Subsistence Department and workers employed by salt contractors supplying the government.[2] Davis himself decided that workers for gunshops and tanneries supplying the Confederate government and the states came under the "spirit" of the conscription law. The Niter and Mining Corps was allowed to exempt civilians and take details from the army,[3] and Congress authorized the Quartermaster's Department to detail 2,000 shoemakers from the army.[4]

By the fall, however, the armies were obviously short of men. The Adjutant and Inspector General's Office reported an "aggregate present" of only 224,000 men, a decrease of 33,000 from January 1, 1862, before the conscription act.[5] In addition, controversy was bubbling up over the operation of the conscription act. Many complained that men were abusing the professional categories; the number of men claiming to be doctors, teachers, and other professionals suddenly boomed. Governor Milton of Florida reported that the Gulf shores of his state

* Younger, *Kean Diary,* p. 48.

1. Randolph to McKee, April 26, 1862, WDLS, VII, 296; Randolph to Shorter, Aug. 4, 1862, WDTS, XXXIV, 312.
2. Davis to Pettus, May 1, 1862, *OR*-4, I, 1110.
3. General Orders No. 99, Adjutant and Inspector General's Office, 1862 Series, Dec. 5, 1862, *ibid.,* II, 228.
4. "An Act to Provide Shoes for the Army," Oct. 9, 1862, *Statutes,* II, 72.
5. Consolidated Returns, Adjutant and Inspector General's Office, *OR*-4, I, 1176.

swarmed with salt makers professing to work for the government.[6] On the other hand, many important officials, including Randolph and some state governors, felt that the spring legislation had hustled into service too many artisans and mechanics, such as tanners and millers, who would have served the cause better by applying their skills at home, if their avarice could be checked.[7] In any case, the time had come to review and overhaul the allocation of manpower.

The President felt that one solution to the shortage of soldiers would be to extend the draft age from thirty-five to forty-five, and Congress passed the necessary act on September 27, 1862.[8] Randolph advised that the supply situation would make it impractical to call up the total number allowable by this act. Randolph estimated that taking men up to age forty, after the necessary deductions for areas lost to the enemy and the usual proportion of rejects, would give the army a total of 500,000 men. "It is questionable whether a larger number can be fed, clothed, and armed," he commented. "We shall gain more after reaching a certain point by proper attention to subsistence and equipments than by mere addition to the numerical strength of our forces."[9] Consequently, the immediate call embraced only men from thirty-six through thirty-nine.[10]

For the better part of September Congressmen gingerly tossed about the hot issue of exemptions. Some protested the whole concept of exemptions, stressing that the discontent at home and in the army would do more harm than could be justified by the alleged services of those exempted.[11] However, this was the opinion of a minority. The Exemption Act of October 11, 1862, placed severe restrictions upon the professional and official exemptions, a salutary move to weed out skulkers.[12] It also restricted the number of exemptable railroad workers, a move necessary to cull out draft dodgers but also one capable of injuring transportation if too many men were taken. Responding to pressure, Congress opened up new categories for men whose skill was considered more valuable for supplying the army and the civilian population than for bearing arms: saltmakers who produced twenty bushels per day; herders; one overseer per twenty slaves for plantation police; shoemakers, tanners, blacksmiths, wagon-makers, millers, and

6. Milton to Florida Congressional Delegation, Sept. 11, 1862, *ibid.*, II, 93–95.

7. *Ibid.;* Randolph to Chestnut, May 13, 1862, *ibid.*, I, 1121.

8. "An Act to Amend an Act Entitled, 'An Act to Provide Further for the Public Defence, April 16, 1862,' " Sept. 27, 1862, *Statutes,* II, 61–62.

9. Randolph to Davis, Oct. 20, 1862, *OR*-4, II, 132.

10. *Ibid.*

11. *Debates,* XLVIII, 182.

12. *Ibid.*, XLVI, 20–22.

millwrights, on the condition that their profits were not to exceed 75 per cent or a rate fixed by the Secretary of War. Wool and cotton operatives and managers were again to be exempted at the discretion of the Secretary of War, with the new provision that they, too, were not to charge more than 75 per cent profit on the cost of production, and this category was extended to paper and wool card manufacturers. The bill tightened up on exemptions for munitions workers and miners, as well as all workers in naval manufacturing, by requiring that these workers be certified by some responsible public officer. Finally, the President could exempt persons on the grounds of "justice, equity, or necessity."[13]

The exemption law of October 11, 1862, remained the focal point of manpower allotment until 1864. There was inevitable grumbling about each category of exemption, especially about the "twenty nigger law," and one congressman declared that the act "stunk in the nostrils of the people."[14] In fact, however, the act, based as it was on six months' experience with conscription, improved conscription policy. The increased exemptions of skilled workers and artisans and the attempt to place controls on the domestic market demonstrated that the government was adjusting its concepts to a long war of economic attrition. There were still the caste inequities of substitution and the over-large professional and political exemption categories. Moreover, the entire concept of exemption classes rather than individual details from the army provided too many loopholes for an unworthy escape from military service, a waste which would become increasingly unbearable as manpower shortages grew more critical. For conditions in the autumn of 1862, however, conscription policy represented one of the more efficient war policies of the Confederate government.

By the spring of 1863 the aggregate present totals had surpassed 300,000[15] and although Congress held lengthy debates on altering exemption categories, it made only one significant change. In this instance, Congress scrutinized the supply bureaus. Many had come to the conclusion that there was one category of details that could be erased completely—details of able-bodied men working in the offices of

13. "An Act to Exempt Certain Persons from Military Duty, and to Repeal an Act Entitled 'An Act to Exempt Certain Persons from Enrollment for Service in the Army of the Confederate States,' Approved 21st April, 1862," Oct. 11, 1862, *Statutes,* II, 77–79. 14. *Debates,* XLVI, 20–22.

15. Abstract of returns, Jan. —, 1863, *OR*-4, II, 380; abstract of returns, April 30, 1863, *ibid.,* p. 530.

the commissaries and quartermasters. Congressmen denounced the "hale, insolent and impertinent conscripts" who "filled" the supply services; they complained that "every little post quartermaster throughout the country has his clerk, messenger, agent, &c., &c."[16] On April 22, 1863, Congress passed an act forbidding supply officers to employ as clerks men liable to military service. If possible, commanding officers were to detail disabled men for these duties.[17]

If the conscription system was a decently equitable method of getting men into the ranks, the War Department's system of detailing men from the ranks was ineffective. The army commanders, Lee foremost among them, quite naturally objected to losing any men from the fighting line, or even from the winter camps, and did not hesitate to point out the demoralizing influence of allowing a few men to escape the privations of camp life.[18] On the other hand, details for shoemaking and railroad work and other special assignments usually represented valuable man-hours for production as compared to idling in camp, and the supply chiefs did not hesitate to make this point to the Secretary of War. The problem lay in the fact that the various Secretaries, especially Seddon, would not take the final responsibility on this matter. Seddon, after sifting requests from his bureau chiefs and deciding which details had merit, simply recommended them for favorable consideration to the army commanders, who naturally refused them. At one point Seddon became so perturbed by Lee's routine refusal of all his recommended details that he wrote Lee, explaining that he did not recommend details casually and that he did not expect them to be refused.[19] Still, Seddon would not make his recommendations an order, and friction between the supply bureaus and the armies over the proper allotment of men continued.

. . .

Impressment was another policy, or rather practice, that required examination. In the year 1861 impressment of needed articles had been local and sporadic, indulged in primarily by local commanders when they deemed it essential. The power of impressment for the good of the

16. *Debates,* XLVIII, 109.

17. "An Act to Amend an Act Entitled 'An Act to Provide for an Increase of the Quartermaster and Commissary Departments,' Approved February 15, 1862," April 22, 1863, *Statutes,* II, 114–115.

18. Lee to Randolph, July 12, 1862, Dowdey and Manarin, eds., *The Wartime Papers of R. E. Lee,* p. 231; Lee to Cooper, Nov. 15, 1862, *OR*-1, XXI, 1012.

19. Seddon to Lee, Feb. 11, 1863, WDLS, XI, 123–124.

service had also been given to the supply chiefs, but again, to be used only occasionally in cases of extreme exigency. Through the course of the year 1862, however, the practice of impressment had turned into something quite different.

By the fall of 1862 War Department officials and army commanders had greatly extended the range and incidence of impressments. Authorities took medical supplies from blockade runners and from speculators;[20] they seized quartermaster hardware, forage, and horses in the hands of unco-operative sellers; and the Secretary of War authorized the impressment of such major items as railroad iron, distilleries, and niter caves.[21] The government attempted to make its confiscatory actions as palatable as possible. Officials paid on the spot the high prices prevailing on the market, handed out receipts and certificates in profusion, and theoretically made out reports to superiors.[22] At the same time, the War Department peppered army officers with orders containing severe strictures against capricious and unnecessary impressments. General Orders No. 56, August 6, 1862, is a typical example:

> Necessity alone can warrant the impressment of private property for public use; and wherever the requisite supplies can be obtained by the consent of the owner at fair rates, and without hazardous delay, the military authorities will abstain from the harsh proceeding of impressment.[23]

Although the government impressed a sizeable amount of medical, quartermaster, and ordnance stores, it was the extensive and persistent seizure of food which created nationwide irritation. During the autumn the constant seizure of beef, bacon, and other provisions provoked outraged protests from patriots and speculators alike and encouraged resistance, evasion, hoarding, and the destruction of surplus food. To stem the mounting uproar Assistant Secretary of War John A. Campbell

20. General Orders No. 73, Adjutant and Inspector General's Office, 1862 Series, Oct. 1, 1862, *OR*-4, II, 105; Randolph to Mercer, Sept. 16, 1862, WDTS, XXXIV, 348.

21. Randolph to Beauregard, Nov. 4, 1862, WDTS, XXXIV, 404; General Orders No. 14, Adjutant and Inspector General's Office, 1863 Series, Feb. 3, 1863, *OR*-4, II, 380–381.

22. General Orders No. 31, Adjutant and Inspector General's Office, 1863 Series, March 19, 1863, *OR*-4, II, 441.

23. General Orders No. 56, Adjutant and Inspector General's Office, 1862 Series, Aug. 6, 1862, *ibid.*, p. 39; Special Orders No. 28, Army of Tennessee, Dec. 18, 1862, *OR*-1, XX (2), 453.

dispatched orders to the army commanders telling them that their quartermasters and commissaries should not "repose quietly and lazily on the highways," waiting to use the "strong hand" to impress needed supplies when "private enterprise should bring the resources they stand in need of."[24] In September, with the Virginia flour crop short, Secretary of War Randolph prohibited the exportation of flour from the state and directed a routine seizure of stocks of flour held in the state, paying market rates to producers and cost prices to speculators.[25] The resulting outcry kept Randolph busy soothing ruffled Congressmen and local politicians.

Despite public opposition to the impressment methods of the War Department, Seddon, the new Secretary of War, at the instigation of the Subsistence Department, intensified the practice by imposing a nationwide uniform price schedule for purchase and, if refused, impressment. Ruffin and Northrop, in statements to the Secretary of War, denounced the citizens' refusal to sell to the government at fair prices while holding out for the artificially high prices offered by the speculators, and they predicted that "If this state of things is permitted to continue the army cannot be fed."[26] They insisted that government purchasing and/or impressment required "universality"—a fixed price per article for the whole country. They suggested that a fair price schedule could be created by taking a five-year prewar average of commodity prices as the base and then allowing a percentage increase that would reflect relative availability of each item on the current market. The percentage of increase suggested ranged from 100 per cent to 250 per cent for most items upward to 733⅓ per cent for coffee and 900 per cent for salt.[27] Seddon accepted the arguments and suggestions and on December 26 published a price schedule for provisions, forage, labor, and transportation. Railroads were exempted. Impressing agents were to pay on the spot if possible, leave enough subsistence for the family, use written forms, and display written authorization; and the

24. Campbell to Pemberton, Nov. 12, 1862, WDLS, IX, 138; see also Campbell to Hill, Nov. 11, 1862, *ibid.*, VII, 192–193; Randolph to Martin, Oct. 31, 1862, WDTS, XXXIV, 400.

25. Randolph to Galt, Sept. 23, 1862, WDLS, VIII, 34; Randolph to Galt, Oct. 4, 1862, *ibid.*, p. 71; Randolph to Jones, Oct. 1, 1862, WDTS, XXXIV, 365–366; Randolph to Jones, Oct. 3, 1862, *ibid.*, p. 367; Randolph to Jones, Oct. 6, 1862, WDLS, VIII, 80.

26. *Communication from [the] Secretary of War Enclosing the "Orders of Impressment, together with the Instructions and Regulations under the same, Recently Issued by the War Department or Any Bureau Thereof"* (Richmond, 1863), p. 10. 27. *Ibid.*, p. 12.

supply bureaus were to keep records of impressment activities for official scrutiny.[28]

Seddon had given executive sanction to a method of procurement which the situation at that time demanded. Impressment, once local and occasional, had become a regular, nationwide method of War Department procurement, a practice often abused but more often used as a weapon of defense against an inflated general market over which the War Department had no economic or legal control. The uniform price system, once in operation, set a standard for impressing officers. However, it was to prove unsatisfactory because it discounted local variations in values and set up such unrealistic percentage ratios that schedule prices fell well below current market prices.[29]

The general hue and cry which followed the promulgation of the schedule was a protest not only against the price level, but also against the formal declaration of the War Department that it was sanctioning impressment as an official policy without Congressional authorization. By February 1863 newspapers around the country, undoubtedly reflecting the attitudes of most Confederate citizens, were raising a

28. *Ibid.*, pp. 7–8.

29. Impressment rates can be compared with market prices by considering the following schedules:

A. War Department five-year base, 1856–1860*
B. War Department Schedule Price, Dec. 26, 1862†
C. Market Prices in Richmond *Dispatch,* January 30, 1863‡
D. Virginia Schedule of Prices under Impressment Act, May 18, 1863§
E. South Georgia Schedule of Prices under Impressment Act, June 15, 1863//

	A.	B.	C.	D.	E.
Bacon/lb.	$00.10½	$00.35	$1.00	$1.00	$00.75–$00.85
Flour/bbl. of 196 lbs.	8.00	17.50	24.50	$22–$28	40.00
Sugar/lb.	.08	.28	1.15	1.00	.75
Coffee/lb.	.12	1.00	5.00	3.00	—
Lard/lb.	.10	.30	1.00	1.00	—
Meal/bu. of 50 lbs.	.95	2.20	4.00	4.20	1.60
Candles/lb.	.12½	.50	1.25	1.00	.50
Soap/lb.	.04½	.20	1.10	.30	—

* *Communication from* [*the*] *Secretary of War Enclosing the "Orders of Impressment, together with the Instructions and Regulations under the Same, Recently Issued by the War Department or Any Bureau Thereof,"* pp. 12 ff.

† *Ibid.*

‡ Jones, *War Clerk's Diary,* I, 250.

§ General Orders No. 65, Adjutant and Inspector General's Office, 1863 Series, May 21, 1863, *OR*–4, II, 559–560.

// *Ibid.*, pp. 561–562.

chorus of complaint.[30] The Richmond newspapers, acutely sensitive to the shortage of food in the city markets, declared that farmers were hoarding their products rather than trying to bring them into Richmond and thus face impressments. The *Daily Richmond Examiner* laid the policy at Northrop's door, commenting bitterly about "conceit and folly" and demanding that the government "abandon the nefarious, illegal and insane policies of monopolies and impressments without just compensation, encourage the production of food, and its exhibition in the public markets by securing its safety and paying the full comparable value. . . ."[31]

In the face of these virulent attacks, Seddon defended his actions vigorously, as in this letter to Congressman Martin:

> The department holds that it is competent to itself to accumulate supplies for the necessities of the army. . . .
>
> The difficulty of supplying the army in consequence of the spirit of speculation that raged through the land, and the greed of those who withhold the means in their power, to render those supplies abundant can hardly be properly represented—The duty imposed upon this department is in the highest degree responsible and embarrassing. Its orders and actions have been directed to the performance of this duty with the least inconvenience or mischief to the community at large.[32]

Seddon did not hesitate to discharge this "embarrassing" duty himself when he felt it necessary, but in so doing he precipitated a crisis. In March, in the midst of a provisioning crisis, he directed the widespread seizure of the flour held by Virginia speculators in order to send it to Lee's troops, but the speculators secured an injunction from the Virginia courts.[33] "Theft and robbery,"[34] trumpeted the *Daily Richmond Examiner* about the impressments; "Acts of banditti, defiant of human law and divine."[35] It was now questionable whether the War Department could continue impressment on its own authority.

Congress then exerted its authority. Seddon himself had suggested the

30. For example, see the Atlanta *Southern Confederacy,* March 11, 1863; *Daily Richmond Examiner,* Feb. 23, 1863; *Daily Richmond Whig,* Feb. 5, 1863.

31. *Daily Richmond Examiner,* March 11, 1863. See also the Richmond *Daily Dispatch,* March 13, 1863.

32. Seddon to Martin, Jan. 12, 1863, WDLS, XV, 419.

33. Jones, *War Clerk's Diary,* I, 279–280. For details see *Daily Richmond Examiner,* March 24, 1863; Richmond *Enquirer,* March 25, 1863.

34. *Daily Richmond Examiner,* March 5, 1863.

35. *Ibid.,* March 24, 1863.

necessity of Congressional action to clarify the situation, and Congressional committees considered numerous bills regulating impressment. Congressmen witnessed the hullabaloo in Richmond over Seddon's flour seizures and provided numerous peppery opinions of their own during the debates on the "wild and uncertain" impressment practices of the War Department.[36] Congress debated every aspect of the impressment problem at length: "market prices" versus "just compensation"; one schedule, many schedules, or no schedule; appraisement by state commissioners or local appraisers; immediate compensation by impressing officers or delayed compensation by disbursing officers; the liability of everyone to impressment or the liability of speculators only; and so on.[37]

The bill as finally produced authorized supply minions, if "exigencies of any army in the field were such as to make impressments of forage, articles of subsistence or other property absolutely necessary," to impress from both producers and nonproducers, with a different method for each but in all instances paying on the spot. The producer could reserve a quantity of goods to subsist himself and his family for an indeterminate period and to carry on his occupation; the remainder was subject to impressment at an evaluation agreed on by producer and agent, presumably at current market prices, though this was not specified. Any disagreement about the amount to be reserved from impressment or about the value of the good liable to impressment would go to two local persons, one chosen by the agent and one by the producer. These local appraisers, who had the final decision, could call in a third appraiser in case of disagreement.

In the case of nonproducers, impressing officers would pay the prices given in the impressment schedule promulgated by the state Commissioners of the particular state in which the act of impressment occurred. These Commissioners, as created by the bill, consisted of two Commissioners, one chosen by the President and one by the governor; the two Commissioners could call in a third person in case of disagreement. The state schedules of appraisement were to be republished at least every two months. If nonproducers and impressing agents disagreed as to what category in the schedule certain goods belonged, the local appraisers would decide; but the impressing agent could appeal to

36. *Debates,* XLVII, 126.

37. *Ibid.,* pp. 126–128, 148–150; *ibid.,* XLVIII, 82–85, 112–113, 124–125, 132, 213–214, 240–279; *ibid.,* XLIX, 7–9, 12–17; *Journal,* III, 20–21, 50, 72, 115, 122–134, 142–148, 173, 189–194; *ibid.,* VI, 23, 100–102, 178–179, 213–218.

the State Board if dissatisfied. The bill further interlarded all of this complex procedure with oaths, affidavits, receipts, and vouchers.

Additional provisions empowered the Secretary of War, when he judged necessary, to confer on "subordinate officers" the power to impress property; this allowed field officers to impress supplies for their commands in case of emergencies. The government was made liable for paying compensation for the damage of temporarily impressed property, the rates to be fixed by local appraisers. The bill carefully hedged about with restrictions the impressment of slaves. The whole act was vitiated, however, by one omission—there were no provisions for punishment of resistance or evasion.[38]

The President had hardly signed the bill when incidents of local appraisement indicated that Congress had created an inflationary bomb. The act had intended that the impressing officer would offer the market rates and that the producer would accept, but Senator Hunter had predicted a different result during the debates:

> Persons from the vicinage [the local appraisers] would assess the property at a high price, because they would thereby be putting up the price of their own property. . . . When the two facts, the depreciation of the currency, and the real scarcity of articles of prime necessity were considered it would be easily seen that rapidly increasing inflation must be the consequence.[39]

The Senator had correctly "appraised" his fellow citizen. In all too many instances, the producer refused the market price offered by the impressing officer, and the local appraisers set extravagant valuations on the property. In an instance of impressment near Richmond, local appraisers set the price of hay at $20 per hundred pounds, as compared with $4 per hundred called for by the state Commissioners, whose price schedule at this time approximated current market prices.[40] Such actions infuriated the War Department and produced consternation in Congress. Kean noted in his diary that "The new impressment law bids fair to ruin the country and the cause. . . . The farmers are the worst extortioners we have to deal with and at this rate will wholly break up the supply of the army."[41] Senator Hill thundered: "This is a gross

38. "An Act [to] Regulate Impressments," March 26, 1863, *Statutes,* II, 102–104. 39. *Debates,* XLVIII, 205. 40. *Ibid.,* XLIX, 177.

41. Younger, *Kean Diary,* pp. 52–53. The Confederate officials were not the only ones to lay a large share of the blame on the farmers. The Confederate press occasionally took a potshot as well. The "farmers have signalized themselves in this

imposition on the Government, and the names of the parties to the transaction should be published in every paper in the country, that they might be a hissing and a byeword among the people."[42] To rectify this situation, Congress rushed through an act allowing impressing officers to appeal to the State Board of Appraisers any judgment of the local appraisers, while holding the property in question.[43] The *Daily Richmond Examiner,* which like most of the Confederate press had supported the original impressment bill,[44] commented bitterly that the supplementary bill gave the Subsistence Department "unlimited power over everything that grows on the ground of every farmer in the Confederacy"[45] and that "The people of the country should not be without defense against the ignorance, rapacity, and domineering insolence of Quartermasters and Commissaries."[46]

Impressment of military supplies had now been legalized and would remain government policy, in one form or another, until late in the war. Students of the Confederacy have both condemned forced procurement for compounding Confederate economic problems and defended it as an unpleasant necessity pressed upon the government. It is indeed difficult to decide what should have been done. The military and an increasing number of civilians needed regular, extensive, and continuous procurement of supplies. Factory-produced supplies could be secured because the government exercised tight controls over raw materials and labor, but it was a different question with agricultural supplies. Exemptions touched only a small part of the agricultural labor force and Mother Nature controlled raw materials. Scarcity and inflation had created both speculation and hoarding where foodstuffs were concerned, and the earlier "illegal" impressment, with the accompanying offers of high prices, had intensified this hoarding. Bales of inflated money would not guarantee regular sales. A combination of stringent tax laws, controlled output of currency, price laws, rationing, punishment for hoarding, and impressment regulations might have kept the domestic market in manageable condition; but the property

---

war as the most flinty-hearted of the extortionate," commented the *Daily Richmond Examiner* on April 15, 1864. See also *Richmond Daily Dispatch,* Jan. 13, 1864. 42. *Debates,* XLIX, 177–178.

43. "An Act to Amend an Act Entitled 'An Act to Regulate Impressments by Officers of the Army,'" April 27, 1863, *Statutes,* II, 127–128.

44. *Weekly Columbus Enquirer,* April 28, 1863; *Daily Richmond Whig,* March 27, 1863; Richmond *Enquirer,* March 26, and April 13, 1863; Augusta *Tri-Weekly Constitutionalist,* Aug. 26, 1863.

45. *Daily Richmond Examiner,* April 23, 1863. 46. *Ibid.,* April 25, 1863.

holders would not tax themselves, and the other measures were too radical for the period. The only alternative remaining appeared to be to force sales. As the war continued, impressment lost its utility because of intensified hoarding, the lack of punitive provisions in the impressment law, and resistance on the part of local authorities. Finally, late in the war, the bureaus lacked the money to pay for those goods that could be located for impressment.

But this is judging impressment too rigidly by looking ahead to 1864–65, when impressment was brought down as a part of a general economic collapse. In 1863 the practice was already in existence and had to be either curtailed or put on a legal basis. Even Congress, despite its sensitivity to public hostility, found impressment an unavoidable necessity for carrying on the war. It does appear to have aided the supply bureaus in ferreting out supplies for at least another year. On the basis of the latter point alone and in the light of conditions of the spring of 1863, the legalization and continuation of impressment appears to have been an action of responsibility on the part of the Confederate government.

. . .

In dealing with conscription and impressment, the Confederate government had modified or clarified old practices. The intensification of railroad problems, however, pointed to the creation of new public policy. After the Manassas tie-up, except for a general indifference to handling commissary supplies, the railroads had transported government supplies with passable dispatch. During the spring of 1862 the quartermasters undertook the added responsibility of arranging shipments of cotton for foreign exchange to the seaports without encountering any undue difficulty. The railroads had handled even the commotions and alarms of spring withdrawals with reasonable efficiency.

In April Myers attempted to bring even more efficiency into his bureau's railroad arrangements and produced a tidy small bureaucratic plan, directed at speeding up the constant loadings and unloadings at the connection points of the many small railroad lines. Myers directed that quartermasters forwarding shipments which were to continue past the terminus of the railroad employed would wire the quartermaster at that junction, so that the quartermaster would be ready to expedite the unpacking and repacking of the shipments. He requested each railroad president to notify the president of the connecting railroad to have the freight cars at the junction. The quartermaster and president thus communicated with were to notify the next set of officials, and so on.[47] This was a setup pleasing perhaps for a bureaucrat, but it was hardly the type of arrangement to be given consideration by the railroad people.

In the summer of 1862 the sum total of government regulation of the railroads consisted of Myers's paper system, the round-robin rates agreements, and the exemption of railroad personnel from conscription. The only other connection between the two involved the subsidies to particular companies to close gaps in the railroad network. The government continued this policy by the advance of $12,000 to the Pensacola and Georgia Railroad to connect that line with the Savannah, Albany and Gulf, and thus to provide a rail link with Florida.[48] Congress further appropriated $1,122,480.92 in Confederate bonds for a loan to build the Blue Mountain Railroad link from the vicinity of Anniston, Alabama, to Rome, Georgia, and thus to connect Mississippi by rail with the rest of the Confederacy.[49]

By September, however, there had been enough friction with the railroads for Myers to alter his outlook on the proper relationship between the government and private enterprise. Deterioration of equipment and service had become noticeable. The railroads were showing a much greater interest in transporting the goods of private citizens and speculators at the prevailing high freight rates than in shipping government freight at lower rates. Despite this, Myers told a Congressional group that he still opposed intereference with railroad operations from military commanders in the field. He also opposed general government seizure because it would demoralize civilian personnel and bring the government under obligation to the stockholders. He suggested, instead, the appointment of "an able, methodical, and energetic person" under the direction of the Quartermaster General to be chief of transportation and make regulations and attempt to bring the railroads into "harmonious action."[50] Congress, however, took no action on the matter.

The War Department acted on its own shortly thereafter. A series of impressments of railroad property by local army commanders, coupled

47. Myers to Railroad Presidents, April 25, 1862, QMDLS, XVI, 128; Quartermaster's Department Circular, April 25, 1862, *ibid.*

48. Randolph to Myers, April 2, 1862, WDLS, VII, 208.

49. "An Act to Enable the President of the Confederate States to Provide the Means of Military Transportation by the Construction of a Railroad between Blue Mountain in the State of Alabama, and Rome, in the State of Georgia," *Statutes,* II, 66.

50. Myers to Chilton, Oct. 3, 1862, *OR*-4, II, 108–109.

with prohibitions upon citizens using the railroads, brought a rash of complaints from speculators, Congressmen, and even from state governors. The War Department was kept busy pacifying complainers and ordering commanders to refrain from interfering with the railroads, and Randolph and Davis decided that the time had come to appoint a general railroad superintendent to put his full time into working out an efficient, enforceable government railroad policy.[51] Randolph summed up the situation in a letter to a complaining Governor Shorter of Alabama:

> The Confederate Government has never attempted to exercise any control over the railroads of the Country farther than to claim a preference in the transportation of munitions and supplies for the Army. Conscious, however, that the Government transportation intereferes with the commerce of the Country, and desirous of avoiding such interference the Department is now engaged in selecting a Superintendent of Railroad transportation, who will be charged with the duty of regulating it, so far as the power of the Government extends.[52]

The War Department settled on William M. Wadley, President of the Vicksburg, Shreveport and Texas Railroad and a noted railroad builder and manager. He was duly appointed Lieutenant-Colonel and his duties outlined in General Orders No. 98, December 3, 1862. Wadley's assignment was "to take supervision and control of the transportation for the Government on all the railroads in the Confederate States." He was empowered to make contracts and agreements and to make disposition of government men and machines connected with the railroads, even to the extent of detailing men from the army.[53] In fact, Wadley had little power, for the government had little control over the railroads. Wadley was supposed to report directly to the Secretary of War via the office of the Adjutant and Inspector General.[54] Myers lost no time in sending an official complaint to the Secretary of War, in which he declared that such an agreement would

51. Randolph to Galt, Nov. 12, 1862, WDTS, XXXIV, 414; Campbell to Brett, Foster, and Company, Nov. 7, 1862, WDLS, VIII, 171; Cooper to Pemberton, Nov. 29, 1862, *OR*-1, XVII (2), 770.

52. Randolph to Shorter, Nov. 12, 1862, WDLS, VIII, 202.

53. Randolph to Wadley, Nov. 11, 1862, WDTS, XXIV, 411; General Orders No. 98, Adjutant and Inspector General's Office, 1862 Series, Dec. 3, 1862, *OR*-4, II, 225.

54. *Ibid.*

divide authority and "occasion difficulty and embarrassment to this department."[55] He received no answer.

The adventures of Wadley among the railroad owners and railroad lines of the Confederacy have been extensively recounted by Robert S. Black in *Railroads of the Confederacy* and need no recapitulation here. It is sufficient to say that the winter's experience transformed the ex-railroad president into an advocate of government railroad regulation, to go hand in hand with railroad subsidies. As Wadley put it on January 26, 1863, the government should be empowered to "take possession of any railroad that failed to perform promptly, Government transportation."[56]

Others were also coming around to a consideration of government regulation. Davis had recommended in his report to Congress "the control of the roads under some general supervision, and resort to the power of impressment."[57] Seddon and Myers were growing increasingly irritated by transportation difficulties, but were not yet ready to act as the winter dragged on.

Meanwhile, the War Department officials did what they could to streamline transportation. Northrop and Myers both told Seddon that the system of sending agents and messengers to speed up individual shipments (arranged by Wadley) had accomplished nothing and that the War Department should disregard the plan.[58] Northrop suggested that the quartermasters at posts note losses and damages to government freight in order to fix responsibility on the proper railroad lines, and Myers sat down to translate this suggestion into regulations. He created three new forms and gave his subordinates until July 1 to master his new system.[59] Myers did succeed in creating a series of army supply trains from Charlotte to Richmond, but that was as far as he could—or would—go unless ordered to impress trains, a policy which he opposed.[60] There was little else for Myers to do except to follow the progress of shipments and put his signature on the quarterly statements of disbursements for railroad transportation.

The scurrying about of War Department officials during the winter transported little meat to the Army of Northern Virginia. On January

55. Myers to Seddon, Dec. 9, 1862, *ibid.*, pp. 231–232.

56. Wadley to Seddon, Jan. 26, 1863, *OR*-4, II, 373–374.

57. Davis to the Senate and House of Representatives, Jan. 12, 1863, *ibid.*, p. 348.

58. Northrop to Seddon, Feb. 4, 1863, *ibid.*, pp. 384–385.

59. *Ibid.;* Myers's endorsement, Feb. 11, 1863, on same, *ibid;* Myers to Quartermasters at posts, Feb. 13, 1863, QMDLS, XVII, 18; Myers to Wadley, Feb. 14, 1863, *ibid.*, pp. 19–20.

60. Myers to Chilton, Oct. 3, 1862, *OR*-4, II, 108–109.

26 Lee announced that he had eight days' meat rations left and that he had virtually exhausted the supply of forage.[61] As the Army of Northern Virginia continued on a hand-to-mouth basis day by day through February, March, and into April, the responsibility for feeding 75,000 men made Seddon more and more irascible. He sent telegrams and letters to the wandering Wadley, fuming about "dilatory and irregular transportation" and "gross inattention" on the part of the railroads, while threatening to stop and load passenger trains.[62] He demanded that Wadley force the railroad presidents to agree to the principles of through freight schedules and intermingling of stock that they had rejected in December, noting irritably:

> I suppose[d] this course had long been pursued, as it seems to me manifestly required to give full efficiency, to the railroad facilities as well as to their own interest, but learn that, owing to the jealousies and conveniences of special roads, it has never even been practiced. The least calculation will show that if the railroads will in good faith give preference to Government freight and will steadily and continually run their freight trains by through schedule rates more than all the supplies needed for the Government can be transported on the leading lines. Harmony, co-operation, and reasonable energy on their part only are required. . . . It would be difficult for the roads to agree on such schedules, but they might, I think, be shown the necessity of the matter to the Government as well as their own interest as to come into the schedules arranged by you.[63]

Of more practical value was Seddon's appeal to Vance to aid in unsnarling the perpetual railroad tie-ups in eastern North Carolina. Vance, in a co-operative mood, transferred ten cars originally promised for the transportation of state supplies to the use of the Confederate government in hauling food and forage out of eastern North Carolina.[64] As noted before, Seddon had also given Colonel Carrington authority to impress needed railroad transportation to bring out forage. As the transportation crisis persisted into April, Seddon called for a general

61. Lee to Seddon, Jan. 26, 1863, *OR*-1, XXV (2), 597.

62. Seddon to Wadley, Feb. 5, 1863, WDTS, XXXIV, 456; Seddon to Wadley, March 25, 1863, *OR*-4, II, 457.

63. Seddon to Wadley, March 25, 1863, *OR*-4, II, 457.

64. Seddon to Vance, Feb. 10, 1863, WDLS, XI, 117.

railroad conference in Richmond, where Congress might observe friction between the government and the railroads.[65]

The Richmond Convention assembled on April 20, 1863, and by its adjournment the next day had clearly defined its idea of solving railroad problems: government aid but no government regulation.[66] To ensure a minimum performance, railroad managers of the Confederacy declared that they would need an additional 31 engines and 930 cars. Merely to keep the two main lines to Richmond supplied with adequate rolling stock would mean building 24 new engines and 710 cars. Maintaining adequate roadbeds would require production of 50,000 tons of rails.[67] The labor involved would demand the detailing of hundreds of mechanics from the army. Such needs were utterly beyond the capacity of private or public enterprise in the Confederacy of 1863. Far from producing rails, the government was taking up side-line rails to armor-plate naval vessels and to repair worn-out spots on main lines.[68] The Tredegar works and the Atlanta foundries together had a capacity to produce only 20,000 tons of rails per year, and these works were committed to ordnance production.[69] The War Department had allowed commanders in the field to veto additional details for railroad construction work, a shortsighted permissiveness on the part of Seddon. The railroads refused to consider any possibility of government control and ended the convention by calling for more public assistance while they once again raised the rates on government transportation.[70] The government would not help the railroads to regain their former efficiency by subsidizing private management, and the railroads refused to allow the government to regulate their declining physical strength for the primary interests of the war effort.

Even before the railroad magnates convened, Seddon had become exasperated with the situation and had drafted a bill giving the government broad powers over the railroads.[71] On the day the railroad convention opened, the bill had appeared on the Senate floor with a favorable report from the Senate Committee on Military Affairs.[72] After the railroad men left town, Seddon wrote Senator Wigfall that it was apparent that the railroad officials were too jealous of their rights

65. Black, *Confederate Railroads,* p. 119. 66. *Ibid.,* pp. 119–120.

67. Wadley to Seddon, April 14, 1863, *OR*-4, II, 483–485; Jones, *War Clerk's Diary,* I, 302–303.

68. Randolph to Beauregard, Nov. 4, 1862, WDTS, XXXIV, 404.

69. Jones, *War Clerk's Diary,* I, 302–303.

70. Myers to Smith, April 23, 1863, QMDLS, XVII, 301.

71. Younger, *Kean Diary,* p. 55. 72. Black, *Confederate Railroads,* p. 121.

to make any voluntary arrangement with the government and that centralized control of transportation regulations and the power to seize unco-operative carriers were definitely necessary for the good of the war effort.[73] Congress went to work on the bill, and the matter aroused such hot passions and was considered to be so politically dangerous that the two houses finally pushed the bill to passage in secret session on April 29.[74]

Davis apparently opposed interference with private enterprise to the extent provided in this railroad bill and despite his earlier recommendations and Seddon's urgings debated whether or not to veto it.[75] While he hesitated, the railroads themselves may have tipped the balance. Some weeks earlier the War Department had negotiated an agreement with the proper railroads for the forwarding of 120,000 pounds of meat per day into Richmond.[76] By April 30, as the new bill lay on the President's desk, no meat had arrived in Richmond for a week, and there was rising consternation and indignation. Special agents went south to find the shipments and hurry them forward.[77] Eventually the shipments came, but the capital and the army had received a bad scare. The President signed the bill.

The new act lodged great potential power in the hands of the Confederate executives. The Secretary of War, "under the direction of the President," was authorized, when necessary in his judgment, to require that any or all of the railroad companies not owned by the states devote "all means and resources" to support the armies, with the exception of one passenger train each day.[78] The bill gave the Quartermaster General the power of immediate supervision of railroad affairs and authority to create railroad regulations. In addition, the Quartermaster General was to arrange through freight schedules and intermingle the rolling stock of the railroads as circumstances might dictate. He might take equipment and rails of any railroad for use on another line if necessary. If any railroad refused to co-operate, the Secretary of War "under the direction of the President" could seize the railroad and

73. *Ibid.* 74. *Journal,* III, 354–355, 429; *ibid.,* VI, 472–473.

75. Younger, *Kean Diary,* p. 55. 76. *Ibid.,* p. 54.

77. Myers to Jacobs, April 30, 1863, QMDLS, XVII, 338; Seddon to Wadley, April 30, 1863, WDTS, XXXV, 20.

78. "An Act to Facilitate Transportation for the Government," May 1, 1863, Charles W. Ramsdell, ed., *Laws and Joint Resolutions of the Last Session of the Confederate Congress (November 7, 1864–March 18, 1865) Together with the Secret Acts of Previous Congresses* (Durham, N. C., 1941), pp. 167–169.

force all employees of conscription age to continue working on that line. To sweeten the bitter pill, Congress included various clauses to ensure proper compensation for seizure and/or damages.[79] Congress ignored the office of Railroad Superintendent, a War Department creation, and on the last day of the session disposed of the Superintendent by declining to confirm Wadley's appointment as colonel.[80]

Although Northrop had pleaded for controls, none of the Confederate officials directly responsible for railroad transportation had really campaigned for government control of the railroads. Rather, near-disaster for the Army of Northern Virginia had forced a reluctant Congress to give a reluctant Executive the power to rule the railroads for the good of the cause. How, or if, this power could be used, remained to be seen.

• • •

The most radical proposition demanding a decision was the policy of trading for supplies through enemy lines.[81] Earlier in the war, Congress had forbidden trade in staples with the United States or trade with the cities of the Confederacy inside the Union lines. However, authorities made no check on ships putting out to sea if a ship's papers indicated some neutral port as its destination. Commanders who suspected that certain traders were sailing to Northern or to Union-held Confederate ports were told by the War Department not to interfere with the ships unless the commanders were certain that the ships would be taken by the blockaders or unless the commanders could prove that ships were bound out to the enemy or were just in from an enemy port.[82]

The law of Congress was soon flouted. Increasingly, citizens surrep-

79. *Ibid.* 80. *Journal,* III, 426.

81. "An Act to Prohibit the Exportation of Cotton from the Confederate States, Except through the Seaports of Said States, and to Punish Persons Offending Therein," May 21, 1861, *Statutes,* I, 152–153; "An Act to Extend the Provisions of an Act Entitled 'An Act to Prohibit the Exportation of Cotton from the Confederate States Except through the Seaports of Said States, and to Punish Persons Offending Therein,' Approved May Twenty-one, Eighteen Hundred and Sixty One," Aug. 2, 1861, *ibid.,* p. 170; "An Act to Prohibit the Transportation and Sale of Certain Articles in any Part or Place within the Confederate States, in the Possession of the Enemy, and to Prohibit the Sale, Barter, or Exchange of Certain Articles Therein Named, to Alien or Domestic Enemies," April 19, 1862, *ibid.,* II, 46.

82. Benjamin to Milton, Nov. 30, 1861, *OR*-1, XVI, 857; Randolph to Jones, April 14, 1862, Confederate States of America Archives, Executive Departments, War Department, Duke University Manuscript Department; Seddon to Whiting, Dec. 30, 1862, WDTS, XXXIV, 435.

titiously traded through the enemy lines, often in connivance with Union commanders.[83] Although Confederate authorities, especially certain zealous military commanders such as Pemberton, sometimes punished the guilty parties,[84] the cotton trade increased everywhere along the military frontier. The trade was greatest along the banks of the Mississippi River, but it was also prevalent in eastern North Carolina and in Virginia.[85] The government was generally ineffective in preventing it. In the fall of 1862 the question arose as to whether or not the government should also trade cotton through the lines with Union connivance to get commodities needed by the troops.

The first pressure on the Confederate government to modify its official non-intercourse policy came from the states. By the summer of 1862 the general salt shortage had reached crisis proportions in the Confederate Southwest, both for the people and for the commissaries trying to pack the government meat. The Union army and navy were apparently willing to let salt come through the lines in exchange for cotton, and the state governors wanted to know if the Confederate government would let such trade pass through their lines. Governor Shorter of Alabama broached the subject in a tentative way to Randolph in July, but it was Governor Pettus of Mississippi who became persistent on the subject.[86] In October, Pettus authorized citizens to bring cotton to Ponchatoula, Louisiana, in exchange for salt brought through the Confederate lines.[87] Technically, no one knew anything about the destination of the cotton or why the salt had been allowed through the Union lines. Davis chose to view the trade as internal, and Randolph promulgated orders that the ships carrying salt by authority of the governors of Alabama and Mississippi would be exempt from

83. It is generally accepted that General Benjamin F. Butler in New Orleans and authorities in Memphis encouraged or allowed trade through the lines for cotton. For example, see An English Merchant [W. C. Corsan], *Two Months in the Confederate States, Including a Visit to New Orleans under the Domination of General Butler* (London, 1863), pp. 35–64. After the war, Northrop termed Butler's offers "unlimited"; see Northrop to Davis, May 23, 1878, Rowland, *Jefferson Davis,* VIII, 457. See also Joseph H. Parks, "A Confederate Trade Center Under Federal Occupation: Memphis, 1862 to 1865," *Journal of Southern History,* VII, No. 3 (Aug. 1941), 289–314.

84. Davis to Pemberton, Jan. 14, 1862, Rowland, *Jefferson Davis,* V, 416–417.

85. Younger, *Kean Diary,* p. 41.

86. Shorter to Randolph, July 30, 1862, *OR*-4, II, 21–22.

87. Betttersworth, ed. *Mississippi in the Confederacy,* p. 154; Davis to Pettus, Sept. 25, 1862, *OR*-1, XVII (2), 713; Pettus to Davis, Oct. 17, 1862, *OR*-4, II, 126; Davis to Pettus, Oct. 25, 1862, Rowland, *Jefferson Davis,* V, 360–361.

impressment.[88] At the same time the War Department instructed Pemberton not to allow trade with New Orleans under any circumstances.[89]

Meanwhile the Commissary General had reached a decision. Desperately short of meat and coffee, Northrop perused the offers of Jephtha Fowlkes of Grenada, who offered to bring in from the Memphis area ten thousand hogsheads of meat for certain and perhaps twenty thousand more, if he could take cotton across the Confederate lines into Memphis. Fowlkes claimed that there was enough cotton in the Confederate-held areas adjacent to Memphis to feed and clothe the entire army.[90] Northrop endorsed the letter in strong terms, urging acceptance of the Fowlkes proposition and maintaining that he could not feed the army unless the Confederate government would allow a certain amount of trading with cities in Northern hands.[91]

The fervor of Northrop's plea apparently persuaded Randolph, who also took into account Myers's difficulties with contracts; for the Secretary of War sent the papers on to the President with the following endorsement:

> The alternative is thus presented of violating our established policy of withholding cotton from the enemy or of risking the starvation of our armies. Regarding the former as the less evil, I advise that the Commissary General be authorized to contract for bacon and salt, and the Quartermaster-General for blankets and shoes, payable in cotton, and that the general commanding on the Mississippi be instructed to permit the cotton delivered under these contracts to pass our lines.
>
> The amount of purchases should be limited to what is absolutely necessary to feed the Army and supply it with blankets and shoes.
>
> I have examined the statutes prohibiting trade with the Confederate ports in the possession of the enemy and I am of the opinion that they do not apply to the Government, nor do I know

88. Randolph to Pettus, Oct. 28, 1862, WDTS, XXXIV, 396; Randolph to Shorter, Oct. 28, 1862, *ibid.*

89. Randolph to Pemberton, Oct. 17, 1862, *ibid.*, p. 385.

90. "Substance of the testimony of Col. Frank G. Ruffin of Virginia, late Lieut. Col. in the Confederate Bureau of Subsistence, given before the joint select committee of the two houses of the Confederate Congress, on the means of public defense on the 23rd of January, 1865," Virginia State Library.

91. Randolph to Davis, Oct. 30, 1862, *OR*-4, II, 151; Jones, *War Clerk's Diary*, I, 79.

of any principle of public law which prohibits a government from trading with the citizens or subjects of a hostile power. . . .

I am fully aware that in permitting the enemy to obtain a partial supply of cotton we are conceding an advantage to him and licensing an objectionable trade, and nothing less than the danger of sacrificing our armies would induce me to acquiesce in such a departure from our established policy. But the Commissary-General, whose duty it is to study the question of subsistence and to inform himself of the sources of supply, and who has had the benefit of eighteen months' experience, having recorded his opinion that the Army cannot be subsisted under the present arrangements, I must decline the responsibility of overruling him and entering upon an experiment which may result in ruin.[92]

Davis hesitated. His subordinates were united and vigorous in their view that the time had come to forget principles and to yield to the realities of war. The President apparently objected to the idea because such a practice was detrimental to morale. He also had a more practical objection. He replied to Randolph:

Is there necessity for immediate action? Is there satisfactory evidence that the present opportunity is the last which will be offered? Have you noted the scheme of the enemy for the payment of their next accruing interest on their public debt? You will not fail to perceive the effect of postponing the proposed action until after January 1st, 1863, if it be necessary at any time to depart from the well defined policy of our govt. in relation to Cotton.[93]

Northrop kept up the pressure on Randolph, and the Secretary of War, troubled by recurring complaints from Lee, was still convinced that the time had come to make a break in policy. Randolph asked Major Ruffin, Northrop's meat specialist, to prepare an analysis that could be sent on to the President. Ruffin dutifully presented a report which indicated that the number of slaughtered hogs was down by two fifths from last year and that packing totals in 1862 ensured only enough meat until January.[94] Randolph passed Ruffin's report on to the President on November 12 with the comment: "Unless the deficiency

92. Randolph to Davis, Oct. 30, 1862, *OR*-4, II, 151.
93. "Ruffin Testimony," PRSD, p. 4.
94. Ruffin to Randolph, Nov. 8, 1862, *ibid.*

be made up by purchases beyond the limits of the Confederacy I apprehend serious consequences."[95] The President replied on November 13 with a stinging rebuke: the figures "did not sustain the conclusion presented." Davis said that he needed a "comparative view" based on the Adjutant and Inspector General's report of troops to be fed and concluded: "The resources of every portion of the Confederacy must be considered in order to reach a just estimate."[96]

At the same time that the top executives were becoming heated over this problem, coincidence dictated that a number of men fresh from New Orleans filled the War Department office, men who swore that Butler would trade anything for cotton; and the desks contained an array of offers from firms and individuals to deliver goods from inside the enemy lines for cotton.[97] It was on one of these propositions rather than on the Secretary of War's message that Davis showed some signs of yielding: "As a last resort, we might be justified in departing from the declared policy in regard to exports, but the necessity should be absolute."[98]

November 13, the day of Davis's curt endorsement on Ruffin's report, was also the day of Davis's famous rebuke to Randolph's unauthorized strategic arrangements, a rebuke which apparently led to Randolph's resignation. Analyses of Davis's and Randolph's motives in this affair by students of the Confederacy do not mention the rebuff on trading through the lines, but this issue must have contributed to Randolph's decision to resign, an action received with sympathy by the Confederate press.[99] Randolph had been the best Secretary of War to date in terms of supply management. He had been instrumental in establishing conscription and had expedited new policies in impressment, railroad management, trading through the lines, and overseas purchasing. His successor, however, would be even better—he would learn how to influence Jefferson Davis.

The new Secretary of War, James A. Seddon, did not assume his position until November 21, but the issue of trading with the enemy did not await his arrival. On the sixteenth, Northrop sent in new

95. *Ibid.* 96. *Ibid.*, p. 5.

97. Jones to Randolph, Nov. 7, 1862, *OR*-4, II, 173–175; Jones, *War Clerk's Diary,* I, 187–191. 98. "Ruffin Testimony," PRSD, p. 5.

99. Besides sympathy for Randolph on the matter of his resignation, the press commented favorably on Randolph's tenure in office. For example, see the Charleston *Mercury,* Nov. 22, 1862; *Charleston Daily Courier,* Nov. 20, 1862; Richmond *Daily Dispatch,* Nov. 20, 1862; *Daily Richmond Examiner,* Nov. 20, 1862; Richmond *Enquirer,* Nov. 17, 1862.

evidence to support his case, endorsing dispatches concerning conditions in Tennessee. Myers joined Northrop in calling for trade through the lines when he endorsed a letter from Lee concerning the supply situation.[100] On the eighteenth, Northrop sent in the "Comparative View" called for by Davis on the thirteenth, arguing again the case for trading through the lines. Davis still temporized, asking new questions and disputing points which Northrop had made.[101] Shortly thereafter Northrop again wrote, claiming a 43 per cent deficit in meat and maintaining that only one third of the potential hog supply was inside the present military lines. He discounted other sources of supply, saying that the price outside the lines in cotton was cheaper than the price inside the lines in notes and that he would have to make arrangements immediately if the troops were to be fed from this source. He feared that Union authorities might end their permissive policy. Besides, the whole proposition was not new, according to Northrop. Private and state authorities, he claimed, imported 1,200,000 hogs across the lines in 1861, and state and Confederate soldiers had consumed 300,000 of these.[102] Davis did not reply.[103]

Davis was apparently determined in any case to wait until January 1, 1863, so that Confederate cotton could not be used to save the Union's financial obligations, or, as Ruffin interpreted it, so "that their credit would explode, and the war speedily cease from the bankruptcy of our assailants."[104] Ruffin later summarized Davis's other objectives: the Union wanted the cotton trade in order to discover navigable streams and in general to spy out the land; the trade would be demoralizing; cotton exported by way of New Orleans "would make Europe think we had caved in . . . [and they would] decline to recognize us, or to intervene."[105] According to Ruffin, Davis told Seddon before leaving for the South in December that he could make contracts should it become absolutely indispensable, but that in his opinion it was not then indispensable.[106] Kean, Chief of the Bureau of War, contended that the President had received support in this stand from cabinet members Reagan, Watts, and Benjamin.[107]

Discarding such puerile objections as "spying out the land," Davis

100. Northrop endorsement, Nov. 16, 1862, on Cummings to Northrop, Nov. 10, 1862, PRSD; Myers endorsement on Lee to Randolph, Nov. 14, 1862, *OR*-1, XIX (2), 718. 101. "Ruffin Testimony," PRSD, pp. 6–7.

102. Northrop Report, Nov. [21], 1862, *ibid.* 103. *Ibid.*

104. "Ruffin Testimony," PRSD, pp. 12–13. 105. *Ibid.*

106. *Ibid.*, p. 12. 107. Younger, *Kean Diary*, pp. 47–48.

and company had acted upon sophisticated morale and economic-diplomatic considerations, but these considerations were too theoretical to apply to the immediate situation. The opportunities along the open military frontier would erode civilian morale whether or not the government traded cotton, and the relatively small volume of government cotton contemplated for exchange could not have been a major factor in Union finance or European diplomacy.

The bureau chiefs had the more realistic approach. They argued that it was folly to allow private citizens to make a profit and vitiate the economic weapon that cotton theoretically presented while the troops were going ragged and hungry and the factories and railroads were deteriorating for lack of supplies. Kean apparently spoke for nearly all the officials of the War Department when he jotted this succinct comment in his diary: "The question is simply whether they suffer more for the comparatively small quantity of cotton, say 100,000 bales, or we for the indispensable articles of salt, meat, clothing, medicines."[108]

Facts forced a decision where reports and arguments had not. In December Seddon began to arrange for trading through the lines.[109] A series of losses in running goods through the blockade, together with growing problems in feeding and clothing the Army of Northern Virginia, made trading through the lines appear advisable, although at this early point in his service Seddon found the prospect distasteful.[110] The main arrangements which evolved during the winter were as follows: the government would give no permits to private parties to trade in enemy-held cities; however, authorities were not to harass these parties too zealously, and when unlicensed private individuals returned with their contraband, military officials were to seize the goods and give remuneration at cost plus a profit not to exceed 75 per cent.[111] In other words, for violating the law, smugglers were to receive the same percentage of profits as any other government contractor. Some men even made official contracts with the department to be "caught" bringing in supplies through the lines.[112] Another method was for the Secre-

108. *Ibid.*, p. 32.

109. Barriere and Brothers contract of Dec. 19, 1862, may be found in Garner to Gordon, Oct. 15, 1863, *OR*-1, XXVI (2), 415–419.

110. Seddon to Pemberton, Jan. 18, 1863, *ibid.*, XVII (2), 839–840.

111. Godwin to Seddon, Jan. 7, 1863, *OR*-4, II, 302; Seddon to Godwin, Jan. 10, 1863, *ibid.*, pp. 334–335; Seddon to Malloy, Jan. 29, 1863, WDTS, XXXIV, 452; Seddon to Adams, Feb. 20, 1863, *ibid.*, p. 464.

112. Younger, *Kean Diary*, pp. 46–47.

tary of War to make a few large contracts with parties to deliver goods through the lines for cotton to be taken out; bureau heads could authorize particular agents to make arrangements to have supplies brought in locally and to have cotton taken out. The War Department encouraged field commanders in the Southwest, Virginia, and eastern North Carolina to make arrangements on their own to get supplies for their men.[113] State governors could also make arrangements for agents to bring in needed supplies for their citizens, and the military would not interfere.[114] Finally, the manufacturers could make arrangements to bring in materials necessary to keep up their production.[115]

This varied array of policies actually produced meager results. Davis and Seddon were apparently half-hearted in prosecuting trading through the lines and did not press a unified policy. The trade was further complicated during the winter of 1862–63 by the fact that the Washington authorities and the local Union and Confederate commanders fluctuated markedly in their response, sometimes permitting the trade, sometimes prohibiting it.[116] As a result, few contracts came to fruition and the golden opportunities once presented by Butler at New Orleans passed.[117]

• • •

Beset by shortages at home, the Confederacy continued to rely heavily on supplies from abroad. Bedeviled by changing circumstances, the government could not devise an efficient arrangement. In the au-

113. Seddon to Hill, March 26, 1863, WDLS, X, 354; Seddon to DeBraun, March 19, 1863, WDTS, XXXIV, 479–480.

114. Seddon to Moore, March 6, 1863, WDTS, XXXIV, 472.

115. Seddon to Smith, April 3, 1863, WDLS, XI, 341.

116. Studies on trading through the lines are numerous though perhaps not definitive. The principal collection of information can be found in U. S. Congress, House of Representatives, "Trade with Rebellious States," *House Reports,* No. 24, 38th Congress, 2nd Session. Standard studies include Walter L. Fleming, "Blockade Running and Trade through the Lines in Alabama, 1861–1865," *South Atlantic Quarterly,* IV, No. 3 (July 1905), 256–272; E. Merton Coulter, "Commercial Intercourse with the Confederacy in the Mississippi Valley, 1861–1865," *Mississippi Valley Historical Review,* V, No. 4 (March 1919), 377–395; Joseph H. Parks, "A Confederate Trade Center under Federal Occupation: Memphis, 1862–1865," *Journal of Southern History,* VII, No. 3 (Aug. 1941), 289–314; T. H. O'Connor, "Lincoln and the Cotton Trade," *Civil War History,* VII, No. 1 (March 1961), 20–35; L. H. Johnson, "Contraband Trade during the Last Year of the Civil War," *Mississippi Valley Historical Review,* XLIX, No. 4 (March 1962), 635–652.

117. Younger, *Kean Diary,* p. 45; Northrop endorsement, Sept. 4, 1863, on Hillyer to Bragg, Aug. 25, 1863, *OR*-1, XXX (4), 550; Northrop to Davis, May 23, 1880, Rowland, *Jefferson Davis,* VIII, 457.

tumn of 1862 the government was following two main policies evolved during 1861 and the winter of 1861–62. Agents purchased for individual bureaus with monies sent from home, and the government awarded contracts to private parties to ship to the Confederacy goods which would be paid for in cotton that could be exported to Europe. With these policies came two major difficulties. Contractors were not delivering the goods while government cotton sat idle, and the Confederacy was running out of specie to furnish the agents. The obvious solution was to ship cotton abroad. Although some cotton had been shipped abroad under the Hypothecation Act, by September 1862 the Confederate depository, Fraser, Trenholm, and Company, had received only dribbles of cotton to sell.[118] The War Department agent, Caleb Huse, was running up an enormous debt, and Navy Department agents had to suspend operations.[119]

The government needed other means of using cotton for credit, and Memminger devised schemes for placing cotton bonds, cotton certificates, and cotton warrants in England to provide credit for purchasing. For example, the Treasury Department planned to place $5,000,000 in 8 per cent cotton warrants in England for the use of the War and Navy departments, allowing a 50 per cent discount based on cotton valued at 6*d*. per pound.[120] Memminger also urged Mallory and Seddon to turn over the funds earmarked for overseas purchase to the Treasury Department, whose agents would purchase cotton on which Memminger could base additional interest-bearing cotton certificates for sale in Europe.[121] These credit forms were put to immediate use by War Department purchasing agents. Huse gave cotton warrants totaling five million pounds of cotton valued at 5*d*. per pound to Isaac, Campbell and Company to pay for goods already shipped by that company.[122] These measures extended Confederate credit during the fall and winter of 1862 until the War Department made new arrangements for future foreign supply, but the sale of certificates and bonds and the use of warrants lagged and never furnished a significant amount of money.[123]

In the spring of 1863 the government made another attempt to use its cotton as an instrument of credit by arranging for the Erlanger loan. The Erlanger banking house handled the sale of $15,000,000 in

118. Mallory to Bulloch, Sept. 20, 1862, *ORN*-2, II, 268–271.
119. Todd, *Confederate Finance*, p. 179. 120. *Ibid.*, p. 181.
121. Mallory to Bulloch, Nov. 3, 1862, *ORN*-2, II, 288–289.
122. Todd, *Confederate Finance*, p. 185. 123. *Ibid.*, pp. 185–186.

Confederate twenty-year 7 per cent bonds, the interest convertible into cotton at 6*d*. per pound. After a tortured financial history the government finally realized $7,675,501.25, a poor return technically; but the money accrued proved valuable in paying off obligations and contracting for supplies.[124] As bonds, warrants, loans, and other methods of using cotton as credit failed to provide adequate specie for overseas procurement, it soon became apparent that the arrangement which would provide the most secure income was for the government to ship its cotton abroad. However, cotton shipments faced the problem of shortage of cargo space. Private blockade runners were not furnishing sufficient cargo space to ship out government cotton to pay for current contracts, let alone an expanded cotton sale; and to combat this shortage, the War Department turned to government-owned blockade runners. The idea of government-owned shipping was not new. In the fall of 1861 the Navy had purchased the *Fingal,* which had come into Savannah with a valuable cargo of supplies before being sealed up at Savannah by the Union blockade fleet.

In the spring of 1863 the War Department created two systems of government-owned shipping. Under one plan the Ordnance bureau began buying a number of steamers to run in its saltpeter, arms, and lead from Bermuda and Nassau.[125] These ships brought in the ordnance and medical supplies which Huse was procuring. The other plan involved a partnership with private interests, primarily to bring in commissary and quartermaster supplies. Partly impelled by the meat crisis of the winter, the War Department entered into an agreement with the Richmond firm of Crenshaw and Company. The War Department purchased three fourths interest in a number of blockade runners to be built or purchased abroad to carry government cargoes into Confederate ports and run government cotton out.[126] Crenshaw and Company associated themselves with Collie and Company of England to take the remaining quarter of the cargoes, with the understanding that goods brought in on the account of the two private companies could also be purchased by the Confederate government at domestic market prices. The government made the arrangement even more lucrative by allowing a system of purchasing commissions and tariff rebates.[127]

To finance this arrangement, Seddon had hoped to acquire some of

124. *Ibid.*, pp. 48–51.

125. A full discussion of the Ordnance Department's arrangements may be found in Vandiver, *Confederate Ordnance,* pp. 90 ff.

126. Seddon to Mason, Dec. 18, 1862, *OR*-4, II, 244–245.

127. *Ibid.*

the cotton already collected by the Treasury agents from the produce loan and other sources, but Memminger informed the Secretary that the Treasury Department would need all of the available cotton to back its credit schemes abroad.[128] Memminger offered to put Treasury agents at the War Department's disposal to facilitate the purchase of more cotton, and Seddon accepted.[129] The War Department thus faced substantial delays in buying and transporting cotton to finance this ambitious Crenshaw-Collie project, and Captain William G. Crenshaw began to make arrangements in England for advances to purchase and construct the necessary ships. While Crenshaw negotiated abroad, Seddon instructed the bureau chiefs to put whatever proportion of their funds they cared to allot for overseas purchases into the hands of the Treasury agents, who would mark each bale to the credit of the bureau which had purchased it.[130] After the cotton had been purchased, it would receive priority over other government railroad shipments and would be hurried to Wilmington and Charleston, where the Collie steamers, as they were called, would carry the cotton to England. Crenshaw was to sell the cotton on commission and use the receipts to pay for the supplies which agents had contracted for on separate bureau accounts. Payment would be made in proportion to the cotton receipts accruing to the bureau on each particular cotton shipment. If any money was left over after each shipment because supplies on contract were not immediately available, the remaining funds were to be applied to payments for the ships.[131] Seddon appointed Major Thomas L. Bayne to superintend arrangements for supplying the cotton and coal needed for both the Collie and the Ordnance steamers.[132] Finally, the War Department pushed to completion a railroad to the coal fields at Deep River, North Carolina, in order to provide stockpiles of coal at Wilmington so that the steamers would not be delayed in making return trips.[133] The Subsistence Department for the first time laid plans for large-scale shipments of meat from abroad. Previously, when the government had been dependent on private blockade runners, little foreign meat had come in because it was bulky and owners of blockade

128. Memminger to Seddon, May 11, 1863, *ibid.*, pp. 550–551. 129. *Ibid.*

130. Gorgas to Cuyler, March 3, 1863, *ibid.*, p. 416; Myers to Calhoun, July 30, 1863, QMDLS, XVII, 601.

131. Seddon to Crenshaw, May 23, 1863, *OR*-4, II, 565–571; Seddon to Crenshaw, June 21, 1863, *ibid.*, pp. 599–602.

132. Special Orders No. 174, Adjutant and Inspector General's Office, 1863 Series, July ——, 1863, *ibid.*, p. 660.

133. Seddon to Crenshaw, May 23, 1863, *ibid.*, pp. 565–567.

runners had preferred to bring in more profitable items of less bulk.[134]

While the new systems for shipping out government cotton, paying for supplies, and shipping the supplies into the Confederacy would in time become more efficient, they did not solve overseas procurement problems immediately. The contracted steamers would not be available for months; and when they were, much of their outbound cargo space would have to be devoted to taking out cotton to pay for their construction. It was the outgoing cargo space that provided the "money" for purchasing supplies, and the government was especially pinched for such space. Thus by 1863 the government had not yet worked out a satisfactory shipping policy.

Other developments complicated overseas purchasing considerations. During the year a new entryway into the Confederacy opened at Matamoros, Mexico, near the mouth of the Rio Grande opposite Brownsville. A friendly local strong man, General Vidaurri, allowed ships to unload merchandise there to be sent across the river into Texas. At the same time, Confederate agents made arrangements in Mexico for small amounts of lead, copper, saltpeter, shoes, blankets, and firearms.[135] The Quartermaster's Department dispatched an agent to Brownsville, authorizing him to buy cotton in Texas, haul it to Brownsville, and use it to pay for unsolicited goods which might arrive and to meet contracts payable in Confederate cotton.[136] The War Department's interest in this port of entry, however, was tempered by the knowledge that few of the goods arriving at Matamoros would get across the Mississippi.

It was also coming to the attention of the War Department that the expanding but unco-ordinated network of government agents abroad was beginning to dissolve into chaos. Confederate agents overesas had begun to quarrel among themselves. Major Ferguson reported that Huse paid 50 per cent more for quartermaster stores than necessary, and Myers indignantly asked Seddon to put all monies for quartermaster purchasing exclusively in the hands of Ferguson.[137] Huse would not co-operate with Crenshaw, the naval agents were not on speaking terms, and everyone was confused as to who was to handle receipts

134. Ruffin to Northrop, Oct. 18, 1864, *OR*-4, III, 739.

135. The basic source of information on Confederate political and economic relationships with Mexico is the John T. Pickett Papers of the Library of Congress.

136. Myers to Washington, April 9, 1863, QMDLS, XVII, 245.

137. Myers to Seddon, April 22, 1863, QMDSW, p. 348; Myers to Seddon, May 16, 1863, *ibid.*, p. 354.

from bond sales.[138] Confederate Commissioner Slidell wrote from Paris, commenting upon the "very great embarrassments" arising from the "alienation" of the agents. Slidell suggested that one person handle disbursements and assign priorities.[139] For the time being, however, the War Department refrained from unscrambling the overlapping powers of its numerous agents.

Meanwhile events abroad continued to produce evidence that the system of awarding contracts to private parties was a failure. Bulloch, the Navy Department agent, wrote to Mallory in September 1862 that little would actually come of these contracts because of the irregular financing engaged in by the parties, such irregularity stemming from an obvious lack of capital.[140] At home government officials were becoming increasingly exasperated in their efforts to secure something from their contracts with private parties. The War Department's standard contract paid 50 per cent on invoice plus freight charges in cotton at Confederate prices. Under the pressure of replenishing losses in the spring disasters of 1862, Myers found that contractors in June were demanding 100 per cent profit on invoice plus charges, and endorsed on one of these contracts, "The necessities of the Government are such as to demand imperatively supplies of the articles proposed to be furnished. I do not feel authorized to advise against the execution of the contract, though the profit required . . . is enormous."[141]

By September the demands of contractors were scaling upward astronomically. Randolph felt it necessary to accept an offer of Chamberlain and Company of London to furnish all supplies needed by the Ordnance, Medical, and Quartermaster's bureaus, for payment in cotton at European prices or in Confederate funds at 300 per cent on invoice. The company guaranteed in return to submit the goods to inspection by Confederate agents abroad and to certify that the goods had been purchased at current European wholesale rates. The company also assumed the usual shipment risks.[142] Late in the fall and into the winter the Quartermaster's Department received a number of offers to supply goods at 300 per cent on invoice. When one contractor went so far as to take out his cotton payment in advance, sell it, buy with a part of the

138. Mason to Benjamin, Dec. 10, 1862, *ORN*-2, III, 617–618.

139. Slidell to Benjamin, June 21, 1863, *ibid.*, pp. 810–812.

140. Bulloch to Mallory, Sept. 24, 1862, *ibid.*, II, 274–278.

141. Myers to Randolph, June 26, 1862, QMDLS, XVI, 341–342.

142. Randolph to Myers, Moore, and Gorgas, Sept. 25, 1862, *ibid.*, VIII, 44–45; Randolph to Huse, Oct. 1, 1862, *OR*-4, II, 106.

proceeds the goods contracted for, and ship the goods back to the Confederacy, Myers decided that it was time to examine the policy of awarding private contracts.[143]

Myers had observed that contractors were now so eager to get cotton that they were besieging the government to trade it through the Union lines, and he persuaded Seddon that better terms could be arranged on these private contracts. Myers argued that the speculators' greed for cotton and the new foreign procurement policies of selling cotton abroad and using government steamers for shipment would make the government's need for private parties less pressing. Hence, the government could exact more advantageous terms: "The desire to obtain cotton is general among Capitalists and the Govt. can control the use of the staple, so as to accrue its supplies upon very favorable terms."[144] In particular, Seddon approved Myers's suggestion that all contracts should state specific, reasonable prices for each unit item contracted for and that they should also specify a fixed valuation on the cotton.[145] The era of the "per cent on invoice" chicanery was ended. Nevertheless, the War Department still hoped to use private individuals abroad as a source of supplies; and it continued the policy of awarding contracts which promised enormous profits but secured few supplies.

By the spring of 1863 the Confederate government had evolved most of its domestic procurement policy, but it still groped about for an efficient system of foreign supply. The government now employed cotton as the medium of exchange in a variety of arrangements, in theory providing ample financial backing for overseas purchasing, but this program was not yet effective. Cotton as credit was of limited usefulness, cotton paid to private parties had secured meager returns, cotton sales in Europe were dragging for lack of cargo space, and the agents were quarreling over the employment of their meager resources. The government was entering the third year of the war without an efficient importation system.

. . .

By early 1863 the Confederate government had settled on basic national policies in the field of domestic procurement, policies which it

143. Myers's endorsement on Gerard and Powell proposals, Dec. 23, 1862, QMDELR, pp. 50–51; Myers's endorsement on Haynes and McNally proposal, Jan. 27, 1863, *ibid.*, pp. 65–66; Myers's endorsement on Alexander and Allen proposals, Jan. 30, 1863, *ibid.*, pp. 67–68.

144. Myers's endorsement on Maynes proposition, Dec. 23, 1862, *ibid.*, p. 52.

145. Myers's endorsement on Speed, *et al.* proposal, Jan. 29, 1863, *ibid.*, pp. 66–67.

pursued, with modifications, to the end of the war. Congress had agreed to drastic measures proposed by the Executive in the areas of conscription, railroad regulation, and impressment; the War Department had decided to implement *sub rosa* cotton trade with the United States when and where it was advantageous. In foreign procurement, however, policy was still in the process of transition. The government proliferated methods of using cotton to secure supplies from abroad but still had not found solutions for contract, shipping, and disbursement problems.

Domestic procurement policies, with the exception of the imponderables of impressment, represented, on their face, perceptive and efficient answers to Confederate shortages in material products. Nevertheless, the initiative for these policies had come in whole or in part from the bureau heads, who had to persuade their civilian chiefs that innovations were necessary. While it was undoubtedly healthy for subordinate specialists to have good ideas, it was a somber portent that the bureau chiefs, especially Northrop, often had to combat an ingrained conservatism on the part of the politicians over them. Indeed, such potentially sound policies as trading through the lines and co-ordination of the railroads were vitiated by the reluctance of Davis to employ them. Seddon, too, opposed trading through the lines. Thus, the only efficacious policy wholeheartedly pursued at the top was the conscription-exemption system, and that policy would soon require a major change in order to cope with the burgeoning manpower shortage.

A more serious criticism of the war effort up to early 1863 does not involve the efficiency or the sources of the supply policies. Rather, it concerns the fact that the Confederate administration continued its essentially negative habit of formulating policy by reacting to circumstances instead of planning ahead. Admittedly, the administrators had to contend with severe supply problems, many of which had not come to light until the government had engaged in a war of attrition on a continental scale. Such unprecedented problems obviously defied snap solutions. As the weaker adversary, however, the Confederacy desperately required the hard-headed weighing of assets and liabilities and the creation of a basic plan involving the co-ordination of resources and the assignment of priorities in order to make the most efficient use of the country's resources. Instead, separate policies, unrelated to each other, had been gropingly and haltingly evolved only as the mounting pain and pressure of adverse circumstances forced the issue. More specifically, policy was formulated as events and the opinions of subordinates modified or solidified Jefferson Davis's personal outlook. By 1863, with no end of the war in sight but with the virtual certainty that shortages would increase, the Confederate civilian leaders had displayed little foresight, had evolved only a few effective supply policies, and had imperfectly husbanded dwindling resources. In addition, all innovations, salutary or not, had been carried out in the teeth of increasing resistance from the Confederate citizens. Had the Davis administration done too little too late?

CHAPTER FIVE

MIDWAR BUREAUCRACY

Maj. Lanier asked me why it was you had so little confidence in him—I told him that you were probably under the impression that he drove fast horses—gambled occasionally—kept a woman—and drank a quart of whiskey per day—all of which he says is true, *but nevertheless thinks himself capable of making a good officer and promises to do his duty*
—— W. A. Broadwell to L. B. Northrop, June 7, 1862.*

By 1863 the administration of the Confederate supply system had reached maturity. Little administrative evolution or expansion took place for the rest of the war. In overcrowded and inflation-ridden Richmond, the War Department at mid-war provided a concentrated case of the mushrooming supply bureaucracy. The Department had scattered its component bureaus through buildings around Capitol Square, and a growing number of clerks and desk officers kept pace with an increasing volume of paper work. In the central office the Secretary of War, the Assistant Secretary of War, and the head of the Bureau of War, or chief clerk, tried to keep up with top-level correspondence and paper work. Adjutant and Inspector General Cooper employed 61 clerks and 3 messengers to transmit orders to officers in the field and to receive reports. In the bureau offices around the Square paperwork was equally the tale of the hour. The Surgeon General's Office employed 21 clerks; the Quartermaster General's Office, 88 clerks and 1 messenger; Subsistence, 36 clerks and 1 messenger; Ordnance, 24 clerks and 1 messenger; Niter and Mining, 11 clerks; Engineer, 3 clerks and 1 messenger; Conscript Bureau, 2 clerks; the Exchange Bureau, 6 clerks; and Army Intelligence, 1 clerk—a total of 273 clerks and 8 messengers.[1]

In the midst of this paper-shuffling furor, the routine of decision-making ground forward. The starting point was the President's office, located conveniently near the central office of the War Department, since nothing of consequence in supply policy was accomplished with-

* Confederate States of America; Army, Commissary Department; Lucius Bellinger Northrop, Commissary General, New York Public Library. Cited hereinafter as New York Public Library: Northrop Papers.

1. RG 109, Vol. 87, War Department Payrolls.

out the President's approval. Secretary of War Seddon held numerous daily conferences with the President, and many reports and communications went back and forth between the two offices. Later in the war the presence of General Bragg as special military adviser to the President led to a strange situation because the areas of authority of the General and the Secretary, apparently never defined, often overlapped. Presumably, Bragg had authority from the President to give commands to the lower echelons of bureau officials and field officers.

The heads of the bureaus usually communicated with the Secretary of War; only rarely, apparently, did they see the President in person or write him directly. Their reports to the Secretary of War were usually written, and Seddon often passed their communications on to the President with his comments. No matter who made the final decision or gave the crucial opinion or advice—Davis, Bragg, or Seddon—all formal directives to the bureaus were given on the authority of the Secretary of War.

By 1863 each of the supply bureaus had evolved its peculiar administrative arrangement. In the Subsistence Department the Commissary General rested at the apex of a pyramidal structure from which, with the advice of special staff officers, he correlated the work of the Chief Commissaries of the several states. These Chief Commissaries in turn directed the work of civilian and army purchasing agents, controlled depot management, and handled the requisitions of the army units.[2]

The Ordnance Department, on the other hand, was not "pyramided." Rather, the commanding officer of each depot and arsenal reported directly to the Chief of Ordnance, who maintained a sizable staff in Richmond to co-ordinate bureau affairs.[3] Gorgas's manufacturing system had reached maturity with the exception of the central laboratory at Macon, which was still under construction and waiting for machinery. Besides heavy casting and production done by contract with the Tredegar Works at Richmond, a huge powder plant had been set up at Augusta and cartridge-making arsenals established at Richmond, Augusta, Charleston, Macon, Fayetteville, Columbus, Atlanta, Selma, Danville, Lynchburg, Montgomery, and San Antonio.[4] Cannon foundries were established at Macon and Augusta; a foundry for shot and shell at Salisbury; small-arms manufacturing armories at Richmond, Macon, Fayetteville, and Asheville; pistol factories at Macon

2. Circular, Subsistence Department, April 15, 1863, *OR*-4, II, 290–295.

3. General Orders No. 13, Adjutant and Inspector General's Office, 1863 Series, Jan. 31, 1863, *ibid.*, pp. 379–380.

4. Vandiver, *Gorgas Diary,* pp. 90–91.

and Columbus; a leather shop at Clarksville, Virginia; and a number of depots.[5]

The Niter and Mining Bureau officials in Richmond received reports from plants such as the copper and lead smelting works at Petersburg and the sulphuric acid manufacturers at Charlotte,[6] but most of their time was spent in correlating reports from the officers administering the various districts and zones which had been created in order to produce a maximum output of raw materials. By mid-war St. John had divided the mineral-bearing areas of the Confederacy into three supervisory districts, fourteen niter districts, three mining districts, and three iron service districts.[7] The Niter and Mining Bureau was noteworthy for the small number of officers in Richmond and around the country who supervised the labor of over ten thousand Negroes and whites in remote locations and distributed their productions about the country with the proper priorities.

Although the Medical Service is not in the scope of this study, it is worth noting in passing that by 1863 Surgeon General Samuel P. Moore had assembled a tidy little industry of his own. Shops for manufacturing medicine were located in Lincolnton, Charlotte, Columbia, Macon, Atlanta, Mobile, and Montgomery; and alcohol was distilled at Salisbury, Columbia, Macon, and Wilcox County, Alabama.[8] Despite these shops, however, Surgeon General Moore reported that most of the medicine came in through the blockade and through the enemy lines.[9] In addition, medical officials were plagued by their dependence on the other bureaus, by run-ins with state governments, and by the perversity of human nature in the guise of defaulting contractors. The Surgeon General complained, for instance, that the Quartermaster's Department would not furnish enough cotton goods, fuel, and transportation.[10]

While detailed information concerning the personnel and structure of the Confederate supply bureaus is generally unavailable, there is enough information about the Quartermaster's Department to give an illustration in depth of wartime bureaucratic proliferation. The Quartermaster's Department was the largest supply bureau. It attempted to

5. *Ibid.*

6. RG 109, Entry 38, Niter and Mining Bureau Correspondence and Reports, Dec. 31, 1864.

7. *Ibid.*

8. Moore to Breckinridge, Feb. 9, 1865, *OR*-4, III, 1073–1076. The comprehensive study of the Medical Department is Horace H. Cunningham, *Doctors in Gray: The Confederate Medical Service* (Baton Rouge, 1958).

9. Moore to Breckinridge, Feb. 9, 1865, *OR*-4, III, 1073–1076.

10. *Ibid.*

discharge so many responsibilities that, in addition to its extensive network of paymasters and unit quartermasters in the field, the Quartermaster bureau organization comprised three separate staff systems. First, like the Subsistence Department, procurement was centralized under a chief quartermaster for each state, who reported to the Quartermaster General.[11] Second, like the Ordnance Department, individual manufacturing establishments reported directly to the Quartermaster General. Finally, a number of special organizations were supervised by a designated chief who reported to the Quartermaster General—the Tax-in-Kind Office, the Railroad Superintendent's Office, and the Inspector-General of Field Transportation's Office. In addition, as the war progressed, a number of quartermaster officials with special assignments began to accumulate in Richmond. These officers had such duties as supervising correspondence, directing pay and office accounts, "general duties," purchasing forage and fuel, settling claims for impressed property, directing the Richmond clothing depot, paying soldiers' and officers' accounts and travel claims, forwarding medical stores, supervising wagon transportation in and around the city, directing wagon and ambulance construction and the production of horseshoes and nails, supervising canal and river transportation, paying hospital accounts, and supervising state soldiers' relief associations.[12]

Outside Richmond a network of depot and post quartermasters reported directly to the main office in Richmond and sets of purchasing agents in each state reported to the chief Quartermaster for that state. The special organizations also spread officials across the land, coordinated by a hierarchy of districts and subdistricts. The total effect of this system was to blanket each state with overlapping layers of quartermasters.

Georgia represents an average sample of the bureaucratic network of the Quartermaster's Department. Depot and shop personnel under the direct control of the Quartermaster General's Office could be found in Augusta, Forsyth, Fort Gaines, Macon, Atlanta, Athens, Columbus, Calhoun, and Cuthbert.[13] The Superintendent of Railroad Transporta-

11. Circular, Quartermaster General's Office, March 24, 1863, *ibid.*, II, 453–456.

12. Myers to Seddon, Feb. 16, 1863, QMDSW, pp. 273–275; Lawton to Seddon, Dec. 9, 1863, *ibid.*, p. 394.

13. The information in this section is extracted from lists provided in RG 109, Vol. 228, Station Book of Quartermasters; RG 109, Vol. 230, Assignment Record of Quartermasters; unsigned report, Nov. 4, 1864, RG 109, Entry 45, Quartermaster's Department file of letters received.

tion had his headquarters in Augusta, and he directed transportation agents at Americus, Cassville, Columbus, Macon, and West Point. Tax-in-kind officers supervised depots in Augusta, Athens, Albany, Americus, Griffin, Macon, Marietta, and Thomson. Augusta was the headquarters of the Second Field Transportation District, with inspectors at Dublin, Augusta, and Savannah and also with the Army of Tennessee. More exotic positions in the field transportation system included the inspector of Negro transportation at Macon, supervisors of animal purchasing at Columbus, Macon, Augusta, and Americus, a horse-infirmary director at Oconee, and a wagon-shop director at Augusta. The quasi-official forage office was replaced by a grain purchaser for the Army of Northern Virginia at Augusta and a forage-depot supervisor for the Army of Northern Virginia at Albany. And so it went in every state.

With the rapid expansion of supply administration had come inefficiency and some corruption. The Subsistence and Quartermaster's bureaus in particular grew steadily in public disfavor. This is explained in part by the fact that these bureaus were the ones most frequently in contact with the civilians and in part by their administration of unpopular regulations such as impressment. The public was unfamiliar with the work of the supply bureaus and not appreciative of their unromantic but essential services to the army.

Part of the supply bureaus' unpopularity, however, lay in the indifferent quality of their men. Many of the supply minions were responsible and efficient men, of course, but others were inefficient or ignorant, disregarding regulations and executing their duties in an arbitrary and wasteful manner. Vouchers, reports, forms, accounts, bonds—all these traditional methods of control existed in the Confederate bureaus, but the supervisors and inspectors themselves were too inexperienced to instill discipline and efficiency in their subordinates. Some men were exceedingly cavalier in handling public money. In the spring of 1864, for example, over nine hundred quartermasters, some handling over $1,000,000 quarterly, had not turned in their accounts for the first two quarters of 1862.[14]

Beyond inefficiency, supply officials great and small were accused of corruption. Undoubtedly corrupt individuals did infest supply services. The opportunities to abuse public money and property abounded, and

14. Lawton to Taylor, correspondence series in QMDLS, IX: Feb. 4, 1864, 23–26; March 10, 1864, 80–88; March 25, 1864, 118–119; April 9, 1864, 156–158; April 28, 1864, 198–200.

some who began their careers as honest men undoubtedly ended up by indulging in speculation, extortion, collusion, and outright theft. By mid-war the Southern press kept up a constant barrage of accusations of incompetence and peculation intertwined with calls for investigation and reorganization. The Savannah *Daily News* demanded

> a searching inquiry into the acts of the Commissary and Quartermaster's Departments . . . to clear up or prove and punish the general suspicion in the public mind, that peculation and plunder, and misuse of authority for private purpose, have often been put before public duty and public service. . . .[15]

The *Daily Richmond Whig* spoke of "many leakages, countless inaccuracies, possibly a little corruption."[16] The Richmond *Enquirer* commented that "Quartermasters sometimes get rich—they ought never to get rich,"[17] and continued, "Unfaithful, incompetent, or dishonest quartermasters or commissaries could plunge the country into ruin. . . . Let the best men be cherished and honored. Unfit men must be discharged."[18] Later the *Enquirer* decided that discharge was too lenient for quartermasters accused of fraudulently filling in blank impressment forms signed by farmers: "We mean to insist on their being made to suffer the extreme penalty. They cheat both soldiers and farmers and the government and the public. Half a dozen of them hanged up in a row would be an edifying sight."[19] Nevertheless, little in the way of evidence of corruption turned up, investigations were rare, and no malfeasance was ever proved.[20]

Undoubtedly, the basic causes of inefficiency and corruption were the pell-mell pace of the expansion of the Confederate supply effort and the wholesale utilization of untrained men that this expansion demanded. Still, while inefficiency and corruption impeded matters, they were not crucial factors in Confederate supply failures. That sense of responsibility and public service necessary for efficient administration could have come only with time and training. Such a luxury was unavailable to the Confederacy's wildcat supply effort.

· · ·

15. Savannah *Daily News,* Aug. 1, 1863.
16. *Daily Richmond Whig,* June 24, 1863.
17. Richmond *Enquirer,* Aug. 21, 1863. 18. *Ibid.,* Oct. 7, 1862.
19. *Ibid.,* Feb. 11, 1863.
20. The only major investigation involving supply officers and the awarding of contracts, which concerned Major Ruffin and Haxall, Crenshaw, and Company, ended in complete vindication. See *Report of Committee on Quartermaster and Commissary Departments on Case of Major Frank G. Ruffin* (Richmond, 1863).

The independence of the Confederacy depended almost exclusively on the success of the armies east of the Mississippi, and this study has concentrated on the evolution of supply policy and administration in relation to this predominant effort. Military actions in the Trans-Mississippi and naval operations, never major aspects of the war, became less and less relevant to survival as the conflict progressed. These subordinate elements of the war effort have been dealt with extensively in other studies, and only a brief survey of supply arrangements in these areas will be given here.

Beginning with the fall of New Orleans early in 1862, the Trans-Mississippi had been gradually cut off from the main body of the Confederacy, a process virtually completed with the fall of Port Hudson and Vicksburg in mid-1863.[21] For most of its history it received only sporadic attention from the Union except for the abortive Red River campaign in the spring of 1864, and it received little more notice from Richmond administrators. There were only about forty thousand troops in the section, a small proportion of the Confederate army;[22] but even this small number of men had its supply problems, for the vast area west of the Mississippi had definite limitations in resources. With impressive potential for agricultural and industrial development, it had little for immediate use except an abundance of food. During the early stages of the war the Richmond bureaus had been anxious to secure wool, leather, and beef on the hoof from this section and had enjoyed a limited success for a time; but after 1863 little of consequence came east across the river. Even less crossed over the Mississippi heading west. Desperately in need of money and small arms, the commanders in the Trans-Mississippi received but a few dribbles of each.[23] Cut off in the Mississippi Valley and by blockade, the Confederates had to turn to the Mexican port of Matamoros, a few miles up the Rio Grande, for their source of supplies.

For the Confederate government two problems, both stemming from a shortage of funds, dominated the supply situation in the Trans-Mississippi. First, there was the problem of paying for supplies that were

21. A number of studies shed light on supply arrangements in the Trans-Mississippi. Among those of particular importance are Joseph H. Parks, *General Edmund Kirby Smith, C.S.A.* (Baton Rouge, 1954); James Nichols, *The Confederate Quartermaster in the Trans-Mississippi* (Austin, 1964); Florence Holladay, "The Powers of the Commander of the Confederate Trans-Mississippi Department, 1863–1865," *Southwest Historical Quarterly,* XXI, No. 3 (Jan. 1918), 279–298; No. 4 (April 1918), 333–359. Cited hereinafter as Holladay, "Trans-Mississippi."

22. Average of field returns given in *OR*-4, II, 615, 1073. *Ibid.,* III, 520, 989.

23. Magruder to Gorgas, May 30, 1863, *OR*-1, XXVI (2), 24–25.

being brought to Matamoros and offered for sale; second, there was the question of preventing private parties from taking all of the valuable cotton out through neutral Matamoros, as Confederate law allowed. The cotton planters of Texas were busily shipping out their cotton through Matamoros to sell at high prices in Europe, and they were not interested in selling their cotton at a lower price to the Confederate government on credit or for Treasury notes. In 1862 General John B. Magruder, the commander of the Texas District, decided that his troops must be supplied, law or no law. Wielding his trumps, military force and control of wagon transportation between the cotton lands of northeast Texas and the Rio Grande, he installed a permit system which allowed planters to ship out cotton only if they invested a part of the proceeds in military goods that the planters would sell to the Confederate government on credit.[24] These regulations violated the Confederate intercourse acts, and the outraged cries of planters and politicians eventually reached all the way to Richmond, with the result that Seddon ordered Magruder to revoke his regulations.[25] Immediately a great cotton exodus began in the spring of 1863, and Major Simeon Hart, the quartermaster agent in Texas charged with buying goods for the general Confederacy from the Matamoros trade, found that he could get no cotton on credit in order to buy the goods that were piling up in that city.[26] He asked Myers for the authority to impress, Myers asked Seddon, and Seddon asked Davis, who vetoed the idea in July 1863 except as a last resort.[27] In the meantime, events were taking a radical turn in the Trans-Mississippi.

In February 1863 Edmund Kirby Smith was ordered to duty as the commanding general of the Trans-Mississippi, now shrunk to the size of Texas, southeastern Indian territory, southwestern Arkansas, and northeastern Louisiana.[28] Independent of Richmond in all practical aspects, and fortified with Davis's approval for independent action,[29] Kirby Smith began to organize the department for self-sufficient operations and in so doing flouted the government's trade policy. He created the supply bureaus for his department from his personal staff, and the

24. Magruder to Cooper, March 31, 1863, *ibid.*, XV, 1030–1032.

25. Campbell to Hitchcock, Feb. 14, 1863, *OR*-4, II, 399–400; Smith to Cooper, June 8, 1863, *OR*-1, XXVI (2), 62; Younger, *Kean Diary,* pp. 59–60.

26. Myers to Seddon, July 15, 1863, QMDSW, pp. 368–369.

27. *Ibid.;* Jones, *War Clerk's Diary,* II, 53.

28. Cooper to Kirby Smith, Feb. 9, 1863, *OR*-1, XV, 972.

29. Davis to Kirby Smith, July 14, 1863, Rowland, *Jefferson Davis,* V, 552–553.

supply officials were made responsible to him rather than to the supply chiefs in Richmond.[30] Supply bureau headquarters were located with Army Headquarters at Shreveport, Louisiana, with the exception of the Ordnance bureau at Marshall, Texas.[31] The Trans-Mississippi Subsistence bureau divided the military department into four procurement districts but concentrated the supply depots in northeastern Texas at Bonham, Paris, Marshall, and Dallas, where supplies could move in any direction to support forces in action in the Indian Territory, Louisiana, Arkansas, or the Texas coast.[32] The Quartermaster's bureau controlled the clothing production of the Texas State Penitentiary and set up clothing and shoe shops and depots at Houston, Austin, Tyler, San Antonio, Jefferson, and Huntsville, all in Texas, and at Shreveport, Louisiana, and Washington, Arkansas; the chief tax-in-kind depot was at Marshall, Texas.[33] The Niter and Mining Bureau began working Arkansas and Texas nitrate deposits, and powder and cartridges were produced at San Antonio and Tyler.[34] By 1864 Kirby Smith had succeeded in adequately feeding and clothing his small army. Independence of the Trans-Mississippi was confirmed by Congress when it enacted legislation setting up in that area independent branches of the subordinate bureaus of the War and Treasury departments.[35]

Kirby Smith needed forty thousand small arms to complete his military preparations, and he moved to get them by way of Matamoros.[36] He sent an agent to Europe to begin rounding up the guns on contracts payable in England in cotton sales proceeds.[37] To pay off current debts and to secure the goods already in Matamoros, he ordered his commanders to impress cotton to the extent they deemed

30. General Orders No. 31, Trans-Mississippi Department, 1863 Series, July 25, 1863, *OR*-1, XXVI (2), 579; General Orders No. 19, Trans-Mississippi Department, 1863 Series, June 15, 1863, *ibid.*

31. Holladay, "Trans-Mississippi," p. 334. 32. *Ibid.*, p. 335.

33. *Ibid.;* for a special survey of activities of the Clothing and Equipage Bureau, see Wharton to Turner, Oct. 12, 1863, *OR*-1, XXVI (2), 305–308.

34. Vandiver, *Confederate Ordnance*, pp. 140–192.

35. "An Act to Authorize the Appointment of an Agent of the Treasury Department West of the Mississippi," Jan. 27, 1864, *Statutes*, II, 176; "'An Act to Authorize the Organization of an Auxiliary Bureau of the War Department, West of the Mississippi River," Feb. 17, 1864, *ibid.*, pp. 202–203; "An Act to Be Entitled, 'An Act to Establish and Organize Two Bureaus in Connection with the Agency of the Treasury, for the Trans-Mississippi Department, One of Which Is to Be Known as the Bureau of the Auditor and the Other as the Bureau of the Comptroller for the Trans-Mississippi Department,' " Feb. 17, 1864, *ibid.*, pp. 230–231.

36. Magruder to Gorgas, May 30, 1863, *OR*-1 XXVI (2), 24–25.

37. Magruder to Stanard, Oct. 14, 1863, *ibid.*, pp. 321–322.

necessary.[38] To secure a future supply of cotton to sell in Europe, he created the Cotton Bureau, which imposed a new and stringent set of regulations in defiance of the Confederate laws. Planters were obliged to sell one-half of their crop to the government and to accept in return cotton certificates pledging specie payment when specie was available, or payment in some medium that Congress might later authorize. In return, the planters were allowed to export the other half of their crops free from government impressment, and the government would provide transportation. If a planter refused, all of his cotton was liable to impressment.[39]

Planters resisted the Cotton Bureau, however, justifying resistance on the grounds that it had no sanction in law,[40] and the state of Texas undercut the Bureau by making arrangements with planters to ship out their cotton under state protection.[41] Kirby Smith appealed to Governor Murrah in early 1864, and the governor co-operated by issuing a proclamation urging the farmers to support the government by selling their cotton to it.[42] Shortly thereafter Texas withdrew from competition.[43] Seddon ordered Kirby Smith to follow the new regulations for overland commerce with Mexico drawn up subsequent to the passage of a new intercourse act of February 17, 1864, but Kirby Smith ignored them as being impractical.[44] With the arrival of representatives of the Treasury Department, the Cotton Bureau was disbanded, and the Treasury took over the purchase of cotton, in conformity with policies then current in the East.[45]

In spite of Kirby Smith's stringent efforts to obtain supplies, inadequate amounts came in. He allowed a limited amount of trading cotton through the lines along the Mississippi River to supplement supply importations from abroad, but he abandoned this policy under pressure from local officials.[46] As small as his army was and as ill-

38. Kirby Smith to Magruder, June 27, 1863, *ibid.*, pp. 94–96.

39. "Announcement of Cotton Bureau to Cotton Planters of Texas," Dec. 4, 1863, *ibid.*, XXVI, 480–482.

40. Kirby Smith to Davis, May 12, 1864, *ibid.*, XXXIV (3), 821–822.

41. Kirby Smith to Murrah, April 5, 1864, *ibid.*, p. 734.

42. *Ibid.*

43. Holladay, "Trans-Mississippi," p. 350. For a discussion of Trans-Mississippi cotton policy emphasizing different points from those of this study, cf. Holladay, "Trans-Mississippi," pp. 348–352.

44. "Regulations to Carry into Effect the Foreign Intercourse Act—Overland Commerce with Mexico," March 11, 1864, *OR*-4, III, 206–207; Kirby Smith to Murrah, Aug. 25, 1864, *OR*-1, XLI (2), 1082–1083.

45. Holladay, "Trans-Mississippi," p. 352.

46. Kirby Smith's endorsement on Stevenson to Broadwell, Aug. 24, 1863,

armed and poorly provided with field transportation as he claimed it to be, he was able to repulse the main Union effort against him, the advance up the Red River on Shreveport. In the last months of the war his little, underequipped army stood by until the collapse in the east allowed honorable capitulation.

. . .

The early activities of the navy had included contracting for heavy plate production with the Etowah and Tredegar ironworks, undertaking ship construction at Norfolk and New Orleans, constructing shops for naval ordnance and machinery at these spots, and opening a powder factory at Petersburg.[47] The disasters of the spring of 1862, with the losses of New Orleans and Norfolk, crushed any hopes for effective domestic ship construction and also forced the rearrangement of the manufacturing system. Between the spring of 1862 and the fall of 1863 the navy worked steadily on new arrangements and created a new industrial complex.

The Navy Department relied on the Niter and Mining Bureau to supply niter, metals, and coal, and usually found these materials supplied in satisfactory amounts until the fall of Chattanooga strained coal and copper production.[48] Henceforth, Alabama coal supplied the Mobile, Columbus, and Savannah stations, coal from the Egypt mine in North Carolina serviced the ships at Wilmington and Charleston, and the Virginia mines supplied Richmond and Charlotte shops.[49] Iron was a constant problem. Iron contractors defaulted, and even the efficient Niter and Mining Bureau was unable to supply enough iron to the navy.[50] To secure iron, the department was forced to tear up branch

---

Edmund Kirby-Smith Papers, Southern Historical Collection, University of North Carolina; Smith to Taylor, Jan. 15, 1865, Letter Book, *ibid.;* McHenry to Davis, Jan. 5, 1865, *OR*-1, XLVIII (1), 1316.

47. Report of the Secretary of the Navy, Feb. 27, 1862, *ORN*-2, II, 149–157; the information in this section is based on the *Official Records.* The standard references for histories of the Confederate Navy, which give little additional information on naval supplies, are: J. Thomas Scharf, *History of the Confederate States Navy: From Its Organization to the Surrender of Its Last Vessel* (New York, 1887); Joseph T. Durkin, *Stephen R. Mallory: Confederate Navy Chief* (Chapel Hill, 1954); James D. Bulloch, *The Secret Service of the Confederate States in Europe; or, How the Confederate Cruisers Were Equipped* (New York and London, 1959).

48. Report of the Secretary of the Navy, Nov. 30, 1863, *ORN*-2, II, 534.

49. Mitchell to Mallory, Nov. 6, 1863, *ibid.*, p. 544.

50. Report of the Secretary of the Navy, April 16, 1862, *ibid.*, p. 246.

railroad lines such as the one to Brunswick, Georgia, to ease the situation.[51]

Industrial production for the navy was divided between private contracts and government shops. The Etowah and Tredegar works supplied plates, cannon, shot and shell, rolled iron, and other heavy castings in more than adequate supply. The Navy set up its own plants at Charlotte, Selma, and Richmond to cast heavy guns and to manufacture carriages, engines, and machine parts.[52] The Charleston plant made projectiles.[53] The Charlotte plant contained a steam hammer for heavy forging.[54] An excellent powder mill at Columbia furnished all of the powder needed, and a rope works at Petersburg manufactured a tar-treated cotton rope in lieu of hemp.[55]

To supply the resident naval force of between five thousand and six thousand men, the Navy Department worked to stockpile food and clothing. By 1864 from four to eight months' supply of all the chief commodities had been secured at all of the posts, and large accumulations were salted away in the main depots at Charlotte, Montgomery, Charleston, and Augusta.[56] Supply officials at Augusta and Albany directed meat packing.[57] So successful was the department in building up a surplus that it used the food for barter.[58] For clothing, the supply officials bought in the open market and participated in auctions of blockade goods, but eventually the Navy Department turned to contracts with the Graniteville mill in South Carolina, contracting to take one-tenth of that mill's output.[59] Navy clothing shops were set up at Richmond, Savannah, and Mobile.[60] These shops also made shoes, but woolens, blankets, and shoes continued in short supply and had to be sought abroad. Near the end of the war the industrial production of the navy was stifled by the lack of skilled workmen. As early as 1862 Secretary Mallory told his agents in Europe to search out skilled men who would migrate to the Confederacy for good wages, but few came

51. Miner to Mallory, Nov. 24, 1862, *ORN*-1, XIII, 816–817.

52. Brooke to Mallory, Nov. 25, 1863, *ORN*-2, II, 547–552.

53. *Ibid.*

54. Williamson to Mallory, Aug. 15, 1862, *ibid.*, pp. 240–241.

55. Brooke to Mallory, Nov. 25, 1863, *ibid.*, p. 549; Mitchell to Mallory, Nov. 6, 1863, *ibid.*, pp. 544–545.

56. De Bree to Mallory, November 14, 1863, *ibid.*, pp. 552–557; Semple to Mallory, Oct. 18, 1864, *ibid.*, pp. 762–763.

57. *Ibid.*

58. De Bree to Mallory, Nov. 14, 1863, *ibid.*, pp. 552–557.

59. Lawton to Mallory, Sept. 3, 1864, QMDLS, XX, 163.

60. De Bree to Mallory, Nov. 14, 1863, *ORN*-2, II, 552–557.

over.[61] Near the end of the war naval ordnance production was paralyzed by the lack of two hundred skilled workmen.[62]

Deficiencies in textiles, shoes, iron, machinery, and engines fostered a diligent search on the part of the navy for a means to procure European goods. Agents on ship-building missions in Europe were ordered to find and purchase shipping space for desperately needed machinery, plates, and woolens.[63] Mallory took a one-quarter interest in the Crenshaw shipbuilding scheme[64] and also shipped out on private vessels 3,100 bales of cotton in 1863.[65] The department also bought its own steamer, the *Coquette,* to run in the needed goods and to take the cotton payments out.[66]

Near the end of the war the navy became increasingly subordinated to the army in the field of domestic procurement. Already dependent on the Niter and Mining Bureau for minerals and iron, the navy agreed to retire from the food markets, having already provided for itself a sizable reserve, and to allow the Subsistence Department to supply rations. To make the reserves last longer, the ration was reduced, although the navy ration continued to be larger than the army one.[67] The Navy Department also gave up its cotton textile contracts in return for the pledge of the Quartermaster's Department that all reasonable demands for clothing would be satisfied.[68]

The navy's position in the war effort was a strange one. In theory it had had an opportunity for great service; it might have saved the Confederacy by keeping the sea lanes open for the unrestricted importation of supplies. The Confederacy had been unable to build up a fleet from nothing, however, and the navy's efforts became increasingly irrelevant to the war effort. In the autumn of 1864, for example, army commanders insisted that Confederate cruisers which had taken refuge in Wilmington be sent away because their presence had brought a large portion of the Union fleet to the mouth of the Cape Fear, interfering

61. Mallory to Bulloch, Oct. 8, 1862, *ibid.,* p. 280; Mallory to Bulloch, April 11, 1864, *ibid.,* pp. 623–624.

62. Mallory to Davis, July 1, 1864, *OR*-4, III, 520–521 and enclosures, 521–523.

63. Mallory to Bulloch, Feb. 22, 1863, *ORN*-2, II, 368.

64. Mallory to Crenshaw, Feb. 22, 1863, *ibid.,* p. 369.

65. Mallory to Bulloch, Dec. 29, 1862, *ibid.,* p. 568.

66. Bulloch to Mallory, Oct. 22, 1863, *ibid.,* p. 511.

67. De Bree to Mallory, April 28, 1864, *ibid.,* p. 643; Semple to Mallory, Nov. 5, 1864, *ibid.,* pp. 762–763.

68. Lawton to Cunningham, Sept. 29, 1864, QMDLS, XX, 160; Lawton to Mallory, Sept. 3, 1864, *ibid.,* p. 53.

with blockade runners trying to enter with precious supplies for the army.[69] At the very end the navy appeared to be getting in the way.

. . .

In 1863 the various bureaus, despite reorganization and expansion, began to feel the mounting pressures of unavoidable shortages and military reverses. In addition, the bureaus were becoming frustrated with the inadequate general supply policies of their superiors. To begin with, the wastage of war began to put considerable strain on the Ordnance Department. The surrender of Vicksburg and Port Hudson and the defeats at Gettysburg and Lookout Mountain–Missionary Ridge had cost the Confederacy 75,000 small arms, large amounts of field artillery, and huge quantities of ammunition.[70] The Ducktown copper mines had been lost, and a number of iron mines, iron forges, and niter caves as well.[71] Still, Gorgas reported in the autumn of 1863 that he had been able, partly through successful importations, to make up the losses in small arms and artillery and to continue an adequate supply of ammunition.[72] Small-arms production had risen modestly to a total of 3,500 monthly from government and contracting shops.[73] Since September 1862, 113 pieces of field and coastal artillery had been manufactured and 239 purchased, with the result, according to Gorgas, "that the army is now adequately supplied on this side of the Mississippi with artillery quite equal to that possessed by the enemy."[74]

Hampered by lead and copper shortages, the Ordnance Department found that its main problem continued to be the production of cartridges. Efficient home production of niter and continuous success in importing had produced an adequate raw material base for the Augusta mills to turn out a plentiful quantity of powder, but there remained the problem of mining and importing lead to meet the voracious annual consumption of 36,000,000 rounds of small-arms cartridges and 300,000 rounds of field ammunition.[75] The bureau struggled to maintain an issue of 40 rounds of ammunition for each man in the field and 100 rounds per man in reserve, but Gorgas, in order to reduce the wastage, was forced to order a modification in which only 3 cartridges instead of 40 would be issued to men not in the face of the enemy.[76]

69. The involved correspondence on this matter can be found in *OR*-1, XLII (2), (3). 70. Vandiver, *Confederate Ordnance,* p. 196.
71. St. John to Seddon, [Oct. 1, 1864], *OR*-4, III, 695–697.
72. Gorgas to Seddon, Nov. 15, 1863, *ibid.,* II, 955–959. 73. *Ibid.*
74. *Ibid.* 75. *Ibid.* 76. Vandiver, *Confederate Ordnance,* p. 197.

A new development, this time at sea, severely unsettled the Ordnance Department. In July 1863 the Union navy invested Charleston and prevented further importations through that port. The cutoff of importations alone would have been a severe blow to Confederate supply operations, for Charleston ranked second only to Wilmington in importations, but there were other problems as well. The defense of the now-useless port consumed an enormous amount of cannon powder and pressed the resources of Gorgas's bureau to the utmost, at the same time monopolizing coastal railroads in the face of competing demands for the shipment of quartermaster and subsistence stores to Virginia and of export cotton to Wilmington.[77] The most grievous result of the siege of Charleston concerned nearby Wilmington. The Charleston blockading squadron moved northward to reinforce the Wilmington squadron at the mouth of the Cape Fear River, and the augmented patrolling force captured so many Confederate blockade runners that the operations of the supply bureaus were badly damaged. Until August the four Ordnance steamers, later increased to five, had been running saucily in and out of Wilmington without mishap, having completed twenty-two round trips since January.[78] The fleet brought in small arms at the rate of ten thousand a month, plus tons of saltpeter, lead, ordnance stores, and medicine. Then in quick succession Union ships captured or destroyed three of the Ordnance steamers, and the efficient Ordnance Department importation service was wrecked.[79] Gorgas, momentarily staggered when the losses of the Tennessee mines and his steamers hit him at the same time, is reported to have declared that bureau saltpeter supplies would not last beyond January 1, 1864.[80] However, the Ordnance Department was fortunate that the interruption came as the campaigning was drawing to a close. During the winter of 1863–64 the bureau labored to secure resources from home and abroad to supply the arms for the next campaigning season.

• • •

The Quartermaster's Department had faced the 1863 campaign in its best condition since the opening of the war. The bureau had outfitted the armies with necessary quartermaster goods and officials looked to the future with confidence. The new staff-line reorganization had

77. Gorgas to Seddon, Nov. 15, 1863, *OR*-4, II, 957.

78. Vandiver, *Gorgas Diary,* p. 57; Bayne to Benjamin, Aug. 29, 1863, *ORN*-2, III, 882.

79. Lawton to Waller, Dec. 17, 1863, QMDLS, XVIII, 442.

80. Jones, *War Clerk's Diary,* II, 94.

promised to reduce competition for quartermaster supplies. The gathering and processing of raw materials needed by the bureau had been regulated to the degree requisite to ensure adequate quantities. As with the other bureaus, however, there were shortages and problems that could not be controlled by the quartermaster officials, no matter how efficient or perceptive such officials might be. Draft animals were being used up faster than natural increase could replenish them, and fodder distribution faced the same vagaries in weather and railroad transportation that tormented the Subsistence Department. Wool and leather needs could be met only by importation, and satisfactory arrangements had finally been instituted, although importations still meant dependence on luck. The bureau was apparently supplying the armies with little complaint, except for its failure to equip Johnston's new army in Mississippi, a failure to be discussed later. In sum, the Quartermaster's Department appears to have been as well organized and as efficient as circumstances would allow.

In light of these considerations, it came as a shock to both government officials and the general public when Davis dismissed Myers from his post as Quartermaster General. Kean noted in his diary on August 9, 1863: "The event which has put the gossips agog in the last two days is the taking off of the Quartermaster General's head."[81] Gorgas, in his diary, commented: "[Myers] has fulfilled his duties very well. . . . [The President] has, I fear, little appreciation of services rendered, unless the party enjoys his good opinion."[82] This action of the President and public reaction to it, especially the reaction in Congress, was a famous political altercation in Confederate history, and some recapitulation is necessary. There is no concrete evidence of Davis's reasons, but some averred that it stemmed from old U. S. army feuds.[83] Others said that early in 1862 the former Assistant Secretary of War, A. T. Bledsoe, had told Mrs. Davis that Mrs. Myers had called her a squaw.[84] Ironically enough, Congress, in its efforts to reward Myers for what it considered good management of quartermaster affairs, provided the weapon the President subsequently seized upon to "behead" him.[85] Congress had passed the following act on March 20, 1863:

81. Younger, *Kean Diary,* p. 89. 82. Vandiver, *Gorgas Diary,* p. 58.

83. *Daily Richmond Examiner,* Aug. 17, 1863. See also "Orient" article in *ibid.,* Sept. 1, 1863.

84. Younger, *Kean Diary,* p. 90; Wigfall to Clay, Aug. 13, 1863, Clement Claiborne Clay Papers, Duke University Manuscript Department.

85. Favorable comments on Myers may be found in *Debates,* XLVI, 232–234.

The Congress of the Confederate States of America do enact, That from and after the passage of this act, the rank, pay and allowances attached to the office of Quartermaster General of the army of the Confederate States, shall be those of a Brigadier General in the provisional army.[86]

Davis knew that it was the intention of Congress to promote Myers, who enjoyed powerful Congressional support, to brigadier general, but the President had no intentions of having Congress promote anybody. He reasoned that the law could be interpreted to mean that an existing brigadier general could be appointed or "assigned to duty" as Quartermaster General. Consequently, the President began to look around. In May he had Seddon approach Howell Cobb, a brigadier, but Cobb refused on the grounds that he was not qualified to take charge of "so important a bureau in the midst of the war when its business is heaviest and most complicated."[87] All through June it was common knowledge that the President was hunting for a man to replace Myers despite the warnings from Congressmen and Senators who got wind of the matter.[88] Finally, the President spotted his man: Alexander R. Lawton, a former brigade commander under Lee, then convalescing from a wound received at Antietam and without a command. On August 7, 1863, by Special Orders No. 187, Lawton was "assigned to duty as Quartermaster-General," and Myers was given an extended leave of absence after staying on a few days to explain arrangements to Lawton.[89]

The dismissal of Myers is difficult to evaluate. By Confederate standards his bureau was well run, and his contemporaries praised him. On all major policy innovations Myers had been at or near the forefront, except for railroad regulation, where he shared the conservative

86. "An Act to Amend 'An Act for the Establishment and Organization of a General Staff for the Army of the Confederate States,'" March 20, 1863, *Statutes,* II, 99.

87. As Seddon put it to Cobb: "A Quarter Master of high capacity, energy and administrative mind would be of invaluable service to the government, and this may be said without any disparagement of Col. Myers, who is a very good Bureau officer and a very pleasant official to deal with. With you however . . . I should have a far fuller assurance of efficiency and success." Seddon to Cobb, May 5, 1863, R. P. Brooks, ed., "Howell Cobb Papers," *Georgia Historical Quarterly,* VI, No. 4 (Dec. 1922), 366. See also Cobb to Seddon, Ulrich Bonnell Phillips, ed., *The Correspondence of Robert Toombs, Alexander H. Stephens, and Howell Cobb* (Vol. II of the *Annual Report of the American Historical Association* for 1911; Washington, D. C.: 1913), p. 616. 88. Jones, *War Clerk's Diary,* I, 79.

89. *OR*-4, II, 697; Younger, *Kean Diary,* p. 136.

outlook of the President. His removal may have been caused by personality clashes with Davis, Seddon, or some field commanders; to some degree he was the victim of Executive-Legislative feuding.

Hardly had Lawton taken office as the new Quartermaster General when the fortunes of war presented him with a major problem. The bureau had already been faced with the problem that the demands of summer campaigning had exhausted its reserves, and that the armies were running out of shoes, blankets, and footwear with months of autumn campaigning still to come.[90] No one in the bureau was particularly alarmed, however, because arrangements for the importation of shoes and winter clothing from abroad had been in progress since the spring.[91] Major J. B. Ferguson, the Quartermaster agent abroad, had contracted for the delivery of goods at English ports, and Lawton's predecessor had struggled to get the necessary funds remitted to close the deals in England and ship the goods.[92] The first two steamers built on the Collie contract had loaded up almost exclusively with quartermaster goods and were on their way over the Atlantic. The Quartermaster's Department had rented two or three more private vessels for shipments, and large amounts of quartermaster stores deposited at Nassau and Bermuda by private parties were available to the bureau if supplies from the continent proved inadequate.[93]

The Union navy smashed all these plans. In September and October the Collie steamers, the *Hebe* and the *Venus,* freighted with winter clothing and shoes, were lost off Wilmington, the latter steamer containing most of the supplies from Nassau.[94] In a wink the bureau found itself without any prospects that supplies would be arriving from abroad for months to come. Lawton immediately put every effort into accumulating winter supplies, but he quickly ran into an insuperable obstacle, inability to transmit funds to pay for new supplies. Under the complex system of financing overseas purchases then in vogue, the Quartermaster's Department took a part of its funds to buy cotton and sent the cotton to Europe or to the islands to pay for supplies. Lawton found that this plan was blocked at the very beginning, for the Treasury Department would not provide the currency with which to buy the

90. Lawton to Lee, Oct. 12, 1863, *OR*-1, XXIX (2), 784–785.

91. Myers to Waller, May 14, 1863, QMDLS, XVII, 382–383.

92. Myers to Seddon, June 21, 1863, *OR*-4, II, 599; Myers to Seddon, July 29, 1863, *ibid.,* p. 683.

93. Lawton to Waller, Sept. 28, 1863, *ibid.,* pp. 828–829; Lawton to Waller, Oct. 23, 1863, *ibid.,* pp. 895–896.

94. Lawton to Waller, Oct. 23, 1863, *ibid.,* pp. 895–896.

cotton. Expenses of the War Department were running twenty to thirty million dollars ahead of the currency that the Treasury Department could legally furnish for the use of the various bureaus. Some War Department requisitions had to go unfilled, and the requisitions of the Quartermaster's Department were the ones usually ignored because other bureaus marked their requests "special."[95] Myers had struggled against this trend, but by August Quartermaster requisitions totaling over $47,000,000 lay unfilled in the Treasury Department.[96] In addition, Lawton had to fight to keep his bureau from being downgraded when the Secretary of War divided the proceeds of the Erlanger loan.[97]

Trying to get something for the troops before winter arrived, Lawton immediately battered away at his money problems. He wrote frequently to the War Department agents on the islands, telling them to contract for whatever supplies they could, as "the depots are bare," and promising that he would eventually get cotton out to them. He obtained, so he thought, Seddon's permission to have the agents ship quartermaster stores in preference to all else until the emergency was over,[98] but Seddon at the same time instructed the same agents privately that top priority should go to provisions, niter, and lead.[99] Dissatisfied with the proportion of money from the Erlanger loan which Seddon had determined would be spent on quartermaster supplies, Lawton tried to by-pass Seddon. He wrote to Major Ferguson asking Ferguson to persuade Colin McRae, the financial agent, to give the Quartermaster's bureau special priority in allotting payments for contracts being immediately paid off.[100] He also wrote directly to McRae:

> [Major Ferguson] cannot, I assure you, present the necessities of this department in too strong a light. I have but recently assumed the control of affairs, and the condition in which I find our supplies is the occasion of great anxiety. The depots are quite bare; the domestic resources, in many particulars limited at best, nearly exhausted, and a season of the year is rapidly approaching which renders indispensable many articles of clothing, such as shoes, blankets, and overcoats, which it is impossible to provide here. . . . I do not mean to disparage the wants of other branches of the service, but I feel a strong conviction that at this particular

95. Lawton to Seddon, Aug. 26, 1863, *ibid.*, p. 755. 96. *Ibid.* 97. *Ibid.*
98. Lawton to Heyliger, Oct. 23, 1863, *ibid.*, pp. 896–897.
99. Seddon to Heyliger, Oct. 17, 1863, *ibid.*, p. 877.
100. Lawton to Ferguson, Oct. 23, 1863, *ibid.*, p. 895.

juncture, in view of the great scarcity of the supplies referred to and the near approach of winter, some demands made by them might be postponed for a brief season to provide for the urgent necessities of this department.[101]

In other actions Lawton sent inspectors to the bureau clothing shops to check on production; he ended the selling of cloth to officers until the men were supplied, not scrupling to deny even such notables as General Hardee, at that time commander of the Army of Tennessee.[102] In addition, he opened a new shoe factory at Montgomery. Despite previous failures with private contracts, Lawton entered into a large contract with James L. Tait of Richmond, a contract approved by the Secretary of War, for the importation in three months from January 1, 1864, of 50,000 units each of overcoats, suits, and flannel shirts and a 100,000 units of blankets, pairs of shoes, and pairs of socks at a fixed price per unit plus 5 per cent commission.[103]

All of Lawton's acts, while displaying administrative energy, did not produce clothes for the troops, and Lawton had to face the complaints of the field commanders, now steadily rising in volume. Fortunately for him, the steamer *Dee* arrived in early October with a complete load of quartermaster stores. Shoes, blankets, and flannel shirts from the vessel were rushed up to the Army of Northern Virginia and out to the West.[104] For weeks after the *Dee* arrived, however, very little came in, and Beauregard, Johnston, and Bragg continually pressed Lawton with reports of cold and shoeless men.[105] It was Lee, however, who complained most often about the condition of his men during October and November.[106] Lawton sent Lee, in addition to most of the *Dee*'s cargo, 16,000 pairs of shoes, the entire output of the government shops, 15,000 overcoats, the last batch, and 6,500 blankets.[107]

In November and December after Lee's men had gone into winter quarters, a series of successful blockade runners deposited considerable

101. Lawton to McRae, Oct. 13, 1863, *ibid.*, p. 872.

102. Lawton to Hardee, Dec. 18, 1863, QMDLS, XVIII, 441.

103. Cross to Dillard, Dec. 26, 1863, *ibid.*, p. 469; Lawton to Tait, Dec. 19, 1863, *ibid.*, pp. 447–448.

104. Lawton to Lee, Oct. 12, 1863, *OR*-1, XXIX (2), 784–785.

105. Johnston to Lawton, Sept. 22, 1863, *ibid.*, XXX (4), 686; Seddon to Beauregard, Nov. 16, 1863, WDLS, XIV, 190.

106. Lee to Seddon, Oct. 23, 1863, *OR*-1, XXIX (2), 800; Lee to Seddon, Nov. 10, 1863, *ibid.*, p. 830.

107. Lawton to Lee, Oct. 12, 1863, *ibid.*, pp. 784–785; Lawton to Lee, Oct. 16, 1863, QMDLS, XVIII, 222; Lawton to Lee, Oct. 27, 1863, *ibid.*, p. 264.

amounts of quartermaster stores on the Wilmington docks, and the bureau began methodically to fulfil the demands of the various armies. The Quartermaster's Department rushed some sixty bales of blankets from three blockade runners to Atlanta and distributed them to the Army of Tennessee and to Longstreet's command in the northeast tip of Tennessee and thus satisfied their wants for the winter.[108] Shoes went up by the thousands from government shops and the Wilmington docks to the Army of Northern Virginia.[109] However, any hopes that the bureau might have had of building up a supply reserve faded during mid-winter when Union blockaders off Wilmington captured or destroyed two more ships loaded with quartermaster stores and three others with mixed orders.[110] In February 1864 Lawton ruefully estimated that blockade-running losses off Wilmington alone during the fall and winter amounted to 100,000 pairs of shoes and 100,000 blankets.[111] When the Union navy lifted the siege of Charleston and reduced the blockading squadron off Wilmington, supplies again appeared with regularity at both Wilmington and Charleston. By the spring it appeared that once more the bureau was meeting regularly all of the requisitions for supplies, but at an undoubted cost of confidence on the part of the field commanders.

The vagaries of importation during 1863 spurred Lawton to tighten his controls over the domestic resources and in particular over textile manufacturing. Myers had made a patchwork of agreements with private textile concerns outside the state of North Carolina, agreements usually specifying a certain fixed amount of cotton cloth per month or a certain proportion of the factory's monthly output, at varying rates, ranging from about 50 per cent profit over cost of production in Georgia to 75 per cent profit for Virginia firms.[112] Beginning in early 1864, Lawton moved to construct a more uniform and more rigorous system, using as a lever government controls over raw materials, transportation, and manpower.[113] Starting with the Georgia firms and then putting pressure on the Virginia firms, Lawton negotiated new contracts in which he agreed to exempt operatives in the plants and to sell raw materials to the factories.[114] In return, the

108. Lawton to Lee, Jan. 20, 1864, QMDLS, XVIII, 554–555.
109. *Ibid.;* Lawton to Cone, Jan. 26, 1864, *ibid.,* p. 573.
110. Lawton to Lee, Jan. 20, 1864, *ibid.,* pp. 554–555.
111. Lawton to Johnston, Feb. 9, 1864, QMDLS, XIX, 15.
112. Lawton to Ferguson, Sept. 12, 1864, *ibid.,* XX, 96.
113. Lawton to Miller, Sept. 28, 1864, *ibid.,* p. 158.
114. Lawton to Ferguson, Sept. 12, 1864, *ibid.,* p. 96.

Quartermaster's Department usually took two-thirds of the factory's production, allowing a profit of 33⅓ per cent.[115] Lawton was careful to check on rigged figures for the "cost of production" base for determining profit.[116] For example, with one firm he contracted to sell cotton at $1 per pound in return for two-thirds of the shirting and sheeting output at $1.75 per yard, all tent cloth at $2.25 and half of the cotton yarn at $20 per bunch, representing a profit of 33⅓ per cent.[117] Major Cunningham at Atlanta was given control of textile manufacturing arrangements from South Carolina to Mississippi, while Lawton supervised the Virginia factories.[118] In another important move Lawton determined to end the agreement with North Carolina in which that state had agreed to furnish her own men with clothing and the Confederate government had agreed not to contract for textiles in the state.[119] Lawton was not willing to continue to exempt forty factories from service to the Confederate government, and he began to press, through control of details, to have the North Carolina factories shift from state contracts to Confederate contracts, much to the dismay of Governor Vance, who protested vigorously.[120] Lawton persisted, however, although in the case of North Carolina factories he was willing to contract for only one-third in categories where he usually demanded two-thirds of the production.[121] At the same time Lawton vigorously upbraided that state for having built up large reserves and sometimes allowing clothing to wait in depots for over a year while refusing to share with others or to allow the Confederate government to buy at cost.[122] The struggle between the state and the Quartermaster's Department for the control of North Carolina textiles was still going on when the war ended. Lawton did not always attempt to monopolize production. For example, he withdrew from Florida's only operative cotton mill so that the state might use the mill for aid to soldiers' families.[123] While all these measures assured the Quartermaster's bureau of enough cotton fabrics, the critical shortage of woolen materials continued as before.

Meanwhile, Lawton experienced the same difficulties in achieving

115. Lawton to Cunningham, April 23, 1864, *ibid.*, XIX, 186. 116. *Ibid.*

117. Lawton to McDonald and Sons, Sept. 21, 1864, *ibid.*, XX, 139.

118. Lawton to Cunningham, April 23, 1864, *ibid.*, XIX, 186.

119. Lawton to Chisman, Aug. 24, 1864, *ibid.*, p. 385; Lawton to Miller, Sept. 2, 1864, *ibid.*, XX, 48. 120. Vance to Seddon, Sept. 17, 1864, *OR*-4, III, 671–672.

121. Lawton to Seddon, Sept. 28, 1864, *ibid.*, pp. 690–692. 122. *Ibid.*

123. Lawton's endorsement, July 25, 1864, on Milton to Seddon, July 11, 1864, *ibid.*, pp. 499–500.

effective co-operation with the field commands as Myers had had. Lee, for example, was continually looking for ways to improve his men's comforts. He wrote the Quartermaster General that his men had been out looking for leather and had found hides instead. Leather held by tanners was priced so high that Lee felt these hides should be exchanged for smaller amounts of leather.[124] In addition, he wanted the Quartermaster's Department to send leather and tools from its shops to his army where the men in the various brigades would make shoes, also noting that many of the shoes of the Quartermaster's Department were inferior in quality.[125] Lawton encouraged Lee to get all the hides that he could and promised to send tools to allow the men in camp to make shoes.[126] He would not, however, agree to an exchange of hides for leather, a move which he considered wasteful in the long run; nor would he close down the bureau's shoe shops, observing that Lee's own staff had approved the Richmond shoe shop.[127] He answered Lee's complaints of a need for underwear and cotton shirts by acidly commenting that the bureau had a "large excess" on hand but that Lee's own quartermasters had stopped shipments on the grounds that they had enough. Further, Lawton noted that when he had suggested that Lee's men should have fresh underclothing before campaigning, there had been no reply.[128]

In his first months in office the new Quartermaster General had proved to be an energetic and resourceful organizer along traditional lines, drawing praise from the press.[129] Lawton's experience in his new office transformed his outlook on staff-field relationships, and the former brigade commander now unhesitatingly took the bureau point of view in areas of dispute. He had been unable to create any solutions for chronic shortages in wool, leather, and field transportation, but these chronic shortages were beyond solution. Lawton displayed other limitations. He did not suggest improvements in foreign supply and participated in cut-throat competitive arrangements with other bureaus; on railroad regulations, as we shall see, he retained the same negative conservatism as his predecessor.

124. Lee to Lawton, Jan. 19, 1864, *OR*-1, XXXIII, 1098.

125. Lee to Lawton, Jan. 18, 1864, *ibid.*, pp. 1094–1095; Lee to Lawton, Jan. 30, 1864, *ibid.*, pp. 1131–1132.

126. Lawton to Lee, Feb. 5, 1864, *ibid.*, p. 1146.

127. *Ibid.*

128. Lawton to Lee, April 26, 1864, *ibid.*, p. 1313.

129. Richmond *Daily Dispatch* editorialized on May 12, 1864: "There never was a time when our armies, so far as this Department was concerned, were better supplied, and when there was more satisfaction with its workings exhibited by the press and the public."

As a matter of fact, during the winter of 1863–64, it looked as if Lawton might have to surrender his position to his predecessor. When Congress reassembled in December 1863 the Senate, fuming over Davis's dismissal of Myers, lost no time in challenging the President. On December 10, led by Senator Sparrow of Louisiana, one of Myers's allies and the chairman of the Senate Committee on Military Affairs, the Senate inquired of the President:

> Whether the Quartermaster-General is now discharging the duties of that office, and if not, by whom they are discharged, and whether the person discharging such duties had been appointed to the office of Quartermaster-General by and with the advice of the Senate . . . and whether the person now discharging the duties of the Quartermaster-General was previously to and at the time of his assuming said duties, in the military service of the Confederate States, and under what law he had been appointed.[130]

The Senators thought that they had the better of the President on several technicalities. Lawton's appointment as Quartermaster General had not been sent to the Senate for confirmation. Furthermore, Lawton's rank had been confirmed only by the Provisional Congress and had not been reconfirmed by the Permanent Congress. As far as the Senate was concerned, not only was Myers the Quartermaster General, but Lawton was not even a brigadier general.

In two replies the President reviewed the whole case and presented an ingenious argument. His main point was that the office of Quartermaster General was not an office subject to confirmation by the Senate, but was rather a staff duty to which the President could assign army officers. The President concurred in the Senate's view that the rank of any army officer would have to be confirmed and sent in Lawton's name.[131] He added:

> My own observations of the manner in which those duties had been discharged had previously satisfied me that the public interests required an officer of greater ability and one better qualified to meet the pressing emergencies of the service during the war.[132]

In answer, the Senate passed a resolution on January 21, 1864, by a vote of 15–6,[133] which declared:

130. *Debates,* L, 27; *Journal,* III, 456.
131. *Debates,* L, 109–112; *Journal,* III, 483, 627–628.
132. *Debates,* L, 111; *Journal,* III, 627; Younger, *Kean Diary,* p. 136.
133. *Debates,* L, 309.

1st. That in the opinion of the Senate, A. C. Myers is now Quartermaster General of the Confederate States army, and is by law authorized and required to discharge the duties thereof.

2nd. That A. R. Lawton is not authorized by law to discharge the duties of said office.[134]

Despite this braggadocio, Congress surrendered to the President by confirming Lawton's army rank and appointment to office on February 17, the last day of the session.[135] In the meantime, Lawton, disgusted with his "responsible and thankless" office and particularly upset over the current furor, tendered his resignation, but Davis declined to accept it.[136]

. . .

During 1863 a combination of old and new problems began to destroy the effectiveness of the Subsistence Department. From a theoretical standpoint, 1863 should have proved a good year rather than an evil one for the bureau. Good weather in the lower South, combined with extensive agricultural conversion, promised a superabundant harvest of corn and vegetables;[137] experiments in growing wheat in the Cotton States had been successful; the increase in corn and fodder was stimulating bacon and beef production. In addition, the new centralized administrative system of the Subsistence Department and the tax-in-kind promised a more efficient procedure of collection and distribution.[138]

Despite such apparently favorable prospects for subsisting the military, adverse factors began to take effect from the beginning of 1863. Lee had made an agreement with Northrop that reserve depots would be set up in Virginia to reduce the vulnerability of his army to the vagaries of railroad transportation.[139] However, Northrop reported that the Army of Tennessee had, against his protests, eaten up so much of

134. *Ibid.*, pp. 273–274, 307–309; *Journal*, III, 604, 621–622.

135. *Journal*, III, 725, 812.

136. Lawton to Seddon, March 4, 1864, Alexander R. Lawton Papers, Southern Historical Collection, University of North Carolina.

137. For a discussion of agricultural conversion, see E. Merton Coulter, "The Movement for Agricultural Reorganization in the Cotton South during the Civil War," *Agricultural History*, I, No. 1 (Jan. 1927), 3–17. See also Benjamin to Mason, May 20, 1863, *ORN*-2, III, 774. Reports on the crops can be found in the Richmond *Daily Dispatch*, May 4, 1863; *Daily Richmond Examiner*, May 20, 1863; *Richmond Enquirer*, June 2, 1863.

138. [Northrop to Seddon, Nov. 20, 1863,] *OR*-4, II, 970.

139. Lee to Northrop, Aug. 5, 1863, *OR*-1, XXIX (2), 625.

the general reserve at Atlanta that little could be sent up immediately for storage in Virginia.[140] The Collie-Crenshaw importation scheme had produced only "a few mouthfuls" and trading through the lines had brought in little.[141] Sarcastically, Northrop reported to Seddon that he did have one new source of supply:

> In consequence of the insufficient quantity and inferior quality of salt among the inhabitants, much of their meat is spoiling. The high prices fixed by the county committees, and the fear that the commissioners of appraisement might not reach prices high enough to satisfy avarice, has doubtless stimulated every one who could spare any meat to bring it out, and the fear of its being fly-blown and spoiled in their hands has strengthened the patriotic desire of feeding the soldiers.[142]

Despite "patriotic" sales, Northrop in his usual manner cast gloomy predictions about the future supply of meat. He did not feel that his bureau and the armies could collect enough meat to maintain the "standard" ration until the fall meat-packing season. For the campaign season of 1863 the Subsistence Department had accumulated about 9,000,000 pounds of salt bacon and 8,000,000 pounds of beef.[143] At the new standard issue of one-half pound of salt meat and one pound of beef, the bureau could supply 400,000 men for sixty days. Local accumulations by the armies and additional bureau purchases from limited civilian stocks might stretch this out to the end of the summer, but several months would elapse after that time before the Subsistence Department could secure the products of the fall meat packing.

Because of these adverse factors, Northrop proposed a new daily standard ration of salt meat: one-quarter pound for troops on garrison duty, one-third pound for troops in camp, and one-half pound for troops on active duty.[144] "The condition of the troops," he added, "that is, health and appearance—proves that it is enough, as evinced by observing those who have for a long time been on reduced rations."[145] Seddon, who felt that Northrop exaggerated to suit his purposes, balked at the idea; but Northrop dunned his superiors through June and into July and finally obtained permission to order a general reduction in the meat ration of all the armies to one third pound when not on

140. Northrop to Lee, July 23, 1863, *ibid.*, LI (2), 738.
141. *Ibid.;* Northrop to Seddon, June 4, 1863, *OR*-4, II, 574–575.
142. Northrop to Seddon, June 4, 1863, *OR*-4, II, 574–575.
143. *Ibid.*, p. 575. 144. *Ibid.* 145. *Ibid.*

active duty.[146] Northrop ordered that the remaining reserve at Atlanta, plus an additional 11,500 cattle, be held exclusively for the Army of Northern Virginia and the Army of Tennessee during the ensuing months. Other commanders were apparently expected to supply themselves. Despite his problem in collecting meat, Northrop was still able to gather an additional reserve of 500,000 pounds at Richmond for Lee's army.[147] There were few official complaints about subsistence for the rest of the campaigning season.

While the armies were being regularly supplied, albeit on a reduced basis, through the latter months of 1863, prospects for the following year were steadily deteriorating. Incessant rains in Virginia ruined the 1863 wheat crop.[148] This destroyed any hope of building up substantial flour reserves in Virginia and of lessening dependence on railroad transportation. Loss of the Mississippi Valley had curtailed accumulation of sugar and molasses as a substitute for meat, and these products passed out of the regular field ration, joining coffee and tea as items reserved exclusively for the sick and convalescent.[149] The temporary collapse of blockade running in the autumn of 1863 prevented the importation of some three million pounds of meat which Crenshaw had sent to Bermuda, meat which was progressively rotting away.[150] Importation of cattle across the Mississippi, a project so important that Seddon had ordered Kirby Smith and Johnston to co-operate to effect it,[151] continued at a slow and irregular pace, and there is little evidence that the cattle brought across went any farther than the stomachs of the troops in Mississippi. Northrop's superiors in the War Department still shrank from a vigorous program of trading through the lines for meat, and consequently this source was yielding little. Most important, Tennessee was now almost completely in the hands of the enemy, just at meat-packing time. In 1862 some twelve million pounds of meat had come from Tennessee, and the Confederate armies had barely gotten through the winter on this meat.[152] Now, Northrop reported that he could expect nothing from Tennessee.[153]

Embarrassments in collection and distribution of supplies were fast

146. Northrop to Lee, July 23, 1863, *OR*-1, LI (2), 738.

147. *Ibid.;* Northrop to Seddon, June 4, 1863, *OR*-4, II, 574–575; Northrop to Lee, July 23, 1863, *OR*-1, LI (2), 738.

148. Vandiver, *Gorgas Diary,* p. 56; see also French to Northrop, Aug. 3, 1863, *OR*-1, XXIX (2), 656.

149. Northrop to Seddon, Nov. 20, 1863, *OR*-4, II, 970.

150. *Ibid.*

151. Seddon to Kirby Smith, Nov. 19, 1863, WDLS, XV, 237.

152. [Northrop to Seddon, Nov. 20, 1863,] *OR*-4, II, 969.

153. *Ibid.*

proving as damaging as the failure in sources of supply. As will be discussed later, the deterioration of the financial system which undergirt impressment practice was fast paralyzing domestic purchasing and resulted in diminishing returns. Consequently, heavier reliance had to be placed upon securing foodstuffs through the tax-in-kind. The tax-in-kind had contributed abundantly to the provisioning of the Confederate armies with breadstuffs throughout the campaigning season of 1863, but the returns had proved uneven, and the tax-in-kind was not bringing in meat. The once cotton-mad Deep South now contributed the great bulk of provisions, and Bragg had predicted late in 1863 that receipts from the tithe could feed the Army of Tennessee for a year with any decent management of transportation.[154] In Virginia, however, because of bad weather and war devastation, the tax-in-kind returns were nil.[155] The swollen population in Richmond and the Army of Northern Virginia found cold comfort in collection statistics from Alabama. The War Department had tried to simplify the clumsy collection procedures of the act of 1863 by encouraging producers to deliver their tithes early in the fall of 1863 directly to army unit commissaries rather than to post quartermasters, and the commissaries would give the official tax-in-kind receipts.[156] The farmers responded in an encouraging manner but sent in field crops, not meat, which portion of the tithe was not due until 1864 after the winter curing. Thus, by the autumn of 1863 tax-in-kind receipts were limited to the breadstuffs and vegetables of the lower South.

The efficiency of the collection of the tithe was also cut down by the nationwide shortage of wagon and rail transportation. Many farmers could not get their tithes to market, and the depot quartermasters did not have the transportation to go after them. On the other hand, some of the collections in the south were so heavy that the government could not properly store them, and great amounts of perishable vegetables and field crops that were collected at depots along the railroads rotted away.[157] Unauthorized agents collected the tithes from the ignorant and sold them or collected them for army units and gave illegal receipts.[158] Tax-in-kind officers were accused of speculating in the sale of the

154. Fitzgerald Ross, *A Visit to the Cities and Camps of the Confederate States* (Edinburgh and London, 1865), pp. 237–238.

155. Jones, *War Clerk's Diary,* II, 118.

156. Quartermaster's Department Circular, Aug. 8, 1863, *OR*-4, II, 698.

157. Milton to Seddon, Jan. 11, 1864, *ibid.,* III, 14–15.

158. Smith to Seddon, Nov. 7, 1864, *ibid.,* p. 801.

products under their care. Supplementary acts of Congress in 1863 and 1864 further reduced accumulations by exempting small farmers, disabled veterans, and soldiers' widows of small means from paying the tax.[159] The War Department also authorized the sale of local surpluses in danger of spoiling to relief agencies and soldiers' families at market prices.[160] These official measures, while humane, reduced the amount available to the armies. Finally, enemy ravages and general wastage further reduced the amount collected.

With these modifying factors considered, by the spring of 1864 the tithe brought in 30,000,000 rations of flour and 50,000,000 rations of corn meal, enough to feed 200,000 men for one year.[161] In addition, there was enough corn to feed 130,000 animals for one year and enough hay and fodder for 35,000 animals.[162] After discounting the tithe distributed in the fall of 1863 and that purchased by civilians or distributed to industrial workers, and allowing for spoilage and wastage, the Subsistence Department estimated that three-quarters of the tithe gathered actually went to the army.[163] With "aggregate present" totals falling toward 200,000 the tithe collections alone could produce over one-half of the rations for the armies during 1864.

Balancing all considerations, Northrop reported on the contents of his larder in November 1863. He foresaw a surplus of bread for the western armies and garrison troops in the Deep South and enough meat available from Trans-Mississippi cattle, local purchases, and the tax-in-kind accumulations to meet most of the needs of these same troops. For the Army of Northern Virginia Northrop reported small accumulations of flour that would last until January 1 and enough surplus corn and corn meal available in the Deep South to feed soldiers and civilians for the winter if the government could manage railroad transportation efficiently.[164] Bureau meat reserves, however, were inadequate; only 9,000,000 pounds of meat, salt and fresh beef, pork, and mutton, were

159. "An Act to Amend So Much of Section Eleven of the Tax Law As Requires One-Tenth of the Sweet Potatoes Produced This Year to Be Paid to the Government," Dec. 28, 1863, *Statutes*, II, 171; "An Act to Amend an Act Entitled 'An Act to Lay Taxes for the Common Defence and Carry on the Government of the Confederate States,' Approved April Twenty-Fourth, Eighteen Hundred and Sixty-Three," Feb. 17, 1864, *ibid.*, pp. 215–217; "An Act to Amend the Laws Relating to the Tax in Kind," June 10, 1864, *ibid.*, p. 264.

160. Smith's endorsement, Jan. 20, 1864, on Milton to Seddon, Jan. 11, 1864, *OR*-4, III, 18. 161. Smith to Seddon, Nov. 7, 1864, *ibid.*, p. 802.

162. *Ibid.* 163. *Ibid.*

164. [Northrop to Seddon, Nov. 20, 1863,] *ibid.*, II, 968–972.

on hand for all the armies.[165] Even if the bureau held its entire reserve for the Army of Northern Virginia and had allowed none for filling the deficits of the Army of Tennessee or for sale to civilians, the meat supplies would not last beyond March 1.

If the civilians were to be fed, a combination of favorable circumstances was necessary: the tax-in-kind, successful importations, trading through the lines, a revamped currency that would make purchasing feasible, and, above all, regular supply by the railroads.[166] The embattled citizens of Richmond, faced with a dearth of supplies on the market, besieged Seddon to persuade him to sell reserve rations to civilians.[167] Northrop opposed the idea. Upset at Seddon's decision to allow the City of Richmond to buy perishable tithes for the poor of the city, Northrop spoke his mind to diarist Kean: "He said to me very earnestly that the alternative was between the people and the army, and there is perhaps *bread* enough for both but not *meat* enough, and that we have to elect between the *army* and the *people* doing without."[168]

Others suggested a different choice: the army or Northrop. In Congress Representative Foote submitted the following resolution:

> *Resolved,* That in the judgment of this House it is eminently desirable, in order to secure the comfortable subsistence of our valiant armies, and to allay discontents known to exist in certain rural districts, that the present Commissary-General be removed and a suitable successor appointed in his place.[169]

The resolution was tabled by a vote of 46–20, and Foote commented that he had "performed his duty, and was done with the question forever."[170] About this time a Congressional deputation called on Davis to urge Northrop's removal; Davis is alleged to have replied that he thought the Commissary General was a genius and that if Northrop had been in better health he would have been put at the head of an army.[171] Thus the Subsistence Department, as well as the Quartermaster's Department, was finding its task complicated by Executive-Congressional politics.

. . .

165. Abstract of Meat Supplies, Nov. 15, 1863, *ibid.,* 959–960.
166. [Northrop to Seddon, Nov. 20, 1863,] *ibid.,* pp. 968–972.
167. Younger, *Kean Diary,* p. 166. 168. *Ibid.* 169. *Debates,* XII, 302.
170. *Ibid.* 171. Jones, *War Clerk's Diary,* II, 131.

One trend common to the operation of all the bureaus merits comment. One by one the bureaus assumed supreme control over commodities essential to their operations and controlled the allocation of these commodities to those bureaus which had a subordinate interest. Apparently, the head of the bureau most concerned initiated matters and pressed for agreements from the other bureau chiefs after securing approval from the Secretary of War and the President. The Niter and Mining Bureau had inaugurated this centralized control early in the war when it assumed control over mineral extraction and iron production, allocating these materials as it judged best. The Subsistence Department, as we have seen, in return for exclusive purchasing rights in the domestic market, undertook to supply rations for industrial workers in other War Department bureaus and also for army officers, prisoners, and the navy.[172] The Quartermaster's Department came into control of the corn supply, presumably on the assumption that the horses needed it more than the men, and guaranteed to supervise the purchase and transportation of enough corn to satisfy the Navy, Medical, and Subsistence departments.[173] The Quartermaster's Department not only subjected cotton textile manufacturers to a uniform and stringent system of controls but also became the sole agent of the government in the cotton textile market, absorbing the contracts of the other bureaus of the War Department and of the Navy Department, in return obligating itself to furnish all the cotton goods these departments needed.[174] This centralization came too late in the war for results

172. For example, see General Orders No. 41, Adjutant and Inspector General's Office, 1862 Series, May 31, 1862, *OR*-4, I, 1139; "An Act to Repeal Certain Portions of the Act of May the Twenty-First, Eighteen Hundred and Sixty-One, Relative to Prisoners of War," Feb. 17, 1864, *Statutes,* II, 194; "An Act to Allow Commissioned Officers of the Army Rations and the Privilege of Purchasing Clothing from the Quartermaster Department," Feb. 17, 1864, *ibid.,* p. 193; Semple to Mallory, Nov. 5, 1864, *ORN*-2, II, 762–763. The Subsistence Department's difficulties in securing rations prompted the Navy Department and the Niter and Mining Bureau to strike out on their own, buying up provisions at premium rates above the scheduled prices in order to accumulate a six months' supply of provisions. The Niter and Mining Bureau claimed that the rations issued by the Subsistence Department were inadequate to sustain energy for the daily physical labor of their workers, but Northrop in his turn complained that the actions of these bureaus placed "all the restrictions and privations" on the fighting man; see French to Northrop, July 8, 1864, and Northrop endorsement, *OR*-4, III, 535.

173. Lawton to Mallory, Northrop, and Moore, Aug. 10, 1864, QMDLS, XIX, 401.

174. Lawton to Mallory, Sept. 3, 1864, *ibid.,* XX, 53; Lawton to Cunningham, Sept. 29, 1864, *ibid.,* p. 163.

to be measured accurately, but there is evidence that the dependent bureaus believed they did not receive the amounts they needed and that the dominant bureau felt that the requests of the dependent bureaus were exorbitant.[175]

. . .

The events of 1863 had revealed the limitations of the supply bureaus in meeting their responsibilities. On the one hand, the bureaus had demonstrated commendable efficiency in managing those areas under their exclusive control. Generally speaking, these areas involved processing domestic raw materials. Mining operations and ordnance and cotton textile production had been efficiently directed and the collection of the tithe competently handled. Consequently, the Ordnance Department and the Niter and Mining Bureau, the bureaus most involved in processing and the least dependent on other bureaus and on civilian leadership, were the most efficient. On the other hand, the passage of time had revealed a number of chronic problems beyond the control of a single bureau, problems which forced the bureaus to rely increasingly on the effectiveness of their civilian superiors in solving national supply problems—finding a medium and a method for purchasing goods from civilians at home, procuring items in short supply from outside the Confederacy, transporting materials to the front, and retaining enough men to carry on supply operations. The Subsistence Department had become the bureau most dependent on a negotiable currency and on the regular transportation of materials, and all of the bureaus had become dependent to some degree on efficient procurement from the outside. As the war continued during 1863, it became increasingly apparent that the existing policies created by the civilian leadership to meet these major problems were inefficient. In addition, civilian leadership was rent by clashes between the President and Congress over the proper personalities to fill the supply posts. Unless the Confederate leaders could work in harmony and move imaginatively to solve major supply problems, the bureaus, especially the Subsistence Department, would face disaster.

175. On the latter point, see Lawton to Cunningham, June 4, 1864, *ibid.*, XIX, 269–270.

CHAPTER SIX

CONTINUED GROPING AT THE TOP

Among those having control there is no one possessing the faculty to perceive . . . the exact things needing to be done and the energy, determination, and skill to go right to work to do it effectually. —— *Daily Richmond Examiner,* February 4, 1864.

In the first years of the war the Confederacy had continually uncovered shortages of materials and unforeseen problems of administration. While the bureau chiefs had in some instances tried to anticipate problems, the Confederate leadership on the whole had met most of these new shortages and problems by reacting to those circumstances which pressed most insistently, setting up policies which appeared to meet the problems of the moment. As the war progressed each supply bureau had evolved a complex system of domestic procurement and distribution which functioned with tolerable efficiency in the areas controlled by that bureau. The over-all supply policies directed by the civilian leadership, policies on which all the bureaus depended, had not yet proved satisfactory. The civilian leaders, pressed by problems in manpower, finance, and outside procurement that had not been solved by their earlier arrangements, continued to tinker with their haphazard collection of policies in their usual spirit of reaction and improvisation.

By 1863 the conscription-exemption policy demanded re-evaluation. Not only were more fighting men needed, but there was also a growing problem of keeping enough skilled laborers and plantation overseers. In the face of new circumstances, the 1862 exemption formulas were becoming obsolete. The conscription and exemption act of October 1862, a satisfactory act for that period in the war, had raised the aggregate present totals from 225,000 in 1862 to 360,000 in early 1863.[1] However, as the campaigning season wore on, the totals had

1. Abstract of Returns, Adjutant and Inspector General's Office, June 30, 1862, *OR*-4, I, 1176; Abstract of Returns, Adjutant and Inspector General's Office, April 30, 1863, *ibid.,* II, 530.

dropped steadily, falling to 310,000 by mid-summer.[2] After the disaster at Vicksburg, the President called to duty those men aged forty-one through forty-five who were liable for military service under the conscription laws.[3] Despite this directive and the redoubled efforts of the conscription officers, aggregate present totals continued to fall.[4]

Many Confederate leaders believed that fighting men could be culled from the supply bureaus. Under the law of April 22, 1863, the bureaus had been directed to send their able-bodied clerks into the army; but the bureaus had dragged their feet all through the year on the matter of giving up their clerks and had eventually exasperated the President, as indicated in a letter from Davis to Governor Milton of Florida:

> You speak with a just sense of the impropriety of the employment of able bodied men in positions in the Quartermaster's and Commissary Departments, which could well be filled by those whom the casualties of the war have rendered unfit for field duty. . . . finding that suggestions as to the advantages of a substitution of these latter for the former met with no proper response, orders have been issued for this purpose, and a searching investigation instituted which it is trusted will have good results. . . . The law and the instructions issued to chief quartermasters in regard to the appointment of agents and other subordinates employed in the collection of the taxes were imperative, and any appointments to those situations of persons qualified for field service are unauthorized, and if pointed out will be remedied.[5]

By the winter of 1863, however, peremptory orders from Seddon had forced the bureau chiefs to replace their able-bodied clerks doing light duty with over-age men or with women.[6]

Commissaries and quartermasters in the field had offended too many, also, and civilians and politicians pressured the War Department to send these men to the front.[7] While the bureau chiefs grudgingly agreed that clerical work could be handled by the over-age, the handicapped, or women, they pointed out that the strenuous activities of the purchasing agents and tax-in-kind collectors demanded vigorous

2. Abstract of Returns, Adjutant and Inspector General's Office, June 30, 1863, *ibid.*, II, 615.

3. Davis's Proclamation, July 15, 1863, *ibid.*, p. 635.

4. Abstract of Returns, Adjutant and Inspector General's Office, Dec. 31, 1863, *ibid.*, p. 1073; Abstract of Returns, Adjutant and Inspector General's Office, June 30, 1864, *ibid.*, III, 520.

5. Davis to Milton, Sept. 16, 1863, *ibid.*, II, 808–809.

6. Jones, *War Clerk's Diary*, II, 140.

7. For example, see Bonham to Seddon, Aug. 12, 1863, *OR*-4, II, 709.

men; the chiefs doggedly resisted the removal of such men.[8] For example, the Chief Commissary for Georgia, Colonel John A. Locke, successfully fought off Governor Brown and kept his experienced hog and cattle agents who were supplying Bragg's army.[9]

Other classes of exempted workers important to the war effort were also singled out as bloated with inefficient, healthy men who should be sent to the front. The railroads and express companies had too many men, it was averred;[10] the Niter and Mining Bureau received so much opprobrium for allegedly harboring able-bodied shirkers that St. John tendered his resignation—it was not, of course, accepted.[11] The outcry against exempted overseers was constant.[12]

Sometime during the autumn of 1863 Davis and Seddon decided to take drastic steps and prepared a plan that would increase the men in the ranks and also aid in controlling the domestic market. Realizing that the largest immediate supply of healthy men for the front lay in the exempted classes, particularly in the professional and official categories and to a lesser degree in the producing categories, Seddon proposed to Congress when it assembled in December that all exemptions be revoked and that all physically fit men be conscripted, then detailed out for administrative, agricultural, and factory labor at the discretion of the War Department.[13]

The Richmond press weighed in heavily against Seddon's plan. The editors claimed that the government could find enough men by enforcing existing regulations with more efficiency and by eliminating unnecessary details. They denounced Seddon's plan as an unconstitutional centralization of power in the hands of one man.[14] Congress, beset by the press and plagued by violent political pressures, hesitated in the face of Seddon's radical proposition but finally, in an atmosphere of copious and pungent debate, produced most of what Seddon wanted. The Congressmen warmed to their task by enacting a special bill

8. "Ruffin Testimony," PRSD, p. 39.

9. Brown to Seddon, Nov. 24, 1863, *OR*-4, II, 988–989, and endorsement by Locke, Dec. 3, 1863.

10. Preston to Seddon, April 30, 1864, *ibid.*, III, 358.

11. Younger, *Kean Diary*, p. 134.

12. Moore, *Conscription and Conflict in the Confederacy*, pp. 143–144.

13. Seddon to Davis, Nov. 26, 1863, *OR*-4, II, 997; Davis to Senate and House of Representatives, Dec. 7, 1863, *ibid.*, p. 1641.

14. Richmond *Daily Dispatch*, Jan. 11, 12, and 15, 1864; Richmond *Enquirer*, Jan. 7, 1864; *Daily Richmond Examiner*, Jan. 9 and 14, 1864; the *Examiner* and *Enquirer* both finally supported the bill in editorials on February 18, 1864.

eliminating substitutes,[15] and then produced the conscription and exemption act of February 17, 1864.[16] Bowing to political pressure, Congress ignored Seddon and continued the exemptions for professionals and national officials in a tighter form and also retained exemptions for state officials, perhaps the most inequitable constant in the whole series of conscription acts. The bill also exempted the two producing classes of overseers or owners on plantations holding fifteen or more slaves and railroad workers at the rate of one per mile of track used by the military. To these exemptions the administration had no real objection.

The rest of the bill followed the administration's prescription. The President and Secretary were delegated the power to detail from the army men found indispensable to the war effort. Congress gave the Secretary of War authority to detail men temporarily for agricultural work; he could detail "artisans, mechanics, or persons of scientific skill to perform indispensable duties," and could thus keep his textile and munitions workers in the factories, and he could allow bureau chiefs to certify certain employees as "indispensable to the public service."

These broad exemption-and-detail provisions put the government in a general position to control farm and factory labor, and in the face of mounting subsistence shortages, the act, together with subsequent War Department rulings, spelled out government controls over agriculture with even greater precision. The act specified that each exempted agriculturalist must be bonded to deliver to the government one hundred pounds of beef on the hoof or the equivalent in grains. The plantation surplus must be sold to the army and to soldiers' families at the schedule prices of the state commission. Seddon, who was anxious to keep the farms and plantations producing, offered an administrative carrot along with the legislative stick by ruling that small farms within a radius of five miles having together a total of fifteen slaves were the equivalent of a legally exempted plantation and thus entitled to one exempted overseer for police on the prescribed terms of bonded deliveries and sale of surplus. He also detailed men to police groups of small farms which could not meet the fifteen-slave limit, and ruled that

15. "An Act to Prevent the Enlistment or Enrollment of Substitutes in the Military Service of the Confederate States," Dec. 28, 1863, *Statutes,* II, 172; "An Act to Put an End to the Exemption from Military Service of Those Who Have Heretofore Furnished Substitutes," Jan. 5, 1864, *ibid.*

16. "An Act to Organize Forces to Serve During the War," Feb. 17, 1864, *ibid.,* pp. 211–215.

detailed men policing under five hands had only the obligation to sell their surpluses to the government and soldiers' families at scheduled rates.[17]

The conscription act of February 17, 1864, was the final legislative distribution of Confederate manpower. From an administrative viewpoint the act left little to be desired, except for the exemption of officialdom and professionals. If anything, it permitted the taking of too many farmers and factory hands, but the needs of the army allowed little choice. A man must go into the ranks if there was the least doubt of his value as a worker. It had given the government tighter control over procurement and had struck a blow at inflation. It was difficult for legislation to do more.

Good legislation did not mean successful administration, especially in the face of intensified public resistance. During the spring of 1864 as the army's aggregate present totals plummeted toward a disastrous 200,000, Colonel John A. Preston, the head of the Bureau of Conscription, reported that his bureau had conscripted the agricultural and industrial producers to their limits and that it could take few more men without doing more harm than good. The only areas left in which to find any men were the non-producing professional and official categories, but to get any men from these classes, Preston said, the bureau had to engage in an

> hourly contest with every authority, every prejudice, every interest, and every fear which exists in the Confederacy. Governors and judges demand some local convenience; others, pecuniary or other interests, and the needs of every occupation are magnified into public necessities. Towns and cities demand able-bodied men for police; banks and brokers, for clerks; charitable institutions, for wardens; public functionaries, for subalterns, and all on the plea that such are necessary for the public good. . . . Since I took charge of this Bureau, no authority, association, or individual has offered one man to the military service.[18]

By the end of 1864 Preston reported that 86,863 men in the Confederacy of conscript age had been officially excused from active duty. Of these, 67,054 were exempted and 19,809 detailed. Of the exempts,

17. Circular No. 8, Bureau of Conscription, March 18, 1864, *OR*-4, III, 221–222.

18. Preston to Seddon, April 30, 1864, *ibid.*, p. 356. His general points can be found in *ibid.*, pp. 354–358.

however, after deducting the physical, official, and professional exemptions, only 9,700 men, the bonded agriculturalists and the railroad workers, could be classified as producers. Some 5,000 detailed artisans and mechanics carried on industrial work; workers detailed for public necessity, such as millers and tanners, numbered 5,803, nearly all unfit for field duty; finally, 4,612 detailed men helped to keep the bureaus operating.[19] Thus a total of less than 30,000 men of conscript age in the Confederacy, many of these disabled, remained at home supporting the troops, a proportion that approaches the incredible by twentieth-century military standards. Actually, the proportions were too spectacular. If the Confederate administrators continued to bleed the productive categories allowed by Congress, war production would become too crippled to supply the field armies.

. . .

As the war progressed, Davis and Seddon erratically and half-heartedly employed the policy of trading through the lines. At one time or another both men had opposed the practice in principle, and although the trade was allowed because of necessity, the pair insisted on imposing regulations that hampered the bureaus. Convinced that any open admission that the government was trading through the lines, especially with Union connivance, would be detrimental to morale and would hurt the image of the Confederacy abroad, they bent over backward to veto any supply bureau trade schemes that would obviously result in the shipping of Confederate tobacco and cotton from Union ports, nor would they allow any goods to come in or out where evidence indicated that Union officers were privy to the operations. Of course, Confederates from Davis down knew that the bulk of the goods taken out of the Confederate lines eventually found its way to the North or to Europe and that many of the goods coming into the Confederacy had come into Union-held ports with the connivance of the Union officials. As long as there was no direct evidence, however, few questions were apparently asked at the exchange points. Such an approach to trading through the lines thwarted many schemes for importation, and the goods imported amounted to less than would have come in with unrestricted importation. Whether the additional goods brought in under an open policy would have been worth the alleged damage to the morale of the population is a moot point.

19. Preston to Breckinridge, Feb. ——, 1865, *ibid.*, pp. 1101–1109.

Another restriction on trade through the lines involved the tendency of Davis and Seddon to sit and wait for requests from military district commanders rather than to instruct them to assist bureau officials in pushing the trade. Seddon also allowed the military district commanders to end the trade if they objected, an even greater blow to the trade. Commanders in Mississippi and Alabama complained that numerous supply bureau schemes for importations ruined the morale of the soldiers and civilians. The commanders further complained that soldiers were becoming more interested in bribery and speculation than fighting and that the people were becoming seditious when army regulations or operations threatened to frustrate their opportunitites to trade cotton through the lines.[20] In 1864 Seddon, impressed with the morale argument, finally authorized Richard Taylor, the commander of the Department of Alabama, Mississippi, and East Louisiana, to restrict government trading enterprises at his discretion. Consequently, Taylor used this authorization virtually to end the importation operations of the bureaus in his military district.[21] In one instance his cavalry prevented the consummation of a Subsistence Department transaction by turning back cotton trains heading through the lines.[22] Thus little in the way of supplies for the government came into the Cis-Mississippi West during the latter stages of the war.

Despite these restrictions, the supply bureaus, as co-ordinated by the Secretary of War, continued to expand their importation system. At first, as has been noted, the War Department ignored the Congressional acts forbidding private citizens to trade with the enemy[23] by "seizing" the goods brought in by civilians and paying a 75 per cent profit instead of turning the smugglers over to the civil courts. This covert flouting of the laws brought occasional embarrassment. When the Treasury Department hauled a War Department "contractor" into court for smuggling, Seddon suggested quashing the indictment, but the Attorney General refused.[24] As the war progressed, however, the

20. Harris to Bragg, Sept. 7, 1864, *ibid.*, pp. 645–651.

21. Headquarters Circular, Department of Alabama, Mississippi, and East Louisiana, September 22, 1864, PRSD; Seddon to Taylor, September 27, 1864, *OR*-4, III, 638–640. Not until after the fall of Fort Fisher did the War Department, after centralizing contract arrangements under Lieutenant-Colonel Thomas L. Bayne, order Taylor to permit Major Mims, Chief Quartermaster for Mississippi, to trade cotton through the lines. See "Ruffin Testimony," PRSD, p. 22a.

22. "Ruffin Testimony," PRSD, p. 22a.

23. Gordon to Garner, Nov. 16, 1863, *OR*-1, XXVI (2), 415–419.

24. Jones, *War Clerk's Diary,* I, 376.

War Department moved away from a dependence on "seizing" goods as they found them and evolved a permit system. Under this system the Secretary of War and generals commanding military districts issued permits to individuals allowing them to make regular trips back and forth through the lines.[25] The details of the trading arrangements are difficult to uncover, but they usually stipulated that private cotton and tobacco would be taken out and that the food, arms, and medicines brought in would be sold to the government at a specified price or at a profit on invoice.[26]

Despite the fact that the contracts made in the winter of 1862–63 had proved barren, the War Department continued throughout the war to negotiate large-scale contracts for the importation of quartermaster and subsistence stores on the theory that the goods would not come in through Union-held ports or with Union connivance. For example, one party in 1863 guaranteed to deliver steamer-loads of meat on the Tennessee River in Alabama, and another guaranteed the delivery of large supplies of quartermaster stores in Tennessee.[27] However, it is not reported that any of these massive contracts were successfully carried out.

In areas where the commanding generals and the bureau officials co-operated, an increasing amount of supplies came in through the lines as the war wore on. As the trade became more successful—and more necessary—in these areas, Seddon became more enthusiastic. The Subsistence Department, pressed by the meat shortage, pushed trading through the lines to the fullest extent that the Secretaries of War and Treasury and the generals would allow. In Virginia and eastern North Carolina a large and successful trade in subsistence supplies began in December 1863 and grew during 1864 and 1865 after Lee awoke to the possibilities of such trade and overcame his own scruples. The main transaction was the exchange of cotton and tobacco for meat, and the rate varied from a pound-for-pound exchange in North Carolina to the more favorable rate of three pounds of bacon for one of cotton or tobacco in northern and western Virginia.[28] Indeed, so heavy was trade across the Chowan River in eastern North Carolina and the Blackwa-

25. Seddon to Lee, Feb. 19, 1864, WDLS, XVII, 187; Lee to Seddon, March 29, 1864, *OR*-1, LI (2), 842–843.

26. For example, see Lee to Noland, April 12, 1864, *OR*-4, III, 285–287.

27. "Ruffin Testimony," PRSD, p. 22a.

28. Noland to Seddon, April 1, 1864, *OR*-4, III, 261–262. Examples of contract terms can be found in an undated manuscript, "Confederate States of America; Army, Commissary Dept.; Lucius Bellinger Northrop, Commissary General," New York Public Library: Northrop Papers.

ter in southeastern Virginia that the Subsistence Department needed 600 to 800 bales of cotton delivered each week at Weldon, North Carolina.[29] Albeit negative, another indication of the size of the trade was the destruction at Fredericksburg by Union troops of a whole trainload of tobacco and cotton destined for trade through the lines.[30] Major Robert Tannahill, who was in charge of government arrangements along the Blackwater and Chowan, commented after the war that the trade went on "day and night" as a "last resort" and that it was impossible to "approximate the magnitude" or to "appreciate the importance" of the traffic.[31]

As the government diverted more and more of its energies into trading through the lines, it also moved to suppress "wildcat" private smuggling. The combined scrutiny of Lee, Seddon, and the bureau officials kept the trade in Virginia limited to those operating for the government under permit. The results so impressed Seddon that he nervously warned Lee on one occasion when the latter appeared to be vacillating:

> It is of importance that no obstruction should be opposed by the pickets to the persons engaged in the trade, and that those concerned should be facilitated and protected as much as possible. The expectation of the Department is to press it to the fullest extent that it may be found practicable.[32]

But there was no need to prod Lee. Once he understood how important the trade had become in feeding his men, he actively participated in increasing its effectiveness. Not only did he arrange for contracts and permits, but he also suggested that the War Department stiffen its penalties against civilian traffic. He proposed fines and imprisonment in addition to confiscation and suggested that the government seize tobacco, cotton, and naval stores found in the presence of the enemy, on the *prima facie* assumption that the goods were for contraband trade.[33] After the loss of Wilmington, when other resources of the Confederacy were fading out in the general collapse, Ruffin claimed that nearly all of the meat consumed by the Army of Northern Virginia had come in through the lines.[34] Tannahill claimed that if Lee had been

29. Anderson to Cameron, Jan. 19, 1864, *OR*-1, XLVI (2), 1104.
30. Jones, *War Clerk's Diary*, II, 451.
31. Tannahill to Northrop, March 12, 1880, New York Public Library: Northrop Papers.
32. Seddon to Lee, April 1, 1864, *OR*-4, III, 261.
33. Lee to Seddon, Jan. 16, 1865, *OR*-1, XLVI (2), 1075–1077.
34. "Ruffin Testimony," PRSD, p. 36.

able to hold Richmond "there is no telling the amount of supplies we could have gotten from the North in the way of exchange for cotton."[35]

There is little evidence available to indicate the amount of supplies imported for the use of the Confederate armies in the two years that the War Department traded through the lines. Certainly the results of the policy fell short of potential benefits. Although the practical difficulties involved were severe, the efforts of Davis and Seddon were all too often inconsistent and halfhearted. Instead of vigorously pressing the policy if they had decided it was necessary, or suppressing it entirely in the interests of morale or diplomacy, they pushed off the responsibility for effecting the policy on the supply chiefs and the commanders of military districts. It may be argued, of course, that the policy of leaving the responsibility in the hands of the military district commanders provided a necessary flexibility, allowing Seddon to push trade where supplies were necessary and suppress it where morale considerations were paramount. Such a view, however, assumes government control of private traffic as well. As it turned out, suppression in Taylor's military district served only to eliminate government importations without controlling private trade or winning Confederate citizens in that area back to patriotic abstinence. Generally speaking, trading with the enemy was a striking instance of the Confederate government's fatal penchant for too little and too late.

. . .

By 1864 the fevered inflationary spiral in the Confederacy had so vitiated domestic supply procurement that Confederate leaders, who were by no means united on means or ends, were forced to make radical innovations in finance and impressment to sustain the war effort. In early 1863 the government had met domestic procurement needs in a shrinking market by expanding the circulating medium and legalizing forced sales. Impressment, a measure to secure regular purchase in the face of hoarding, was envisioned as a temporary expedient based on public acquiescence until the return of financial stability brought goods out for purchase on the open market. Even with this limited concept, impressment would fail unless it were administered with tact, tolerated by the public, backed with large amounts of currency which retained public confidence, and supplied with legal punitive teeth.

35. Tannahill to Northrop, March 12, 1880, New York Public Library: Northrop Papers.

None of these conditions materialized. In the first place, the inflationary spiral accelerated during 1863. Congress's response was to stiffen the tax laws moderately, issue new bonds, and provide for another outpouring of currency.[36] The act of March 23, 1863, had authorized the output of $50,000,000 of currency per month to match the current expenses of the War Department.[37] After this action by Congress there was a marked rise in the commodity price levels during the summer of 1863, coupled with a notable increase in the incidence of refusal of Confederate notes by producers. These results brought War Department expenses to $70,000,000 a month by the summer of 1863, piling up bills faster than the Treasury Department could print the notes, and once again the various bureaus began to complain that requisitions on the Treasury Department went unpaid.[38] By the autumn the War Department estimated that expenses for the first six months of 1864 would total some $437,000,000, or over $70,000,000 per month.[39]

In this atmosphere of fiscal never-never land the War Department attempted to pursue its business of domestic procurement. Armed with bales of treasury notes and various types of government bonds, the Department went ahead with its customary arrangements for payments on manufacturing contracts and bought what little goods it could find on the open market. The bulk of the domestic purchasing, however, continued to involve impressment proceedings, and therein lay a sad tale. The impressment act of March 26, 1863, had provided for impressment of surplus stocks held by non-producers at state Commissioners' rates and impressment of surpluses of producers at local appraisement rates subject to appeal to the state Commissioners on the grounds of disputes of quantity and value of the items under considera-

36. "An Act Making Appropriations for the Support of the Government for the Period from February First, to June Thirtieth, Eighteen Hundred and Sixty-Three, Inclusive, and to Supply Deficiencies Arising Prior Thereto," Feb. 10, 1863, *Statutes,* II, 94–97; "An Act to Lay Taxes for the Common Defense, and Carry on the Government of the Confederate States of America," April 24, 1863, *ibid.,* pp. 115–126.

37. "An Act to Provide for the Further Issue of Treasury Notes," Sept. 23, 1862, *ibid.,* p. 59; "An Act to Provide for the Funding and Further Use of Treasury Notes," March 23, 1863, *ibid.,* pp. 99–102.

38. Jones, *War Clerk's Diary,* II, 23; Seddon to Memminger, Aug. 25, 1863, WDLS, XIII, 399.

39. The estimates were enacted uncut in "An Act Making Additional Appropriations for the Support of the Government of the Confederate States of America, for the Fiscal Year Ending June Thirtieth, Eighteen Hundred and Sixty-Four," Feb. 17, 1864, *Statutes,* II, 197–202.

tion. Impressing officers would make payment at the time of impressment if currency were available. If out of funds, officers were to present certificates redeemable by authorized military disbursing agents.[40] The Secretary of War, caught between political pressures and procurement needs, found that the vague wording of the act gave him ample room to construe the act to his own satisfaction. Some of his rulings increased the amount of goods impressed; other rulings were restrictive. Under the first category, Seddon, in order to give the power to impress to the greatest number of men, ruled that all field commanders down through the brigade commanders, the commanders of detached units of any size, and also post commanders could order their commissaries, quartermasters, or medical officers to impress. Seddon also authorized the Quartermaster General, the Surgeon General, and the Commissary General to so empower any agents they chose. The Secretary of War speeded up the impressment process by empowering agents to make an offer to producers and simultaneously to notify them that if they refused the offer, officers would appeal under the provisions of the impressment acts and thus bind the goods for the government.[41]

On the other hand, the Secretary sharply reduced the classes of goods subject to impressment. He ruled that producers could hold one year's supply of provisions free from impressment, and he continued in force the traditional War Department prohibition on impressing goods in transit to markets, in order that the civilian consumers might find something at the markets to buy for their families.[42] In addition, he exempted from impressment goods secured by government contractors to feed their employees, supplies for railroad workers, institutional supplies, and goods brought in by city and county agencies intrusted with relief for the poor and for soldiers' families.[43]

While the Secretary of War was busily interpreting the impressment law, the new Commissioners were at work with schedules and interpretations of their own. The prices of the schedules varied markedly at different times and localities, but the schedule prices were nearly always well below market prices and thus acted as a brake on the more unreasonable profiteering elements of the producing classes.[44]

40. "An Act to Regulate Impressments," March 26, 1863, *ibid.,* pp. 102–104.

41. General Orders No. 37, Adjutant and Inspector General's Office, 1863 Series, April 6, 1863, *OR*-4, II, 471–472.

42. Northrop to Seddon, Nov. 20, 1863, *ibid.,* p. 969; "Ruffin Testimony," PRSD, p. 35.

43. Northrop to Seddon, Nov. 20, 1863, *OR*-4, II, 969; "Ruffin Testimony," PRSD, p. 35.

44. Goode to Seddon, July 19, 1863, *OR*-4, II, 544.

By the fall of 1863 it had become apparent that the legalized impressment system was losing the indispensable ingredient of public support. Private citizens and local officials became increasingly hostile and obstructive, and for this the military was much at fault. Bureau officials and line officers often disregarded instructions and operated in such an arbitrary manner that the people were driven in exasperation from acquiescence to resistance. The officers seized goods on the way to markets, and unauthorized agents seized goods and gave worthless certificates.[45] Impressment agents also violated the sections of the impressment act that made it illegal to impress more than was actually needed or to impress at schedule rates unless there was a refusal to sell.[46] The undisciplined cavalry of the southwest exploited the civilians so brutally, often taking everything an individual had, that Seddon issued one of his more peremptory orders, commanding the generals in that area to curb their men.[47] The most general complaint was that impressment agents continually appropriated goods from the areas adjacent to their commands and posts and made little effort to go farther away to impress on an equitable basis.[48] As a result few supplies reached the open market, producers did not willingly declare many surpluses, and hoarding intensified, while the hated impressment agents redoubled their efforts to drag out hidden surpluses. The *Daily Richmond Examiner,* in its relentless war against the Subsistence Department, demanded action against "the emissaries of Mr. Northrop who consider themselves quite equivalent to the satraps of provinces."[49] The *Daily Richmond Whig* trumpeted, "The land is ringing with outcries against the enormities perpetrated by impressing agents, with myriad of proofs of the incapacity, if not insanity, of the Commissary General. . . ."[50]

The public, in the meantime, began to realize that the impressment act contained an Achilles heel—it contained no provisions for punishment of evasions by citizens who swore falsely about amounts of

45. Milton to Florida Senate and House of Representatives, Nov. 23, 1863, *ibid.,* pp. 972–976; Brown to Seddon, Nov. 9, 1863, *ibid.,* pp. 943–944; Vance to Seddon, Dec. 29, 1863, *ibid.,* pp. 1066–1067; Jones, *War Clerk's Diary,* II, 101–102; Vandiver, ed., *The Civil War Diary of General Josiah Gorgas,* p. 69.

46. *Daily Richmond Whig,* Nov. 3, 1863.

47. Seddon to Johnston, Nov. 3, 1863, WDTS, XXXV, 125; Seddon to Johnston, Nov. 7, 1863, *ibid.,* p. 126; Seddon to Johnston, Oct. 30, 1863, WDLS, XIV, 139.

48. Benham to Seddon, Oct. 8, 1863, *OR*-4, II, 863–864.

49. *Daily Richmond Examiner,* Oct. 7, 1863.

50. *Daily Richmond Whig,* Dec. 15, 1863.

surplus goods or who refused to part with goods on receiving notice of impressment. Increasingly the impressment agents met with outright refusals, refusals often backed by the local police and judicial authorities, and agents could not get the products which they knew to be stored away.[51] The department had not generally allowed the use of armed force to aid the impressment officers, as it was well aware of the public abhorrence of military coercion of civilians; but some military commanders apparently did not hesitate to use force when their impressing officers met with refusals or evasions. Some bureau agents arranged for aid from local post commanders.[52] In general, however, flat refusal blocked impressment actions.

By the autumn of 1863 purchasing returns showed almost nothing,[53] a somber prospect for the government. Seddon felt that under the financial circumstances of the Confederacy impressment was a necessary evil, but he hoped that the tax-in-kind would reduce the most frequent type of impressment, that of food.[54] His letter to a complaining Alexander Stephens summarized his views at this time:

> Impressments are scarcely less odious to me than to you but with all deference I believe them the only mode, in the present exceptional condition of the country, to obtain supplies, and of course when resorting to them I must as to prices conform to the laws of Congress. But for impressment just now, only the very patriotic would sell at all, because prices are palpably advancing every day, and the products in kind are preferred to the currency. Both the community and the Government are in effect indebted to the impressment system for supplies, for but the liability to impressment, prices would advance to the most extravagant rates, and yet fail to tempt sales. Congress will I trust devise an early and effectual remedy to the currency. Else there will be no credit, and seizure without payment, be the last alternative. I think a remedy may yet be devised and hope for one from the wisdom of Congress.[55]

Seddon's views apparently had the form if not the full-blooded vigor of Davis's approbation, but a tide of hostility from the public and

51. "Ruffin Testimony," PRSD, p. 31.

52. Carlisle circular, Nov. 20, 1863, enclosed in Milton to Florida Senate and House of Representatives, Nov. 23, 1863, *OR*-4, II, 974.

53. Noland letter of Nov. 14, 1863, quoted in "Ruffin Testimony," PRSD, p. 35.

54. Seddon to Davis, Nov. 26, 1863, *OR*-4, II, 1011–1012.

55. Seddon to Stephens, Nov. 10, 1863, WDLS, XV, 211.

from the less august reaches of officialdom was sweeping impressment away. The Supreme Court of Georgia struck a sharp blow by invalidating the state schedule of appraisements on the principle that a pre-existing schedule of appraisement prices was not evidence of current value in the case of nonproducers' impressed goods.[56] Having once again collided with state judiciaries on matters of impressment, the War Department retreated. In General Orders No. 161 it was announced that if a nonproducer objected when his goods were taken at scheduled prices the impressing officer was to allow local appraisement and then appeal to the state Commissioners if dissatisfied.[57] Thus the government abandoned the distinction between producers and nonproducers set up by the impressment act and made all seizures liable to local appraisement followed by appeal to the Commissioners if the government agents were not satisfied.

Although Congress came to the aid of the War Department in the meat crisis of the winter of 1863–64 by authorizing agents to take up to one half of the meat stocks normally reserved for family consumption,[58] the momentum for restricting the powers of government was irresistible. Seddon had suggested to Congress that it put teeth into the existing law by providing punishments that would be administered in civil courts;[59] instead, Congress, on February 16, 1864, after months of extensive debate and salty opinionating, enacted a measure which sharply constricted the impressment power of the War Department. Congress declared the impressed surpluses of all citizens subject to local appraisement, and the citizens as well as the impressment agents were given the right to appeal questions of value to the state Commissioners, whose powers were now limited to hearing appeals and setting schedules for appeal cases. This last change was more apparent than real, given undoubtedly as a sop to public outcry. In actual fact, the state Commissioners had already received many appeals from government agents, and the Commissioners still had the power to employ their own moderate schedule rates if they saw fit. A much more serious blow in the eyes of procurement officials was the clause which forbade appeals from local appraisement on the question of the quan-

56. Jones, *War Clerk's Diary,* II, 111–112.

57. General Orders No. 161, Adjutant and Inspector General's Office, 1863 Series, Dec. 10, 1863, *OR*-4, II, 1052–1055.

58. "An Act to Authorize the Impressment of Meat for the Use of the Army under Certain Conditions," Feb. 17, 1864, *Statutes,* II, 196–197.

59. Seddon to Davis, Nov. 26, 1863, *OR*-4, II, 1011.

tity of goods liable to impressment. The question of finding voluntarily declared surpluses had always been more of a problem than settling the value of the surplus. Now, only friendly local appraisers held the power to determine what constituted a year's supply of provisions necessary to the support of the citizen and his family. This clause could only diminish the amount of declared surpluses which the War Department could secure, and how seriously this would cripple army procurement only time would tell. Another serious flaw was the continued absence of any civil penalties for those who would not allow their surplus to be confiscated.

The most ominous clause of the general impressment law remains to be mentioned. This clause stipulated that all goods must be paid for by the impressing officer at the time of impressment unless there was disagreement, in which case payment would be suspended awaiting judgment.[60] One can better understand the gravity of this clause by examining the concurrent financial legislation which was aimed at reducing the currency in circulation. In an attempt to curb the runaway inflation and save some semblance of government credit, Congress, on February 17, 1864, funded the old issues of notes by taxing them out of existence and replaced them with new issues of notes at the rate of two dollars of new notes for three of the old. This was a laudable effort to blunt inflation and curb government expenses by reducing the currency by one third. However, the War Department was already incurring bills faster than the old currency could provide notes, and the projected reduction of currency threatened to leave the department far short of means to pay its bills unless price levels took a sudden dive as currency was restricted. The department needed currency to pay the men, to pay off certain types of contracts, and to allow impressment officers to pay on the spot the producers, who would now, it was hoped, accept the lower prices offered because they had confidence in the new notes. To ease the currency strangle, the funding act provided that the War Department might offer in payment for supplies a series of 6 per cent non-taxable bonds or certificates of indebtedness bearing 6 per cent semi-annual interest, the latter payable two years after the ratification of a treaty of peace.[61]

60. "An Act to Amend 'An Act to Regulate Impressments,' Approved March Twenty-Sixth, Eighteen Hundred and Sixty-Three, and to Repeal an Act Amendatory Thereof, Approved April Twenty-Seventh, Eighteen Hundred and Sixty-Three," Feb. 16, 1864, *Statutes,* II, 192–193.

61. "An Act to Reduce the Currency and Authorize a New Issue of Notes and Bonds," February 17, 1864, *ibid.,* pp. 205–208.

By passing the impressment and currency acts of February 1864 Congress had elected to gamble with the domestic procurement system of the War Department. In 1863 the department had managed domestic procurement by impressment and by vast amounts of currency, but public resistance had rapidly destroyed impressment as a system of domestic procurement, and Congress had limited its scope. The new financial legislation staked everything on the proposition that currency reform would regain public confidence to such an extent that prices would fall and enough goods would appear on the open market for the government to buy everything it needed with its reduced funds. Otherwise, in 1864 there would be neither impressment to find goods nor money to pay for them.

. . .

By 1863 Confederate officialdom was all too aware that the Confederate war effort depended for its success on the uninterrupted flow of war materials from overseas. The very existence of the Ordnance Department depended on the importation of massive amounts of saltpeter and metals; the Quartermaster's Department rated the overseas purchases of leather and woolen goods indispensable; and of late the Subsistence Department needed meat desperately. Confederate administrators spent much of their energy grappling with a tangled knot of overseas procurement problems, slowly—too slowly—improving their foreign purchasing system.

Since 1862 the government had used cotton as its currency for overseas procurement and had accumulated enough to pay for its overseas purchases, but the overriding problems continued unsolved—how to get the cotton translated into purchases, and how to get the purchases into the Confederacy. The most direct policy of shipping cotton abroad, selling or exchanging it for materials and shipping the war materials back in, continued to be thwarted by the unco-operative attitude of private shipping interests, who gave government cotton and goods low priority. To ease its burden, the government had continued the admittedly inefficient process of waiting for private contractors to bring goods in and take cotton out in payment, but little came in on this basis, except to the Trans-Mississippi. As the months passed with government cotton rotting in the Confederacy and with European producers selling their goods elsewhere, some answer to the strangulation of transportation was imperative.

One answer was more government-owned ships. As we have seen, the government had acquired a few steamers directly and arranged for controlling interests in others which were to be built over a period of time, but these arrangements were already proving to be inadequate. The government-owned steamers had proved quite successful, running back and forth from Bermuda and Nassau continually in 1863, but such steamers were able to handle only the needs of the Ordnance and Medical bureaus.[62] The partly owned steamers, which were to give priority to quartermaster and subsistence supply needs, the Collie-Crenshaw line, were not so successful. Of a projected twelve, only three were ready by late summer, and three more by the end of 1863.[63] An additional problem was that much of the cotton taken out went to pay for the steamers and could not be put toward paying for supplies.

By mid-1863 the government was losing ground. The supply bureaus, with plenty of cotton to spend, were ordering heavily to meet their projected needs, but they could not get their cotton to Europe. Major Ferguson was making extensive orders for the Quartermaster's Department in Europe to provide winter clothing for the troops;[64] W. G. Crenshaw was ordering and forwarding meat to the islands for the Subsistence Department, and other bureaus were also at work.[65] In addition, private capitalists were making war material available on the islands if the Confederacy could pay for it.[66] Fortunately for the Confederacy, the government was meeting some of its current expenses with proceeds of the Erlanger loan, but this money would not last long. More shipping space for cotton was necessary. The Collie-Crenshaw steamers were not yet ready, and even when completed they would not be sufficient.

Despite all of these pressures, government officials gave no signs of moving to avert the complete collapse of overseas purchasing arrangements until events forced them to take action. The news of the military reverses of July 1863 reached Europe, and Confederate credit nose-dived. Proceeds from the Erlanger loan came to a standstill, and contractors became wary about advancing credit and waiting for payment. That same month Union siege forces moved in to invest Charleston, cutting off that port and freeing the Charleston blockading squadrons for closer investment of Wilmington. Davis and Seddon feared that the

62. Myers to Seddon, July 26, 1863, *OR*-4, II, 682–683.
63. Crenshaw Memorandum, n.d., PRSD.
64. Myers to Seddon, July 29, 1863, *OR*-4, II, 682–683.
65. Crenshaw Memorandum, n.d., PRSD.
66. Myers to Waller, July 22, 1863, *OR*-4, II, 658.

blockade might become fully effective and decided that the government's cotton, tobacco, and naval stores would have to be shipped out immediately.[67] Davis, previously loath to regulate railroads, was now ready to impress ships. On August 11 Seddon telegraphed the government cotton agents at the various ports to enter into agreements with the private shippers that these shippers were to put one half of their vessels' outbound cargo space at the disposal of the government at freight rates and were to bring back a half cargo of useful goods on which the government had first purchasing option. If any shipper would not agree, he would not only be refused cotton, but his ship would also be impressed into the government service.[68] The government claimed no legality except the legality of necessity. Another major sector of Confederate economy had come under government regulation.

During the autumn of 1863, as Union blockaders caught one government-owned ship after another, Davis and Seddon found it necessary to create still another plan for securing cargo space. The government contracted for fleets of ships to run in and out on government account exclusively, exempting these ships from the "regulations," as the new restrictions on private shipping had come to be called. The firms contracted with the bureaus to buy shiploads of goods needed by the government and to bring them into Confederate ports. The government in turn agreed to pay 50 per cent profit on invoice and freight at £25 per ton, payment to be made in cotton valued at 6*d*. per pound. With cotton bringing a net profit of 20*d*. per pound in England, actual profits to the shipping firms ranged up to 850 per cent.[69] The two most important firms, who did much of the shipping for the Quartermaster's and Subsistence departments, were Power, Lowe and Company, and Davis and Fitzhugh.[70] The Confederate administrators were unhappy at having to continue devaluing their cotton, but these firms did deliver goods regularly while the number of ships running under the semi-impressment coercion of the regulations appears to have declined.[71]

While they were in the mood for action about overseas arrangements in the early fall of 1863, the Confederate officials decided to take action on the matter of multiple disbursing agents in Europe. Since 1862 the Confederate diplomatic and fiscal agents abroad had been

67. Seddon to Beauregard, Aug. 11, 1864, *ibid.*, pp. 714–715.
68. *Ibid.* 69. Ruffin to Northrop, Nov. 4, 1864, PRSD.
70. *Ibid.*; "Ruffin Testimony," PRSD, p. 22.
71. "Ruffin Testimony," PRSD, p. 22.

pleading with authorities to end the system under which various Confederate purchasing and bonding agents abroad were all handling both drafts from home and proceeds from bond sales.[72] Most of these complaints had passed over the desk of Benjamin as official diplomatic correspondence, and he finally persuaded Davis to call in Seddon, Memminger, and Mallory to find a solution for the problem. By September 18, 1863, the group had officially decided to make Colin J. McRae co-ordinator of spending abroad with power to assign priorities of payments and to transfer funds from the account of one bureau to another to meet immediate obligations. Bureau agents were limited to arranging contracts, and lines of authority among the major departments were simplified and more clearly delineated.[73] It was an act of simple common sense long in appearing.

Late in 1863, after a harrowing autumn of Union success in disrupting the importation of supplies, the Confederate administrators moved to legalize their impressment actions and to tighten up their control over foreign commerce. From Europe Confederate agents had been pleading with their superiors to go the whole way and take over the export trade completely. As McRae put it, ". . . not another bale should be allowed to come out, not a pound of goods go in, except on government account."[74] However, Davis, Seddon, and Memminger were apparently not convinced that shippers would be interested in braving the blockade for shipping fees alone, and they were determined to ask Congress to give legal sanction to the current system of preempting half-cargo space.

The first regulatory legislation enacted by Congress was the antisumptuary law. It prohibited importation of a long list of non-essentials, items which shed a tragi-comic light on the petty vices of a society fighting for its life: gems, paintings, statuary, muffs, carriages, alcohol, dolls, firecrackers, coin collections, etc.[75]

On February 6, 1864, the bill desired by the administrators entitled "A Bill to Impose Regulations Upon the Foreign Commerce of the Confederate States and to Provide for the Public Defense" was passed

72. For example, see Slidell to Benjamin, June 12, 1863, *ORN*-2, III, 806–807.

73. Benjamin to Slidell, Aug. 17, 1863, *ibid.*, p. 873; Benjamin to Memminger, Seddon, and Mallory, Sept. 15, 1863, *ibid.*, II, 496–498; Benjamin to Memminger, Sept. 20, 1863, *ibid.*, III, 904; Seddon to McRae, Sept. 26, 1863, *OR*-4, II, 824–827; Davis to McRae, Sept. 18, 1863, in Rowland, *Jefferson Davis*, VI, 42–43.

74. McRae to Gorgas, Sept. 4, 1863, *OR*-4, II, 890.

75. "An Act to Prohibit the Importation of Luxuries, or of Articles Not Necessaries or of Common Use," Feb. 6, 1864, *Statutes*, II, 179–181.

by a nervous group of politicians in secret session.[76] The crucial passages read:

> *The Congress of the Confederate States of America do enact,* That the exportation of cotton, tobacco, military and naval stores, sugar, molasses and rice from the Confederate States, and from all places in the occupation of their troops, is prohibited, except under such uniform regulations as shall be made by the President of the Confederate States.
>
> . . .
>
> Sect. 5. That the powers granted by this act . . . to allow or refuse exportation of the articles before mentioned or for the seizure or detention of any of the said articles, shall be exercised in conformity with such instructions as the President may give through the Department of War and of the Treasury, which instructions may impose conditions to the destination and sale of the same, and the investment of the proceeds of the same, or a portion thereof, in military or other supplies for the public service. . . .[77]

Now that Congress had given them *carte blanche* to regulate overseas transportation, Davis and company sat down to write the necessary regulations and blundered. Undoubtedly they were correct in their assumption that the shipping interests needed some concessions to make their blockade running worthwhile, and on that basis it would have seemed wise for the government to continue its lenient policy on freight rates and bonding regulations while retaining absolutely unimpaired its rights to half cargoes. The resulting regulations did neither. On the one hand, the government unnecessarily tightened its restrictions. First, it now demanded one half of the cargo space of each vessel that was inbound as well as outbound. Second, while still paying contracting firms for freight charges in cotton valued at 6*d.* per pound, the administration now lowered freight charges on ships running under the "regulations" to 5*d.* sterling on exported freight and paid for imported freight in cotton valued at 10*d.* In addition, the new regulations now required shippers and exporters to give bond double the value of their ships and shipments and to pledge return voyages from

76. "A Bill to Impose Regulations Upon the Foreign Commerce of the Confederate States to Provide for the Public Defence," Feb. 6, 1864, *ibid.*, pp. 181–183.

77. *Ibid.*

Europe in sixty days from landing. The regulations called for a number of certificates and affidavits to enforce compliance. Third, the government demanded that one-half of the proceeds from the sale of any private cotton carried out be put into useful goods to be returned to the Confederacy for government purchase or paid in specie to Confederate agents in Europe, to be repaid by the Confederate States in cotton valued at 10*d*. per pound.[78]

The shipping interests, already unhappy with the basic proposition, objected strongly to the more stringent regulations. Many ships apparently left the blockade-running trade, and more might have done so if Confederate administrators had not committed a second blunder, damaging the government's rights to half cargoes by providing a loophole that allowed shippers to evade carrying government shipments. The thirteenth and final regulation provided that holders of government bonds, bonds which in some instances pledged payment in cotton valued as low as 4*d*. per pound, could ship out their cotton at will, the government claiming only half the remaining cargo space. Shippers thus could and did buy cotton certificates and load their ships with cheap 4*d*. cotton, excluding the government completely from a share in the cargo space.[79] Just whose ideas were embodied in the final form of the regulations is not known, but diarist Kean avowed that Benjamin and Davis had ruined the more suitable proposals of Seddon.[80]

To expedite matters, Davis and Seddon created a new office, one not directly authorized by statute, the Bureau of Foreign Supplies. The new bureau was placed in the charge of Lieutenant-Colonel Thomas L. Bayne, who had already been managing operations of government-owned vessels.[81] He was made responsible for expediting purchases and sale of cotton and for the over-all management of contracts and shipping arrangements. In addition, he was to manage the $20,000,000 which Congress had appropriated for the War Department to replenish stocks of government-owned staples.[82]

78. "Regulations to Carry into Effect the Foreign Intercourse Act: Sea Regulations," March 5, 1864, *OR*-4, III, 187–189.

79. Bayne to Seddon, May 13, 1864, *ibid.*, pp. 423–424.

80. Younger, *Kean Diary*, p. 141.

81. Special Orders No. 64, Adjutant and Inspector General's Office, 1864 Series, March 17, 1864, *Special Orders of the Adjutant and Inspector General's Office, Confederate States, 1864* (n.p., n.d.), p. 232.

82. "An Act Making Additional Appropriations for the Support of the Government of the Confederate States of America, for the Fiscal Year Ending June Thirtieth, Eighteen Hundred and Sixty-four," Feb. 17, 1864, *Statutes*, II, 199.

As the year 1864 marched on, it was apparent that the government still could not command enough shipping space, despite the employment of four different shipping methods and despite the fact that the Union had lifted the siege of Charleston. Comparative tonnage figures for different periods of the war are notoriously imprecise, but it is known that although the amount of cotton exported on government account rose, government exportations definitely fell far short of supply bureau demands. From August 1863 to March 1864, the period of the informal regulations and the time of greatest losses in blockade running, the War Department shipped out an average of 1600 bales of cotton a month.[83] These figures do not include Navy and Treasury department exports and may not include certain payments on shipbuilding contracts. From March to December 1864 the government, in all its branches and for all purposes, exported about 3,000 bales or 2,000 tons a month.[84] This increase, however, still fell short of the demand. The War Department alone estimated that it would need 6,000 bales or 3,900 tons of cotton exported monthly to meet current needs for the last six months of 1864.[85] This figure apparently did not include cotton needed by the War Department to pay off large outstanding contracts on supplies and shipbuilding. The import gap was worse than the export gap. With 2,000 tons of cargo space monthly at the command of the government, the Subsistence Department estimated that it alone would need 2,300 tons monthly; the Niter and Mining Bureau estimated its needs at 1,600 tons monthly.[86] The problem of inadequate transportation remained unsolved.

New actions by the Confederate administrators best indicate the inadequacy of the government's transportation program. During 1864 administrators backed McRae's efforts in Europe to build and buy a fleet of specially designed blockade runners, to be paid for in sterling proceeds of cotton sales.[87] These ships came increasingly into use during the fall and winter of 1864 and 1865 and became the best investment that the government made during the entire war; but they came on the scene much too late.[88]

Confederate administrators also moved to make contract terms more

83. This is the average of totals given in Bayne to Seddon, March 22, 1864, *OR*-4, III, 241.

84. This is the average of totals given in Seddon to Davis, Dec. 10, 1864, *ibid.*, p. 930.

85. Trenholm to Seddon, Aug. 12, 1864, *ibid.*, p. 587.

86. Bayne to Trenholm, Aug. 12, 1864, *ibid.*, p. 589.

87. McRae to Seddon, July 4, 1864, *ibid.*, pp. 525–526.

88. Thompson, *Confederate Purchasing Operations Abroad*, pp. 76 ff.

efficient by renegotiating contracts based on under-valued cotton. Bayne, Memminger, and Trenholm led the "more pence per pound" push. Trenholm put the case for efficiency in simple and powerful terms. By his calculations, the Crenshaw steamer contract, which called for payments in 6*d*. cotton, would cost the Confederacy 30,000 bales, while buying the same ships out of proceeds of cotton sales in England would have cost only 5,000 bales.[89] As a starter in the program of realizing maximum value from cotton, the Treasury Department stopped the evasion of regulations through the 13th article by ending the sales of cotton certificates; in addition, the government finally canceled many lesser contracts calling for payment in cotton, years after this practice should have been ended.[90]

A clash occurred, however, over the question of ending contracts with the shipping lines that were carrying government cotton and stores for 50 per cent profit plus freight. The particular point of controversy occurred in the late autumn of 1864 when the Power, Lowe and Company contract came up for renewal. This firm had been making 650 per cent profit by bringing in subsistence and quartermaster supplies, and Bayne and Trenholm refused to countenance its renewal, averring that 300 per cent profit was enough for hauling such items as meat.[91] Northrop and Ruffin put up a determined battle to save the contract and in so doing launched a vigorous attack on the whole idea of the "regulations."[92] They admitted that the government was not getting the return it would like for its cotton but pointed out what they considered to be a more important consideration. They claimed that to eliminate such arrangements as those with Power, Lowe and Company or with Crenshaw would smash overseas procurement, for few ships were running under the "regulations."[93] Of 36 dockings between August 19 and November 1, 1864 only 9 ships operated under the regulations of the act of February 6, 1864. All the rest were made by government steamers or contracted ships, and none of these brought in meat.[94] From June to December 1864 the government had imported a total of 2,767,610 pounds of meat. The Crenshaw steamers had

89. Trenholm to Seddon, Aug. 12, 1864, *OR*-4, III, 588.

90. Memminger to Seddon, April 30, 1864, *ibid.*, pp. 364–365; Lawton to Waller, Sept. 21, 1864, QMDLS, XX, 135.

91. Ruffin to Northrop, Nov. 4, 1864, PRSD; "Ruffin Testimony," PRSD, p. 26.

92. The correspondence on the question of the Regulations may be found in Oct.–Dec., 1864, correspondence, PRSD, and in "Ruffin Testimony," *ibid., passim.*

93. Ruffin to Northrop, Nov. 4, 1864, PRSD.

94. *Ibid.*

brought in half, 1,384,050 pounds; contract vessels, 916,150 pounds; vessels running under the regulations, 410,000 pounds; and government vessels, 57,300 pounds.[95] The pair claimed that it was not possible to have efficient use of cotton, no matter how desirable it might be in theory, and also get the needed supplies; for the shippers were apparently not interested in operating under the regulations. As Northrop and Ruffin put it:

> Meat is a bulky article and will not pay and hence blockade runners will not bring it. . . . the trade regulations so far have failed to bring subsistence, and if insisted on as the exclusive policy of the Government, will effectually kill all importations of that character.[96]

Nevertheless, Northrop and Ruffin lost their fight. The administration refused to renew the contract with Power, Lowe and Company right at the time of Lee's third annual mid-winter meat crisis.[97] In lieu of canceled contracts, the Treasury Department offered $168,000 in specie to buy meat, but shortly thereafter the whole question became academic with the fall of Fort Fisher.[98]

Many other aspects of the story of overseas procurement could be discussed, including the disposition of funds overseas and the story of Davis's long and bitter struggle with the states and Congress to prevent weakening of the regulations. Only the logistical side of the problem has been developed here, however, in order to estimate administrative efficiency. A few concluding observations must suffice. The Confederate government would not have solved its transportation problems satisfactorily if it had pre-empted all cargo space. Most shippers would not have braved the blockade for freight rates alone; thus, the government should have demanded not more than one half of the cargo space of private vessels, paying very liberal freight rates in cheap cotton and leaving private half-cargoes unrestricted. If such an arrangement failed to provide enough ships, the government should then have resorted to some contracts of the Power-Lowe type to supplement shipping until enough government ships were bought or built. All purchases of materials and ships should have been from sterling proceeds of cotton sales in Europe under centralized auditing and disbursement.

95. "Ruffin Testimony," PRSD, p. 30.
96. Ruffin to Northrop, Oct. 18, 1864, *OR*-4, III, 739.
97. "Ruffin Testimony," PRSD, p. 28. 98. *Ibid.*

Instead, the Confederate administrators faltered from beginning to end. They waited too late to regulate private shipping while they embarked on a number of wasteful cotton contract schemes. They then mismanaged regulations on private shipping so badly that private shippers left the trade, with the result that the government found itself back to its original problem of too few government-owned and contracted vessels. Meanwhile the government took years to come around to centralized disbursement. As a result, the efficiency of foreign procurement varied widely at various times and among the various bureaus. The Ordnance Department, after a bad start, met minimum obligations because late in the war it enjoyed priority in sterling funds and owned most of the government's shipping. The Quartermaster's Department fluctuated from disaster in 1863 to success in 1864. The Subsistence Department never approached meeting its needs. With more intelligent management from above, all the bureaus would have fared better.

. . .

The record of the civilian leadership during the height of the war is open to severe indictment. Simply put, the Confederate leaders moved too slowly and irresolutely, losing ground on supply problems which threatened to disintegrate the Confederate war effort. Ironically, their most judiciously contrived policy, allocation of manpower, concerned a problem for which there was no remedy. In other areas the leaders had reasonable prospects of overcoming their problems, but their dilatory tinkering never really approached achieving successful results. They improved their policies of trading through the lines and overseas procurement, but such improvement was inadequate and came too late. Domestic procurement, already debilitated by financial anemia, was pegged to a risky financial gamble. All of these fumbling readjustments had been carried out in the now ingrained manner of reacting to pressures grown intolerable rather than trying to plan ahead. Davis and company had given the bureau chiefs and the military commanders little reason to look to 1864 with confidence.

CHAPTER SEVEN

SUPPLY AND STRATEGY: A TROUBLESOME INTERPLAY

. . . it is in consequence of the present system, the most perfect for gleaning the whole country that can be devised, that the armies of Northern Virginia and of Tennessee are enabled to keep the field. ——
—— L. B. Northrop, March 12, 1864*

I cannot see how we can operate with our present supplies. Any derangement . . . would render it impossible for me to keep the army together. . . . We have rations for the troops to-day and to-morrow.
—— R. E. Lee, April 12, 1864†

While the supply administrators struggled with policy, supply problems and deficiencies were affecting campaigning and strategy. By the late spring of 1863, when the Confederate armies went into action from the Rappahannock to Texas, there appeared to be no reason to fear that shortages of food, clothing, arms, or accouterments would be great enough to interfere with the efficiency of the armies.[1] By the end of 1863, however, the fortunes of war, unexpected shortages, and administrative tie-ups had not only intruded supply factors forcefully into strategy but had also begun to produce, on the part of the commanding generals, a defensive attitude that boded ill for the future of the Confederacy.

Ironically, Lee's campaigns in the east were less affected by supply problems than were military operations in the west, although the Army of Northern Virginia lived in a more impoverished area than the western armies and had suffered a disconcerting provisioning crisis in the previous winter. The Chancellorsville campaign, for example, had

* Northrop's endorsement, March 12, 1864, on Polk to Davis, Feb. 22, 1864, *OR*-1, XXXII (3), 745. † Lee to Davis, April 12, 1864, *ibid.*, XXXIII, 1275.

1. Northrop to Seddon, June 4, 1863, *OR*-4, II, 574–575; Gorgas to Seddon, Nov. 15, 1863, *ibid.*, pp. 955–959; Myers to Waller, May 14, 1863, QMDLS, XVII, 382–383.

not been affected by supply factors.[2] The subsequent decision to invade the North appears to have been reached primarily on grounds other than supply considerations, although some supply officials held hope that supplies could be gathered in the wake of Lee's army. During the invasion Lee's army managed to sustain itself adequately from its supply trains, purchases, and increasingly in the later stages by foraging. On the other hand, Lee did have trouble in finding fodder, and his men wore out shoes faster than they could secure new ones.[3] When the army returned, it brought little in the way of extra supplies. The Quartermaster General summed up the administration's disappointment when he replied to a dispatch from Lee's quartermaster in Pennsylvania pleading for shoes: "I have been in anticipation of receiving stores from you and not to supply you."[4]

By the autumn, however, supply problems had become a factor. Lee's men began to run short of shoes and woolen clothing because Union blockaders had intercepted blockade runners on which the Quartermaster's Department depended. Lee thanked Lawton for his efforts to scrape together enough supplies to enable him to take the offensive but told the Quartermaster General that the planned pursuit of Meade during the Bristoe Station campaign had nevertheless been aborted:

> The want of the supplies of shoes, clothing, overcoats, and blankets is very great. Nothing but my unwillingness to expose the men to the hardships that would have resulted from moving them into Loudoun in their present condition induced me to return to the Rappahannock. But I was averse to marching them over the rough roads of that region, at a season, too, when frosts are certain and snows probable, unless they were better provided to encounter them without suffering. I should otherwise have endeavored to detain General Meade near the Potomac, if I could not throw him to the north side.[5]

If the sole consideration that prevented Lee from moving against Meade was supplies, this campaign is as clear an example as any of the effects of the general supply situation on Confederate strategic planning. The Confederacy's basic deficiencies in wool and leather meant

2. This statement is based on extensive surveys of campaign reports and correspondence in *OR*-1.

3. Lee to Davis, June 23, 1863, *OR*-1, XXVII (2), 298; Lee to Davis, July 16, 1863, *ibid.*, p. 302.

4. Myers to Corley, July 3, 1863, QMDLS, XVII, 539.

5. Lee to Lawton, Oct. 19, 1863, *OR*-1, XXIX (2), 794.

dependence on importing these materials from abroad. Management of overseas importations had been inadequate, and as a consequence the Quartermaster's Department had failed to supply the Army of Northern Virginia adequately and Lee had decided against attacking Meade. The possible results if Lee had attempted such a campaign is the province of experts in military strategy.

Turning to the west, the Confederate commanders there, none of them men of sanguine temperament, felt hamstrung from the beginning by shortages of both men and supplies. Johnston, no man to gloss over obstacles, could not assemble an army that was, by his standards, adequately prepared to take the field to relieve Vicksburg. Even for the small forces at his command he was short in field transportation, not only for moving normal army impedimenta but also for bringing in provisions from the countryside.[6] He was also short of clothing, ammunition, and small arms, and in general Johnston believed that his little command was unfit for active operations.[7] The supply bureaus held stocks in most of the materials that Johnston needed, but communications with Mississippi were so tenuous and the administrative procedures so slow that it was not until the autumn of 1863 that the forces in Mississippi had the supplies they needed; and even then they lacked adequate field transportation.[8]

While the supply situation vitally affected the scope of Johnston's operations, his actions in Mississippi in turn damaged Confederate resources. Johnston's two abandonments of Jackson resulted in the unnecessary destruction of a large amount of rolling stock and a great quantity of supplies.[9] These events increased Davis's antipathy for Johnston. Davis had already laid losses of supplies at Manassas and the loss of Norfolk shipbuilding equipment to what he considered Johnston's precipitate and unwarranted retreats in 1862.[10] Later in the war, in writing to Colonel James Phelan of Mississippi, he alluded to these events and concluded:

> The loss of supplies during the time he was in command had been so great, and our difficulties for the want of them so distress-

6. Johnston to Seddon, June 5, 1863, *ibid.*, XXIV (1), 224–225; Johnston Report, Dec. 24, 1863, *ibid.*, p. 237.
7. Johnston to Seddon, June 5, 1863, *ibid.*, pp. 224–225; Johnston Report, Dec. 24, 1863, *ibid.*, p. 237.
8. Johnston to Lawton, Sept. 22, 1863, *ibid.*, XXX (4), 686; Barbour to Johnston, Oct. 5, 1863, *ibid.*, p. 729.
9. Davis to Phelan, March 1, 1865, Rowland, *Jefferson Davis*, VI, 498.
10. *Ibid.*, pp. 494–495.

> ing, as to cripple our military operations to a far greater extent than can readily by appreciated.[11]

After the war Davis continued to harp on the theme of Johnston's unnecessary wastage of war material.[12] Whether or not Johnston's losses were justifiable, they intensified the Davis-Johnston feud, with all that this feud contributed to the fate of the Confederacy.

As for Bragg, his Army of Tennessee was apparently in condition to fight. Colonel W. P. Johnston, special aide to the President, reported that the Army of Tennessee was in a "high state of efficiency, well clad and armed,"[13] and that the army "lacks no physical element of success."[14] There were some supply problems, of course, typical of a Confederate army—only "tolerable" field transportation and shoe supply and a shortage of "long forage" for the animals.[15] As we have seen, however, a regular supply of subsistence was the biggest problem.[16] Johnston called it the "vital" question that was "very far from satisfactory," but he noted that the men were not grumbling.[17]

The subsistence problem eased with the summer, but the scars of Bragg's spring subsistence shortages figured in strategic planning. In the first place, the very position of the army, in southern Tennessee rather than in the logical strategic position in the Cumberland foothills astride the Nashville-Chattanooga railroad was a consequence of the need to remain in a country more likely to yield provisions. The railroad from Georgia could not bring in enough supplies. The generals talked vaguely of invading Kentucky to gain provision-rich territory, but the presence of large Union forces at Nashville prevented such a move.[18] Actually, Johnston, as over-all commander in the west, was thinking in defensive terms, even of retreat. Although he knew that Bragg would have to defend Georgia's industrial and rail complex, he considered moving the Army of Tennessee to the west, where there was greater room to maneuver.[19] To defend Georgia, however, the Army of Tennessee was already too far to the west of the route Rosecrans would take. As Johnston admitted, Bragg's army was susceptible to a turning movement past its right flank.[20] Still, Johnston did not order any change in dispositions and clung to the more abundant country of

11. *Ibid.*, p. 496.
12. See 1878–1879 Davis-Northrop correspondence, *ibid.*, VIII, *passim.*
13. W. P. Johnston to Davis, April 15, 1863, *OR*-1, XXIII (2), 758.
14. *Ibid.* 15. *Ibid.*, pp. 758–759. 16. *Ibid.*, p. 759. 17. *Ibid.*
18. *Ibid.*, p. 761. 19. Johnston to Davis, April 10, 1863, *ibid.*, p. 745.
20. Johnston to Polk, March 3, 1863, *ibid.*, pp. 659–660.

southern Tennessee. Eventually, during June, after Johnston had gone to try to aid Pemberton, Rosecrans moved on Chattanooga and Knoxville past Bragg's right, and Bragg hastily retreated southeast to interpose himself between Rosecrans and Chattanooga, abandoning his winter encampments with only trifling losses in materials.[21] Thus, although the problem of securing supplies had initially placed Bragg in poor strategic position, he had recovered from this and succeeded in blocking the road to Chattanooga.

The subsequent campaign in the Chattanooga area, with its disastrous results for the Confederacy, is an important episode in the interrelationship of the supply effort and campaigning. As the campaign opened, Bragg in Chattanooga and Rosecrans to the west across the Tennessee River faced the same strategic problems. To strike directly at the enemy in that particular terrain was hazardous, but to outmaneuver the opponent by moving against his supply lines involved crossing the Tennessee River and putting it at the army's back, carrying supplies through barren mountains and giving the enemy the opportunity to cut off units or strike flank and rear. Rosecrans had ample troops, supplies, and transportation, plus the obligation to press the offensive, and he finally moved across the Tennessee and around Bragg's left flank. Bragg, with a smaller army, claimed that he was too deficient in transportation and supplies to take any offensive effort to prevent Rosecrans from advancing across the river.[22] In this case Bragg's choice to remain on the defensive was much more than a routine strategic maneuver. It meant that he would have to abandon Chattanooga in order to interpose his army between Rosecrans and the railroad to Atlanta. Chattanooga's value was immense; besides being the gateway to Georgia it controlled one of the two main trans-Confederacy railroad supply lines to Lee and protected much of the Confederacy's remaining meat and niter supplies and all of its copper production.[23] Bragg should have made a supreme effort in August to prevent Rosecrans from maneuvering him out of one of the most strategic points in the Confederacy.

The battle of Chickamauga and its aftermath raise additional problems in determining the relationship of supply problems to Bragg's campaigning. For example, the strategic-logistical feat of bringing Longstreet's men to the battlefield has been justly praised as an inspir-

21. Bragg to Johnston, Aug. 7, 1863, *ibid.*, XXIII (1), 584.
22. Bragg to Cooper, Sept. 4, 1863, *ibid.*, XXX (2), 21.
23. Vandiver, *Confederate Ordnance*, pp. 201–202, 201 n.

ing example of the railroads' contribution to the Confederacy's war effort.[24] Still, this movement was not entirely beneficial. Bragg had had continual difficulties in bringing up supplies regularly over the Georgia-owned Western and Atlantic,[25] and the movement of Longstreet's troops now completely disrupted the flow of supplies.[26] However, supplies were not a significant problem during the battle. While the maneuvering of Bragg's army and the movement of Longstreet's men had put the troops on short rations before and during the battle, by Bragg's own declaration their morale was excellent.[27] Reports from the unit commanders occasionally mentioned the usual difficulties in distributing ammunition and rations in the confusion of battlefield maneuvering, but the incidence of this was too insignificant to offset the course of the fighting.[28]

There has come down to us considerable controversy as to whether or not Bragg should have pursued the Union troops immediately after Chickamauga or assaulted Chattanooga in the days following. More pertinent to this study, did Bragg fail to follow up his victory because of supply problems? Bragg's short, cryptic reports on the twenty-first and twenty-third, immediately after the battle, mention his losses and make the judgment that the enemy was in "heavy force" and behind "strong defenses."[29] These references suggest that at that time supplies were not the reason why he failed to pursue Rosecrans. In longer reports on September 24, Bragg still emphasized the enemy's strength in Chattanooga and his own losses, but he did introduce problems of short rations, lack of field transportation, and irregularity of supplies.[30] He did not, however, relate these problems clearly to any decision against pursuit.

In December 1863, after subsequent fiascos had made the failure to attempt an assault on Chattanooga a matter of heated controversy, Bragg wrote a long report reviewing his actions. In reference to his abandonment of Chattanooga, he gave the same reasons as before—inferior numbers, gloomy supply prospects, strategic considerations—for

24. Black, *Confederate Railroads,* p. 119.

25. The bulk of this correspondence can be found in *OR*-1, XXXI and XXXII, *passim.*

26. Bragg to Cooper, Dec. 28, 1863, *ibid.,* XXX (2), 36.

27. Bragg to Cooper, Sept. 24, 1863, *ibid.,* p. 24.

28. This statement is based on a survey of reports in *ibid., passim.*

29. Bragg to Cooper, Sept. 21, 1863, *ibid.,* pp. 22–23; Bragg to Cooper, Sept. 23, 1863, *ibid.,* p. 23.

30. Bragg to Cooper, Sept. 24, 1863, *ibid.,* p. 23; Bragg to Cooper, Sept. 24, 1863, *ibid.,* p. 24.

refusing to take the offensive and for maneuvering on the defensive instead.[31] In discussing his failure to pursue Rosecrans after Chickamauga, Bragg continued to put strong emphasis upon tactical problems: "Immediate pursuit . . . would have been fruitless, as it was not deemed practicable, with our weak and exhausted force, to assail the enemy, now more than double our numbers, behind his entrenchments."[32] However, in the same report, Bragg claimed for the first time that supply problems were a major cause of his lack of pursuit. On the morning of the twenty-first, he asserted, his men were out of food, water, and ammunition.[33] He continued, "Our supplies . . . were greatly reduced. . . . These supplies were ordered replenished and as soon as it was seen we could be subsisted, the army was moved forward."[34] Bragg's subordinates, while mentioning many reasons why he should have pursued Rosecrans and assaulted Chattanooga, do not mention the supply situation in any way.[35] Bragg's latter-day stress on supplies as a major factor in not pursuing smacks somewhat of rationalization. One wonders if Bragg would have attempted a pursuit, much less an assault on Chattanooga, even if well-supplied.

For the first time also, in Bragg's December report, we get his ideas about the third controversial point of the Chickamauga-Chattanooga campaign, his decision not to invade Tennessee after his success at Chickamauga. In essence claimed that he could not advance for the same reasons that he could not take the offensive to save Chattanooga in August. Enumerating a list of supporting points he demonstrated to his satisfaction that such a movement was "utterly impossible for the lack of transportation" and that it would have displayed an "entire want of military propriety" strategically.[36] Whatever value military experts might attach to Bragg's strategic reasoning, his transportation deficiencies make a weighty list: one-third of his artillery horses had been killed, he had no pontoons, the bridges over the Tennessee were out and the fords were subject to sudden rises in the river, and Longstreet's men had brought no field transportation.[37] Still, as in the previous cases, one wonders if Bragg would have undertaken the offensive even if properly equipped.

There were no outstanding supply problems which Bragg could blame for the disasters at Missionary Ridge and Lookout Mountain.

31. Bragg to Cooper, Dec. 28, 1863, *ibid.*, p. 27. 32. *Ibid.*, p. 35.
33. *Ibid.*, p. 34. 34. *Ibid.*, p. 36.
35. This statement is based on a survey of reports in *ibid.*, *passim*.
36. Bragg to Cooper, Dec. 28, 1863, *ibid.*, p. 37. 37. *Ibid.*

The troops had ample food, ammunition, and accouterments of war; and although there was some shortage of winter clothing because of the blockade-running losses of the Quartermaster's Department, official reports of the fiasco did not complain about the state of clothing for the men.[38]

How much did supply problems determine the outcome of Bragg's campaign in Tennessee and how much did his campaign affect the supply effort? Bragg was faced with the problems of inferior numbers, inadequate transportation, no immediate supply reserves, and some irregularities in supply service from Atlanta. On the other hand, he had weighty responsibility to protect one of the key centers of the Confederate war effort, and his opponent, although well-supplied, had severe strategic problems in advancing against him. It appears that perhaps Bragg was too much aware of his problems and too little aware of the compelling need to hold Chattanooga and East Tennessee. If he had seen matters in clearer perspective, he perhaps would have been more aggressive, taking the offensive either before or during Rosecrans's move around Chattanooga. Failing that, he should have made a vigorous effort to drive the Union troops out of Chattanooga after Chickamauga. If that too had failed, perhaps he should have taken the offensive into middle Tennessee to draw the enemy out of the Chattanooga area and open a new supply district, although this operation may well have been less feasible than the others. It should be noted, however, that Bragg's superiors had not directed that he fight to save the vital areas of East Tennessee. Indeed, there was little comment about the value of the area anywhere in the leadership circles of the Confederacy until the press began in the autumn and winter of 1863–64 to lament the loss of East Tennessee.[39]

In summary, supply deficiencies did, in fact, hamper Bragg's campaigning and possibly produced an unduly negative effect on his strategic thinking. Furthermore, it is certain that Bragg's conduct of affairs in Tennessee resulted in a disastrous blow to the Confederate war effort. Not only had he surrendered railroads, food, and minerals to the enemy, but he had also opened the gate to Georgia and thus to the

38. This statement is based on a survey of the reports in *ibid.*, XXXI, *passim.*

39. *Daily Richmond Examiner,* Oct. 31, 1863, and Jan. 28, 1864; a few others also realized the value of Chattanooga: see W. M. Polk to Davis, Oct. 4, 1863, *OR*-1, XXX (2), 66. Kean gloomily noted, "The enemy are rapidly confining their hold on Tennessee, its *flour* and *meat* so much needed by us. Alas, for our prospects this winter." Younger, *Kean Diary,* p. 111.

industrial, agricultural, and transportation backbone of the Confederacy. How might the war have gone if the Union army had still faced the Appalachian barrier in the spring of 1864?

. . .

In a pursuit of the theme of the interrelationship of supplies and campaigning, two situations merit close attention: the second winter of supply problems for the Army of Northern Virginia and the controversy over the condition of the Army of Tennessee. In the first situation, divided authority and intrenched prejudices at the highest levels of policy-making failed to prevent or mitigate a recurrence of another winter food shortage for the Army of Northern Virginia.

In the autumn of 1863 Northrop, worried about the future supply of subsistence to Lee's army and harassed by irregular railroad transportation, pressed for more effective methods of collecting supplies. Northrop suggested to Lee that he order his field officers to inaugurate a continuous system of impressing all private surpluses in Lee's district.[40] Lee objected, and the issue developed into a three-way argument among Lee, Seddon, and Northrop, an argument ranging into legal and moral questions and ultimately displaying an example of a leadership vacuum. Lee objected to being the only military commander to be called upon to impose sweeping and continuous local impressment at a time when the people were resisting the impressment system of the act of 1863.[41] He argued that general orders of the War Department allowed generals to use impressment powers only under circumstances of temporary local emergency and claimed that any order for continuous local impressment would have to come from the War Department.[42] Further, Lee did not think that conditions warranted impressment.

Caught between Lee and Northrop, Seddon claimed that he did not have legal authority to order commanding officers to impress all private surpluses and that the officers alone were the judges of military necessity that overrode the current legal restrictions that allowed only the impressing of hoarders' stocks.[43] He agreed with Lee, however, that in any case the situation was not yet severe enough to warrant such

40. Northrop to Lee, Nov. 22, 1863, *ibid.*, XXIX (2), 843–844.

41. Lee to Northrop, Nov. 23, 1863, *ibid.*, p. 844; Lee to Seddon, Nov. 19, 1863, *ibid.*, p. 837; Jones, *War Clerk's Diary,* II, 104.

42. Lee to Seddon, Nov. 19, 1863, *OR*-1, XXIX (2), 837; Lee to Seddon, Dec. 7, 1863, *ibid.*, p. 862; Lee to Northrop, Jan. 5, 1864, *ibid.*, XXXIII, 1064–1065; Lee to Northrop, Jan. 13, 1864, *ibid.*, pp. 1087–1088.

43. Seddon to Lee, Nov. 20, 1863, *ibid.*, XXIX (2), 838.

action.[44] From November 1863 to January 1864 Northrop tried to persuade Lee to order both the field commissaries and the agents of the Subsistence Department to comb Lee's military district and to impress all supplies not immediately held for family consumption, citing the impressment act and subsequent army orders for technical justification.[45] Northrop's main argument, however, went beyond adept citation. He claimed that bureau agents impressing from hoarders alone had failed to produce a reserve and that impressment by field officers was absolutely necessary.[46]

In the end nothing was done. Lee conceded that Northrop was technically right, but he claimed that the logical result of having each commander impress all the supplies in his own district would mean each army's fending for itself and the creating of a wide variety of prices, the very antithesis of Northrop's own system of centralized purchasing and distribution for the accumulation of a general reserve for all the armies.[47] In any event, Lee still did not feel it necessary to impress and refused to act unless ordered by Seddon. Seddon was becoming convinced of the need for immediate impressments but declared that he had no legal power to order them. Northrop reiterated that the need was there, that there was legal justification, that normal impressment regulations were not securing the food, and that for the time being impressment in Lee's district was the only answer for the Army of Northern Virginia, theories of centralized procurement notwithstanding. Still neither Seddon nor Lee would assume power. Lee's letter to Seddon on December 7, 1863, neatly summarized the whole impasse. Lee wrote:

> The power that you desire [that of general and continual impressment of all surpluses] rests, in my opinion, with the War Department, . . . [except] in casual emergencies provided for, and can be more uniformly and judiciously exerted than by the commanders of the armies.
>
> I shall endeavor to collect all the supplies for this army that I can legitimately do, and keep it in the best condition I can. But

44. *Ibid.,* p. 839.

45. Lee to Seddon, Nov. 19, 1863, *ibid.,* p. 837; Northrop to Lee, Nov. 22, 1863, *ibid.,* pp. 843–844; Lee to Northrop, Jan. 5, 1864, *ibid.,* XXXIII, 1064–1065; Lee to Northrop, Jan. 13, 1864, *ibid.,* pp. 1087–1088.

46. Northrop to Lee, Nov. 22, 1863, *ibid.,* XXIX (2), 843–844.

47. Lee to Northrop, Jan. 13, 1864, *ibid.,* XXXIII, 1087–1088.

unless it is supplied with food, it will be impossible for me to keep it together.[48]

On this Northrop endorsed cryptically: "The power of meeting the present crisis, as far as is possible, rests somewhere, because that necessity is absolute which has no law to limit it."[49] Seddon's endorsement was lame enough: "I know, as an officer, no greater necessity than to obey the law."[50] Northrop may have exaggerated his problems and his suggestions may not have been efficient, but he was trying to meet his responsibilities. In contrast, Seddon and Lee had been inert and negative, not only denying the gravity of the situation but also refusing to suggest possible remedies if the supply crisis should become severe.

As it turned out, Northrop had correctly estimated the gravity of the subsistence situation. By January the small supply of flour and fresh meat in reserve at Virginia depots was being rapidly consumed.[51] Every mouthful of food and fodder for future consumption would have to come in by train. The railroads up to this time had not brought in enough provisions to feed the army on a continuing basis, and the prospects for an adequate food supply in the future were bleak.

To account for the railroads' inefficiency, we must consider the nature of the government's administration of the railroads since the passage of the railroad regulation act of May 1, 1863. This act had authorized the government to create a set of through freight schedules and to enforce them at its discretion. Fragmentary evidence indicates, however, that the regulatory provisions were not invoked during 1863, primarily because (if absence of complaints signifies anything) the railroads delivered government freight and moved troops with a tolerable degree of efficiency, except for their ingrained dilatoriness in moving fodder. The imposition of through freight schedules would have improved performance, but apparently nothing was done on this score, even though Northrop and Seddon were strong advocates of this approach. The only change in government administration was to subordinate the Railroad Bureau, now under Lieutenant-Colonel F. W. Sims, to the Quartermaster General[52] and to create a new set of government officials. Civilian transportation agents were now dispatched to all the

48. Lee to Seddon, Dec. 7, 1863, *ibid.*, XXIX (2), 862. 49. *Ibid.*
50. *Ibid.* 51. French to Northrop, Jan. 3, 1864, *ibid.*, LI (2), 808.
52. Special Orders No. 133, Adjutant and Inspector General's Office, 1863 Series, June 4, 1863, *OR*-4, II, 579.

crucial railroad junctions to take up permanent residence and speed the shipments of government freight.[53]

During the fall and winter of 1863, problems with government railroad shipments began to build up. Long forage had already been in chronic short supply all over the Confederacy for some time, and during the summer the local supply of fodder for the Army of Northern Virginia failed completely. By late fall Lee's army depended on daily delivery of some 20 box cars or 5,000 bushels of corn from as far away as Georgia to keep his animals at minimum condition. This massive shipment of corn added enormously to the burden of the railroads, which were increasingly strained with shipments of subsistence, quartermaster, and ordnance stores, cotton, and troops.[54] The railroad companies were reluctant to ship corn if any other kind of freight was at hand, and thus the needed amounts of forage did not arrive in Virginia. Lee had to return to his expedient of the previous winter of scattering his cavalry and artillery over Virginia and North Carolina to find subsistence locally.[55] As a matter of fact, the Richmond administration never did regulate railroad transportation so as to ensure an adequate fodder supply, with the result that the weakened Confederate cavalry contributed mightily to the disasters of 1864.

To harassed officials who thought they had already experienced every possible railroad problem in the previous winter's debacle, there arose a new headache—stealing. During the fall and winter of 1863, reports poured in concerning consignments of subsistence being methodically robbed en route, and incoming trains constantly arrived with proper invoices but short shipments. Often, meat shipments would be loaded by the piece at Richmond and sent up the line to Lee, only to arrive at Gordonsville short. For example, in eight days after December 30, 1863, over 3,000 pounds of meat was stolen between Richmond and Gordonsville.[56] Since supplies traveled at government risk, it became necessary for commissaries and quartermasters at depots to put guards on the trains to frustrate stealing, but still meat and other subsistence supplies disappeared or were fraudulently invoiced at the

53. Myers to Shaw, May 28, 1863, QMDLS, XVII, 422–423.

54. Cole Memorandum, n.d., in RG 109, Entry 43, Quartermaster's Department Telegrams Received; Lawton to Longstreet, March 9, 1864, *OR*-1, XXXII, 598–599.

55. For information on Lee's horse and forage problem, see Charles W. Ramsdell, "General Robert E. Lee's Horse Supply, 1862–1865," *American Historical Review,* XXXV, No. 4 (July 1930), 758–777.

56. Lee to Davis, Jan. 11, 1864, *OR*-1, XXXIII, 1079.

beginning of the shipment. During 1863 some 617,847 pounds of bacon disappeared, over 500,000 pounds of it lost in transit from Atlanta.[57] In addition, thousands of pounds of beef, peas, lard, potatoes, and rice were stolen.

Adverse fortunes of war also helped to strangle the shipment of supplies. Union armies took Knoxville and Chattanooga during the autumn of 1863, severing the heavy-duty supply line from Atlanta to Richmond. Supplies from Georgia depots now had to go by more circuitous routes, either by Augusta, Kingstree, Charlotte, and Greensboro to Weldon or by Macon, Savannah, Charleston, and Wilmington to Weldon. From Weldon all supplies now had to be funneled over a single track to Richmond. The Greensboro-Danville link, which would have provided two entirely separate Atlantic seaboard routes from Georgia to Richmond, had not been completed, although the money for the line had been appropriated two years previously. The feeding of the animals and men of the Army of Northern Virginia and of a large proportion of the city of Richmond depended on a shaky, rundown railroad system culminating in 85 miles of single track.

In January 1864 the Army of Northern Virginia was put on quarter-pound salt meat rations,[58] and this state of affairs prompted Lee to think of new ways to get more food and better quartermaster supplies for his men. Lee objected to the practice of letting the officers at posts buy rations at cost for themselves and for their families, for they thus consumed supplies that might have gone to the men.[59] Northrop disputed Lee's points but then recommended that the meat component be omitted from rations sold to officers. Seddon approved Northrop's suggestion, but Northrop changed his mind and recommended that the War Department await the action of Congress, which was then considering legislation on the matter of furnishing rations to officers.[60] Seddon then agreed to Northrop's second proposal, and Jones, noting the procedures, snorted: "Here are twenty days gone, and the Commissary General has his own way still. He don't hesitate to bully the Secretary and the highest generals in the field."[61]

57. *Ibid.*, p. 1078.

58. Davis to Northrop, Jan. 4, 1864, William James Rucker Papers, Alderman Library, University of Virginia; Lee to Davis, Jan. 2, 1864, *OR*-1, XXXIII, 1061.

59. Lee to Seddon, Jan. 22, 1864, *OR*-1, XXXIII, 1114–1115.

60. Endorsement of Lee to Seddon, Jan. 22, 1864, *ibid.*, pp. 1115–1116; Northrop endorsements, Jan. 27, 1864, and Feb. 9, 1864; Seddon endorsement, Feb. 11, 1864.

61. Jones, *War Clerk's Diary*, II, 147.

On February 28 Lee's chief commissary reported the army down to two days' bread and only a few days of meat.[62] In his endorsement of the report, Northrop circumspectly twitted his superiors for allowing the railroads to do as they pleased about transporting stores and then declared that there was an abundance of supplies in the south if the railroads could only get them up. He estimated that only one third of the needed flour had arrived over the last few months because only one eighth of the transportation of the railroads had been used to ship government freight. He strongly recommended that passenger trains be stopped: "Nothing should be allowed as a sufficient reason to delay an immediate accumulation of supplies of food at this point."[63] Lawton, who was responsible for railroad management, apparently offered no suggestions. It should be noted that the decision-making process in the War Department, obscure already, had become absolutely enigmatic by the elevation of Bragg to the post of military adviser to the President. Northrop's endorsement was passed around among Seddon, Davis, and Bragg for some days in early March, producing only some idle speculation about what Wadley might do to cure the railroad problem if recalled.[64] The *Daily Richmond Examiner* attacked the railroad companies savagely, declaring that "the impression is universal" that the railroads were "managed in the interest of speculators and extortioners,"[65] with whom the government officers and speculators were "apparently in partnership."[66]

Finally, Davis, perhaps pressured by Lee, directed Seddon to act. On March 11, under the authority of the regulatory act of May 1, 1863, Seddon "authorized" the Quartermaster General "to stop passenger trains upon any line of Rail Road on which either forage or subsistence for the army may be delayed, until the same or such portion thereof as may be necessary to the public service is removed."[67] By the fourteenth, before any good could come from this measure, and with the Army of Northern Virginia out of meat and down to one day's ration of bread, Seddon notified the commanding officers at posts to provide military force if necessary to "sustain" the action of the quartermasters in managing the trains.[68]

62. *Ibid.,* p. 161.

63. Northrop endorsement, March 6, 1864, on Lee to Davis, Jan. 6, 1864, *OR*-1, XXXIII, 1077.

64. *Ibid.,* p. 1078.

65. *Daily Richmond Examiner,* March 4, 1864.

66. *Ibid.,* Feb. 4, 1864.

67. Special Orders No. 59, Adjutant and Inspector General's Office, March 11, 1864, WDLS, XVIII, 92; Special Orders No. 60, Adjutant and Inspector General's Office, March 12, 1864, *OR*-4, III, 209.

68. Seddon to Post Commanders, March 18, 1864, WDLS, XVII, 222.

On March 16 the government further tightened its controls over the railroads. The regulations of March 11 had been only temporary and local, applying to cases of delayed shipments. The new orders placed the entire Augusta-Charlotte-Weldon railroad network under military control. Only one passenger train was allowed to run daily, "all other rolling stock to be devoted to moving government freight."[69] Results were gratifying. Fifteen days' supply of meat, figured on the short rations of the Army of Northern Virginia, arrived in twelve days, plus three thousand bushels of corn meal per day.[70] Lawton, in answering the outraged protests of the President of the Wilmington and Weldon Railroad, commented, "The *results* have fully vindicated the act of the War Dept. More Govt. stores have been transported from Wilmington & Charlotte to Richmond in the last five days, than ever before, during this war, in the same space of time."[71]

On March 30 the War Department returned to its earlier regulations under which passenger trains would be suspended only when there was a jam-up of freight.[72] It is not clear who gave this order to end strict military control of railroad transportation. Northrop claimed that Seddon bowed to political pressure.[73] However, considering the facts of decision-making in the Confederate administration and Seddon's pronounced interest in government control of the railroads, it is probable that Davis made the decision. Meanwhile, Lee had written to the War Department urging the Quartermaster's Department to do its duty, concluding: ". . . all the difficulties can be overcome by attention, energy and diligence on the part of the officers in charge of transportation."[74] Lawton wasted no time in replying to his former commander. He summarized all of the extraordinary actions taken to supply the Army of Northern Virginia and said:

> If there is an officer who can discharge the duties with satisfaction, and with fair prospect of accomplishing what you think quite possible, I beg that you will not hesitate to indicate him, that the

69. Lawton to Post Quartermasters, March 16, 1864, QMDLS, XIX, 97.

70. Lawton to Lee, April 16, 1864, *ibid.*, p. 175.

71. Lawton to Fremont, March 18, 1864, Confederate States of America, Quartermaster General's Office Papers. Virginia Historical Society. Not everyone in the government was pleased. Navy Department officials fumed at the army's monopoly of transportation as iron plates destined for the construction of ironclads on the North Carolina rivers remained in Richmond: Mallory to Seddon, March 11, 1864, *OR*-1, XXXIII, 1217–1218.

72. Quartermaster's Department Circular, March 30, 1864, QMDLS, XIX, 131.

73. Northrop to Davis, April 21, 1878, Rowland, *Jefferson Davis,* VIII, 182; see also Jones, *War Clerk's Diary,* II, 188.

74. Quotation in Lawton to Lee, March 21, 1864, *OR*-1, XXXIII, 1237.

assignment may be made . . . I am willing to be stimulated to the discharge of my duty, general, and shall always be glad to know your wants and your views, but I beg of you not to expect impossibilities.[75]

As soon as the government lifted strict controls, shipments fell off. Again the Commissary General returned to the attack. He reported on April 7 that over a million pounds of meat was on its way and that there was a general abundance of supplies in the south.[76] He repeated his suggestion that the passenger trains be stopped until the reserves could be built up. Later he went into Seddon's office to request that the President see his report. At the same time, Lee reported to Davis that he was down to a day's supply of food.[77] Davis referred Northrop's report to Bragg, noting that "the matter is that of which we have repeatedly conversed."[78] Bragg did not answer until the twentieth, but his reply urged that the government stop temporizing. He began by noting that in addition to all previous difficulties the railroads now had to move troops up to reinforce Lee. Bragg said that he had "no hope of any important result" from voluntary actions of the railroads.[79] He wanted through schedules, military supervision of the railroads, and one passenger train daily with space reserved first to government travelers. Bragg then brought up a new point. He felt that there were too many noncombatants in Richmond and suggested that the government should prune personnel to "reduce consumption."[80] Davis referred Bragg's suggestion to Seddon for remarks. Jones deduced from this that Bragg "seems to *rank*" Seddon.[81] Davis in the meantime called a cabinet meeting, and Seddon's opinion came in the next day as per directions.[82] The Secretary of War predictably concurred with Bragg that "military possession" and "complete management" of the railroads was necessary and also agreed that "all supernumeraries or others in various offices and posts under the control of the Government who can be spared should be sent away."[83]

75. *Ibid.* 76. Northrop to Cooper, April 7, 1864, *ibid.*, LI (2), 851.

77. *Ibid.;* Lee to Davis, April 12, 1864, *ibid.*, XXXIII, 1275.

78. Davis's endorsement on Northrop to Cooper, April 7, 1864, *ibid.*, LI (2), 851.

79. Bragg's endorsement, April 20, 1864, on Northrop to Cooper, April 7, 1864, *ibid.*, pp. 851–852. 80. *Ibid.*, p. 852.

81. *Ibid.;* Jones, *War Clerk's Diary,* II, 190.

82. Jones, *War Clerk's Diary,* II, 190; Seddon endorsement, April 22, 1864, on Northrop to Cooper, April 7, 1864, *OR*-1, LI (2), 852.

83. Seddon's endorsement, April 22, 1864, on Northrop to Cooper, April 7, 1864, *OR*-1, LI (2), 852.

All of Davis's subordinates, including his confidant Bragg, had suggested that the government should use its full powers under the railroad law, but Davis would not listen. He wrote to Seddon:

> Due effort should be made to secure the co-operation of railroad companies in the most effective plan before proceeding to take possession of the railroads. I am not encouraged by the past to expect that all difficulties would be removed by transferring the management of these extensive organizations to the agents of the War Department.[84]

It was obvious that the President, whether for personal or political reasons, was determined to overlook years of frustration in railroad affairs, as well as the recent success in bringing in food by government control, if he could salve his conscience with promises from the railroads that they would voluntarily improve their service. Railroad officials, then meeting at Columbia in a convention which represented only a fraction of the railroads of the Confederacy, spotted their cue and promised to send daily into Virginia ten thousand bushels of corn plus the needed meat.[85] With this promise, and cheered by the arrival of subsistence materials, the President not only refused to order more extensive military controls or through schedules, but he also terminated the existing arrangements to send on delayed freight shipments. Meanwhile, aided by the return of grass and vegetables in the spring, the Army of Northern Virginia began to eat regularly, if simply, again, but Northrop was unable to build up any sizable reserves.

While the President refused to interfere with the freedom of the railroad companies, he did not hesitate to take the unprecedented, autocratic step of supervising the removal of government employees from Richmond and precipitating severe derangements of family affairs for the lowly clerks and laborers. The population of Richmond had expanded from 50,000 at the outbreak of the war to an estimated 130,000.[86] The swollen population had always been faced with the most inflated prices in the Confederacy, prices which had destroyed their incomes. During the last winter there had been an actual scarcity of provisions.[87] A shocked Gorgas termed Bragg "a *little cracked*" when the latter speculated that future campaigns might result in the cutting of railroad lines to Richmond, causing the people to leave in order to

84. Davis's endorsement, April 23, 1864, on Northrop to Cooper, April 7, 1864, *ibid.*

85. Jones, *War Clerk's Diary*, II, 196.

86. Vandiver, *Gorgas Diary*, pp. 91–92.

87. For example, see Jones, *War Clerk's Diary*, II, 156, 168–169.

escape starvation and the pillaging of hungry troops.[88] Davis pressed his subordinates to rid the city of as many of their employees as possible. Memminger ordered the lady note-singers to Columbia, and the prisoners and parolees were removed. Gorgas began transferring ordnance shops out of the city while other bureaus sent off all who could administer their jobs away from the capital.[89]

In light of the various features of the great winter supply crisis, Northrop appears to have been more victim than villain. His superiors had already magnified his general procurement problems by their inept management of trading through the lines, foreign procurement, and domestic finance. As Lee's supply problems became more acute, the Subsistence Department actually had food available in its Deep South depots, but Davis had not allowed adequate transportation to be assembled until disaster impended. Davis then removed controls before reserves for the men or even adequate supplies for the animals could be assembled. The Army of Northern Virginia might have been adequately fed if Davis had allowed it.

Perhaps the best example of the depressing effect of supply problems on the strategic outlook of the Confederate generals was the winter and spring conflict among Confederate leaders over the condition and future of the Army of Tennessee. This conflict reveals the growing fears of the military commanders that the system of supply administration now centralized in Richmond would not provide adequately for their armies. This episode also suggests that the commanders allowed these fears to combine with other factors to paralyze their strategic thinking. Bragg's Chattanooga campaign had given some evidence of the generals' pessimism, but the Army of Tennessee's spring paralysis clearly revealed the new military mentality.

By December 1863 Confederate authorities had begun to look toward the next campaigning season. The prime question was whether the Confederacy should attempt the offensive in 1864, and if so, whether it should undertake that offensive in the east or in the west. There was almost unanimous agreement among the generals and administrators that the Confederacy must undertake an offensive, and only Seddon felt that the major effort should again be an invasion of Pennsylvania in order to make the United States sue for peace. Seddon argued that the Confederacy should make no effort in the west, at least no effort for the reason of obtaining supplies. He maintained that there

88. Vandiver, *Gorgas Diary,* p. 95. 89. *Ibid.,* pp. 94, 99.

was enough food for the next year if authorities would administer distribution somewhat more efficiently than before.[90] The rest of the leaders, however—Davis, Lee, Johnston, Bragg, Longstreet, and Polk—eventually came to an agreement that the Confederacy should make its effort in the west. The usual strategic considerations such as relieving pressure on Lee were advanced, but the recapture of the productive areas of Tennessee was also a prime factor.[91] Apparently the top leaders had finally realized the value of the territory they had given up in 1862 and 1863.

The instrument for Confederate strategy in the west was, of course, the ill-starred Army of Tennessee. In December 1863 the army was camped at Dalton, Georgia, under the command of General Hardee, busily refitting and making good the losses in quartermaster and ordnance stores incurred in the autumn disasters. Hardee himself seems to have been of two minds about his command as he readied it to be turned over to Johnston. To Adjutant General Cooper on December 17, at a time when blockade-running losses had stripped the supply bureaus bare, Hardee dwelt on the "infinite trouble" that he was meeting in supplying and re-equipping his men. He felt that it might be necessary to invade Tennessee and Kentucky to get supplies even though the army was too weak, in his opinion, to fight in Georgia.[92] Davis, on reading the letter, must also have been considering the necessity of reconquering Tennessee, for he commented that "The general propositions are too obvious for discussion."[93] Shortly thereafter, however, Hardee wrote to Johnston and gave an entirely different picture of the condition of the Army of Tennessee. He said that the army was in comfortable quarters and that the health of the men was "unprecedentedly good." In addition, he said that although there had recently been a "great deficiency" of shoes and blankets, these supplies had finally come. The ration was "now uniform and full" and the men rearmed. Only the artillery, Hardee felt, needed some attention and reorganization after the disastrous losses and demoralization of recent battles.[94]

90. Younger, *Kean Diary*, pp. 116–117.

91. Davis to Johnston, Dec. 23, 1863, *OR*-1, XXXI (3), 856–857; Longstreet to Lee, March 4, 1864, *ibid.*, XXXII (3), 582–583; Bragg to Johnston, March 7, 1864, *ibid.*, p. 592; Lee to Bragg, March 8, 1864, *ibid.*, p. 595; Lee to Davis, April 2, 1864, *ibid.*, pp. 736–737.

92. Hardee to Cooper, Dec. 17, 1863, *ibid.*, XXXI (3), 839–841.

93. Davis's endorsement on Hardee to Cooper, Dec. 17, 1863, *ibid.*, p. 841.

94. Hardee to Ives, Dec. 24, 1863, *ibid.*, p. 860.

At the same time that Johnston received this cheerful report on the condition of his new army, he received an important message from Davis, in which the President analyzed the condition of the army from the reports reaching him in Richmond. Davis spoke of the army's being "tolerably" supplied with clothing and said that there was an accumulation of thirty days' supply of food on hand and that the artillery, in his view, was in as good a condition as before Chickamauga.[95] In any event, Davis felt that the army was in good enough condition to fight and to take the offensive, especially "in view of the necessity of reoccupying the country, upon the supplies of which the proper subsistence of our armies materially depends."[96]

Johnston, however, on viewing his men at Dalton, felt somewhat differently about their condition than either Hardee or Davis. In the first place, Johnston was a hearty opponent of the centralized system of bureau procurement and distribution and had complained about the system constantly for over a year.[97] He had been especially incensed over the failure of the bureaus to outfit his men in Mississippi properly in the summer of 1863 and continued to doubt the capacity of the supply bureaus to outfit his men adequately. Johnston wrote several letters to the President and to Bragg during early 1864, in which he vaguely agreed that some move against the enemy was necessary but maintained that the condition of the army prevented immediate action.[98] He further maintained that the army was short of food because the railroad from Atlanta was mismanaged, but after a round of letters, analyses, and explanations involving Lawton, Davis, Governor Brown, and Johnston, this long-standing situation was straightened out to the extent that supplies of subsistence went forward to the army regularly.[99]

Johnston then returned to his old grievance. He claimed that he had no reserve supplies for an offensive and that he could not accumulate them because the supply officials were loyal to the supervisors in Richmond and not to him.[100] Typical of Johnston's feelings about the centralized supply system was his comment to Longstreet that a campaign in the West was "a greater undertaking, I think, than anything

95. Davis to Johnston, Dec. 23, 1863, *ibid.*, pp. 856–857. 96. *Ibid.*, p. 857.

97. For Seddon's reaction to Johnston's hostility, see Seddon to Johnston, Oct. 31, 1863, *ibid.*, pp. 613–614.

98. Johnston to Davis, Jan. 2, 1864, *ibid.*, XXXII (2), 510–511; Johnston to Bragg, March 12, 1864, *ibid.*, pp. 613–614.

99. The bulk of this correspondence can be found in *ibid.*, pp. 510–612, *passim.*

100. Johnston to Bragg, March 30, 1864, *ibid.*, pp. 714–715.

yet accomplished by those Departments, and if they succeed it will not be very soon."[101] Northrop, who reciprocated Johnston's contempt, commented:

> It is because of the present system which General Johnston has assailed, that his army has been subsisted. In the fall of 1862, when all of East Tennessee was open to him, he had to call on the supplies of this Bureau, because the previous system [field armies' procuring their own subsistence] would not suffice.[102]

Northrop called on Johnston to indicate how it could be done better than at present and

> how long it is since he wanted to advance and was prevented as aforesaid; . . . I accept the issue. General Johnston's army has been subsisted precisely because of the present system. He never could have subsisted it otherwise. He has not been unable to move for want of subsistence since an advance was practicable, for the same subsistence which has so long sustained his army stationary could have sufficed to feed it moving.[103]

Northrop then appended a paper from the depot commandant at Atlanta, Major Cummings, who had written, "I have advised General Johnston that I can furnish him thirty days' supplies, should he at any time desire to make a movement."[104] In addition, Major Locke, Chief Commissary of Georgia, complained that the Army of Tennessee had committed "many abuses in overdrawing rations through incorrect returns."[105]

By March 1864 the pressures on Johnston to take the offensive were mounting. All signs indicated that the main Union effort of the new year would come against Atlanta or Richmond or both. Davis and others felt that a Confederate offensive in the West would put the Union forces off balance in that area. Longstreet's command in the northeastern part of Tennessee had spent an uncomfortable winter, but their commander was anxious to combine with somebody in order to invade Kentucky or middle Tennessee.[106] Beauregard's men, now that

101. Johnston to Longstreet, March 13, 1864, *ibid.*, XXXII (3), 618.

102. Northrop's endorsement, April 13, 1864, on Johnston to Bragg, March 30, 1864, *ibid.*, p. 717. 103. *Ibid.*

104. Cummings to Northrop, Feb. 13, 1864, *ibid.*

105. Locke to Northrop, March 8, 1864, *ibid.*, p. 597.

106. Longstreet to Davis, March 16, 1864, *ibid.*, pp. 637–641; Longstreet to Beauregard, March 15, 1864, *ibid.*, pp. 627–628.

Union forces had lifted the siege of Charleston, were also available. Lee himself was convinced that the best plan of attack was in the west in order to get supplies and to relieve the pressure on Virginia, and he was willing to have Longstreet combine with Johnston.[107]

A conference involving Davis, Longstreet, Lee, Bragg, and officials of the War Department was held on March 14, in the midst of the Virginia provisioning crisis. Precisely what happened is unknown, but apparently the participants agreed that the forthcoming effort should be a concentration in the west for the reasons already mentioned.[108] Bragg wrote to Johnston and instructed him to combine with Longstreet in east Tennessee after receiving reinforcements from Polk and Beauregard, increasing his army from 41,000 to 75,000 men.[109] He directed Johnston to move between Chattanooga and Knoxville, cross the Tennessee River, and move into middle Tennessee, so that he could try to take Nashville, cut the railroads and flush out the Union armies at Chattanooga and Knoxville, and thus open up the west. Bragg assured Johnston that supplies of ammunition and subsistence stores were ample and concluded: "It is needless, general, for me to impress upon you the great importance, not to say necessity, of reclaiming the provision country of Tennessee and Kentucky."[110] Bragg also stressed the need to get more recruits for the depleted armies.[111] If such sentiments reflected Bragg's own thinking as well as official policy, his change of attitude since he commanded the Army of Tennessee is striking. General Hood, in charge of one of Johnston's corps, wrote confidentially to Davis that the army needed to advance, that it was "well clothed, well fed, and the transportation . . . excellent, and in the greatest possible quantity required."[112] "We have a vast quantity of supplies," he concluded.[113]

Still Johnston resisted. Both he and Longstreet discounted Bragg's plan. They agreed that it would be dangerous to try to unite in East Tennessee in the presence of Union forces at Chattanooga and Knoxville, and Longstreet also agreed with Johnston that if his own scheme of invading Kentucky had fallen into disfavor, it would be better for him to join Johnston in Georgia and to try to invade Tennessee from Alabama or Mississippi.[114] Johnston, however, began to shift the basis

107. Lee to Longstreet, March 8, 1864, *ibid.*, pp. 594–595.

108. Longstreet to Johnston, March 16, 1864, *ibid.*, p. 637.

109. Bragg to Johnston, March 12, 1864, *ibid.*, pp. 614–615.

110. *Ibid.* 111. *Ibid.*

112. Hood to Davis, March 7, 1864, *ibid.*, pp. 606–607. 113. *Ibid.*

114. Johnston to Longstreet, March 13, 1864, *ibid.*, p. 618; Longstreet to Davis, March 16, 1864, *ibid.*, p. 639.

of his arguments with the War Department. In the teeth of the clamor from all sides to march out and fight, he altered his supply-shortage excuses for not attacking and at the same time began to advocate a purely defensive stand. He now admitted that he apprehended "no difficulty in procuring food (except meat) and forage,"[115] but he now claimed that he did not have enough animals and wagons to move his artillery and to carry the necessary fodder, supplies, ammunition, and bridge trains through the barren mountains. He suddenly announced that he would need a thousand more wagons.[116] At the same time, he claimed that it would be better to wait and face attack in Georgia and defeat the enemy there than to try to march around him and be defeated in transit. He felt that the Confederacy should attempt invasion only if the enemy did not attack first and then not from East Tennessee but rather from northern Alabama.[117] Finally, he reported that he had heard of reinforcements for Sherman at Chattanooga.[118]

April was now at hand, and Johnston had done nothing. Davis dispatched General William Pendleton, Lee's chief of artillery, to investigate the condition of the artillery of the Army of Tennessee and to carry to Johnston Davis's reasons for immediate action. Pendleton found that certain perfunctory changes would put Johnston's artillery in fighting condition.[119] He presented Johnston several reasons which the administration offered for taking the offensive, reasons that included the morale factor, relief of pressure on the Army of Northern Virginia, protection of Georgia by drawing the enemy away, and the necessity of reclaiming "productive territory."[120] Johnston countered with several reasons why he could not take the immediate offensive. He was understrength in men, he would expose communications, he was short on transportation, he expected no supplies enroute, and he could not carry enough.[121] Johnston concluded that the risk of losing the army was too great for the potential achievement.[122]

In the meantime the Quartermaster General sent Major A. H. Cole, the Inspector General of Field Transportation, to see what could be done for Johnston. Cole found confusion and shortage, in part substan-

115. Johnston to Longstreet, March 13, 1864, *ibid.*, p. 618; Johnston to Bragg, March 19, 1864, *ibid.*, pp. 653–654.

116. Johnston to Bragg, March 19, 1864, *ibid.*, pp. 653–654.

117. Ewell to Johnston, April 29, 1864, *ibid.*, pp. 839–842; and enclosure, Ewell to Bragg, April 20, 1864, *ibid.*

118. Johnston to Bragg, May 1, 1864, *ibid.*, XXXVIII (4), 654.

119. Pendleton to Cooper, March 29, 1864, *ibid.*, XXXII (3), 684–709.

120. Pendleton to Johnston, April 16, 1864, *ibid.*, XXXVIII (3), 622–623.

121. *Ibid.*, pp. 622–624. 122. *Ibid.*

tiating Johnston's claims, but he stressed the fact that the army command had let the problem drag on for months without effective action and implied that Johnston could have been much better prepared for an advance if he had taken proper steps.[123]

In any case, nothing was done. By late April Longstreet had been called back into Virginia to meet extensive Union preparations there, and Beauregard's forces were being appropriated in piecemeal fashion for Virginia. Johnston sent one of his aides to Richmond to assure the President that he was still willing to advance when he found himself ready, but Davis replied to the aide that the inactivity of Johnston had failed to prevent "a formidable attack in Virginia and North Carolina, having for its object the capture of Richmond . . . that to have prevented this was one of the important objects for threatening movements by your army."[124] Davis then told the aide that it was still important for Johnston to move.[125] But Johnston was unready to move, and soon after that Sherman settled the whole matter by moving forward to inaugurate the fateful Atlanta Campaign.

. . .

As the campaigning progressed throughout 1863, supply problems, particularly logistics, had more and more become a determining factor in the inception and conduct of military operations. Of all the commanders, only Lee had been blessed with enough freedom from supply worries to base his movements primarily on strategic considerations, and then only during the spring and summer. By the autumn, however, Lee's supply problems had crippled his activities and by the winter he found himself bound to his railroad supply lines and, thanks in part to Davis's fondness of laissez-faire railroad transportation, almost starved.

The commanders in the west launched the campaign year distrusting the new supply policies, which took arrangements out of their hands and centralized them in the bureaus. This lack of confidence in Richmond's management of supplies, combined with actual shortages of men and field transportation, precluded in their minds any movement that smacked of taking the offensive. Johnston in Mississippi and later in North Georgia and Bragg in Tennessee both pleaded supply, transportation, and manpower problems as one of their major justifications for not taking the offensive in 1863 or planning to do so in 1864.

123. Cole to Gibbons, April 11, 1864, *ibid.,* XXXII (3), 772–774.

124. Ewell to Johnston, April 29, 1864, *ibid.,* p. 840.

125. *Ibid.*

Undoubtedly their problems were severe, but in many instances, especially the question of whether or not the Army of Tennessee was ready to undertake an offensive in the spring of 1864, supply problems appear to be a rationalization rather than a legitimate justification for remaining on the defensive. It is a significant question as to how much of this negative attitude sprang from a responsible weighing of supply factors and how much was the result of pessimistic temperament complicated by a too-rigid adherance to traditional military concepts of effective supply. What a Lee, a Jackson, or a Forrest might have done with the western armies is, and has been, an enticing matter of speculation.

CHAPTER EIGHT

"COME HOME TO ROOST"

They [the Union] think these little reverses are evidence of exhausted resources, but really we are better off now than we were two years ago when no one doubted our ability to wage the War. The only point against us is the scarcity of men to fill up our Armies. —— Josiah Gorgas, September 29, 1864*

The truth is we are prostrated in all our energies and resources. —— Robert G. H. Kean, December 25, 1864†

The supply situation at the beginning of the 1864 campaign season displayed both positive and negative elements. Industrial production was undoubtedly the strongest sector of the war effort. The Niter and Mining Bureau, despite the loss of niter caves and works on the western Appalachian slopes and the headaches of reconstructing and relocating saltpeter works, continued to maintain the niter production rate of the last two years.[1] On the other hand, the output of metallic ores and finished metals, which had never been adequate despite new smelting plants, flagged as crucial mines were lost. Consequently, the bureau had to place increasing reliance on importations.[2] St. John expected to increase niter production as soon as he solved some minor problems in creating plants for the manufacture of artificial niter. Throughout 1864 the bureau mantained production and continued to have good fortune in importations; thus St. John was able to report in the autumn that he had met all the "pressing" demands of the army and navy for saltpeter and all demands for metals except navy iron.[3]

With an adequate supply of raw materials, Ordnance Department production also maintained previous levels. Copper deficiencies rendered cartridge production capricious and forced the substitution of iron for bronze in artillery production, but Gorgas claimed to have met all demands for powder and cartridges and to have produced artillery that was "satisfactory in both quantity and quality."[4] Small-arms

* Vandiver, *Gorgas Diary,* p. 143. † Younger, *Kean Diary,* p. 181.

1. St. John to Seddon, Oct. 1, 1864, *OR*-4, III, 695–702.

2. *Ibid.;* Vandiver, *Confederate Ordnance,* p. 202.

3. St. John to Seddon, Oct. 1, 1864, *OR*-4, III, 695.

4. Gorgas to Seddon, Oct. 13, 1864, *ibid.,* pp. 733–734; Gorgas to Seddon, Dec. 3, 1864, *ibid.,* pp. 987–988.

production, however, had dropped to one-third because of short-sighted conscription of skilled workers and bad luck on importations.[5] Still, Gorgas reported a number of small arms on order and in transit. He also cited a favorable battlefield capture ratio and claimed to have a reserve supply equal to that of 1863.[6]

Summary figures on the industrial output of the Quartermaster's Department are not available, but fragmentary evidence and subsequent reports by Lawton indicate that the bureau continued to secure an abundant supply of cotton goods from the textile factories as a result of its stringent new controls. Heavy spending and good fortune on importations during the spring and summer of 1864 enabled the bureau to build up a reserve of shoes and woolen clothing and to convert woolen cloth to uniforms at its various clothing factories.[7] Lawton emphasized, however, that this comeback had been retarded by inefficient ordering on the part of army commanders and by waste, barter, and sale of issues by troops.[8]

Non-industrial aspects of the war effort were less comforting but by no means gloomy. The total output of subsistence in the Confederacy was sufficient for both civilians and the armies during the summer of 1864. However, geographical variations in production dissipated this abundance to some extent because the cotton states had surpluses while Virginia was in short supply. Because of increased production of foodstuffs, the tax-in-kind, and the new "gleaning" system, the Subsistence Department claimed that the commissaries could accumulate enough bread and meat for the troops in the cotton states and enough bread for the troops and civilian workers in Virginia if other bureaus could maintain transportation.[9] Northrop admitted that maintaining the meat ration for the troops in Virginia would be more problematical and would depend on the fortunes of importation, on trading with the enemy, and on small surpluses shipped up from the south. If these factors held good, there would be sufficient meat to last the Army of Northern Virginia until the autumn; otherwise, there would be trouble, for only one third of the Confederacy's cattle and bacon reserves were within easy reach of the army and the industrial workers in Virginia.[10] In addition to bread and meat, the bureau continued to furnish irregularly, depending on the vicissitudes of transportation, coffee, rice, peas,

5. Gorgas to Seddon, Oct. 13, 1864, *ibid.*, p. 733; Gorgas to Seddon, Nov. 15, 1863, *ibid.*, II, 956.

6. Gorgas to Seddon, Oct. 13, 1864, *ibid.*, III, 731.

7. Lawton to Corley, Dec. 12, 1864, *OR*-1, LII (3), 1269.

8. *Ibid.*

9. Northrop to Seddon, May 4, 1864, *OR*-4, III, 379–380.

10. *Ibid.*

sugar, vinegar, and soap, with supplements of local vegetables in season.[11]

Transportation constituted much more of an imponderable than production. Wagon transportation was a constant headache, both at home and at the front; shortages of animals and wagons affected both campaigning and the accumulation of subsistence severely, if not fatally. The railroad companies were unable to replace or repair worn out materials, and rails and rolling stock rapidly deteriorated. Still, the railroad situation at the opening of the 1864 campaigning season was by no means desperate, for the trains continued to distribute both war materials and civilian goods around the country and into Virginia. However, the railroads were stretched to their utmost capacity; if rail transportation were disrupted, the war effort would grind to a halt.

The more pressing supply questions of 1864 were whether or not the civilian leaders could hammer out efficient outside-procurement policies, unsnarl fiscal policies that threatened to abort domestic procurement, and find the fortitude to take over full control of railroad transportation. In the background loomed the fundamental problems of manpower, morale, and moral authority. Were there enough men to work and fight? Were the armies large enough and military leadership effective enough at least to protect war production, ports, and the distribution network even if the Confederates could not take the offensive? Had time and privations sapped the morale of the soldier and the fortitude of the commanders? Could the government persuade the people to follow the harsh policies necessary for the maintenance of Confederate independence?

As Lee prepared to face Grant on the line of the Rapidan and Rappahannock, Colonel Walter, Lee's adjutant, reported the men in good spirits and good condition.[12] This may have been true of the infantry and artillery, but the cavalry and field transportation displayed definite signs of deterioration.[13] The supply officials had failed to procure either remounts for the troops or draft animals for the wagons, and the animals on hand were semi-starved and weak from

11. *Ibid.;* Ransom to Cooper, June 12, 1864, *OR*-1, XXXVI (3), 898–900; Northrop to Seddon, Dec. 12, 1864, *OR*-4, III, 930–931.

12. Douglas Southall Freeman, *R. E. Lee, A Biography* (4 vols.; New York and London, 1934–35), III, 268. Cited hereinafter as Freeman, *Lee.*

13. For a general discussion of Lee's animal problems, see Charles W. Ramsdell, "General Robert E. Lee's Horse Supply, 1862–1865," *American Historical Review,* XXXV, No. 4 (July, 1930), 758–777.

inadequate food during the provisioning crisis of the previous winter.[14] The supply bureaus had failed the cavalry; soon the weakened cavalry would fail to protect supply operations. Numbers constituted the most severe problem. While the Army of Northern Virginia itself reported its usual sixty thousand men,[15] Lee had no supporting troops to defend the lines of communication.[16] The results were nearly fatal. Lee's inability to protect his supply lines immobilized him and almost starved him out.

Lee's army, marooned in a wasteland and now dependent on railroad transportation for all its subsistence and much of its ordnance and quartermaster supplies, was thus doomed to the defensive. The supply officials, hoping simply to keep the army functioning, looked at logistical prospects with tempered confidence at the beginning of 1864, in spite of earlier crises. Railroad transportation problems would be eased when the engineers completed the Piedmont Railroad link between Greensboro and Danville.[17] When the Piedmont Railroad opened, Lee would have four major railroad lines from four important sources of supply. One, the Virginia Central, would bring the limited grains and provender the Shenandoah and James River valleys could provide. The second, the Virginia and Tennessee, would bring in substantial supplies of beef and foodstuffs from southwestern Virginia and northern Tennessee. The third would bring supplies from the Southwest and from the southeastern Piedmont through Atlanta, Augusta, Charlotte, and Greensboro over the new Piedmont line to Danville and on to Richmond and Petersburg. Finally, the traditional source of heavy supply from the south, the Petersburg and Weldon, brought in goods from Georgia, Savannah, Charleston, and Wilmington. This fourth route also carried crucial imported woolens and meats to Lee's men from the Wilmington docks. As the campaign opened, supplies were going forward to Virginia with gratifying regularity after the late winter nightmare. In response to Lee's earnest request, the supply bureaus toiled to build up a reserve in Richmond in case the fortunes of campaigning interrupted railroad services.[18]

14. *Ibid.*

15. "Abstract from field returns of the Army of Northern Virginia, April 20, 1864," *OR*-1, XXXIII, 1297–1298.

16. Abstracts of returns from departments of Western Virginia, Henrico, Richmond, Cape Fear, Richmond Local Defense, *ibid.*, pp. 1298–1301.

17. Rives to Seddon, May 7, 1864, *OR*-4, III, 392.

18. Northrop to Seddon, May 4, 1864, *ibid.*, pp. 379–380; Lee to Davis, June 16, 1864, in Freeman, *Lee's Dispatches,* pp. 246–247.

The Union commanders were aware of the logistical difficulties of the Army of Northern Virginia. During May and June while Lee and Beauregard fended off Grant and Butler in one desperate encounter after another, Union cavalry ripped up each of the four major railroad supply routes, destroying bridges on the main line to Weldon and destroying 419,000 rations at Beaver Dam. In general, they so disrupted the flow of supplies that Lee's men and the civilian employees at Richmond consumed all reserves and feared starvation.[19]

Confederate authorities recouped before Lee's men actually ran out of food. On the twenty-fifth of May the first trains pushed forward over the now-completed Piedmont Railroad, bringing in both troops and corn.[20] The Quartermaster's Department reported to Lee's anxious quartermaster, Colonel Corley, that once the northbound reinforcements had been moved, the railroad could transport 6,000–7,000 bushels of corn per day for the army.[21] Lee dispatched troops to the Valley to reclaim that area in time for the wheat harvest. Wagons closed the double break in the railroad to Wilmington; and the breaks in the Virginia Central, the Richmond and Petersburg, and the Richmond and Danville were repaired.[22] Gorgas noted in his diary with relief: "Provisions are coming in somewhat more freely. The trains laden with corn are constantly arriving, the fear of starvation has, therefore, nearly subsided."[23] Lee's meat ration, temporarily at one-quarter pound, was put up again to the now standard one half pound ration; and as the fighting continued during May and into June, Northrop ordered special issues of coffee and sugar to stimulate the troops.[24] As soon as the troops rested from fighting in late June, however, authorities immediately reduced the meat ration to one third pound, now the standard ration for stationary troops.[25]

From late June to mid-August, another series of logistical disasters buffeted Lee.[26] Union raiders in Virginia severely smashed up the railroads leading to the west and southwest, and in August Grant, pushing

19. Black, *Confederate Railroads,* p. 277. 20. *Ibid.*

21. Lawton to Corley, May 11, 1864, *OR*-1, XXXVI (2), 989–990.

22. Douglas Southall Freeman, *Lee's Lieutenants: A Study in Command* (3 vols.; New York, 1951), III, 467.

23. Vandiver, *Gorgas Diary,* p. 110.

24. Northrop endorsement on Ransom to Cooper, June 12, 1864, *OR*-1, XXXVI (3), 899.

25. *Ibid.*

26. A good discussion of operations in Virginia in this period can be found in Freeman, *Lee,* IV, 448–457, 479–491; for operations in the Deep South, see Black, *Confederate Railroads,* pp. 250–253.

his left flank over the main line to Wilmington, quite close to Petersburg, forced Lee to extend his wagon caravans to thirty miles. To compound Lee's logistical agonies, Sherman's raiders cut the Alabama-Atlanta railroad connection, and Sherman himself cut the Atlanta-Augusta segment of the northern artery. A daring Union cavalry squad of fifty burned the railroad bridge over the Oconee River between Macon and Savannah and cut the other main supply route. Thus, Johnston and Hood had failed to protect Lee's main supply routes. To further magnify the nightmare, drought burned up most of the Virginia harvest of corn and vegetables.[27] Faced with an uncertain food supply and starving animals, Lee appealed to the administration for help, but with little result. He asked that the railroads leading to Richmond be put under military control and that only government supplies be brought forward until the army had built up a reserve. If not all lines, Lee begged, the government should at least take over the Piedmont-Danville route, the most inefficient.[28] Davis had done nothing during the May crisis, and he did nothing in July. He gave Seddon, who favored intervention, the obnoxious job of framing a refusal without tendering specific explanations.[29] On the other hand, both Lawton and Seddon pressed Lee to keep Grant off the Weldon Railroad as long as possible.[30] The Quartermaster General limited the Weldon line to goods imported at Charleston and Wilmington and to provisions that came from trading through the lines in eastern North Carolina.[31] All the remaining food, ordnance, and quartermaster stores not supplied from Virginia factories had to move over the Piedmont-Danville line.

The President apparently made one concession by directing the Secretary of War to authorize the Quartermaster General to employ the railroad control formula of March 11 during the summer and into the fall. On occasion, Lawton authorized certain quartermasters to stop private freight and passenger trains when these quartermasters reported pile-ups of government freight at their stations.[32] This limited action, together with some impounding of iron on branch lines and the

27. Vandiver, *Gorgas Diary,* p. 132.

28. Lee to Davis, June 16, 1864, in Freeman, *Lee's Dispatches,* pp. 246–247; quotation found in Seddon to Lee, July 9, 1864, *OR*-1, XL (3), 753–754.

29. Seddon to Lee, July 9, 1864, *OR*-1, XL (3), 753–754.

30. Lawton to Lee, June 23, 1864, QMDLS, XIX, 308; Seddon to Lee, June 24, 1864, *OR*-1, XL (2), 684–685.

31. Lawton to Corley, Sept. 30, 1864, QMDLS, XX, 162.

32. Lawton to Chisman, Sept. 26, 1864, QMDLS, XX, 149; Lawton to Sharp, Oct. 27, 1864, *ibid.,* p. 237; Lawton to Robinson, July 4, 1864, *ibid.,* XIX, 329–330.

impressment of extra rolling stock on the Raleigh and Gaston Railroad, was all the President was willing to take.[33]

With no cavalry or reserve infantry to protect the railroads, the plight of the government was pathetic. A resort to subterfuge by Seddon clearly reveals the sad state of affairs. He did not announce the resumption of service on the Virginia Central and exaggerated the damage done to the Danville line, in hopes that the raiders would not come again.[34]

Except for these minor administrative adjustments, Lee had to rely for food until late August on the local wheat and oats, trickles from the south, and the fortunate cessation of Union cavalry attacks. With the breaks in Georgia and Virginia railroads finally repaired, supplies arrived regularly into the autumn until Sherman began his march to the sea.

In the east, supply and manpower shortages had immobilized Lee, and the Army of Northern Virginia had survived only by desperate logistical juggling. In the west, the Army of Tennessee, while beset with its own manpower problems, nevertheless enjoyed easier logistical circumstances and more abundant supplies, at least where it stood on the defensive at Dalton. Still, supply shortages, in the eyes of its commander, had immobilized the army and prevented it from taking the offensive and regaining the lost western territories.

As he slowly retreated to the environs of Atlanta, Johnston did not claim that supply problems affected his defensive strategy, and on his removal he reported that he had left his troops "well-equipped and abundantly supplied."[35] Hood did not dispute this but did assert that under Johnston's management the army had lost one third of its men and that its organization and efficiency were "seriously diminished."[36] Hood then proceeded to lose Atlanta's manufacturing and railroad resources and thereby opened the way for Sherman to crush the backbone of the Confederate war effort and cut Lee's logistical life line. In the evacuation of Atlanta, mismanagement reminiscent of the Nashville debacle cropped up. The arsenal, clothing, and shoe-making machinery were sent off safely, but the reserve ordnance train was blown up in the confusion; haste and mismanagement resulted in unnecessary

33. Lawton to Robinson, July 4, 1864, *ibid.*, pp. 329–330; Seddon to Lee, June 25, 1864, *OR*-1, XL (2), 686–687.

34. Seddon to Lee, June 29, 1864, *OR*-1, XL (2), 701–702; Lee to Seddon, June 28, 1864, *ibid.*, XXXVI (2), 697; Jones, *War Clerk's Diary*, II, 239.

35. Johnston to Cooper, Oct. 20, 1864, *OR*-1, XXXVIII (3), 618.

36. Hood to Cooper, February 15, 1865, *ibid.*, p. 629.

losses of quartermaster and commissary supplies.[37] A court of inquiry censured Colonel M. B. McMicken, the Chief Quartermaster of the Army of Tennessee, for not supervising the removals more carefully.[38]

It was after the loss of Atlanta that Hood set out to do that which Johnston had felt unable to do in the spring: invade Tennessee, open new territories for supplies, disrupt Union communications, and force Sherman to retreat. In the crucial delays in north Alabama and in the subsequent disasters in Tennessee, supply problems played an important role. When Hood arrived at Gadsden on October 20, at a time when Sherman's supplies were still in confusion and when he might have been forced to fall back, Hood found "a thorough supply of shoes and stores."[39] Beauregard claimed that the Army of Tennessee was "in good spirits" and "confident of success."[40] Hood was prepared to cross the Tennessee immediately, but unable to communicate with Forrest, he delayed the crossing and moved on to the Florence-Tuscumbia area.[41] He then idled away weeks at Florence because the railroads were unable to accumulate a ration reserve and other supplies for the march of the army.[42] Subsistence existed in abundance in central Alabama and eastern Mississippi, but the roads into north Alabama were in such poor condition that the decrepit railroads had to be galvanized into use. This involved shipping goods from Alabama west into Mississippi, then north to Corinth and back east again to Florence. Bridges had to be rebuilt, and track had to be laid, a process severely delayed by incessant rains.[43] Once in Tennessee, Hood had few troubles with food and ammunition, and the inspector general reported the army in good condition; but subordinate officers complained of shortages of clothing, shoes, and tents.[44] Such shortages must have contributed to poor morale and subsequently to the defeat at Nashville.

Meanwhile Sherman was busy knocking the Confederate war effort to pieces. He concentrated on the destruction of transportation, the most lethal onslaught possible. Ordnance Department production at

37. Special Orders No. 51, Adjutant and Inspector General's Office, 1865 Series, March 2, 1865, *ibid.*, pp. 991–992.

38. *Ibid.* 39. Hood to Cooper, Feb. 15, 1865, *ibid.*, XXIX (1), 802.

40. Beauregard to Cooper, April 15, 1865, *ibid.*, XLV (1), 650.

41. Hood to Cooper, Feb. 15, 1865, *ibid.*, XXXIX (1), 802.

42. *Ibid.*, pp. 801 ff.; Hood to Cooper, Feb. 15, 1865, *ibid.*, XLV (1), 652–656.

43. Black, *Confederate Railroads*, pp. 264–267; see also Frank E. Vandiver, "General Hood as Logistician," *Military Affairs*, XVI, No. 1 (Spring 1956), 1–11.

44. Johnston to Cooper, Jan. 8, 1865, *OR*-1, XLV (1), 676.

Macon was only temporarily disrupted. The vital powder works at Augusta and the Columbus arsenal continued to function without interruption.[45] On the other hand, Sherman thoroughly smashed the Macon-Savannah railroad and thus permanently severed Lee from his south Georgia subsistence and from the ordnance production of Columbus and Macon, although Lee still drew for a time on the central Georgia foodstuffs that came out by a railroad running to Augusta.[46] However, Sherman's movements in South Carolina in January and February nailed the lid on Lee's coffin by cutting Lee off from his Deep South supply source. When Sherman reached Branchville, South Carolina, he cut Lee's connection with Augusta and Central Georgia, and he captured intact the large armory at Columbia.[47] The evacuation of Charleston combined with the fall of Fort Fisher and Wilmington to cut off Lee's indispensable sources of foreign supply. The loss of the ports would have had disastrous long-range effects on the Ordnance Department as well, but the war did not last that long.

It is unnecessary to pursue the details of the Confederacy's military disintegration in the latter months of the war. The 1864 campaigning season had revolved around the question of whether the two main Confederate armies could hold off the Union armies from the vital productive areas of the country. The Army of Northern Virginia had been able to defend the capital, but the Army of Tennessee continued its ill-starred role in the destruction of the Confederate war machine. In 1862 it had lost the provision and manufacturing areas of Kentucky and two-thirds of Tennessee; in 1863 it had lost eastern Tennessee provisions, mining, and railroads; in 1864 it had lost the subsistence and transportation backbone located in Georgia.

. . .

The lost battles, the fallen cities, and destroyed farms and factories were the external road to Confederate collapse, and the Army of Tennessee was only one of the agents of destruction. There was an internal road to ruin, and the civilian administrators in Richmond presided over this process. To begin with, the Confederate officials allowed the domestic procurement of the War Department to grind to a

45. Walthall to Strange, Jan. 3, 1865, *ibid.,* p. 725; Capers to Garden, Jan. 4, 1865, *ibid.,* p. 735; Smith to Porter, Jan. 23, 1865, *ibid.,* p. 740; Forrest to Mason, Jan. 24, 1865, *ibid.,* pp. 759–760.

46. Black, *Confederate Railroads,* pp. 258–260.

47. Vandiver, *Confederate Ordnance,* pp. 260–261.

halt from financial malnutrition. Entering 1864, the War Department had spent nearly all of its huge appropriations. Only the Subsistence Department had any noteworthy unexpended sums, about $63,000,-000;[48] this surplus had occurred for the ominous reason that the people had so evaded and resisted impressment that the bureau had not been able to find foodstuffs on which to spend its money. Congress, as was its late-war habit, appropriated, unpared, the War Department estimates, some $437,000,000 for the first six months of 1864, or over $70,000,000 per month, most of which the department needed in currency.[49] At the same time, as we have seen, Congress had legislated a reduction of the currency, offering new alternatives to currency payments by authorizing bonds and certificates of indebtedness, and it had limited the Secretary of the Treasury to a total issue of $50,000,000 of Treasury notes a month for the use of the entire government.[50]

These competing laws soon led to disaster. Price levels did not drop. The people spurned the bonds and certificates and would accept currency only grudgingly. Yet, at best, the War Department could expect to get in currency only half of the $70,000,000 monthly authorization.

The War Department tried to co-operate with the Treasury Department by translating as much of its disbursements as possible into bonds and certificates, but its consumption of new currency was heavy. From February to June 1864 the Treasury Department had issued over $57,000,000 in new bank notes, most of which had been spent by the War Department.[51] With the prospect that Congress would limit note production to $100,000,000, Memminger wrote Seddon urging "the absolute necessity of witholding your requisitions for money and instead thereof, making use of certificates of indebtedness."[52] Memminger wanted to reserve money requisitions for paying the troops and wished to have general purchasing and contracts with railroads and factories done with bonds and certificates.[53] Seddon replied by pointing out that the people were already resisting paper currency and refusing outright to accept bonds or certificates under impressment proceed-

48. WDAA, XL ½, 39, 42.

49. "An Act to Make Additional Appropriations for the Support of the Government of the Confederate States of America, for the Fiscal Year Ending June Thirtieth, Eighteen Hundred and Sixty-four," Feb. 17, 1864, *Statutes*, II, 197–202.

50. "An Act to Reduce the Currency and Authorize a New Issue of Notes and Bonds," Feb. 17, 1864, *ibid.*, pp. 205–208.

51. Memminger to Seddon, June 2, 1864, *OR*-4, III, 465.

52. *Ibid.*

53. *Ibid.*

ings.[54] The impressment act, he reminded Memminger, did not have any provisions to force the people to accept the bonds or certificates. Seddon maintained that the War Department must have money; if not, procurement of subsistence under the impressment act would expire and payments for industrial goods would be aborted. Seddon concluded, "I trust every effort will be made at once to raise money by the sale or hypothecation of a loan. Otherwise, I fear the machinery of the Government will stop."[55]

The machinery of domestic procurement, at least, faltered markedly in the summer and ground to a halt by the winter for want of currency. Since 1863 virtually the only method of obtaining subsistence on the domestic market had been by forced sales, but the people had resisted the operation of impressment, and Congress had made impressment operable only if money were offered on the spot in payment. By the autumn of 1864 the Subsistence Department had no currency to offer for impressed goods and none with which to purchase goods coming in through the lines or to pay off debts for goods already delivered. The Quartermaster General could not pay the troops or the factories, the latter needing a portion of their contract money in notes to pay workers and to meet taxes.[56]

By the new year the Treasury Department had fallen so far behind in providing currency to pay War Department debts that figures lost all meaning. On December 29, 1864, in response to Seddon's queries, the Subsistence Department reported unpaid requisitions of over $34,000,000; the Quartermaster's Department, $108,000,000; and Seddon calculated the Trans-Mississippi arrears at over $60,000,000.[57] On January 8 Assistant Secretary of War Campbell estimated that the War Department had $178,000,000 in unpaid requisitions in the Treasury Department and that the War Department still had $180,000,000 in authorized appropriations for which it had not put in requisitions.[58] Mr. Trenholm professed to be astonished that his department had fallen so far behind, but War Department officials insisted that they had kept him informed.[59] The state of fiscal insanity in early 1865 can be illustrated by the fact that although the Subsistence Department alone was entitled to draw on the Treasury for $774,193 per day,

54. Seddon to Memminger, June 4, 1864, WDLS, XIX, 1. 55. *Ibid.*

56. Lawton to Seddon, Sept. 8, 1864, *OR*-4, III, 626–628.

57. Northrop to Seddon, Dec. 29, 1864, *ibid.*, pp. 974–975; Lawton to Seddon Dec. 29, 1864, *ibid.*, p. 974; Seddon to Trenholm, Dec. 29, 1864, *ibid.*, p. 975.

58. Younger, *Kean Diary*, pp. 184–185. 59. *Ibid.*

the Treasury Department signed requisitions totaling only $500,000 per day for all government expenses.[60]

Figures are meaningless in indicating the practical nature of the collapse of the War Department's procurement system. Two extracts from reports of harried supply officers in the field tell the story. A subsistence officer, Captain Charles S. Taylor, wrote:

> I now owe $1,200,000. A great portion of this sum has been due since early last spring. During the past summer the railroad connections were cut by the enemy, and large supplies were promptly loaned by the people to sustain the Army in its emergency. From the exhausted condition of the country I have been unable to return a very large proportion of these borrowed stores. They have expressed a readiness to receive payment instead, yet in but few instances have I had it in my power even to do this, for want of funds. Whilst such delay naturally causes much dissatisfaction and want of confidence in those who have heretofore acted with patriotic energy in support of the Government, the future is more unpromising.[61]

Quartermaster George Brent wrote from Montgomery:

> [We suffer a] total want of quartermasters' funds. Owing to this, all the branches of the service are at a standstill, transportation is embarrassed, supplies slowly and with difficulty obtained, and impressments also totally impossible. Certificates of indebtedness will not be received by the people, and the indebtedness of the different departments has become so great as to become a source not only of embarrassment to public officers in the discharge of their duties but also one of suffering and discontent to the citizens. . . . Whilst the army is in Tennessee every effort should be made to add to our stock. But one difficulty stares us right in the face—the want of money.[62]

The bureaus tried every possible method to compensate for lack of funds. With cotton, they bought Union greenbacks and gold with which to buy goods through the lines and horses and mules.[63] The

60. Strother to St. John, March 11, 1865, *OR*-1, XLVI (2), 1302.

61. Taylor to Noland, Jan. 6, 1865, *OR*-4, III, 1005–1006.

62. Brent to Beauregard, Dec. 18, 1864, *OR*-1, XLV (2), 704–706.

63. Lee's endorsement, Feb. 28, 1865, and Trenholm's endorsement, March 21, 1865, on Cole to Corley, Feb. 20, 1865, *ibid.*, XLVI (2), 1242–1243; Seddon to Lawton, Oct. 20, 1864, *OR*-4, III, 741–742.

Quartermaster's Department forced the railroads and factories under its control to take every possible dollar in bonds.[64] Northrop proposed that the government accept disbursing officers' vouchers from citizens for payment of taxes, but Trenholm was not interested.[65] Seddon succinctly pointed out to Trenholm the bitter fruits of financial incompetence as the war dragged on toward its end:

> I am satisfied that the discredit of the Government has arisen, in a measure, from the delay that has been made in the liquidation of . . . pressing, urgent, and meritorious claims. I am aware of the many strong considerations that induce a restriction of issue as far as practicable; but I venture to suggest that the currency itself probably suffers more discredit from the failure to meet the engagements of the Government than could result from inflation by the issue necessary to redeem them.
>
> You can scarcely realize to what extent the inability or failure to meet the obligations of the Department has been prolific of mischief. It has been the occasion or excuse for desertion, marauding, sale of clothing and equipments among soldiers; it has prevented the accumulation of supplies; it has affected the efficiency of transportation; it has produced carelessness or indifference among contractors; officers are resentful, and soldiers reckless, discontented, and suffering.[66]

The Confederate administrators had done little to stem the disintegrating effects of the financial system on domestic procurement. In the face of their other major problem, manpower, they did take an active step—and thereby worsened the situation.

The Confederate government decided it could no longer spare thirty thousand men to produce goods for the war effort. By the autumn of 1864, with Union forces deep inside the Confederacy, the government had to secure men from some source to put into the ranks. Unable to corral tens of thousands of skulkers, draft dodgers, and deserters, and politically balked from drafting thousands of professionals and state "officials," the administration surveyed those men over whom it did exercise control and finally decided upon the desperate expedient of raiding the industrial details for soldiers. On October 8, 1864, General

64. Lawton to Cunningham, July 28, 1864, QMDLS, XIX, 372; Lawton to Magrath, July 28, 1864, *ibid.*, p. 374.

65. Northrop to Seddon, Jan. 11, 1865, *OR*-1, XLVI (2), 1035.

66. Seddon to Trenholm, Dec. 29, 1864, *OR*-4, III, 975.

Orders No. 77 revoked all industrial details of men eighteen to forty-five and allowed reassignment to work of only those whom the bureau chiefs could certify as "experts" or as "absolutely indispensable to the public service." As a check on veracity, bureau heads were ordered to describe the employment of every man for whom they asked reassignment.[67]

Gorgas and St. John must have protested strongly, for shortly thereafter Seddon and Davis granted them a "concession" by announcing through General Orders No. 82 that the public service would be satisfied if the Niter and Mining Bureau and the Ordnance Bureau would make a flat, across-the-board cut of one-fifth in their current detail rolls.[68] The other bureaus were not so favored.

The order revoking details was supported by the Richmond press.[69] Nevertheless, it would appear that this reduction of industrial details constituted a blunder on the part of the administration which equaled its fiascos in financial and railroad management. The measure severely hampered production without producing any corresponding gain in fighting manpower.[70] Kean took this point of view:

> The conscription has been pressed to its utmost limits, and beyond any reasonable ones, by the revocation of details. General Order 77, which prostrated the industrial interests, private and public, went further to break the spirit of the people than any administrative act of the war.[71]

. . .

Heading into the winter of 1864–65, the industrial bureaus, even in the truncated Confederacy and despite financial derangement and manpower problems, still managed to produce ammunition and clothing and by means of priorities to get some of the supplies to the armies despite widespread railroad disruption. On the other hand, the collapse of domestic procurement through lack of funds and through the inability of the railroads to function with regularity ruined the Subsistence Department and brought on the third straight winter famine for Lee's

67. General Orders No. 77, Adjutant and Inspector General's Office, 1864 Series, Oct. 8, 1864, *ibid.*, p. 715.

68. General Orders No. 82, Adjutant and Inspector General's Office, 1864 Series, Oct. 20, 1864, *ibid.*, p. 741.

69. See the Richmond *Daily Dispatch*, Sept. 9, 1864; Richmond *Enquirer*, Oct. 5 and Oct. 8, 1864; *Daily Richmond Examiner*, Oct. 15, 1864.

70. Vandiver, *Confederate Ordnance*, pp. 262–263.

71. Younger, *Kean Diary*, p. 181.

army. Meager returns from the tithe because of poorly packed meat, chronic inefficiency among the field supply officers, and conflicts in overseas procurement policies all contributed to the failure of the bureau.

Because of lack of money, impressments of breadstuffs in the south had fallen off so markedly that Lee's men had to consume the small emergency reserve in Virginia. Alabama, Mississippi, and Georgia were the only states from which subsistence could be drawn, but transportation from the first two was almost impossible. Besides, these states were feeding the Army of Tennessee in its last campaign. The only meat coming in for the Army of Northern Virginia was that brought in by trading through the lines and by the contract steamers at Wilmington. Thirty days' efforts in the Deep South in August and September to find and transport subsistence, mostly breadstuffs, had resulted in an amount suitable for only one week's rations for the armies and the large number of civilian dependents.[72] Collections in Georgia in October had yielded "not a pound."[73] With Sherman in Atlanta it appeared likely that transportation from the Deep South would cease entirely.

On December 5 Commissary officials reported that reserve stocks had almost run out. Richmond had only 130,000 pounds of meat on hand and a meager 170,000 were enroute from North Carolina and South Carolina, a total of nine days' supply for 100,000 men, a figure which excluded the civilian dependents.[74] There were 3,000,000 pounds of meat in the islands, but few ships were bringing it in. The bureau could anticipate only thirty days' supply of breadstuffs, and two thirds of this was enroute from the south and might never arrive.[75] A telegram from Lee to Davis on December 14, stating that the Richmond depot was out of salt meat and was now doling out its last two days' supply of fresh meat brought Davis into action.[76] Kean reported the President and the Secretary of War "greatly alarmed" when they realized that "not a pound remained in Richmond."[77] However, Davis was not alarmed enough to take over the railroads.

Just as the army was running out of meat, prospects momentarily

72. French to Northrop, Sept. 15, 1864, *OR*-4, III, 653–654.

73. French to Northrop, Oct. 18, 1864, in "Ruffin Testimony," PSRD, pp. 42–44.

74. Ruffin to Seddon, Dec. 14, 1864, *OR*-4, III, 941.

75. *Ibid.*

76. Lee to Davis, Dec. 14, 1864, Freeman, *Lee's Dispatches,* pp. 307–308; Davis to Lee, Dec. 15, 1864, Rowland, *Jefferson Davis,* VI, 417–418.

77. Younger, *Kean Diary,* p. 181.

brightened. Sherman had now passed through Georgia to Savannah, and the commissaries in Georgia once again began to find supplies in central Georgia to ship out via Augusta and Branchville to Charlotte and points north. The Augusta officials reported that they could secure 60,000–70,000 bushels of corn, with funds, and might be able to ship 1,000 bushels of corn a day.[78] In North Carolina Charlotte officials reported breadstuffs accumulating in "considerable amounts,"[79] and Goldsboro officials reported that they had been able to accumulate corn in eastern North Carolina. It was estimated that some 743,000 rations of bread were available in North Carolina or on the way to Richmond, but even that amount would feed the army for only seven days.[80] Blockade runners materially aided the cause during December. Three ships alone had brought approximately 950,000 rations of meat into Wilmington. Another 1,000,000 rations from various sources were en-route from Wilmington or were in Richmond. In all, there was enough on hand to feed 100,000 men for 20 days.[81] What would happen if Sherman cut the railroad from Augusta or if the fortunes of blockade running proved adverse, no one dared to say.

The breakdown of the Piedmont Railroad denied Lee's men their Georgia cornbread and English tinned beef. The railroad was poorly constructed, understocked, and built on the wrong gauge.[82] The Confederate authorities had a surplus of wide-gauge stock suitable for the railroads south of Salisbury and north of Danville, but the North Carolina railroad from Salisbury through Greensboro and the Piedmont Railroad from Greensboro to Danville were narrow gauge and were short of cars. Therefore, supplies moved far too slowly through North Carolina. The Confederate government wished to widen the tracks between Salisbury and Danville so that the Deep South route would have transportation facilities adequate to its needs, but Governor Vance prevented this.[83] Even under "normal" circumstances supplies piled up at Charlotte and Greensboro.

As the bottleneck in North Carolina continued, Davis relented in the face of the agonies of the Army of Northern Virginia and those of the Subsistence Department and finally invoked the railroad act. On January 3, 1865, Lawton ordered his Greensboro quartermaster to impress "all trains reaching Greensboro" for use on the Piedmont

78. "Report of Resources," Jan. 2, 1865, PRSD. 79. *Ibid.* 80. *Ibid.*
81. *Ibid.* 82. Black, *Confederate Railroads,* pp. 228–229.
83. Vance to Breckinridge, March 25, 1865, *OR*-1, XLII (3), 693–694.

Railroad.[84] He further authorized the Chief Quartermaster of the Army of Northern Virginia to stop the movement of passenger trains on all railroad approaches to Petersburg if the latter felt that it would benefit the arrival of supplies.[85] War Clerk Jones claimed that private freight shipments were forbidden between Georgia and Virginia and that the Piedmont Railroad had been impressed outright.[86] Nature and Fortune, however, overwhelmed these belated acts of administrative energy. A fire in Charlotte burned up twenty-two thousand sacks of grain and other subsistence stores, and on January 11 word reached Richmond that torrential rains had washed out culverts on the Piedmont Railroad, making it inoperable over a twenty-mile stretch and causing a ten-day interruption in service.[87]

The news of the breakdown of the Piedmont Railroad sounded like the stroke of doom to the officials of the War Department. On January 11, the day he heard the news, Seddon ordered impressing officers along the Virginia railroads to go to producers within easy reach of rail transportation and impress all surpluses over a six months' supply instead of allowing them to hold the traditional one year's reserve.[88] He also telegraphed Lee: "I fear the extraordinary power reposed in commanding generals of impressing without limit will have to be resorted to by you."[89] However, Seddon proposed an alternative: "A call by you on the people would be more influential in inducing acquiescence, perhaps voluntary contributions, than from any other source."[90] Seddon's impressment scheme fell flat. Lee replied that there was nothing in reach of the army to impress.[91] The bureau chiefs thought that heavy-handed impressments, either by bureau agents or by Lee, were impracticable in view of public opinion, and they preferred to stress appeals. Lawton wrote to Lee "to suggest that word from you in this emergency would assist us in aid from the people, whose supplies have already been sadly reduced, but disposed to lend, if made to understand that it is necessary."[92] Meanwhile Northrop (ignoring his earlier

84. Lawton to Chisman, Jan. 3, 1865, QMDLS, XX, 396.

85. Lawton to Corley, Jan. 10, 1865, *ibid.,* p. 411.

86. Jones, *War Clerk's Diary,* II, 373.

87. Lawton to Lee, Jan. 11, 1865, QMDLS, XX, 413; Hoke to Cooper, Jan. 7, 1865, *OR*-1, XLVI (2), 1023.

88. Special Orders No. 9, Adjutant and Inspector General's Office, 1865 Series, Jan. 12, 1865, *ibid.,* pp. 1041–1042.

89. Seddon to Lee, Jan. 11, 1865, *ibid.,* pp. 1034–1035.

90. *Ibid.*

91. Lee to Seddon, Jan. 11, 1865, *ibid.,* p. 1035.

92. Lawton to Lee, Jan. 12, 1865, QMDLS, XX, 418.

stand on appeals)[93] wrote to Seddon on the twelfth that he felt "a few lines" from Lee "would stimulate the people and voluntarily they would contribute." He continued:

> The [impressment] action you propose as a substitute would be less effective, is liable to opposition except from the good, and so far from shielding General Lee from odium, will throw it on him, while it has neither the sanction of law nor the force to effect your measures. . . .
>
> Permit me to urge that never can there occur a more critical moment or occasion in which General Lee's popularity or hold on the Confidence of the people . . . can find a more fitting opportunity for testing its efficiency in saving the cause.[94]

Lee did issue an appeal for aid, promising "to pay promptly for all supplies delivered under this appeal, or to return the same in kind as soon as practicable."[95] On the sixteenth Lee informed Seddon of his appeal and of the good responses, concluding, "I am glad to say that so far as I know the crisis in relation to this matter is now past."[96] Seddon's endorsement reveals the bankruptcy of civilian management of the supply system: "Noted with pleasure. It was the most effectual mode of obtaining supplies—more effective, I doubt not, than the coercive action of the Department."[97] Virtually the only power left to the supply administrators was that of a general's "popularity"!

. . .

In January 1865 it seemed that General Lee held one of the few safe reputations in the Confederacy. Gorgas's solid record of achievement had been acknowledged by his promotion to Brigadier General,[98] but the pressures of multiplying disasters spurred increased public outcry against the supply services. Congress responded with new investigations and new legislative proposals to reform or punish the supply services. Northrop was cleared by one investigating committee of abus-

93. Earlier in the war Northrop had curtly refused to consider appeals, saying that he had no experience in making arrangements for public appeals. See Northrop endorsement on Lee to Seddon, Jan. 26, 1863, *OR*-1, LI (2), 674–675; Northrop endorsement on Jones to Davis, Feb. 19, 1863, *OR*-4, II, 405.

94. Northrop to Seddon, Jan. 12, 1865, *OR*-1, XLVI (2), 1040.

95. Enclosure in Lee to Seddon, Jan. 16, 1865, *ibid.*, pp. 1074–1075.

96. Lee to Seddon, Jan. 16, 1865, *ibid.*, p. 1074.

97. Seddon endorsement, Jan. 19, 1865, on Lee to Seddon, Jan. 16, 1865, *ibid.*

98. *Journal*, IV, 273, 275.

ing U.S. prisoners,[99] but a more general investigation of the war effort continued throughout the winter. Legislation was proposed to require quartermasters and commissaries to make regular statements of personal property and bank accounts, but this proposal, objected to as casting aspersions on a whole group, failed to pass.[100] A bill authorizing the President "to appoint by and with the consent of the Senate, a Commissary-General, with the rank, pay and allowances of a Brigadier General,"[101] aimed at Northrop's decapitation, sped towards passage.

The latest subsistence agony had exasperated Congress too much for that group to be satisfied with the removal of the men at the top. Congress passed a bill conscripting all post, impressing, and purchasing quartermasters and commissaries, no matter what their position, who were under forty-five years of age, to be replaced by bonded civilian agents who were overage, disabled, or medically exempted. The same act also revoked all details to those departments except the skilled laborers in the factories.[102] One field commissary who got wind of Congress's intentions remarked laconically, "I am very indifferent about the Bill looking to our decapitation. I have no idea that it will pass muster, and if it does 'LET 'EM RIP.' "[103] Davis vetoed the bill, lauding Congress for their good intentions of getting more men for the ranks but claiming that the bill would hurt more in removing experienced officers from duty than it would provide strength in furnishing men.[104]

In this atmosphere of recrimination, latent antagonisms inside the War Department came out in the open. Although only Davis's appreciation of the Subsistence Department's tribulations had kept them in office, Northrop and Ruffin, in open rebellion, testified before Congress that Seddon and Davis had frustrated all their good ideas.[105] Meanwhile, their subordinates began openly to "abuse the President grossly."[106] Although they may have assisted in building up pressure for Seddon's removal, they also hastened their own departure. Kean reported Seddon "deeply pained" at Ruffin's and Northrop's activities

99. *Ibid.*, pp. 342–343.
100. *Ibid.*, VII, 411–415, 439, 440, 569, 572, 574–575, 578.
101. *Ibid.*, IV, 494, 496, 541, 555, 557.
102. Davis to the Senate, March 11, 1865, *Messages*, I, 559–561.
103. Emmerson to Henry, Feb. 2, 1865, Arthur Emmerson Papers, Duke University Manuscript Department.
104. Davis to the Senate, March 11, 1865, *Messages*, I, 559–561.
105. "Ruffin Testimony," PRSD, *passim.;* Vandiver, *Gorgas Diary*, p. 163.
106. Vandiver, *Gorgas Diary*, p. 165.

behind his back: "His view is that when they reached the conclusion that they could not carry on the commissariat with him, they were bound themselves to resign instead of attacking their superiors, in the Congress."[107]

Seddon meanwhile, aware of Congressional opposition, including that of the Virginia delegation, to his remaining in office, resigned despite Davis's wish that he remain. There was no particularly good reason to demand Seddon's removal, but the Confederacy was losing and needed some official scapegoat. It is always difficult to assess the performance of a Confederate Secretary of War, given his peculiar relationship to the President, and much depends on the plane of responsibility that one envisions for the office. If it is necessary for a good Secretary of War to plan ahead with the President and others to find out what is necessary to win the war and to work out systematic programs to utilize domestic and foreign resources, Seddon was a failure. On the other hand, assuming that no Confederate politician had the background or insights for centralized planning, and that a Secretary of War could only translate the concerns of the supply chiefs into propositions that might elicit the President's approval, Seddon was a success. Although he was too solicitous of the field commander's points of view and sometimes did not carry out sound policies, Seddon usually seized upon the avenue of approach that would best ease the problem at hand. Usually these approaches stressed the necessity of coercion for the general good rather than safeguarding individual liberty, and usually they represented the unpopular side of the issue. He favored close controls over the railroads and over shipping, he defended impressment as the only possibility under the given conditions, he believed that some men would have to be kept out of the ranks to work in the factories, and he wanted severe wartime taxation to control finances. Since most of Seddon's conferences with Davis were private and oral, no one knows how much the more radical subordinate influenced the more cautious chief. Perhaps there would have been no railroad law, no shipping law, no tithe, no impressment law, and no liberal interpretation of the exemption and conscription acts without his counsel.

After Seddon's departure General John C. Breckinridge filled his position. A veteran of multitudinous campaigns, Breckinridge was given the opportunity to prove what many a field officer must have long

107. Younger, *Kean Diary,* p. 103.

felt, that an experienced field commander could do better than a civilian. He is alleged to have demanded the ouster of Northrop as a condition to his acceptance,[108] but for a few weeks it was embarrassingly apparent that it was easier to find a new Secretary of War than a new Commissary General. Since Northrop's tenure amounts to the history of the Subsistence Department, evaluation of his career will be postponed until the concluding chapter; but one incident reveals the nature of that embittered eccentric in the last days of his career. As diarist Kean recorded it:

> General Lee wrote that his troops beyond Petersburg had been in line of battle three days and nights in snow, hail and rain *without a mouthful* of meat; that they would be so weakened by exposure and privation as not to have the physical strength to march and fight. It gave the saddest picture of the sufferings of the soldiers I have ever seen. Colonel Northrop was present when General Breckinridge [the new Secretary of War] received it and he showed it to him. "Yes," the old stoic remarked, "It is just what I predicted long ago." And he went on to rehearse the record without a single suggestion of relief. General Breckinridge inquired, "But Colonel, what shall we do?" "Well, I don't know. If my plans had been carried out instead of thwarted etc., etc."
>
> The Secretary sent the letter up to the President, who presently returned it with a very sharp endorsement to the effect that this was the result either of gross incapacity or criminal neglect, and soon after, the President wrote the Secretary a note that meat and whiskey must be borrowed, or impressed, and should be sent over before the commissary officers slept that night. This too Colonel Northrop saw but laid cooly [*sic*] aside, remarking to Lawton *soto* [*sic*] *voce,* that it was "sensational"; to the Secretary that he could not borrow because he had already borrowed more than could be returned, nor impress because by law the money had to be tendered; that it was partly General Lee's fault, and wholly Mr. Seddon's etc. And no suggestion of any means of relief was so much as offered by him. This probably hastens his fate which was sealed before.[109]

While the less charitable had flayed Northrop's idiosyncrasies, Lee had usually referred to them with the more moderate word "peculiari-

108. Jones, *War Clerk's Diary,* II, 395; Augusta *Tri-Weekly Constitutionalist,* Feb. 8, 1865.

109. Younger, *Kean Diary,* p. 200.

ties."[110] Now, however, worried about increasing desertion among his hungry and dispirited men, Lee pronounced more severe judgment:

> I know there are great difficulties in procuring supplies, but I cannot help thinking that with proper energy, intelligence, and experience on the part of the Commissary Department a great deal more could be accomplished. There is enough in the country, I believe, if it was properly sought for. I do not see why . . . [supplies can not be collected] in such a manner as to have more on hand at a given time. The fact that they are collected at all is proof that they exist, and it must be possible to gather more in a given time than is now done. It will not answer to reduce the ration in order to make up for the deficiencies in the subsistence department. The proper remedy is increased effort, greater experience in business and intelligent management. It may be that all is done that can be, but I am not satisfied that we cannot do more.[111]

On February 8, with his army out of food, Lee wrote to Seddon: "If some change is not made, and the Commy Dept. reorganized, I apprehend dire results."[112] Lee had spoken; Davis and Seddon had been alienated; the next day the bill making the Commissary General a Brigadier General passed Congress;[113] three days later Davis signed the bill;[114] one week later Northrop and Ruffin, although not officially removed,[115] disappeared from positions of authority.

Isaac St. John was appointed Commissary General on February 16, 1865, and pursuant to the new law, Congress promoted him to the rank of Brigadier General.[116] The effects of the new personality at the head of the Subsistence Department merit attention. St. John, with his excellent record in the Niter and Mining Bureau, was received with enthusiasm from all quarters. Gorgas thought that the change would "save the army and perhaps the cause."[117] Lee commented that "under the reorganization of the Commissary Department . . . the army will

110. Davis to Northrop, March 17, 1879, Rowland, *Jefferson Davis,* VIII, 369.
111. Lee to Seddon, Jan. 27, 1865, *OR*-1, XLVI (2), 1143.
112. Lee to Seddon, Feb. 8, 1865, *ibid.,* XLVI (1), 381.
113. *Journal,* IV, 564, 583; VII, 558.
114. Ramsdell, *Laws and Joint Resolutions of the Last Session of the Confederate Congress,* p. 41.
115. Thomas R. Hay, "Lucius B. Northrop: Commissary General of the Confederacy," *Civil War History,* IX, No. 1 (March, 1963), 19–20.
116. *Journal,* IV, 569.
117. Vandiver, *Gorgas Diary,* p. 170.

be better supplied than heretofore, and . . . we can accumulate some provisions ahead."[118] St. John was a much better psychologist than Northrop, for he stressed the positive side of subsistence questions. His method was first to let it be known to all that there was enough food in the country to feed the armies and later to follow with such *if*'s as money and transportation. Actually, Northrop had held the same views, but years of frustration had made him see the hole rather than the doughnut.

Besides attempting to buoy up public confidence with optimistic pronouncements, St. John was willing to try all possible methods for obtaining supplies, including an appeal to the farmers for a voluntary contribution, sale, or loan. Coming into office in the midst of a provisioning crisis and noting Lee's January success, St. John moved immediately. He conferred with farmers and millers and asked for the co-operation of the clergy in broadcasting his appeals.[119] He armed himself with the favorable response of the North Carolina congressional delegation and used this information in a letter to Governor Vance to request his support in promulgating public appeals in North Carolina.[120]

St. John's forthright appeals brought a forthright response. In the hour of need the Confederate farmers proved more generous than the jaundiced administrators might have expected. Commissary officials termed the response "most cheering and satisfactory"[121] and reported that depots on the railroads were "rapidly filling up with flour, meal, corn and bacon."[122] There was no doubt that St. John's activity had encouraged the people, besides achieving the practical result of building up a temporary reserve for Lee's army. St. John hardly had time to get settled in his office before Lee wrote to commend him on his "prompt and vigorous measures."[123] Enthusiasm touched the toilers in the lower echelons as well, tempting one unknown commissary to the nether reaches of doggerel:

Our reverses have not increased the source of our Supply.
So Set your Agents all to work,—tis root hog or die
Go proclaim it boldly to this patriotic nation

118. Lee to Longstreet, Feb. 22, 1865, *OR*-1, XLVI (2), 1250–1251.

119. A Lady of Virginia [Mrs. Judith W. McGuire], *Diary of a Southern Refugee during the War* (New York, 1868), p. 334; Vandiver, *Gorgas Diary*, p. 169.

120. St. John to Vance, Feb. 24, 1865, *OR*-1, LI (2), 1063–1064.

121. Claiborne to St. John, March 10, 1865, *ibid.*, XLVI (2), p. 1298–1299.

122. Williams to St. John, March 10, 1865, *ibid.*, p. 1298.

123. Lee to St. John, Feb. 21, 1865, *ibid.*, p. 1246.

And call upon the Commissaries for active co-operation
Tell them bread and meat is wanted or Richmond must fall
Bread and meat is wanted, proclaim this fact to all
In deference to public Sentiment respected you must be
For on you depends the feeding of the army under Lee,
Awake my St John and leave the nitre bureau
It has been determined that Col Northrop now, must go
So go to work my boys, and we'll get a good supply,
The preachers will assist us, for tis root hog or die[124]

Appeals could be only a temporary expedient for raising supplies, however; and no one knew this better than St. John. His real responsibility was to maintain a regular system of supply, and here he faced the same problems that had plagued Northrop—money and transportation. On March 10 St. John reported his immediate successes to the Secretary of War and outlined his views of the subsistence situation.[125] He dismissed voluntary contributions as "simply auxiliary and not to be relied upon as a permanent source of supply."[126] Although Wilmington had fallen, he felt that the Army of Northern Virginia could be subsisted from meat held within reach of the Confederate armies in North Carolina, Virginia, and Tennessee. He estimated that he could obtain 12,500,000 rations of bread and 11,000,000 rations of meat in the next few months from Virginia, with proper protection and transportation.[127] Eastern Tennessee, now back in Confederate control, could yield 15,000,000 rations of bread and 5,000,000 pounds of meat if the bureau could get $500,000 in coin and $150,000 daily in Treasury notes, plus protection and transportation.[128] Meanwhile his supply depots in North Carolina and Virginia reported 2,250,200 meat rations and 1,572,300 bread rations in reserve and seven days' supply of rations on hand at the front[129]—rations gathered under Northrop. He had set up, in addition, a chain of depots that stretched all the way from Charlotte to Washington, Georgia, to provide supplies for any armies that might have to retreat in that direction.[130]

124. Anonymous manuscript, Arthur Emmerson Papers, Duke University Manuscript Department.

125. [St. John] to Breckinridge, March 10, 1865, *OR*-4, III, 1137.

126. *Ibid.*

127. French to St. John, March 10, 1865, *OR*-1, XLVI (2), 1297.

128. *Ibid.*; Williams to St. John, March 10, 1865, *ibid.*, p. 1298.

129. St. John to Breckinridge, March 30, 1865, Lee Headquarters Papers—Folder V, Virginia Historical Society.

130. "Ruffin Testimony," PRSD, p. 6; St. John to Davis, July 14, 1873, Rowland, *Jefferson Davis,* VIII, 352–355.

With all of this optimism St. John stressed the fulfilment of two major conditions for the continued supply of the Army of Northern Virginia: "Prompt payment in funds that will be received without compulsion are [*sic*] considered indispensable in arranging a certain supply for the future; without this all efforts will be paralyzed;"[131] and "the Army of Northern Virginia must be supplied, by distant railroad transportation; from Abingdon, Va., and Goldsboro and Charlotte, N.C., 120 tons of commissary supplies daily."[132] Assistant Secretary of War Campbell commented: "[The] Commissary-General requires the fulfillment of conditions, though not unreasonable, nearly impossible."[133]

For the armies and units south of Virginia, St. John held few fears. He felt that the troops of the southwest and the Army of Tennessee in North Carolina would be able to subsist off the land without having to use the supplies in reserve depots.[134] He was undoubtedly right about the Deep South troops, which as usual found no subsistence difficulties, especially now that few troops were left to consume stores. The Macon depot, for example, reported on March 31, 1865, 274,394 pounds of bacon on hand and 491,199 pounds of corn, 87,529 pounds of peas, 29,429 pounds of sugar, and other reserves.[135] The troops in Mississippi had in reserve over 1,500,000 pounds of meal and flour, 10,000 cattle, 5,000 pigs, 2,000 sheep, and a large amount of other stores.[136]

Food was available for the armies as the war drew to a close. On April 2, the day lines were broken at Petersburg, all requisitions for food in previous days had been met, and rations of meat to the following amounts were on hand in the depots: Richmond, 300,000; Lynchburg, 180,000; Danville, 2,000,000; Greensboro, 1,500,000. Hospital rations of tea, coffee, and sugar were also available if needed.[137] Not until the night of April 2 did the order come from Lee's staff to move the subsistence stores at Richmond down the Richmond and Danville Railroad, and by then it was too late; for the Richmond stores were already in the hands of the mobs. Lee was pushed off the Danville line

131. [St. John] to Breckinridge, March 10, 1865, *OR*-4, III, 1137. 132. *Ibid.*

133. Campbell to Breckinridge, March 5, 1865, *OR*-1, LI (2), 1066.

134. *Ibid.*

135. Robertson to Allen, March 31, 1865, George Robertson Letter Book, Duke University Manuscript Department.

136. Report of Subsistence Stores in Mississippi and East Louisiana, Dec. 15, 1864, *OR*-1, XLV (2), 737–738.

137. Williams to St. John, Sept. —, 1865, Lee Headquarters Papers—Folder L, Virginia Historical Society.

too soon for trains to arrive from that city, and the trains from Lynchburg were seized by Sheridan at Appomattox Station on the night of April 8 just before Lee could reach them, a fact that helped determine his surrender.[138] Johnston's army had apparently used Greensboro depot supplies until he surrendered. The depots in South Carolina and Georgia, waiting for the troops which never came, served only to feed the fleeing Davis and his bodyguard.

St. John's six-week record, up to the time of the collapse in Virginia, has received the commendation of historians, and for good reasons. His previous solid reputation and his guarded optimism had encouraged his contemporaries; his efforts in distributing his subsistence among a series of local depots confirmed the fact that he was a man of initiative and energy. For all these reasons he was undoubtedly an improvement upon Northrop. Still, St. John faced the same problems that had plagued Northrop—inadequate transportation, no importations, and a deficit of funds. St. John fully realized that the Subsistence Department's major problems lay in the realm of economics and logistics, over which it had little control, rather than in administrative efficiency and quality of personnel. As he commented retrospectively to Lee in June 1865:

> I feel it a duty to add as one who was ordered to an unwelcome duty at a singularly unfavorable moment, and therefore in no manner committed to the controversies of the Commissary Department—That my own adverse opinion founded on public report was greatly changed upon personal observation. Among its officers I found some of the finest men of the service—in ability, vigor and devotion. They were contending under Extreme disadvantages with the nearly Crushing Embarrassments of an insufficient supply of purchasing funds, and very deficient transportation. Otherwise their record would have been very different.[139]

• • •

There is no need to narrate supply measures, decisions, and plans of the spring of 1865, for they had no effect on the war. Confederate officials proposed plans and promulgated regulations, Congress legislated on issues great and small, and army leaders shuffled their dwin-

138. *Ibid.;* a concise summary may be found in Black, *Confederate Railroads,* pp. 284–286.

139. St. John to Lee, June 30, 1865, Lee Headquarters Papers—Folder L, Virginia Historical Society.

dling units about to little avail. However, one concluding encounter with the Confederate supply situation is of importance: the attempts of Assistant Secretary of War John A. Campbell to use the supply situation to justify a negotiated peace.

Campbell, Associate Justice of the Supreme Court in 1861, had been a reluctant Confederate but once committed had toiled faithfully in the War Department under three Secretaries of War. He had toiled with such intelligence and discrimination that Kean declared: "Judge Campbell is invaluable; his capacity of labor infinite; his breadth of view great. His endorsements are . . . judicial, deciding questions rather than cases. . . ."[140] Gorgas pronounced Campbell "the mainstay of the War Department."[141] Mainstay or not, Judge Campbell apparently prided himself on his grasp of realities; for by the autumn of 1864 he had become convinced that the Confederacy lacked the resources to prosecute another campaign.[142] In contrast to his gloomy outlook, he heard Seddon report to Congress in December 1864 that "All essential supplies have been afforded. . . . The Army had been subsisted, clothed and provided for in adequate measure, and there had never been deficiency of transportation, munitions, or supplies for all important operations";[143] he also heard Davis claim that "military supplies essentially requisite for public defense will be found, as heretofore, adequate to our needs."[144] Such statements Campbell apparently viewed either as mere official bombast or more ominously as an indication that Davis and Seddon were determined to take the Confederacy down unnecessary last miles to defeat. In response, as Campbell put it, "I was incessantly employed in making the facts known . . . [but] to no result."[145] Campbell forced Trenholm to admit he had understated the proportions of the public debt. He also brought deficiencies to Davis's attention and pushed for negotiations for peace.[146] When these efforts seemed fruitless, he took it upon himself to prepare a memorandum in January 1865 in which he listed those measures

140. Younger, *Kean Diary,* p. 33.

141. Vandiver, *Gorgas Diary,* p. 169.

142. Campbell to Curtis, July 20, 1865, *Century Illustrated Monthly Magazine,* XXXVIII, No. 6 (Oct., 1889), 951.

143. Seddon to Davis, Nov. 3, 1864, *OR*-4, III, 767.

144. Davis to the Senate and House of Representatives, Nov. 7, 1864, *Messages,* I, 485.

145. Campbell to Curtis, July 20, 1865, *Century Illustrated Monthly Magazine,* XXXVIII, No. 6 (Oct., 1889), 951.

146. *Ibid.*

which needed immediate attention. He stressed such obvious problems as financial reform and correction of army absenteeism, but he also asked that the supply bureaus be guaranteed freedom to operate without interference.[147]

After the Hampton Roads conference, where he had been a Confederate commissioner, had ended hopes for a negotiated peace, Campbell immediately returned to his efforts to expose the facts of the hopeless military conditions of the Confederacy. On February 7, the day that the new Secretary of War, John A. Breckinridge, took office, Campbell persuaded Breckinridge to call on each bureau head for a statement "of the means and resources you have on hand for carrying on the business of your Bureau, and your ability for carrying it on, what impediments exist and what is necessary for that purpose."[148] Although Campbell must have hoped that the replies of the bureau chiefs would validate his opinion of the prostration of Confederate resources, he was doomed to disappointment. No bureau head would admit that he was defeated, and some reports were optimistic. Gorgas reported:

> As to "impediments", I know of none which I cannot overcome, except the persistent and continuous interference with our workmen on account of military operations. . . . I will answer for the supply of the ordnance and ordnance stores to the Army.[149]

Lawton claimed that he had enough summer clothing and shoes to supply the army for the campaigning season and possibly enough wool for the next autumn and winter if he could get money and workers.[150] Bayne's optimism in regard to the Bureau of Foreign Supplies bordered on the incredible. Despite the loss of the major ports, he claimed, "I think all general supplies . . . [from overseas] can be obtained."[151] Sims and Cole, reporting through their chief, Lawton, were less sanguine about the state of rail and field transportation. Sims reported that the railroads were worn out and complained of the lack of effectual government control over what was left.[152] Cole reported that the army needed ten thousand animals from Cis-Mississippi sources,

147. Younger, *Kean Diary,* p. 189.
148. War Department Circular, Feb. 7, 1865, *OR*-4, III, 1064.
149. Gorgas to Breckinridge, Feb. 9, 1865, *ibid.,* p. 1071.
150. Lawton to Breckinridge, Feb. 16, 1865, *ibid.,* pp. 1086–1093.
151. Bayne to Breckinridge, Feb. 9, 1865, *ibid.,* pp. 1071–1072.
152. Sims to Lawton, Feb. 10, 1865, *ibid.,* pp. 1091–1093.

Texas, Mexico, and through the lines. To obtain the animals and to put the armies in condition for field operations required the immediate expenditure of large amounts of gold and cotton, neither of which had as yet been forthcoming.[153] Neither man, however, pronounced his task impossible if the administrators would co-operate. Northrop's report on subsistence was the most pessimistic, as befitted the temper of the Commissary General and the exigencies of the Subsistence Department. After reciting his usual tale of financial strangulation, transportation deficiencies, enemy devastation, and frustration in obtaining supplies from outside the Confederacy, Northrop concluded that he could not subsist the armies unless there was "an administration of the other branches of the service (whose operations underlie those of this bureau) different from the past."[154] Consistent with his latter-day outlook, he severely criticized the Secretaries of War for not better co-ordinating the efforts of the bureaus.[155]

Thus, the bureau chiefs, like their superiors, claimed to see the supply situation in a startlingly optimistic light. Give them enough workers and money, efficient administration of transportation and outside procurement, more efficient superiors, and a military stand-off, and they would supply the army. Given all these conditions, they were undoubtedly right.

Balked by the positive tenor of the bureau chiefs' February reports, Campbell bided his time while he worked out a more complicated plan for bringing the Confederate authorities to their senses about the futility of carrying on the war. His plan was to call for new reports from the bureaus, to add Lee's pessimistic opinions, and then to persuade Davis to send all reports together to Congress for its consideration.[156] While this authoritative information weighed heavily on the minds of the Congressmen, Senator William A. Graham of North Carolina would introduce a resolution, written by former Congressman William C. Rives of Virginia, calling for an armistice as a prelude to reconstruction.[157] On March 5 Campbell put his plan into operation by sending a letter to Breckinridge painting a ominous picture of the Confederate war effort.[158] He stressed existing shortages in subsistence,

153. Cole to Lawton, Feb. 1, 1865, *ibid.,* pp. 1087–1089.

154. Northrop to Breckinridge, Feb. 9, 1865, *OR*-1, XLVI (2), 1211–1212.

155. *Ibid.*

156. Campbell to Curtis, July 20, 1865, *Century Illustrated Monthly Magazine,* XXXVIII, No. 6 (Oct., 1889), 952.

157. *Ibid.*

158. Campbell to Breckinridge, March 5, 1865, *OR*-1, LI (2), 1064–1067.

forage, and animals and blamed them on rotten finance, lack of manpower, administrative deficiencies, and war losses rather than on bureau mismanagement. He also forecast medical and ordnance collapse with the loss of the ports. Campbell concluded by declaring that these conditions pointed to the need for reconstruction. He asked that Breckinridge make a "candid inquiry" into the resources of the bureaus, that Lee be requested to give his opinion, and that all this information be sent by the President to Congress "to invite their action."[159] Breckinridge obligingly issued a new call for reports and opinions.[160] Some of the second round of replies are missing but the available reports were optimistic, again thwarting Campbell. St. John and Morton, the new chiefs of the Subsistence and the Niter and Mining bureaus, both indicated that they could do their duty under existing conditions if money were available.[161] Lawton felt that he could control enough transportation to supply Lee if Lee could hold the Richmond and Danville Railroad.[162] As Campbell expected, however, Lee, who had to judge results from existing conditions, had a gloomy outlook. On March 9 he wrote in answer to Breckinridge:

> It seems almost impossible to maintain our present position with the means at the disposal of the Government. . . . The country within reach of our present position has been nearly or quite exhausted. . . .
>
> Unless the men and animals can be subsisted, the army cannot be kept together, and our present lines must be abandoned. Nor can it be moved to any other position where it can operate to advantage without provisions to enable it to move in a body.
>
> The difficulties attending the payment and clothing of the troops, though great, are not so pressing and would be relieved in a measure by military success. The same is true as to the ordnance supplies, . . .[163]

Breckinridge, who may have been supporting Campbell's efforts, duly gathered up the replies and brought them to the President's attention. At this point, however, Davis, presumably unconsciously,

159. *Ibid.* 160. Breckinridge to Lee, March 8, 1865, *ibid.*, XLVI (2), 1292.

161. [St. John] to Breckinridge, March 10, 1865, *OR*-4, III, 1137; Morton to Breckinridge, March 24, 1865, *ibid.*, p. 1164.

162. John A. Campbell, *Reminiscences and Documents Relating to the Civil War during the Year 1865* (Baltimore, 1887), p. 35. Cited hereinafter as Campbell, *Reminiscences.*

163. Lee to Breckinridge, March 9, 1865, *OR*-1, XLVI (2), 1295–1296.

ruined Campbell's plans.[164] It is unlikely that Campbell had expected Davis to urge Congress to end the war, but he did perhaps expect Davis to send over the papers with comments on the seriousness of the situation and possibly with recommendations for sweeping changes in finances and army organization. Davis would thus reinforce the impression of the seriousness of the situation and open the way for Senator Graham to move for an armistice. Instead, Davis sent a special message to the House of Representatives on March 13 in which he declared that Congress was about to adjourn without fulfilling its obligations. He suggested a mixture of controversial proposals and half-way reforms which in themselves did not indicate that the country was in serious difficulties.[165] Davis sent the reports that Campbell had so heavily relied on to the House of Representatives in a separate message on the same day, making no comments on them except to say that they would serve to "elucidate" the main message.[166] Congress stayed in session a few days longer and passed some of the legislation, but the Senate put its energies into a peppery reply to what it termed the President's "effort to excite discord and dissension."[167] Congress apparently disregarded the reports in its eagerness to get in a lick at the President, and Senator Graham felt it useless to introduce the resolution.[168] Thus Campbell's effort to use the supply situation to justify a negotiated peace dissolved in the heat of Executive-Legislative rancor.

Twenty-four days later Lee surrendered.

. . .

On the face of it, the Confederate armies had begun the 1864 campaign season adequately supplied with the materials of war, with the productive centers of the Confederacy protected behind them. In fact, however, it turned out that the armies were fatally immobilized. They were too short of men, field transportation, and supply reserves to take the offensive, and too short of infantry and cavalry to defend their supply lines. With the initiative in the hands of the Union, the Confederate forces were outmaneuvered and worn down until they

164. Campbell to Curtis, July 20, 1865, *Century Illustrated Monthly Magazine,* XXXVIII, No. 6 (Oct. 1889), 952.

165. Davis to the House of Representatives, March 13, 1865, *Messages,* I, 544–551.

166. *Ibid.,* p. 552.

167. *Journal,* IV, 726–731.

168. The text is given in Campbell, *Reminiscences,* pp. 33–34.

delivered the railroad network and the remaining ports to the enemy, bringing the war effort to a halt. In the final months of the struggle, the dissolving armies wandered about the country while the factories produced and the storehouses held supplies that could not be moved to the troops. Shortages had hamstrung the armies; the armies had failed to protect the supply effort.

Meanwhile, the Richmond administrators did their part to hasten the end, prostrating already inefficient policies by calamitous blunders in finance, conscription, and railroad policy. At the end, Richmond had abdicated responsibility for the supply effort amid a welter of recriminations and intrigue.

CHAPTER NINE

RETROSPECT

The Confederate war effort began under the cloud of what might have been. The eleven Confederate states contained only a fraction of the resources which the fifteen Slave States as a group could have employed in a war with the Free States. The loss of the Border States denied to the Confederacy large productive areas of grain and meat and the greater part of the modest industrial strength of the Slave section. It also left most of the valuable agricultural and industrial areas that remained in the Confederacy perilously exposed to Union invasion.

Without the Border States Confederate resources displayed few positive characteristics. The enormous size of the country was as much a handicap as an aid. Although there was an abundance of fertile soil to produce both food for the military services and cotton to exchange for military products, the Confederacy's patchwork transportation and communications network rendered it difficult to collect and distribute military supplies and vitiated efficient administration. Other disturbing conditions existed. Although the Confederacy had the potential for bountiful food production for the future, the food crops were badly located. The bulk of the grains and meat were either exposed to the enemy in Tennessee and Virginia or virtually inaccessible in Texas. Except for cotton textiles, located safely in the southeastern piedmont, the Confederacy's tiny industrial production of coal, iron, clothing, and shoes was concentrated in Virginia, Tennessee, and New Orleans, exposed to attack by land and sea. There was little surplus capital. Manpower, that least replaceable of resources in a war of attrition, was barely adequate to fight a defensive war and included few of the skilled operatives necessary to sustain the fighting men. All in all, the Confederacy displayed a formidable catalogue of material deficiencies, if it became necessary to wage an extended war for independence.

The Confederacy's deficiencies might have been eased and perhaps overcome by carefully laid plans to husband available domestic resources and to import goods from abroad until domestic production could be developed to take over a larger proportion of the supply burden. Existing iron and textile production should have been monopolized, the railroads integrated to secure efficient transportation of supplies, agricultural conversion from cotton to foodstuffs implemented, and manpower carefully allocated between the army and the factories and farms. Available specie and cotton should have been sent to Europe for the purchase of immediate supply needs and for the purchase of government cargo ships to continue importations. By such planning the Confederacy might have managed and developed its resources with maximum efficiency until the Union grew weary of its massive invasion effort or until foreign powers intervened.

Though scanty resources called for vigorous planning and centralized controls, the Confederate leaders provided few blueprints. In the beginning most of the Confederate leaders hoped for a short war, but when this mirage faded away they did not methodically plan for the future in an attempt to control events. Of course, creating a centralized and omnipotent bureaucracy which would allocate persons and property for the general welfare was foreign to every tradition which had nurtured these men. Nor would the Confederate citizens, being the Americans who had taken most pride in their nineteenth-century libertarian ethos, have submitted to any such imposition of authority. Still, while the politicians could not have been expected to create a coldly efficient warfare state, they could have indulged in careful estimation of resources and worked out plans to conserve and allot goods and men within the accepted traditions of "constitutional" war-making. There is no evidence, however, that the civilian leaders at any time sat down together and made plans and programs from estimates of current resources. Rather, as the war unfolded in its vast dimensions across the continent and took on the nature of a war of attrition, the leaders had to be forced by adverse circumstances to invent a series of unco-ordinated, stringent measures in an attempt simply to keep the fighting going. Many of these measures were ignored or evaded by both the civilians and the military. The result was the accidental accumulation of a number of the characteristics of a centralized state, but without producing the efficiency which would have justified it. Confederate centralization was planless, unco-ordinated, tardy, and impotent.

The key figure in Confederate administrative drift was Jefferson Davis. A politician of conservative stripe, he was hardly a man to plan knowingly for the subordination of individual liberties to the necessities of the state. Still, he arrogated to himself all of the final decisions on important matters pertaining to the conduct of the war, including basic supply policies. Davis's mind is therefore a key to the tone and tempo of the supply effort. Allowing events to move him haphazardly towards a centralized administration as the war progressed, he often delayed and defeated centralizing measures deemed necessary by others, only to embrace these same measures himself at a later time, often when it was too late. Actually, Davis held quite inconsistent views of national control, for the efficient Secretary of War in his make-up warred with the constitutionalist politician. When he was dealing with such secretaryish matters as furnishing "goods" to the army, be it uniforms, ordnance, or men, he showed few scruples about imposing government regulations upon persons and property, supporting controls over private agricultural and industrial production, conscription, impressment, and government manufacture of military supplies. On the other hand, he was slow to see the necessity of regulating the supporting elements of the war effort. He did not regulate the shipping interests and co-ordinate an efficient purchasing system abroad until the war was more than half over. He initially opposed trading through the lines and then allowed the policy to proceed, but so shackled with conditions that this source of supplies never reached its potential. Most damaging of all, he prevented effective military control over the railroads throughout the war, in particular prostrating Lee's army and the Subsistence Department. While it may be too harsh to say, as did the Assistant Secretary of War, John A. Campbell, that Davis was "an incubus and a mischief,"[1] it is true that the actions of the President of the Confederate States, as much as any other single factor, contributed to the inefficiency of the Confederate supply effort.

Traditionally in American history, the duties of co-ordinating policies and formulating plans fell to the Secretary of War, but since Davis controlled all important decisions, be they strategy, personnel, or supplies, the Confederate Secretaries of War could do little to bring order out of chaos. Under Davis's domination, three of the five Secretaries, Walker, Benjamin, and Breckinridge, serving a combined total of some fifteen months, contributed nothing worth remembering to the war effort. Randolph tried to exercise some independent judgment both in strategic matters and in backing the plans for trading through the lines proposed by the supply chiefs. The blunt rebukes he incurred from Davis on these matters and irritation at the encroachments of the President led to his departure after nine months, before he was able to do anything of note to aid the development of an efficient supply

1. Campbell to Curtis, July 20, 1865, *The Century Illustrated Monthly Magazine*, XXXVIII, No. 6 (October, 1889), 952.

system. Seddon presided over the War Department for some twenty-six months in the latter half of the war, and his tenure may be considered a success only in terms of the circumscribed limits which the President allowed a Secretary of War. Unlike Randolph, Seddon never pressed to such lengths as to incur his own removal propositions which the President opposed. His role became that of an intermediary between the President and the bureau chiefs, reducing the zone of friction between their aggressive pragmatism and Davis's aggressive idiosyncrasies. While in office, however, Seddon became an advocate of nearly all of the pragmatic, if unco-ordinated, centralizing measures that the supply chiefs proposed and used his influence to persuade the President to countenance such measures. Still, his major responsibility was to co-ordinate the activities of the bureaus and to plan ahead, and in this regard he failed as badly as the President, for he deferred too much to the autonomous proclivities of the field commanders and drifted along with the pressure of events.

The Confederate Congress also held responsibility for furthering the war effort but provided little initiative. In most of the legislation dealing with supply matters Congress dutifully followed the recommendations of the executives, and when such recommendations were deficient, did little to improve them. When Congress did take an independent stand, it was usually detrimental to the supply effort. For example, following political dictates, it weakened conscription legislation and fought shipping regulations. Above all, it refused to enact stringent tax laws or price control measures, while flooding the country with bonds and notes. Coupled with scarcity, the resulting hoarding and inflation first forced the supply bureaus to resort to impressment. Later, however, Congress weakened impressment and the entire domestic procurement system by reducing the amounts of currency without curbing prices and hoarding.

Despite the fact that the civilians responsible for the war effort hampered both foreign and domestic procurement, the supply chiefs compiled a competent record in those areas where they were allowed to operate on their own initiative. In general, the bureau heads planned ahead to meet responsibilities in their realm much more efficiently than their superiors did in theirs, and they consistently pressed for permission to make innovations. The bureaus often competed with each other, and bureau friction existed to some degree throughout the war; but in the later stages the supply chiefs worked out an increasing amount of inter-bureau co-operation, usually on their own initiative.

On the whole, the bureau chiefs kept their organizations a close step behind the expanding scope and complexity of the war.

The greatest failure in bureau operation was civilian resistance to the war effort, resistance caused by inefficient bureau performance. The chief supply officers were unable to enforce bureau regulations and to compel honesty and efficiency among the myriads of lesser personnel operating over the countryside. The bureaus had expanded so rapidly that there had been little opportunity to instill efficiency and a sense of responsibility in the new men. The efficiency of supply service diminished in direct proportion to the distance from Richmond, and in the remote areas of the Confederacy the depot and purchasing commissaries and quartermasters apparently managed on their own as they saw fit. Impressment, conscription, and the tax-in-kind antagonized a population unused to government regulation, and the inefficiencies and occasional corruptions of the supply officers offered a pretext for resisting the war effort. Certainly the supply bureaus were detested by the public in the last months of the war. On the other hand, the Confederate citizens were growing steadily more disenchanted with the general burdens of the war and progressively more unwilling to make the necessary sacrifices. In such an atmosphere it was easy to rationalize hoarding and other forms of non-compliance by blaming the inequities of the government's supply procurement policies.

It is difficult to compare the degrees of efficiency of the individual supply bureaus because they differed so markedly in duties and manner of operation. Generally speaking, a bureau achieved greater success to the extent that it manufactured its own supplies, to the degree that it was not obligated to collect from private sources, and to the degree that it was independent of other agencies for distribution of materials. Faced initially with few shops or skilled workmen or mines on which to build an ordnance complex, the Niter and Mining Bureau and the Ordnance Department forged one of the most impressive chapters in Confederate history. St. John developed mineral and niter production and controlled iron production with notable skill, although he was still unable to produce enough iron for all needs, and could manufacture only half the nitrates needed by the army. Aided initially by battlefield captures, Gorgas succeeded in building up an ordnance production complex that furnished all of the powder and artillery and a fraction of the small arms needed, and his productive capacities for small arms would have been greatly increased if he could have had the necessary workmen. Gorgas was the only bureau chief to create a system of importations adequate to meet his particular responsibilities; throughout the war, he was able to import enough nitrates, minerals, incidental supplies, and small arms to complement domestic production.

The record of Quartermaster's Department was mixed. Both Myers and Lawton planned soundly to anticipate future needs but occasionally lacked vigor in pushing their plans through their quiescent civilian superiors to approval. Generally speaking, domestic resources were efficiently controlled, although the bureau could have moved somewhat faster in setting up these controls. Cotton textile production was regulated and leather production monopolized. The bureau was definitely slow in arranging for a systematic supply of woolens, shoes, and other quartermaster stores from overseas, but Myers and Lawton were hampered in part by their low priority in expenditures of the already inadequate funds earmarked for purchases abroad, and in part by the fortunes of blockade running and captures. By the later stages of the war, however, the bureau had been successful in the importation of clothing and accouterments to the extent that it supplied the wants of the armies and began to build up a reserve.

The greatest failure of the Quartermaster's Department was its management of field and rail transportation. Not all of this was a consequence of the shortcomings of supply officials. Quartermaster officials worked zealously at providing field transportation, even to the extent of evolving a set of special administrators to ferret out new horses and wagons and repair the old, as well as trying to devise effective ways to bring horses across the Mississippi, but they failed. Inadequate field transportation contributed to the growing immobility of the Confederate armies. In railroad transportation there was a failure of vision as well as of resources. Myers opposed military regulation of the railroads, and it was rather through the efforts of Northrop and Seddon that Davis and Congress were persuaded to countenance the theory, if not the fact, of government supervision. Lawton appears to have been willing to use the railroad control law in specific cases if directed to do so, but he does not appear to have advocated its general use. The two Quartermaster Generals therefore contributed to the continuing inefficiency of railroad transportation.

The Subsistence Department has been considered the black sheep of the Confederate supply bureaus, but unjustly so. The bureau and its chief have been condemned, among other things, because the Confederate armies were on short rations while foodstuffs rotted in the lower South. This condition, while all too true, was not the result of incompetence on the part of Commissary General Northrop or of the Subsistence Department as an organization. There were undoubtedly more practical and less cantankerous men than Northrop, such as St. John, who would have been better able to hold the public confidence. To this extent the commissariat could have been better managed. Any other Commissary General, however, would, like Northrop, have been hamstrung by circumstances beyond his control. Military reverses deprived the Subsistence Department of the flour- and meat-producing regions in the vicinity of the armies faster than the railroad network could supply the deficiency from new food-producing areas of the lower South. Procurement of the available domestic stocks in the hands of producers was retarded and then ruined by inflation, requiring resort to impressment as the only method to force sales, followed in turn by producer resistance and currency collapse which destroyed domestic procurement. Those stocks actually secured by the government were dissipated, to some degree by bureau inefficiency but much more directly by the inefficiency of the railroads in carrying food and fodder to the armies, an inefficiency that the Quartermaster's Department and the civilian authorities would not mitigate by more stringent regulation. Hampered at home, Northrop advocated trading through the lines and formulated special arrangements with blockade runners to secure food from abroad, but his plans were hamstrung by restrictions imposed by his superiors. It is not surprising, therefore, that Northrop ceased being grateful for Davis's publicly expressed confidence and turned against Davis and Seddon for not taking action to correct unsatisfactory policies that produced failure and condemnation for the Commissary General.

Supply administration in the field also hampered the Confederate war effort. The men, for example, were wasteful of supplies individually, and the commanders often caused unnecessary destruction of supply accumulations and unnecessary shortages by not warning bureau officials of impending movements for retreat or advance. The field supply officers, loyal to their commanders and not to the bureaus, would not co-operate with bureau regulations for proper requisitioning and distribution, and this caused unnecessary shortages and more waste. The top field commanders operated virtually independently of Richmond, and early in the war competed with each other and wasted supplies to such an extent that their actions forced the usually compliant Seddon to transfer the management of supplies from the commanding generals to the supply chiefs.

The quality of the Confederate supply effort cannot be judged exclusively in terms of administration. It was carried out amidst the march of military events, and policies and campaigns became cause and effect. In 1861 the Confederate government was unable to supply adequately the men called into the field, even when the government's efforts were supplemented by extensive state and private contributions. Happy circumstance allowed the Confederacy to win the only military action of consequence for that campaigning season, but the inadequate supply situation played a major part in preventing Confederates from following up Manassas and bringing the war to a quick finish. Following Manassas, state and private contributions faded into insignificance, and the Confederate government began to step up preparations for the full-scale activities envisioned for 1862, increasing efforts to secure articles from the domestic market and making arrangements for importations from abroad. The latter arrangements, however, were hampered by the policy of withholding cotton from Europe to coerce early recognition and intervention. During the winter conscription was inaugurated and cotton then sent abroad to pay for supplies.

In the spring of 1862, shackled by a policy of defending fixed points, the Confederacy was too weak in men and materials to repel the many-pronged Union assault. In this invasion the Confederacy lost most of its naval bases and ports of supply, regular access to the Trans-Mississippi, much of the valuable meat, iron, and grain country of Tennessee, access to Kentucky provisions, and the meager reserves of the bureaus. These defeats also brought the western armies of the Union close to the Appalachians, which contained crucial mineral production centers and the main east-west Confederate railroad line, and which protected the transportation and ordnance complex developing in Georgia. Good generalship halted the Union advance and launched temporary offensives in the late summer and early autumn, but Bragg's proclivities to turn victory into defeat in the west and the fortunes of war in the east ended all real prospects of foreign intervention and transformed the struggle into a war of attrition.

During late 1862 and throughout 1863, in response to the increasing magnitude of the struggle, the Confederate authorities produced a conglomeration of measures and policies aimed at utilizing men and materials to outlast the United States' interest in invasion. These measures became the basic program for the Confederate supply effort, a program little modified except for intensification during the remainder of the war. They included the modification of conscription and impressment and the inauguration of the tax-in-kind, trading through the lines, and railroad and shipping regulation. The supply bureaus expanded into swollen agencies which regulated private production, built up a system of government shops, and increasingly wrested control of supply operations from the field armies. The location of government shops in the southeast and the conversion of agriculture from cotton to foodstuffs in the lower South had shifted the center of production away from the exposed border areas into the protected areas of the Confederate heartland.

In 1863, as the Confederacy contracted under Union blows, the cause-and-effect relationship of supplies and campaigning intensified. The loss of Vicksburg, occasioned in part by lack of materials and men for Johnston's relieving army, was not a vital blow in terms of supply management, for the two sections of the Confederacy had long since ceased to rely on each other. More serious in terms of the supply situation was the seige of Charleston, which resulted in intensified blockading of Wilmington and the loss of ordnance and quartermaster stores intended to supply the armies for the following winter. This lack of winter clothing and shoes in turn thwarted Lee's plans for a late autumn campaign. The most serious single blow to the supply system in 1863 was Bragg's bungling of the Chickamauga—Lookout Mountain—Missionary Ridge campaign. Bragg lost one of the main railroad supply lines from Georgia to Virginia, surrendered much of the niter and nearly all of the copper production, and also gave the Union the Appalachian gateway to Georgia. After two years of devastation, Virginia supply resources had failed, and this, combined with shrinking manpower and increasing feebleness in cavalry and field transportation, reduced Lee to dependence on the railroads and relative immobility in the face of his increasingly powerful enemy.

Shortsighted leadership from Richmond compounded supply difficulties. The increasing dependence of Lee on railroad transportation demanded the use of existing statutes to curb inefficiency, but Davis would not allow it. The progressive deterioration of the fiscal structure of the country produced a galloping inflation which increased reliance on forced sales at fixed prices. This in its turn caused hoarding, resistance, and a diminution of supplies for the armies in a country that was still highly productive. Military losses had forced an increasing reliance on importation from overseas and through the lines, but effective governmental policies in these areas developed at a snail's pace.

By 1864 manpower shortage had surpassed supply deficiencies as the major problem of the Confederate armies. In the west the disparity of numbers, plus Johnston's questionable dissatisfaction with his supply situation, immobilized the Army of Tennessee until Sherman was ready to move forward on Atlanta. In Virginia Lee, immobilized by his dependence on the railroads, could not maneuver. In both east and west the task of defense was complicated by the decay of the cavalry arm because of persistent shortages in animals and fodder. In the last months of the war the Confederate armies were too feeble to prevent Sherman and Grant from destroying the transportation network, eventually cutting off Lee from his supplies and thus precipitating Lee's surrender and the Confederacy's disintegration. On the home front domestic procurement collapsed as resistance to impressment became insurmountable; factory production fell off as workers were sent to the armies; and all hope of importations ended with the fall of the last ports. At the end, abundant crops and idle factories attested to the Confederacy's productive potential, but there were no factory workers, no money, and no transportation to turn that potential into supplies for the army, and the armies themselves had dwindled away.

By 1862, when it had become obvious that the Confederacy's survival depended on winning a war of attrition, the Confederate leaders became responsible for husbanding and augmenting the nation's resources with foresight and efficiency. The unprecedented dimensions and changing character of the Civil War undoubtedly precluded complete efficiency, but Confederate civilian leadership fell short of even reasonable standards of supply management. Reacting rather than planning, often arriving at workable policies too late, and making too many mistakes, Davis and those around him bungled supply management and thus contributed in large measure to the defeat of the Confederacy.

SELECTED BIBLIOGRAPHY

Primary Sources

Manuscripts

James D. Bulloch Papers. Southern Historical Collection, University of North Carolina.

Clement Claiborne Clay Papers. Duke University Manuscript Department.

Confederate States of America; Army, Commissary Department; Lucius Bellinger Northrop, Commissary General. New York Public Library.

Confederate States of America: Quartermaster General's Office. Virginia Historical Society, Richmond, Virginia.

Confederate States of America Archives: Executive Department; War Department. Duke University Manuscript Department.

Jefferson Davis Papers. Duke University Manuscript Department.

Jefferson Davis Papers. Louisiana Historical Association Collection, Tulane University.

Arthur Emmerson Papers. Duke University Manuscript Department.

General Records of the Department of the Treasury. Confederate Records (Record Group 56), National Archives.

Governor's Letter Book Series. North Carolina State Department of Archives and History.

Edmund Kirby-Smith Papers. Southern Historical Collection, University of North Carolina.

Mrs. Mason Barret Collection of Albert Sydney and William Preston Johnston Papers. Louisiana Historical Association, Tulane University.

Alexander R. Lawton Papers. Southern Historical Collection, University of North Carolina.

Lee Headquarters Papers. Virginia Historical Society, Richmond, Virginia.

Fontaine W. Mahood. "History of the Commissary Department of the Confederate States of America." Virginia Historical Society, Richmond, Virginia.

Charles Beatty Mallett Papers. Southern Historical Collection, University of North Carolina.

J. W. Mallett. "Memoranda of My Life—for My Children." Alderman Library, University of Virginia.

Stephen R. Mallory Diary. Southern Historical Collection, University of North Carolina.

William Porcher Miles Papers. Sothern Historical Collection, University of North Carolina.

John T. Pickett Papers. Library of Congress.

George Washington Rains Papers. Southern Historical Collection, University of North Carolina.

George Wythe Randolph Papers. Confederate Museum, Richmond, Virginia.

George Robertson Letter Book. Duke University Manuscript Department.

William James Rucker Papers. Alderman Library, University of Virginia.

Frank G. Ruffin. "Substance of the testimony of Col. Frank G. Ruffin of Virginia, Late Lieut Col. in the Confederate Bureau of Subsistence, given before the joint select committee of the two houses of the Confederate Congress, on the means of public defense on the 23rd of January 1865." Virginia State Library.

Mr. and Mrs. Benedict Joseph Semmes Papers. Southern Historical Collection, University of North Carolina.

Papers Relating to the Subsistence Department, C. S. A. Virginia Historical Society, Richmond, Virginia.

William H. Thomas Papers. Archives Department, Howard-Tilton Memorial Library, Tulane University.

Leroy Pope Walker. Official Letter Book. Library of Congress.

War Department Collection of Confederate Records (Record Group 109). National Archives.

William L. Yancey Papers. Department of Archives and History, State of Alabama.

Published Records of the Confederate Government

Communication from [the] Secretary of War Enclosing the "Orders of Impressment, together with the Instructions and Regulations under the Same, Recently Issued by the War Department or Any Bureau Thereof." Richmond, Virginia, 1863.

Communication of [the] Secretary of War Transmitting a Report from the Quartermaster General on the Number of Quartermasters in the Service. Richmond, Virginia, 1865.

Journal of the Congress of the Confederate States of America, 1861–1865. 7 vols. Washington: Government Printing Office, 1904–1905.

Miscellaneous Correspondence and Orders of the Adjutant and Inspector General's Office and Correspondence of the Quartermaster General's, Ordnance and Engineer Bureaus of the Confederate States, 1861. Washington: 1876.

Patrick, Rembert W., ed. *The Opinions of the Confederate Attourneys General 1861–1865*. Buffalo, New York; Dennis and Company, Inc., 1950.

Proceeding of the Court of Inquiry Relative to the Fall of New Orleans. Richmond: R. M. Smith, Public Printer, 1864.

[Proceedings of the First and Second Congresses of the Confederate States of America], *Southern Historical Society Papers,* XLIV–LII (June, 1923–1959).

Public Laws of the Confederate States of America, Commencing with the First Session of the First Congress; 1862. Edited by James M. Matthews. Richmond: R. M. Smith, Printer to Congress, 1862.

Public Laws of the Confederate States of America, Passed at the Second Session of the First Congress; 1862. Edited by James M. Matthews. Richmond: R. M. Smith, Printer to Congress, 1862.

Public Laws of the Confederate States of America, Passed at the Third Session of the First Congress; 1863. Edited by James M. Matthews. Richmond: R. M. Smith, Printer to Congress, 1863.

Public Laws of the Confederate States of America, Passed at the Fourth Session of the First Congress; 1863–4. Edited by James. M. Matthews. Richmond; R. M. Smith, Printer to Congress, 1864.

Public Laws of the Confederate States of America, Passed at the First Session of the Second Congress; 1864. Edited by James M. Matthews. Richmond: R. M. Smith, Printer to Congress, 1864.

Ramsdell, Charles W., ed. *Laws and Joint Resolutions of the Last Session of the Confederate Congress (November 7, 1864–March 18, 1865) Together with the Secret Acts of Previous Congresses*. Durham, N. C.: Duke University Press, 1941.

Regulations for the Future Guidance of Officers of the Subsistence Department, Embracing All Amendments and Substitutions Heretofore Made, But Not Printed in the Regulations of Said Depart-

ment—to Take Effect from Date, Richmond, October 1, 1864. Richmond, 1864.

Report from the Quartermaster General with Regard to the Number of Quartermasters on Duty in the City of Richmond. Richmond, February 16th, 1863. Richmond, 1863.

Report of the Committee Appointed under the Resolution of Congress "To Enquire into the Organization and Administration of the Medical, Commissary, and Quartermaster's Departments, and to report What Changes in the Laws and Regulations Are Necessary and Proper." Richmond, 1861.

Report of [the] Committee on Quartermaster and Commissary Departments on Case of Major Frank G. Ruffin. Richmond, 1863.

Report of the Special Committee on Pay and Clothing. Richmond; Enquirer Book and Job Press, [1865].

Report of the Special Committee, on the Recent Military Disasters at Forts Henry and Donelson, and the Evacuation of Nashville. Richmond; Enquirer Book and Job Press, 1862.

Richardson, James D., comp. *A Compilation of the Messages and Papers of the Confederacy, Including the Diplomatic Correspondence, 1861–1865.* 2 vols. Nashville: United States Publishing Company, 1906.

Special Orders of the Adjutant and Inspector General's Office, Confederate States, 1861–1865. 5 vols. n. p.: n. d.

The Statutes at Large of the Provisional Government of the Confederate States of America, from the Institution of the Government, February 8, 1861, to Its Termination, February 18, 1862, Inclusive. Edited by James M. Matthews. Richmond: R. M. Smith, Printer to Congress, 1864.

Published Records of the United States Government

Agriculture of the United States in 1860; Compiled from the Original Returns of the Eighth Census, under the Direction of the Secretary of the Interior, by Joseph C. G. Kennedy Superintendent of [the] Census. Washington: Government Printing Office, 1864.

Manufactures of the United States in 1860; Compiled from the Original Returns of the Eighth Census under the Direction of the Secretary of the Interior. Washington: Government Printing Office, 1865.

Official Records of the Union and Confederate Navies in the War of the Rebellion. 30 vols. and index. Washington: Government Printing Office, 1894–1922.

Population of the United States in 1860; Compiled from the Original Returns of the Eighth Census, under the Direction of the Secretary of the Interior, by Joseph C. G. Kennedy Superintendent of [the] Census. Washington: Government Printing Office, 1864.

"Purchase of Products in States in Insurrection," *House Executive Documents,* No. 16, 38th Congress, 2nd Session. (Serial No. 1223.)

"Report of the Joint Committee on the Conduct of the War," *House Executive Documents,* No. 3, pt. 3, 38th Congress, 1st Session. (Serial No. 1154.)

"Trade with Rebellious States," *House Reports,* No. 24, 38th Congress, 2nd Session. (Serial No. 1235.)

War of the Rebellion: A Compilation of the Official Records of the Union and Confederate Armies. 70 vols. in 127 and index. Washington: Government Printing Office, 1880–1901.

Newspapers

Advertiser and Register (Mobile).

Charleston Daily Courier.

Daily Dispatch (Richmond).

Daily News (Savannah).

Daily Richmond Examiner.

Daily Richmond Whig.

Daily Sun (Columbus).

Enquirer (Richmond).

Mercury (Charleston).

New Orleans Bee.

Sentinel (Richmond).

Southern Confederacy (Atlanta).

Tri-Weekly Constitutionalist (Augusta).

Weekly Columbus Enquirer.

Published Memoirs and Personal Papers

Beauregard, Gen. P. G. T. *A Commentary on the Campaign and Battle of Manassas of July, 1861 together with a Summary of the Art of War.* New York: G. P. Putnam's Sons, 1891.

Brooks, R. P., ed. "Howell Cobb Papers," *Georgia Historical Quarterly,* V, VI (1921, 1922).

Bulloch, James D. *The Secret Service of the Confederate States in Europe; or How the Confederate Cruisers Were Equipped.* New York and London: Thomas Yoseloff, 1959. (Reprint.)

Campbell, John A. *Reminiscences and Documents Relating to the Civil War during the Year 1865.* Baltimore: John Murphy and Company, 1887.

Century Illustrated Monthly Magazine, XXXVIII, No. 6 (October, 1889), 952. (Letter from John A. Campbell to B. R. Curtis, July 20, 1865.)

Chesnut, Mary Boykin. *A Diary from Dixie, as Written by Mary Boykin Chesnut, Wife of James Chesnut, Jr., United States Senator from South Carolina, 1859–1861, and Afterward an Aide to Jefferson Davis and a Brigadier-General in the Confederate Army.* Edited by Isabella D. Martin and Myrta Lockett Avary. New York: Peter Smith, 1929. (Reprint.)

Curry, Jabez Lamar Monroe. *Civil History of the Government of the Confederate States with Some Personal Reminiscences.* Richmond: B. F. Johnson Publishing Co., 1901.

Davis, Jefferson. *The Rise and Fall of the Confederate Government.* 2 vols. London: Longmans, Green and Company, 1881.

DeLeon, Thomas Cooper. *Four Years in Rebel Capitals: An Inside View of Life in the Southern Confederacy, from Birth to Death.* Mobile: The Gossip Printing Company, 1890.

Dowdey, Clifford, and Louis Manarin, eds. *The Wartime Papers of R. E. Lee.* Boston and Toronto: Little, Brown, and Company, 1961.

Du Bellet, Paul P. *The Diplomacy of the Confederate Cabinet of Richmond and Its Agents Abroad: Being Memorandum Notes Taken in Paris during the Rebellion of the Southern States from 1861–1865.* Edited by William Stanley Hoole. Tuscaloosa, Alabama: Confederate Publishing Company, Inc., 1963.

An English Combatant. *Battle-Fields of the South, from Bull Run to Fredericksburg; with Sketches of Confederate Commanders, and Gossip of the Camps.* New York: John Bradburn, 1864.

An English Merchant [W. C. Corsan]. *Two Months in the Confederate States, Including a Visit to New Orleans under the Domination of General Butler.* London: Richard Bentley, 1863.

Freeman, Douglas Southall, ed. *Lee's Dispatches: Unpublished Letters of General Robert E. Lee, C.S.A., to Jefferson Davis and the War Department of the Confederate States of America, 1862–1865, from the Private Collection of Wymberly Jones De Renne*. New York and London: G. P. Putnam's Sons, 1915.

Fremantle, Arthur James. *Three Months in the Southern States: April–June, 1863*. New York: John Bradburn, 1864.

Girard, Charles. *A Visit to the Confederate States of America in 1863; Memoirs Addressed to His Majesty Napoleon III*. Translated by William Stanley Hoole. Tuscaloosa, Alabama: Confederate Publishing Company, Inc., 1962.

Hood, J[ohn] B[ell]. *Advance and Retreat: Personal Experiences in the United States and Confederate States Armies*. Edited by Richard N. Current. Bloomington: Indiana University Press, 1959.

Huse, Caleb. *The Supplies for the Confederate Army: How They Were Obtained in Europe and How Paid For*. Boston: T. R. Marvin and Son, 1904.

Johnston, Joseph E. *Narrative of Military Operations, Directed during the Late War between the States*. New York: D. Appleton and Company, 1874.

Jones, John Beauchamp. *A Rebel War Clerk's Diary at the Confederate States Capital*. Edited by Howard Swiggett. 2 vols. New York: Old Hickory Bookshop, 1935.

A Lady of Virginia [Mrs. Judith W. McGuire]. *Diary of a Southern Refugee during the War*. New York: E. J. Hale and Son, 1868.

Longstreet, James. *From Manassas to Appomattox; Memoirs of the Civil War in America*. Philadelphia: J. B. Lippincott, 1896.

McCarthy, Carlton. *Detailed Minutiae of Soldier Life in the Army of Northern Virginia, 1861–1865*. Richmond: Carlton McCarthy and Company, 1882.

Malet, William Wyndham. *An Errand to the South in the Summer of 1862*. London: Richard Bentley, 1863.

Maurice, Sir Frederick Barton, ed. *An Aide-de-Camp of Lee, Being the Papers of Colonel Charles Marshall, Sometime Aide-de-Camp, Military Secretary, and Assistant Adjutant General on the Staff of Robert E. Lee, 1862–1865*. Boston: Little, Brown, and Company, 1927.

Moore, Frank, ed. *The Rebellion Record: A Diary of American Events, with Documents, Narratives, Illustrative Incidents, Poetry, Etc.* 11 vols.: Vols. I–VI, New York: G. P. Putnam, 1861–1863; Vols. VII–XI, New York: D. Van Nostrand, 1864–1868.

Phillips, Ulrich Bonnell, ed. *The Correspondence of Robert Toombs, Alexander H. Stephens, and Howell Cobb*. Vol. II of the *Annual Report of the American Historical Association* for 1911. Washington, D. C., 1913.

Pollard, Edward A. *Life of Jefferson Davis, with a Secret History of the Southern Confederacy*. Philadelphia, Chicago, St. Louis, Atlanta: National Publishing Company, 1869.

———. *The Lost Cause; A New Southern History of the War of the Confederates*. New York: E. B. Treat and Company, 1866.

———. *Southern History of the War*. 2 vols. in one. New York: Charles B. Richardson, 1866.

Rains, George Washington. *History of the Confederate Powder Works*. Augusta, Georgia: Chronicle and Constitutionalist Printers, 1882.

Reagan, John H. *Memoirs, with Special Reference to Secession and the Civil War*. Edited by Walter Flavius McCaleb. New York and Washington: Neale Publishing Company, 1906.

Ross, Fitzgerald. *A Visit to the Cities and Camps of the Confederate States*. Edinburgh and London: William Blackwood and Sons, 1865.

Rowland, Dunbar, ed. *Jefferson Davis, Constitutionalist, His Letters, Papers, and Speeches*. 10 vols. Jackson, Mississippi, 1923.

Russell, Sir William Howard. *My Diary North and South*. Edited by Fletcher Pratt. New York: Harper and Brothers, 1954.

Scheibert, Justus. *Seven Months in the Rebel States during the North American War, 1863*. Edited by William Stanley Hoole. Tuscaloosa, Alabama: Confederate Publishing Company, Inc., 1958.

Smith, Gustavus W. *Confederate War Papers*. New York: Atlantic Publishing and Engraving Company, 1884.

Taylor, Richard. *Destruction and Reconstruction*. Edited by Richard B. Harwell. New York, London, and Toronto: Longmans, Green and Company, 1955.

Vandiver, Frank E., ed. *The Civil War Diary of General Josiah Gorgas*. University, Alabama: University of Alabama Press, 1947.

Wright, Willard E., ed. "Some Letters of Lucius Bellinger Northrop, 1860–1865," *Virginia Magazine of History and Biography*, LXVIII (October, 1960), 456–477.

Younger, Edward, ed. *Inside the Confederate Government: The Diary of Robert Garlick Hill Kean, Head of the Bureau of War*. New York: Oxford University Press, 1957.

Secondary Sources

Books

Bettersworth, John K., ed. *Mississippi in the Confederacy: As They Saw It*. Baton Rouge: Louisiana State University Press, 1961.

Black, Robert C., III. *The Railroads of the Confederacy*. Chapel Hill: University of North Carolina Press, 1952.

Bragg, Jefferson Davis. *Louisiana in the Confederacy*. Baton Rouge: Louisiana State University Press, 1941.

Bruce, Kathleen. *Virginia Iron Manufacture in the Slave Era*. New York and London: The Century Company, 1931.

Bryan, Thomas C. *Confederate Georgia*. Athens: University of Georgia Press, 1953.

Connor, Henry G. *John Archibald Campbell: Associate Justice of the United States Supreme Court 1853–1861*. Boston and New York: Houghton Mifflin Company, 1920.

Coulter, E. Merton. *The Civil War and Readjustment in Kentucky*. Chapel Hill: University of North Carolina Press, 1926.

Cunningham, Horace H. *Doctors in Gray: The Confederate Medical Service*. Baton Rouge: Louisiana State University Press, 1958.

Durkin, Joseph T., S. J. *Stephen R. Mallory: Confederate Navy Chief*. Chapel Hill: University of North Carolina Press, 1954.

Eliot, Ellsworth, Jr. *West Point in the Confederacy*. New York: G. A. Baker and Company, Inc., 1941.

Fleming, Walter L. *Civil War and Reconstruction in Alabama*. New York: Columbia University Press, 1965.

Freeman, Douglas Southall. *Lee's Lieutenants: A Study in Command*. 3 vols. New York: Charles Scribner's Sons, 1951.

———. *R. E. Lee, a Biography*. 4 vols. New York and London: Charles Scribner's Sons, 1934–1935.

Gates, Paul. *Agriculture and the Civil War*. Impact of the Civil War Series. New York: Alfred A. Knopf, 1965.

Hendrick, Burton J. *Statesmen of the Lost Cause; Jefferson Davis and His Cabinet*. Boston: Little, Brown, and Company, 1939.

Lonn, Ella. *Desertion during the Civil War*. New York and London: The Century Company, 1928.

———. *Foreigners in the Confederacy*. Chapel Hill: University of North Carolina Press, 1940.

Lonn, Ella. *Salt as a Factor in the Confederacy.* New York: W. Neale, 1933.

Massey, Mary Elizabeth. *Ersatz in the Confederacy.* Columbia: S. C., University of South Carolina Press, 1952.

Meade, Robert D. *Judah P. Benjamin, Confederate Statesman.* New York: Oxford University Press, 1943.

Moore, Albert Burton. *Conscription and Conflict in the Confederacy.* New York: Macmillan Company, 1924.

Nichols, James Lynn. *Confederate Engineers.* Tuscaloosa, Alabama: Confederate Publishing Company, 1957.

———. *The Confederate Quartermaster in the Trans-Mississippi.* Austin: University of Texas Press, 1964.

Owsley, Frank L. *King Cotton Diplomacy: Foreign Relations of the Confederate States of America.* 2nd edition, revised by Harriet Chappell Owsley. Chicago: University of Chicago Press, 1959.

———. *States Rights in the Confederacy.* Chicago: University of Chicago Press, 1925.

Parks, Joseph H. *General Edmund Kirby Smith, C.S.A.* Baton Rouge: Louisiana State University Press, 1954.

Patrick, Rembert Wallace. *Jefferson Davis and His Cabinet.* Baton Rouge: Louisiana State University Press, 1944.

Pemberton, John C. *Pemberton: Defender of Vicksburg.* Chapel Hill: University of North Carolina Press, 1942.

Ramsdell, Charles W. *Behind the Lines in the Southern Confederacy.* Baton Rouge: Louisiana State University Press. 1944.

Roman, Alfred. *The Military Operations of General Beauregard in the War Between the States 1861 to 1865, Including a Brief Personal Sketch and a Narrative of His Services in the War with Mexico, 1846–8.* 2 vols. New York: Harper and Brothers, 1884.

Scharf, J. Thomas. *History of the Confederate States Navy: From Its Organization to the Surrender of Its Last Vessel.* New York: Rogers and Sherwood, 1887.

Schwab, John Christopher. *The Confederate States of America, 1861–1865; A Financial and Industrial History of the South during the Civil War.* New York: Charles Scribner's Sons, 1901.

Tansill, Robert. *A Free and Impartial Exposition of the Causes Which Led to the Failure of the Confederate States to Establish Their Independence.* Washington, 1865.

Tatum, Georgia Lee. *Disloyalty in the Confederacy.* Chapel Hill: University of North Carolina Press, 1934.

Thompson, Samuel Bernard. *Confederate Purchasing Operations Abroad*. Chapel Hill: University of North Carolina Press, 1935.

Todd, Richard Cecil. *Confederate Finance*. Athens: University of Georgia Press, 1954.

Vandiver, Frank E. *Ploughshares into Swords: Josiah Gorgas and Confederate Ordnance*. Austin: University of Texas Press, 1952.

———. *Rebel Brass: The Confederate Command System*. Baton Rouge: Louisiana State University Press, 1956.

Wesley, Charles H. *The Collapse of the Confederacy*. Washington: The Associated Publishers, Inc., 1937.

Wiley, Bell Irvin. *The Life of Johnny Reb: The Common Soldier of the Confederacy*. Indianapolis and New York: The Bobs-Merrill Company, 1943.

Yearns, Wilfred Buck. *The Confederate Congress,* Athens: University of Georgia Press, 1960.

Articles

Adams, George Worthington. "Confederate Medicine," *Journal of Southern History,* VI, No. 2 (May 1940), 151–166.

Coulter, E. Merton. "Commercial Intercourse with the Confederacy in the Mississippi Valley, 1861–1865," *Mississippi Valley Historical Review,* V, No. 4 (March 1919), 377–395.

———. "Effect of Secession upon the Commerce of the Mississippi Valley," *Mississippi Valley Historical Review,* III, No. 3 (December 1916), 275–300.

———. "The Movement for Agricultural Reorganization in the Cotton South during the Civil War," *Agricultural History,* I, No. 1 (January 1927), 3–17.

———. "Planters' Wants in the Days of the Confederacy," *Georgia Historical Quarterly,* XII, No. 1 (March 1928), 38–52.

Diamond, William. "Imports of the Confederate Government from Europe and Mexico," *Journal of Southern History,* VI, No. 4 (November 1940), 470–503.

Donnelly, Ralph W. "Confederate Copper," *Civil War History,* I, No. 4 (December 1955), 355–370.

———. "The Confederate Lead Mines of Wythe County, Va.," *Civil War History,* V, No. 4 (December 1959), 402–414.

Fleming, Walter L. "Blockade Running and Trade through the Lines in Alabama, 1861–1865," *South Atlantic Quarterly,* IV, No. 3 (July 1905), 256–272.

Fuller, Major General J. F. C. "A Study of Mobility in the American Civil War," *Army Quarterly,* XXIX, No. 2 (January 1935), 261–271.

Gorgas, Josiah. "Notes on the Ordnance Department of the Confederate Government," *Southern Historical Society Papers,* XII, Nos. 1–2 (January–February 1884), 66–94.

Hay, Thomas Robson. "Lucius B. Northrop: Commissary General of the Confederacy," *Civil War History,* IX, No. 1 (March 1963), 5–23.

Hill, Louise B. "State Socialism in the Confederate States of America," *Southern Sketches,* Series 1, No. 9, general ed., Dr. J. D. Eggleston. Charlottesville, 1936.

Holladay, Florence. "The Powers of the Commander of the Confederate Trans-Mississippi Department, 1863–1865," *Southwestern Historical Quarterly,* XXI, No. 3 (January 1918), 279–298; No. 4 (April 1918), 333–359.

Johnson, Ludwell H. "Commerce between Northeastern Ports and the Confederacy, 1861–1865," *Journal of Southern History,* LIV, No. 1 (June 1967), 30–40.

———. "Contraband Trade during the Last Year of the Civil War," *Mississippi Valley Historical Review,* XLIX, No. 4 (March 1963), 635–652.

Little, Robert D. "Southern Historians and the Downfall of the Confederacy," *Alabama Review,* III, No. 4 (October 1950), 243–262; IV, No. 1 (January 1951), 38–54.

Mallet, John W. "Work of the Ordnance Bureau of the War Department of the Confederate States, 1861–1865," *Southern Historical Society Papers,* XXXVII (1909), 1–20.

McWhiney, Grady. "Controversy in Kentucky: Braxton Bragg's Campaign of 1862," *Civil War History,* VI, No. 1 (1960), 5–42.

Nichols, James L. "The Tax in Kind in the Department of the Trans-Mississippi," *Civil War History,* V, No. 4 (December 1959), 382–389.

O'Connor, Thomas H. "Lincoln and the Cotton Trade," *Civil War History,* VII, No. 1 (March 1961), 20–35.

Parks, Joseph H. "A Confederate Trade Center under Federal Occupation: Memphis, 1862 to 1865," *Journal of Southern History,* VII, No. 3 (August 1941), 289–314.

Ramsdell, Charles W. "The Confederate Government and the Railroads," *American Historical Review,* XXII, No. 4 (July 1917), 794–810.

———. "The Control of Manufacturing by the Confederate Government," *Mississippi Valley Historical Review,* VIII, No. 3 (December 1921), 231–249.

———. "General Robert E. Lee's Horse Supply, 1862–1865," *American Historical Review,* XXXV, No. 4 (July 1930), 758–777.

Roberts, A. Sellew. "The Federal Government and Confederate Cotton," *American Historical Review,* XXXII, No. 2 (January 1927), 262–275.

Ruffin, Frank G. "A Chapter of Confederate History," *North American Review,* CXXXIV, No. 302 (January 1882), 97–110.

Sellers, James L. "The Economic Incidence of the Civil War in the South," *Mississippi Valley Historical Review,* XIV, No. 2 (September 1927), 179–191.

Trexler, Harrison A. "The Opposition of Planters to the Employment of Slaves as Laborers by the Confederacy," *Mississippi Valley Historical Review,* XXVII, No. 2 (September 1940), 211–224.

Vandiver, Frank E. "General Hood as Logistician," *Military Affairs,* XVI, No. 1 (Spring 1956), 1–11.

Webb, Elizabeth Y. "Cotton Manufacturing and State Regulation in North Carolina," *North Carolina Historical Review,* IX, No. 2 (April 1937), 117–137.

Wright, Gordon. "Economic Conditions in the Confederacy as Seen by the French Consuls," *Journal of Southern History,* VII, No. 2 (1941), 195–214.

INDEX